Perspectives on Gerontological Nursing

This book is dedicated to all older adults that I have had the privilege of knowing and who have shared with me their wisdom and caring.

It is also dedicated to my daughter Laura and to my mother Lola, for their love, humor, and prayers.

—Elizabeth Murrow Baines

Perspectives on Gerontological Nursing

edited by

Elizabeth Murrow Baines

SAGE PUBLICATIONS
The International Professional Publishers
Newbury Park   London   New Delhi

For information address:

 SAGE Publications, Inc.
2455 Teller Road
Newbury Park, California 91320

SAGE Publications Ltd.
6 Bonhill Street
London EC2A 4PU
United Kingdom

SAGE Publications India Pvt. Ltd.
M-32 Market
Greater Kailash I
New Delhi 110 048 India

Printed in the United States of America

Library of Congress Cataloging-in-Publication Data

Main entry under title:

Perspectives on gerontological nursing / edited by Elizabeth Murrow
   Baines.
      p.   cm.
   Includes bibliographical references.
   Includes index.
   ISBN 0-8039-3722-9 (c). — ISBN 0-8039-4237-0 (p.)
   1. Geriatric nursing. I. Baines, Elizabeth Murrow.
   [DNLM: 1. Aging—nurses' instruction. 2. Geriatric Nursing. WY
   152 P47]   1991
   610.73'65—dc20
   DNLM/DLC   91-6874
                                                                     CIP

FIRST PRINTING, 1991

Sage Production Editor: Astrid Virding

Contents

Foreword

Perspectives on Gerontological Nursing provides a scientific body of knowledge on which to base nursing care of older adults. It is for nurses, by nurses, and about nursing. The book consists of 21 original chapters written by well-known and widely published scholars on the subject of strategies for intervention to enhance the quality of life during the aging process.

Each contributor was instructed by the editor to include the best scientific evidence to support the interventions that are discussed. Thus the information in the chapters is supported by documentation of a considerable body of the research on the topics with which they deal.

The contributors have presented the challenges and rewards of aging and the role of the nurse in assisting individuals through the aging process. Stressed throughout the book is the theme that theory development, research, education, and service are major avenues by which nurses can continue to improve health care for older adults. We are encouraged to change our vision from one that emphasizes problems of aging to a new vision that includes the promise of active and productive older age. Barriers that make achieving this vision of a high quality life-style for older citizens are dealt with and suggestions for their elimination are offered.

A recurring theme of this book is the positive effect of nursing intervention in the health care of older adults. The scope of gerontological nursing includes direct care in wellness, illness, rehabilitation, investigation of the outcomes of nursing intervention, the theoretical underpinnings of gerontological nursing practice, policy development to address the diverse needs of a diverse aging population, and the nurse's role as advocate for the aged as we seek to build coalitions for problem solving.

Perspectives on Gerontological Nursing truly addresses comprehensive data relevant to the study of gerontological nursing presented in meaningful relationships. This relevant data is presented logically in two major sections: (1) The Promotion of Healthful Aging and the Role of the Gerontological Nurse, and (2) The Maintenance, Treatment, and Restorative Nursing Care of Older Adults Who Have Actual or Potential Health Care Problems.

More specifically, this book addresses several recurring themes that should be of particular concern to nurses providing care for the aged and for other persons in health-related professions involved in the care of aging individuals. These major themes include promotion of independence; demographics and heterogeneity of elders in policy formation, continuum of health care, cost containment, and family caregiving; quality of care including ethical and legal considerations; and respect for cultural diversity among elders.

The desire to remain independent both personally and financially is a major goal of most older persons. Research has proven the capability of older persons to lead independent, productive, and optimally healthy lives if they remain physically active, if they are mentally stimulated by having significant responsibilities, if they are allowed to maintain a sense of control over their lives, and if they receive appropriate support from family and the social/institutional structure of society. The reality of the aging process and the limitations that this process imposes are also documented by research. Equally supported in the literature, however, is the fact that people age at vastly different rates, that the process of aging differs in different time periods and in different places, and that interventions exist that can minimize the limitations that accompany the aging process. Maximum independence as a goal for our aging citizens will significantly decrease the high cost of acute care in both financial and human terms.

The heterogeneity of older adults is another prevalent theme in this text, and the authors suggest the continued need for education regarding the individuality of each person regardless of chronological age. Although demographic projections would suggest that older adults are alike, the older population is in fact neither uniform nor homogeneous. What older people need in South Carolina is not necessarily what they need in California. What the old, old need is not necessarily what the young, old want or need. Consequently, any local, state, national, or international initiative to address health care policy for older adult populations must take into account their diverse nature of needs and wants.

Although the nation's older adults are healthier than ever before, the 65 and older population, nevertheless, uses a disproportionately large share of health care resources. For instance, the 12% of the United States population that was 65 or older during the 1980s used approximately one third of the nation's health care resources. Embedded in this statistic are the facts that older adults require more nursing care than other age groups, are more frequently hospitalized than younger persons and for longer periods of time, occupy more than one half of the beds in intensive care units, and the fact that most nursing homes in the United States have 100% occupancy, most with waiting lists. Although the prospective payment plan initiated in the early 1980s addressed some major cost containment issues in the health care industry, this policy like other social and economic reforms created new problems as older adults began to be discharged earlier from acute care hospitals and with more complex health care problems that continue to be unresolved.

The literature documents that more than 80% of all health care needed by older adults is provided by the family, usually another aging person, even in the presence of professional health care providers. However, less than 5% of the money spent by the government is appropriated for home health care with approximately 45% allocated to hospitals and 21% allocated each for medical care and nursing homes.

As a consequence of spiraling health care costs, due primarily to technological advances and the cost of institutional and medical care, a National Health Care Policy continues to be proposed. Chapter 9 explicates historical and current perspectives of the National Health Care Policy issue. To be sure, the ever increasing aging population will continue to place strains on existing services until there is an increase in funding that is proportionate to the numbers of seniors in the general population. We cannot overlook the existence of ageism in our society and the unfortunate intergenerational conflict encouraged by those who claim that older persons receive a disproportionate amount of government assistance to the detriment of programs designed to assist other segments of the population, particularly children.

Another recurring theme throughout this book is the planning for and the assurance of high quality care for older adults. Subsumed within this theme are the legal and ethical concerns of providing health care, which are addressed by several authors. Despite the relative amount of care provided in the home and in nursing homes, few if any standards of care in these settings have been implemented that are comparable to the exacting controls in place for care in the acute care hospital.

Our goal to decrease or contain health care cost cannot be accomplished at the expense of quality of care. Today's seniors are demanding a right to determine what quality is and how best to achieve it for themselves, including the quality of health care. The barriers to achieving a high quality of life-style and of health care for older citizens must be eliminated.

A final pervasive theme is respect for cultural diversity among elders, given particular emphasis in Chapter 13. We more fully understand that richness of diversity in American life can create both blessings and problems. The author provides strategies for "persons working among different cultural groups for providing more sensitive and relevant services to a wider spectrum of older patients or clients."

This collection of original manuscripts in *Perspectives on Gerontological Nursing* fills a void in the nursing literature by providing a comprehensive, scholarly, research-based text for the teaching and learning of gerontological nursing.

Current demographic pressure on health and other human services should be viewed not as a short-term crisis but rather as an opportunity to change permanently the way we serve the elderly and view them as members of society. As always, education holds the key to our making the best of this opportunity and achieving this long-term vision.

—Opal S. Hipps
Professor and Dean
College of Nursing
Clemson University

Acknowledgments

I would like to express my appreciation to all contributors to this book. Your generosity, scholarship, and hard work are gratefully acknowledged. I would also like to recognize both Kathryn Polski Schindler, MS, RN, and Suzanne Vollrath Keogh, MS, RN, CS, who worked for me as Research Assistants, for their expertise and assistance. I would like to take this opportunity to express my appreciation for the insights and inspiration that I have received from students in Gerontological Nursing. A special thanks to Ms. Christine Smedley, Editor, Sage Publications, for her advice and support in completing this book.

—Elizabeth Murrow Baines

Preface

This book is about aging and gerontological nursing. There are many books on aging and nursing care of the aged, but there are few if any edited nursing texts that provide a synthesis of knowledge, research, and practice by experts, in selected areas of interest to gerontological nurses. Therefore, this book was written to fill this gap in gerontological nursing literature in which experts in specific content areas analyzed the research and critiqued intervention strategies.

The intention not to provide a comprehensive overview of all areas related to gerontological nursing. There are several texts previously published that provide extensive, fundamental approaches to nursing care of the older person. The intention is to select content of importance in advanced gerontological nursing practice and to obtain experts to address these issues in each topic area. In addition, theoretical development in most content areas is based on an electic approach, because there is no one acceptable paradigm for gerontological nursing practice.

This book is written for the graduate student in gerontological nursing and it should be useful for senior-level baccalaureate student nurses. The text should be of interest to in-service educators and nurses in clinical practice settings that care for older adults. The majority of nursing home residents are elderly, at least 50% of the patients in acute care facilities are aged, with even higher percentages in intensive care units, and most home health care nurses visit elderly clients. It is evident that many nurses provide services for older adults and it is hoped that this book will serve as an incentive to give quality nursing care.

The text is also written to serve as a reference for students in other disciplines interested in the health care needs of older adults. It should be of use to upper division baccalaureate and graduate students in architecture, food science, sociology, public health, and related disciplines.

There are two major parts in this text: nursing care of the well elderly, and illness care of the older adult. There are four units including the following areas: introduction, developmental, sociocultural, and actual and potential health care problems.

Chapter 1 provides historical and futuristic perspectives on gerontological nursing and includes a critique of the research in gerontological nursing. Chapter 2 provides selective theoretical and curricular aspects of gerontological nursing.

The second unit includes Chapters 3 through 8 and is based on the developmental theory of aging. Topics in this area include wellness and health promotion, sleep, meaning of life, sexuality, leisure, life-long learning, and death in aging and the role of the clinical nurse specialist.

Chapters 9 through 14 address sociological aspects of aging that impact on the nursing care of older adults. In this unit the following subjects are included: public policy, economics, housing, cultural and cross-national trends. International trends are examined by a nurse, Jean Swaffield, who lives in Scotland. She provides some interesting insights from a European point of view.

Concepts on chronicity care is the first topic in the final unit of this book. This unit is on illness care and the aging person. Topics include physiological and psychological illness care in aging, nutritional status, and urinary elimination. The final chapter is devoted to selected legal and ethical issues in gerontological nursing.

This text should challenge gerontological nurses and persons in related disciples to learn more about older adults and to find better approaches to enhancing the aging process. The book should be of particular interest to practitioners who appreciate the historical, theoretical, and clinical approaches that have influenced the development of gerontological nursing.

P A R T   I

The Promotion of Healthful Aging and the Role of the Gerontological Nurse

INTRODUCTION TO
GERONTOLOGICAL NURSING

1

Historical and Futuristic Perspectives on Aging and the Gerontological Nurse

VERONICA F. REMPUSHESKI

Objectives: At the completion of this chapter, the reader will be able to:

(1) Critique demographic and health care trends of the older adult population in the United States and their relation to gerontological nursing care.

(2) Analyze perspectives in gerontological nursing within a futuristic framework.

(3) Evaluate the role of the Gerontological Nurse Specialist in contributing to the future of professional nursing and elder care.

INTRODUCTION

Whether one accepts as true the living constraints imposed by McCulloch's encroaching "ice age" environment in a *Creed for the Third Millennium* (1985) or the information overload of Naisbitt's *Megatrends* (1984), there is no doubt that the future of gerontological nursing will encompass the challenges of caring for an increasing number of older persons within a context of environmental, informational, and human barriers. A systematic examination of documented history provides data upon which to evaluate the accomplishments of the past; also evident in these data are the gaps that need to be filled, potential tools or strategies that need to be tried, lessons learned, guidelines, and warnings that will determine the success of aging and gerontological nursing in the future.

To grow, mature, make old—that is aging. Aging begins at the time of birth; however, the perspective of aging as a process that occurs in the elderly is the usual way the term is used. Consequently, aging is commonly perceived as the process reserved for individuals in the later years of life. Rather than bluntly state a chronological age of 65 years as the point at which an individual is considered to begin the elder years, think of age in a historical context wherein what designates the "later years of life" is relative to a period of time in history determined by not only predicted life expectancy at birth but also the historical events of the era, some of which contribute to actual life expectancy. The terms "aged," "elderly," "old age," "elder years" are not constants. The chronological age of 65 years as the onset of old age was initially designated in legislation written by Bismarck in the 1880s; legislation continues to guide how the elderly are defined but the chronological age of onset may differ by law. For example, under Title VII of the Older Americans Act—the nutrition program—age 60 is the lower limit; in the Department of Housing and Urban Development (HUD) 202 housing program, it is 62; and in the Medicare program it is 65 (Haynes & Feinleib, 1980). Those persons who encompass the later years of life, be it 60+ years, 62+ or 65+ years, are the clients, patients, and subjects of the gerontological nurse.

Gerontological nursing encompasses the definitions of gerontology (the study of aging), geriatrics (medical treatment of old age and diseases), geriatric nursing (care of an elder during wellness and illness, including promotion and maintenance of health, prevention of illness and disability, care of the ill leading to restoration, rehabilitation, or a peaceful death), and geriatric nursing research (systematic study of nursing action and theory in relation to elder care and responses by elders to care received) (Wolanin, 1983).

This chapter will present some highlights of the past and some hopes for the future combining perspectives on aging and perspectives on gerontological nursing within a framework of six categories proposed by Phillips (1989c) as having an influence on the future of elder care (Figure 1.1). These six categories (Macro Social Situation, Micro Social Situation, Political/Economic Climate, Health Care Milieu, Special Care Requisites, State of Professional Nursing) serve as an outline of the issues that will be addressed in this chapter. Supportive data are condensed and referenced extensively to provide the reader with direction for obtaining details and context from the original sources from which these somewhat cryptic categories and responses are drawn. Consequently, the reader is encouraged to fill in the gaps by referring to the original sources provided at the end of the chapter. These few pages are meant to whet the reader's intellectual curiosity and appetite.

Figure 1.1. Categories of Potential Influence on the Future of Elder Care
Source: Adapted from Phillips (1989c).

MACRO SOCIAL SITUATION

Macro (large) and micro (small) are used in the first two categories to identify relative conditions with regard to circumstances of living together as human beings (social situation). The unit of analysis for the macro social situation is the United States' society and all the variables contained within. Although not addressed per se, assumed to be among the variables are environmental conditions of a global nature, such as the air we breathe and the water we drink. Also assumed as variables are ethnic and spiritual affiliations that may influence the way in which the social situation is interpreted at the macro and micro levels. Some of the variables introduced here are addressed in greater detail in subsequent chapters; in this first chapter the reader is reminded to consider the ways in which these data may present in a different set of circumstances; that is, under a different set of variables, either at the macro or micro level.

Among the issues or subcategories considered in the Macro Social Situation category are (1) aging in American society, (2) health care demography, and (3) assignment of caring responsibility.

Aging in American Society

Twenty-five million individuals or 11.4% of the total population of the United States are 65 years or older. By the year 2030 the national population of elders is predicated to number over 50 million or 17% of the total population (*Census of Population and Housing: 1980,* 1983). More recent predictions, although illustrating change rates every decade that exceed 25%, are more modest. For example, 1990 predictions contrast with 1980 predictions to illustrate a lower percentage distribution of persons 65 years and older; for 1990 they are predicted to be 12.6%; 13% for the year 2000; and 13.9% for the year 2010 (U.S. Bureau of the Census, 1990). The rate of change decreases each decade so it is doubtful that the 1980 predictions will hold. More likely a percentage distribution of persons 65 years and older will be somewhere between 15% and 16%—still a sizable proportion. What is not made clear in these numbers is that the young-old will be caring for the old-old. A larger number of individuals will be in the 75+ age group, whereas the younger age group will decrease in numbers and percentage of the total population. This is illustrated in the predicted rate of change from 1990-2000 wherein the rate of change for the 65-74 year olds is −.7%, whereas the rate of change for the 75+ year olds is 26.2% (U.S. Bureau of the Census, 1990). In other words, the predicted change is a decrease for the 65-74 year olds and a dramatic increase for the 75+ year olds within that decade.

The overall life expectancy at birth in 1986 was 74.8 years. This is more than a full year increase since 1980. The longest life expectancy (78.8 years) is experienced by white females, followed by black females (73.8 years), white males (72.1 years), and black males (65.4 years) (National Center for Health Statistics [NCHS], 1989). Individuals who attained age 65 in 1987 could expect to live an average of another 17 years—to age 82 (National Center for Health Statistics [NCHS], 1990).

Health Care Demography

The first Surgeon General's report on health promotion and disease prevention (U.S. Department of Health, Education and Welfare, 1979) stated a 10-year goal "to improve the health and quality of life for older adults and, by 1990, to reduce the average annual number of days of restricted activity due to acute and chronic conditions by 20 percent, to fewer than 30 days per year for people aged 65 and older" (p. 71). In addition, two subgoals were stated: "to increase the number of older adults who can function independently," (p. 74) and "to reduce premature death from influenza and pneumonia" (p. 78).

In 1979 the restricted-activity rate for elders was at an all time high of 41.9 days. This rate decreased to 30.3 in 1987, and although very close to the projected goal of 30 days, its interpretation and implication are not clear. Thought to be a better indicator of health status of adults aged 65 years and older is the number of bed-disability days. After a high of 16.7 days in 1983 the bed-disability rate decreased to 14.0 in 1987, still above the projected goal of 12.0 days by 1990 (NCHS, 1990).

Elders remain the leading users of health resources. The average number of ambulatory physician contacts for persons aged 65 years and older is 8.9

contacts per person per year. This is an increase of 17% between 1983 and 1987. The average length of hospital stay for elders has declined, however, by a full day during that same 4-year period (NCHS, 1989). Individuals aged 65 years and older account for 40% to 50% of medical, surgical, and psychiatric inpatients in acute care hospitals (Fulmer & Walker, 1990; Rempusheski, 1990a). From one metropolitan teaching hospital the percentage of elders discharged from intensive care units ranged from 47% in medical intensive care to 62% in surgical intensive care. At this same institution, representative of what is happening in other similar institutions around the country, there was a 10% increase in the number of patients 85 years and older discharged from the hospital over a 4-year period between 1984 and 1988 (Rempusheski, 1990a).

Nearing the end of the *Healthy People* decade the five leading causes of death among persons age 65 years and older are: (1) diseases of the heart, (2) malignant neoplasms, (3) cerebrovascular diseases, (4) chronic obstructive lung disease, and (5) pneumonia and influenza. In this 1980-1990 decade the rankings for the five leading causes of death among persons 65 years and older have remained the same except for a shift of pneumonia and influenza from fourth in 1978 to the current rank of fifth (NCHS, 1990).

The gerontological nurse of the future will be expected to assume an even greater responsibility in influencing the health of elders. Not to be overlooked is the health care demography in other age groups, such as birth and fertility rates of women, and the potential influence these rates may have on the elderly. The steady increase in birth rate for women aged 30-45 years during the past two decades has short-term implications for the elderly as older grandparents. Increased stressors associated with preterm infants born to high risk mothers, the environment and care in newborn intensive care units, and the relationship of these variables to the role of older parents, grandparents, and great-grandparents in three- and four-generation families are just beginning to be explored for their effect on the health of elders (Rempusheski, 1990b; Stokes & Gordon, 1988). Unknown as yet are the potential long-term implications of these stressors on grandparents and on parents as elders with teenage and young adult children. As will be addressed by Abdellah in Chapter 9 the health of the elderly in the United States is stipulated as a major concern in the year 2000 objectives for a healthy nation. Leading the way to meet the challenge of accomplishing these objectives for older Americans will be the gerontological nurse specialist.

Assignment of Caring Responsibility

Self-care and care by others are the two major classifications of caring responsibilities. Whether perceived as wellness care or illness care, caring responsibility is a long-term endeavor—something each of us assumes for life. Self-care as an adult or as an older adult is an assumed part of one's activity of daily living, until one is unable to care for self. To whom, at that point in time, is the caring responsibility assigned?

A majority of information and formal caring responsibilities are assumed by individuals in the community—by neighbors, family members, friends, support groups, clergy, and a host of other individuals. Social mores dictate that families assume caregiving responsibility for their elder relatives as the need arises, and a majority of families comply. No laws dictate this responsibility; however, social and legal condemnations are declared on those who do not "honor thy mother and father" and/or neglect to assume the "expected" caring responsibilities for a family member. The bulk of caring responsibilities for elders in the home, especially after discharge from hospital, is shared by family caregivers and professional nurses.

Supporting and caring for informal caregivers and elders are community health nurses. Although society perceives that the least functionally capable elders are in nursing homes, it is estimated that for every individual in a nursing home there are two or three elders living in the community who require equal levels of personal care. Approximately 5% of elders are either home- or bed bound (Mezey & Lynaugh, 1989). Medicare was perceived as supportive of reimbursement for care of elders at home by nurses. The number of U.S. home health agencies approved for federal reimbursement rose from 1,300 in 1965 to over 3,000 in 1988. Costs for home care rapidly escalated; Medicare reimbursement was restricted further with a fixed payment system introduced in 1982. Medicare's prospective payment system, known as diagnostic related groups (DRGs), created an opportunity and a challenge for nurse practitioners in their care of elders in the community; 90% of these elders are over the age of 75 (Burns-Tisdale & Goff, 1989; Mezey & Lynaugh, 1989).

Similar to older adults who are discharged from the hospital to home in need of care that is less acute than is "allowed" in the hospital, yet sicker than able to care for self, are elderly residents returning to a nursing home posthospitalization who may not be at their baseline functional ability. Acuity of residents posthospitalization has been higher than anticipated since 1982; the issues of availability of acute care beds and equipment in nursing homes, level of knowledge and skill needed to care for residents during their acute illness, and the complexity of care for these elders present a challenge in caring to the professional nurses employed in nursing homes.

MICRO SOCIAL SITUATION

The unit of analysis for the micro social situation is the family and all the variables contained within. Assumed to be among the variables are the environmental conditions within a family, such as household composition, community hazards and/or assets. Among the issues or subcategories considered in the Micro Social Situation category are (1) family as the caregiving unit, and (2) quality of caregiving within families.

Family as the Caregiving Unit

An estimated 13.5 million or 7.1% of the U.S. population aged 14 years and older have disabled elderly spouses or parents either at home or in an institution. Approximately 1.8 million women, many of whom are also employed outside the home and caring for children at home, face elder care decisions. One in 12 full-time workers are potential caregivers and one in 60 are active caregivers. Long-term care of elders at home or in institutions is a family issue (Stone & Kemper, 1989). Phillips asserts that "without an orientation that first considers the needs of the elder-caregiver dyad, the health needs of the majority of elders in this country are being neglected" (1989b, p. 795).

Quality of Caregiving Within Families

Nurses in the community are witness to the extremes in care of elders by their family members. On the one hand is the family who gives care that is supportive, compassionate, and adequate, and on the other hand is the family who is neglectful and abusive to the elder (Phillips & Rempusheski, 1985, 1986a, 1986b). Determining nursing interventions in elder-family caregiving situations involves not only an understanding of geriatric nursing, but also an understanding of family nursing and the dynamics among multiple generations in a family, regardless of the geographical distance between the members.

Assessing the nature of an elder-family relationship is the essential first step for intervening in these situations. Phillips (1989b) recommends the need to understand the history of the relationship or the mental "dossier" compiled by members of the family, the social legitimization of roles, nature of the family power structure, and the structure of interactions, before a nurse can assess the image of caregiving, personal images of another, and the nature of family relationships within an elder-family caregiving situation. Protection of an elder's self-esteem may be one rationale used by family members for the way in which they give care (B.J. Brower, 1987). Assisting family members to communicate with elders who may be experiencing pathologic changes (Rempusheski & Phillips, 1988) and to deal with perceived burden (Klein, 1989) and burnout (Lindgren, 1990) are among the more common interventions gerontologic nurses face in these situations.

POLITICAL/ECONOMIC CLIMATE

In 1986, 11% of the U.S. gross domestic product (GDP) was spent on health. This exceeds the percentage spent on health in any one industrial nation in the world. In actual dollars, national health care expenditures average nearly $2,000 per person annually or $458 billion. Of these dollars, 39% is for hospital care, 20% to physician services, and approximately 8% to nursing home care. As a result of the Medicare and Medicaid programs the U.S. government's share of personal health care expenditures has increased from 10% in 1965 to 30% in 1986. In 1986, 28.2 million people aged 65 years and older were enrolled in Medicare. Medicare funds reimbursed an average of $2,870 per person served in 1986 (NCHS, 1989).

Cost containment and the Omnibus Budget Reconciliation Act (OBRA) of 1987 (as an example of current legislation) are the issues considered and briefly mentioned here in the Political/Economic Climate category. Subsequent chapters will address in detail public policy and economics relative to aging.

Cost Containment

The aforementioned health statistics speak to the urgency of containing costs in the health care arena. In an effort to cut costs of health care a number of programs and services for the elderly may be eliminated. Consequently,each cost-related proposal needs to be scrutinized for issues of discrimination due to age, disease or number of chronic diseases, income level or ability to pay for services on the one hand versus the availability of and accessibility to health services by the elderly on the other hand.

OBRA 1987

In an attempt to bring about a measure of quality assurance to nursing homes OBRA was passed by Congress in December 1987. The law amends Medicare and Medicaid statutes in the areas of quality of life of residents in nursing homes, scope of services required under plan of care, certification of residents assessment, provision of services and activities, required training of nurse aides, physician supervision and clinical records, and required social services. Effective October 1, 1990 was the elimination of the distinction between skilled nursing facilities and intermediate care facilities. Of specific concern for nursing is the new requirement for nurse aide training. The requirements of OBRA 1987 include the design and establishment of a 75-hour training program; competency evaluation method to include oral, written, and manual skill components; competency evaluation of aides currently in place; and the establishment of a registry of nurse aides. All of these requirements were to be in place by January 1990. Among the issues not addressed by this legislation, and as yet unresolved, are agency responsible for requirements, liability to nursing, development of evaluation tool, and the related issues of reliability, validity, and usefulness of the tool with the diverse population of nurse aides in nursing homes (Kelly, 1989).

HEALTH CARE MILIEU

The environment in which one receives care influences the outcomes of care. Creating a Health Care Milieu takes into account models of health care, role assignments, and units of care. Related issues within each of these subcategories will vary by setting (e.g., hospital, nursing home, rehabilitation facility, hospice), its philosophy or beliefs, and goals, and the philosophy of the nursing department within the setting, and may be individual or collective in nature. Especially important to this category are the influence of the Robert Wood Johnson Teaching Nursing Home Program (Mezey & Lynaugh, 1989; Mezey, Lynaugh, & Cartier, 1989; Small & Walsh, 1988) and the view of elders within the intensive care environments of acute care hospitals (Fulmer & Walker, 1990; Rempusheski, 1988b, 1990a).

Models of Care

Consider the following questions as issues for models of care within the health care milieu:

- How is the elder viewed? How are elders distinguished from each other? Distinguished as to short- and long-term care needs?
- Does the model of care allow for flexibility in meeting the complex care needs of elders?

Role Assignments

Consider the following questions as issues for role assignments within the health care milieu:

- What is the role of the person who gives direct care to the elder in this setting? How is this determined?
- Are the best possible nurse and other person resources used to meet the complex care needs of elders in this setting? How are nurse resources categorized? How are they accessed?
- What kinds of communication exist among the roles of persons who care for elders in this setting?

- How are collaboration, continuity of care, and consultation viewed among persons assigned specific roles in this setting?

Units of Care

Units of care may be perceived from an individual perspective—that is, a segment of time, space, and energy devoted to delivery of service and treatment to another—or they may be perceived in the collective sense—that is, a structural space within which a health care team delivers care to a group of individuals. Although pertinent issues may be raised about each of these perspectives, the latter will be addressed. Consider the following questions as issues for units of care:

- Are the elderly in this setting located on a single unit, called a "geriatric unit," or are they located throughout the setting on units specific to the diagnosis or care need?
- What is the attitude about elders of a specific age being placed in specialty units, such as coronary care, medical intensive care, surgical intensive care, transplant, and hemodialysis units?
- How are nurses supported in their care to elders on medical units where the percentage of elders or frail elders is high? Is the complexity of care to elders recognized and dealt with appropriately in this setting?

SPECIAL CARE REQUISITES

Among the issues to be considered within the Special Care Requisites are: client diversity, methods of care delivery, and level of complexity of care.

Client Diversity

The generalization of "over 65" does not distinguish the uniqueness of each decade of life beyond 65, and we "know" at least in anecdotal observations that a 75-year-old is very different from a 95-year-old. We also know, however, that we can be caring for several individuals who are the same chronological age and each one is very different physiologically, psychologically, and all the other ways that make each one of us unique. The frail elders at 85+ years old may have more in common with each other than with a younger cohort, but they are nonetheless unique individuals. Other areas of uniqueness, such as ethnicity, will be addressed in subsequent chapters.

Methods of Care Delivery

Primary care, primary nursing care, second generation primary nursing, case management, and patterns of care are some of the titles of methods of care delivery that are seen within health care environments. How each is articulated, despite a similarity of name may, however, vary by such factors as composition and type of nurses employed, size of facility, medical support, collaborating agencies, internal facilities, budget, and acuity or level of complexity of care.

Level of Complexity of Care

An example of special care requisites having become an issue with regard to level of complexity of care was briefly mentioned in the Section on Assignment of Caring Responsibility, above, wherein a rapid rise in the acuity level by residents discharged from hospital to nursing home has created a special care need. Accurate forecasting has become a dominant issue, not only for the demographers, but also for gerontological nurses. Not only understanding but also assimilating the meaning of elder demographic changes over the next decade in association with care needs will prepare nurses for the kinds of restructuring they will need to do to meet adequately the standards of gerontological nursing care.

STATE OF PROFESSIONAL NURSING

Four subcategories will be addressed within the State of Professional Nursing category: (1) certification, (2) gerontological nursing practice standards, (3) geriatric nursing research, and (4) gerontological nurses in the multidisciplinary arena.

Certification

The American Nurses Association (ANA) certification program was established in 1973 for the purpose of providing recognition of professional achievement in specific clinical or functional areas of nursing. The eligibility criteria, requirements for examination, and kind of examination have undergone numerous changes in each of the clinical and functional areas. ANA currently offers certification examinations as a Gerontological Nurse (a generalist certification established in 1974), Gerontological Nurse Practitioner (established in 1979), and Clinical Specialist in Gerontological Nursing (established in 1989). As of January 15, 1990, 8,109 nurses held ANA certification as a Gerontological

Nurse, 1,210 as a Gerontological Nurse Practitioner, and 127 as a Clinical Specialist in Gerontological Nursing ("Numbers of nurses," 1990).

The rise in numbers of nurses seeking ANA certification in one of these three areas of gerontological nursing is positive; however, do three examinations allow for the distinction of a nurse as an expert in gerontological nursing? Other issues, such as the nature of the requirements to qualify for each examination, hours of practice used as a measure of achievement, and guidelines that direct the educational preparation of the nurse are not consistent across the clinical area examinations (Futrell, 1990). Standardization across clinical areas of requirements for certification and recertification, guidelines of educational preparation that recognize the uniqueness of each specialty, and achievement of expertise at the master's level will acknowledge each clinical specialty as contributing in a unique and proportionally important way to the overall diversity of the profession of nursing.

Gerontological Nursing Practice Standards

The first published standards of gerontological nursing practice were published by the American Nurses' Association in 1967. They were revised in 1976 and included a list of "primary factors which are specific to the nursing of older persons," and seven standards (American Nurses' Association, 1976), and revised again in 1987 to include a major revision of the 1981 statement on the scope of gerontological nursing practice and 11 standards (American Nurses' Association, 1987). The most current revision, a 27-page document, classifies standards into organization of gerontological nursing services, theory, data collection, nursing diagnosis, planning and continuity of care, intervention, evaluation, interdisciplinary collaboration, research, ethics, and professional development. The scope of practice briefly summarizes those factors contributing to the practice of gerontological nursing. Demographic changes paralleled with professional nursing strides in gerontological nursing research will necessitate a revision of the scope of gerontological nursing practice within the next decade.

Geriatric Nursing Research

At nearly every international, national, regional, state, and local nursing research conference one can find a nurse who is engaged in geriatric nursing research. Although not necessarily identified as a geriatric nurse researcher, the content, concept, theory, or subject population suggests the researcher's interest in aging and/or the elderly.

Now in its third edition, the Sigma Theta Tau International *Directory of Nurse Researchers* has attempted to capture the nature of nursing research using a classification of topics that includes content, process, and theoretical divisions. Although the survey tool has changed quite dramatically between editions and the directions for respondents have gone from interest area to addressing the specific project(s) with which the researcher is engaged at the time of survey, the results can be compared to give at least one perspective to the number of nurses involved in geriatric nursing research. H. T. Brower (1985) reported on the results of the first edition of this directory, which was published in 1983. Data were received from 820 nurse researchers; 112 or 14% of the total indicated an interest in research on aging. The second edition (Barnard, Kiener, & Fawcett, 1987) reported data received from 3,681 active researchers; 2,299 nurse researchers or 62% of the total indicated they used young-old or old-old human subjects in their studies. Aging as a clinical topic was chosen by 418 researchers or 11% of the total number of respondents. The third edition of this directory (Hudgings, Hogan, & Stevenson, 1990) reported data received from 2,467 nurse researchers. The decrease in number of respondents may be reflective of the directions that requested only those researchers who currently had a study in process to complete the survey. Therefore, it is likely that a nurse just completing a study, or in the proposal stage, although actively involved in some aspect of research may not have responded to this survey. In addition, a major revision in categories took place between the second and third survey by Sigma Theta Tau. In this third edition those researchers who chose a developmental focus of young-old, middle-old or old-old, when cross-referenced for duplication of names, numbered 168 or 7% of the total number of respondents. Those researchers who chose a process focus on aging numbered 156 or 6% of the total number of respondents.

In the past two decades a number of nurses have assessed the state of geriatric nursing and geriatric nursing research from published articles and books dating back to the 1950s. Seven reviews of these data are currently published and are summarized in Table 1.1 by author, date of publication, source of data, dates (of sources used), organization of results, focus (of the assessment), and recommendations (resulting from the review).

Because the Adams (1986) review included published data through 1983, the next few paragraphs will focus on a summary of geriatric nursing research beginning in 1984 through August 1990. The following journals were perused for theory, research, and instrumentation articles that dealt with elder care, aging, or included elders in their sample: *Research in Nursing and Health, Nursing Research, Western Journal of Nursing Research,* and *Image.* The objectives of this review were threefold: to gain a sense of the nature of geriatric nursing research being communicated in a general nursing research forum rather than in geriatric specialty journals, to gain a perspective on the development of geriatric programs of research by individual researchers, and to detect a "filling-in" of the areas of need indicated by previous reviewers of geriatric research.

Table 1.1
Published Reviews of Gerontological Nursing Literature

Author (Date)	Source of Data	Dates	Organization of Results	Focus	Recommendations
Basson (1967)	Nursing literature	1955-1965	438 nursing care & health services publications are classified by types of article, e.g., theory, research, opinion, etc.	Nature of gerontological nursing literature	Need for research in all areas of elder care, theory development
Gunter & Miller (1977)	*Nursing Research* (vol 1=1952)[a] & psychosocial literature	1952-1976	17 studies of aged in *NR*: 5 categorized as clinical, 4 as attitudes of nurses, 8 as surveys of aged problems; 29 studies in psychosocial literature: 9 classified as psychosocial characteristics, 4 as nurse attitudes, 16 nurse interventions	State of research art in gerontological nursing	Need for longitudinal studies; clinical research studies; research utilization
Brimmer (1979)	150 nursing journals in *International Nursing Index* & nonnursing journals in *Index Medicus*	1966, 1971, 1976	Table categorizing articles by percentage, number, topic, e.g., aged, aging, institutions, geriatric nursing	Past, present & future of gerontological nursing; review of literature featured; funding sources, education	Need for research re: social perspective of aging, trends, multidisciplinary, basic human needs; research utilization

Robinson, L. D. (1981)	Nursing journals in *International Nursing Index*, abstracts in *Nursing Research*	1966-11/79	Organized by substantive problem area, framework, method, findings, and trends	Identify body of knowledge in gerontological nursing research	General need in all areas of research on aging; need for nurses educationally prepared to conduct research on elders; need to disseminate new geriatric nursing knowledge to nurse clinicians, educators and researchers
Kayser-Jones (1981)	*WJNR* (vol 1=1979)[a] *RINAH* (vol 1=1978)[a] *JGN* (vol 1=1975)[a] *GN* (vol 1=1980)[a] *Nursing Research*	vol 1 to 7/80; NR = 1/77-7/80	44 research articles categorized: 12 as clinical focus, 7 as attitudes toward aged, 9 as psychosocial problems, 7 as problems of institutionalized elders, 3 as health needs of elder in community, 2 as sexuality in aged, 2 as minority aged, 2 as review of gerontological nurse research	State of gerontological nursing research	Need geriatric/gerontological nursing content in basic and in graduate nurse education; need for elder care research to improve quality care
Wolanin (1983)	Nursing research journals; journals of gerontological/geriatric nursing; dissertations	1952-1982; 1975-1982	Organized into 10 clinical factors: personal care, sleep, movement, medication, relocation, personal space, incontinence, family caregivers, support & stress, changes in mental status	State of the art in clinical geriatric nursing research	5 problems identified in conducting clinical geriatric nursing research with need to improve in these areas: conceptual issues, concern with methods, need for more descriptive studies, instrument construction, analysis of data

(continued)

Table 1.1
Continued

Author (Date)	Source of Data	Dates	Organization of Results	Focus	Recommendations
Adams (1986)	Nursing journals, research conference proceedings: ANA clinical conferences, *GN*, *IJNS*, *JAN*, *JGN*, *NR*, *WJNR*, *RINAH*; RNs as first authors in gerontology journals: *JAGS*, *Geriatrics*, *JG*, *Gerontologist*	vol 1-1983 1980-1983	Organized into 3 categories and subcategories: Enabling physical functioning ADLs, e.g., bathing, dressing, feeding; Enhancing self-esteem, e.g., communication; Optimizing environments of care, e.g., selecting a care environment	State of knowledge in gerontological nursing gained through research	Directions for research; need for: discrimination between age cohorts, measurement tools, replication studies, retirement studies, operation-alization of health in elders

Note: Key to journal titles: GN: *Geriatric Nursing*; IJNS: *International Journal of Nursing Studies*; JAGS: *Journal of the American Geriatric Society*; JAN: *Journal of Advanced Nursing*; JG: *Journal of Gerontology*; JGN: *Journal of Gerontological Nursing*; NR: *Nursing Research*; RINAH: *Research in Nursing and Health*; WJNR: *Western Journal of Nursing Research*.

a. The vol. 1 with a year indicates that the first volume of that journal was published in the year indicated; when volume #1 is indicated in column three it refers to the year the journal was initially published, and thus the review began in different years for different journals.

b. Kayser-Jones begins her review of *Nursing Research* in 1977, which picks up from the review done by Gunter and Miller which reviewed *Nursing Research* from its inception to 1976.

During the 7-year period of this review a gerontological nursing research-related article appeared, on the average, of one per issue per journal reviewed. A few of these articles addressed issues such as gerontological nursing research agendas/priorities (H. T. Brower & Crist, 1985; Duffy, Hepburn, Christensen, & Brugge-Wiger, 1989), the relationship of nurses and elder care, such as choice of career in care of elders (DeWitt & Matre, 1988), attitudes of nurses to elders (McCabe, 1989), and need for gerontological nurses and GNPs (Oakley, 1986; Shamansky & St. Germain, 1987), continuity of elder care, such as discharge planning (Nalor, 1990), congruence between acute care and long-term care research (Engle, 1986a), and resource requirements for long-term care (Gamroth, 1988). Although the majority of these articles addressed topics that "filled-in" the areas of research need indicated by previous reviewers of geriatric research (Table 1.2), many of these studies represent another area of research need—the request for descriptive studies.

Theory development specific to elder care topics was also evident in this review (Pallett, 1990; Phillips & Rempusheski, 1985), as was an increased number of multidisciplinary studies (Brink, Sampselle, Wells, Diokno, & Gillis, 1989; Buckwalter, Cusack, Sidles, Wadle, & Beaver, 1989; Chang, Uman, Linn, Ware, & Kane, 1984, 1985; Given, Stommel, Collins, King, & Given, 1990; Keller, Leventhal, Prohaska, & Leventhal, 1989; Morris et al., 1990). Tracking the multiple studies reported by authors revealed a trend toward developing programs of research in gerontological nursing in contrast to diverse studies from an opportunistic model of research. These include Foreman's work related to confusion in the elderly (Foreman, 1986, 1987, 1989), Gass's studies of widows and widowers (Gass, 1987; Gass & Chang, 1989), Phillips's investigations of elder-caregiver dyads (Phillips & Rempusheski, 1985, 1986a, 1986b; Phillips, Rempusheski, & Morrison, 1989), and Reed's work in religiousness and spirituality (Reed, 1986a, 1986b, 1987, 1989).

Other articles addressed physiological age changes (Frantz & Kinney, 1986), depression related to age/caregiving (Newman & Gaudiano, 1984; Nickel, Brown & Smith, 1990; K. M. Robinson, 1989), and issues nurses and others face in the care of elders at home, in institutions, and in the hospital (Norberg & Asplund, 1990; Pasquale, 1987; Robb, 1985; Roberts & Lincoln, 1988; Ryden, 1984; Shelly, Zahorchak, & Gambrill, 1987; Wilson, 1989). Some areas of research need remain and have been addressed marginally within the context of existing studies or not at all. Life-style or quality of life topics have been studied (Diamond, McCance, & King, 1987; Hoeffer, 1987); however, retirement studies per se have not been addressed specifically. Also absent from the nursing research literature reviewed are studies that discriminate between age cohorts, are replications of prior studies, and are examples of research utilization in gerontology.

Table 1.2

Summary of Gerontological Nursing Research Published Between 1984-1990, Arranged Alphabetically by Author and Data Within Area of Research Need Indicated by Previous Reviewers of Gerontological Nursing Literature

		Areas of Research Need		
Social Perspectives of Aging	*Process Issues: Conceptual, Method, and Analysis*	*Basic Human Needs*	*Operationalization of Health in Elders*	*Developed Tools*
Baillie, Norbeck, & Barnes (1988)	Gueldner & Hanner (1989)	Eating/feeding: Athlin et al. (1989)	Brown & McCreedy (1986)	Bergstrom, Braden, Laguzza, & Holman (1987)
Herth (1990)	Phillips (1989a)	Kayser-Jones (1990)	Burckhardt (1987)	Morris et al. (1990)
Kirschling & McBride (1989)	Robb et al. (1986)	Norberg & Athlin (1989)	Duffy & McDonald (1990)	Phillips, Rempusheski, & Morrison (1989)
Ryan & Austin (1989)		Communication: Buckwalter et al. (1989)	Engle (1986b) Gass (1987)	Stokes & Gordon (1988)
		Comfort:	Gass & Change (1989)	
		Burke & Jerrett (1989)	Johnson et al. (1988)	
		Faherty & Grier (1984)	Reed (1989)	
		Kolanowski (1990)	Rempusheski (1988a, 1990b)	
		Pieper, Cleland, Johnson, & O'Reilly (1989)	Speake, Cowart, & Pellett (1989)	
		White et al. (1987)		
		Sleep:		
		Hoch, Reynolds, & Houck (1988)		
		Kedas, Lux, & Amodeo (1989)		

Safety:
  Janken, Reynolds, &
    Swiech (1986)
  Strumpf & Evans
    (1988)
  Whedon & Shedd (1989)
ADLs:
  Burckhardt (1985)
  Kim (1986)
  Mason (1988)
  Stevenson & Topp
    (1990)
  Travis (1988)
Sex:
  Steinke (1988)

Gerontological Nurses in the Multidisciplinary Arena

Gerontology crosses the lines of many disciplines in the biological, behavioral, social, health care, and medical sciences. The national forum for scientists to meet and share research in gerontology is the annual scientific meeting of the Gerontological Society of America (GSA). Affiliation with the GSA assumes one values and recognizes the multidisciplinary nature of gerontology. As H. T. Brower indicated (1985), a nurse scholar's membership in the GSA is one indicator of this assumed value and recognition. Since 1985, nurse membership in the GSA has risen from 740 nurses or 12.4% of a total of 5,968 members (H. T. Brower, 1985) to the current number of 1,002 nurses or 15% of a total of 6,814 members (Phelan, 1990). As was true in 1985, nurses occupy each of the four designated sections of GSA as well as its noncommitted, member-at-large category. In September 1990 there were 476 nurses or 31% of the total of 1,548 members in the Clinical Medicine (CM) section, 331 nurses or 11% of the total of 3,045 members in the Behavioral and Social Sciences (BSS) section, 153 nurses or 9% of the total of 1,620 members in the Social Research Planning and Practice section, 40 nurses or 9% of the total of 466 members in the Biological Sciences section, and 2 nurses or less than 1% of the total of 135 uncommitted members-at-large. The commitment of the nurse scholar has continued to grow in recognition by GSA colleagues. This is demonstrated by 2 more nurses elected as fellows to the GSA since 1985 bringing that total to 14, nurses elected to hold office in the CM and BSS sections, and a nurse—Elizabeth Nichols, DNS—assuming the position of secretary of the GSA in 1991, the first nurse to receive such recognition in society-wide elections. Chair-elect and vice-chair positions in the Clinical Medicine section will be held by nurses in 1991 (*Gerontology News,* 1990).

SUMMARY

We gain a total perspective on the present when we reflect on the past and predict the future based on what we know today. At one point in time, the present—the Autumn of 1990—the reader has been given a glimpse of what the past has revealed to us about aging and gerontological nursing and what we perceive will be our future. The future of gerontology depends on our systematic, consistent, and careful examination of the macro and micro social situations, political/economic climate, health care milieu, special care requisites, and the state of professional nursing, followed by the appropriate interventions in order to effectively influence elder care and gerontological nursing.

REFERENCES

Adams, M. (1986). Aging: Gerontological nursing research. In H. H. Werley, J. J. Fitzpatrick, & R. L. Tauton (Eds.), *Annual review of nursing research* (pp. 77-103). New York: Springer.

American Nurses' Association. (1976). *Standards of gerontological nursing practice.* Kansas City, MO: American Nurses' Association.

American Nurses' Association. (1987). *Standards and scope of gerontological nursing practice.* Kansas City, MO: American Nurses' Association.

Athlin, E., Norberg, A., Axelsson, K., Möller, A., & Nordstroöm, G. (1989). Aberrant eating behavior in elderly Parkinsonian patients with and without dementia: Analysis of video-recorded meals. *Research in Nursing & Health, 12,* 41-51.

Baillie, V., Norbeck, J. A., & Barnes, L. E. A. (1988). Stress, social support and psychological distress of family caregivers of the elderly. *Nursing Research, 37,* 217-222.

Barnard, R., Kiener, M., & Fawcett, J. (Eds.). (1987). *Directory of nurse researchers* (2nd ed.). Indianapolis, IN: Sigma Theta Tau International.

Basson, P. H. (1967). The gerontological nursing literature. *Nursing Research, 16,* 267-272.

Bergstrom, N., Braden, B. J., Laguzza, A., & Holman, V. (1987). The Braden scale for predicting pressure sore risk. *Nursing Research, 36,* 205-210.

Brimmer, P. F. (1979). Past, present and future in gerontological nursing research. *Journal of Gerontological Nursing, 5,* 6, 27-34.

Brink, C. A., Sampselle, C. M., Wells, T. J., Diokno, A.C., & Gillis, G. L. (1989). A digital test for pelvic muscle strength in older women with urinary incontinence. *Nursing Research, 38,* 196-199.

Brower, B. J. (1987). Intergenerational caregiving: Adult caregivers and their aging parents. *Advances in Nursing Science, 9,* 20-31.

Brower, H. T. (1985). Gerontological nursing: Movement towards a paradigm state. *Journal of Professional Nursing, 1,* 6, 328-335.

Brower, H. T., & Crist, M. A. (1985). Research priorities in gerontologic nursing for long-term care. *Image: Journal of Nursing Scholarship, 17,* 22-27.

Brown, J. S., & McCreedy, M. (1986). The hale elderly: Health behavior and its correlates. *Research in Nursing & Health, 9,* 317-329.

Buckwalter, K. C., Cusack, D., Sidles, E., Wadle, K., & Beaver, M. (1989). Increasing communication ability in aphasic/dysarthric patients. *Western Journal of Nursing Research, 11,* 736-747.

Burckhardt, C. S. (1985). The impact of arthritis on quality of life. *Nursing Research, 34,* 11-16.

Burckhardt, C. S. (1987). The effect of therapy on the mental health of the elderly. *Research in Nursing & Health, 10,* 277-285.

Burke, S. O., & Jerrett, M. (1989). Pain management across age groups. *Western Journal of Nursing Research, 11,* 164-180.

Burns-Tisdale, S., & Goff, W. (1989). The geriatric nurse practitioner in home care: Challenges, stressors, and rewards. *Nursing Clinics of North America, 24,* 809-817.

Census of Population and Housing: 1980. (1983). Washington, DC: U.S. Department of Commerce, Bureau of the Census.

Chang, B. L., Uman, G. C., Linn, L.s., Ware, J. E., & Kane, R. L. (1984). The effect of systematically varying components of nursing care on satisfaction in elderly ambulatory women. *Western Journal of Nursing Research, 6,* 367-386.

Chang, B. L., Uman, G. C., Linn, L. S., Ware, J. E., & Kane, R. L. (1985). Adherence to health care regimens among elderly women. *Nursing Research, 34,* 27-31.

DeWitt, S. C., & Matre, M. (1988). Nursing careers working with the elderly. *Western Journal of Nursing Research, 10,* 335-343.

Diamond, M., McCance, K., & King, K. (1987). Forced residential relocation: Its impact on the well-being of older adults. *Western Journal of Nursing Research, 9,* 445-464.

Duffy, L. M., Hepburn, K., Christensen, R., & Brugge-Wiger, P. (1989). A research agenda in care for patients with Alzheimers disease. *Image: Journal of Nursing Scholarship, 21,* 254-257.

Duffy, M. E., & MacDonald, E. (1990). Determinants of functional health of older persons. *The Gerontologist, 30,* 503-509.

Engle, V. F. (1986a). Bridging the research gap between acute and long-term care of older adults. *Image: Journal of Nursing Scholarship, 18,* 148-150.

Engle, V. F. (1986b). The relationship of movement and time to older adults' functional health. *Research in Nursing & Health, 9,* 123-129.

Faherty, B. S., & Grier, M. R. (1984). Analgesic medication for elderly people post-surgery. *Nursing Research, 33,* 369-372.

Foreman, M. D. (1986). Acute confusional states in hospitalized elderly: A research dilemma. *Nursing Research, 35,* 34-37.

Foreman, M. D., (1987). Reliability and validity of mental status questionnaires in elderly hospitalized patients. *Nursing Research, 36,* 216-220.

Foreman, M. D. (1989). Confusion in the hospitalized elderly: Incidence, onset, and associated factors. *Research in Nursing & Health, 12,* 21-29.

Frantz, R. A., & Kinney, C. K. (1986). Variables associated with skin dryness in the elderly. *Nursing Research, 35,* 98-100.

Fulmer, T. T., & Walker, M. K. (1990). Lessons from the elder boom in ICUs. *Geriatric Nursing, 11,* 120-121.

Futrell, M. (1990). Professional certification and gerontological nursing. *Journal of Gerontological Nursing, 16,* 5, 3.

Gamroth, L. (1988). Long-term care resource requirements before and after the prospective payment system. *Image: Journal of Nursing Scholarship, 20,* 7-11.

Gass, K. A. (1987). The health of conjugally bereaved older widows: The role of appraisal, coping and resources. *Research in Nursing & Health, 10,* 39-47.

Gass, K. A., & Chang, A. S. (1989). Appraisals of bereavement, coping, resources, and psychosocial health dysfunction in widows and widowers. *Nursing Research, 38,* 31-36.

Gerontology News (1990, August). Washington, DC: Gerontological Society of America.

Given, B., Stommel, M., Collins, C., King, S., & Given, C. W. (1990). Responses of elderly spouse caregivers. *Research in Nursing & Health, 13,* 77-85.

Gueldner, S. H., & Hanner, M. B. (1989). Methodological issues related to gerontological nursing research. *Nursing Research, 38,* 183-185.

Gunter, L. M., & Miller, J. C. (1977). Toward a nursing gerontology. *Nursing Research, 26,* 208-221.

Haynes, S. G., & Feinleib, M. (1980). *Second conference on the epidemiology of aging.* Bethesda, MD: National Institute on Aging, Department of Health and Human Services.

Herth, K. (1990). Relationship of hope, coping styles, concurrent losses, and setting to grief resolution in the elderly widow(er). *Research in Nursing & Health, 13,* 109-117.

Hoch, C. C., Reynolds, C. F., & Houck, P. R. (1988). Sleep patterns in Alzheimer, depressed, and healthy elderly. *Western Journal of Nursing Research, 10,* 239-256.

Hoeffer, B. (1987). Predictors of life outlook of older single women. *Research in Nursing & Health, 10,* 111-117.

Hudgings, C., Hogan, R., & Stevenson, J. (Eds.). (1990). *Directory of nurse researchers* (3rd ed.). Indianapolis, IN: Sigma Theta Tau International.

Janken, J. K., Reynolds, B. A., & Swiech, K. (1986). Patient falls in the acute care setting: Identifying risk factors. *Nursing Research, 35,* 215-219.

Johnson, F. L., Foxall, M. J., Kelleher, E., Kentopp, E., Mannlein, E. A., & Cook, E. (1988). Comparison of mental health and life satisfaction of five elderly ethnic groups. *Western Journal of Nursing Research, 10,* 613-628.

Kayser-Jones, J. (1981). Gerontological nursing research revisited. *Journal of Gerontological Nursing, 7,* 217-223.

Kayser-Jones, J. (1990). The use of nasogastric feeding tubes in nursing homes: Patient, family and health care provider perspectives. *The Gerontologist, 30,* 469-479.

Kedas, A., Lux, W., & Amodeo, S. (1989). A critical review of aging and sleep research. *Western Journal of Nursing Research, 11,* 196-206.

Keller, M. L., Leventhal, H., Prohaska, T. R., & Leventhal, E. A., (1989). Beliefs about aging and illness in a community sample. *Research in Nursing & Health, 12,* 247-255.

Kelly, M (1989). The omnibus budget reconciliation act of 1987: A policy analysis. *Nursing Clinics of North America, 24,* 791-794.

Kim, K. K. (1986). Response time and health care learning of elderly patients. *Research in Nursing & Health, 9,* 233-239.

Kirschling, J. M., & McBride, A. B. (1989). Effects of age and sex on the experience of widowhood. *Western Journal of Nursing Research, 11,* 207-218.

Klein, S. (1989). Caregiver burden and moral development. *Image: Journal of Nursing Scholarship, 21,* 94-97.

Kolanowski, A. M. (1990). Restlessness in the elderly: The effect of artificial lighting. *Nursing Research, 39,* 181-183.

Lindgren, C. L. (1990). Burnout and social support in family caregivers. *Western Journal of Nursing Research, 12,* 469-487.

Magilvy, J. K. (1985). Quality of life of hearing-impaired older women. *Nursing Research, 34,* 140-144.

Mason, D. J. (1988). Circadian rhythms of body temperature and activation and the well-being of older women. *Nursing Research, 37,* 276-281.

McCabe, B. W. (1989). Ego defensiveness and its relationship to attitudes of registered nurses toward older people. *Research in Nursing & Health, 12,* 85-91.

McCullough, C. (1985). *A creed for the third millennium.* New York: Harper & Row.

Mezey, M.D., & Lynaugh, J. E. (1989). The teaching nursing home program: Outcomes of care. *Nursing Clinics of North America, 24,* 769-780.

Mezey, M. D., Lynaugh, J. E., & Cartier, M. M. (Eds.). (1989). *Nursing homes and nursing care: Lessons from the teaching nursing home.* New York: Springer.

Morris, J. N., Hawes, C., Fries, B. E., Phillips, C. D., Mor, V., Katz, S., Murphy, K., Drugovich, M. L., & Friedlob, A. S. (1990). Designing the national resident assessment instrument for nursing homes. *The Gerontologist, 30,* 293-307.

Naisbitt, J. (1984). *Megatrends: Ten new directions transforming our lives.* New York: Warner Books.

National Center for Health Statistics. (1989). *Health, United States, 1988.* Hyattsville, MD: Public Health Service.

National Center for Health Statistics. (1990). *Health, United States, 1989.* Hyattsville, MD: Public Health Service.

Naylor, M. D. (1990). Comprehensive discharge planning for hospitalized elderly: A pilot study. *Nursing Research, 39,* 156-161.

Newman, M. A., & Gaudiano, J. K. (1984). Depression as an explanation for decreased subjective time in the elderly. *Nursing Research, 33,* 137-139.

Norberg, A., & Asplund, K. (1990). Caregivers' experience of caring for severely demented patients. *Western Journal of Nursing Research, 12,* 75-84.

Norberg, A., & Athlin, E. (1989). Eating problems in severely demented patients: Issues and ethical dilemmas. *Nursing Clinics of North America, 24,* 781-789.

Nickel, J. T., Brown, K. J., & Smith, B. A. (1990). Depression and anxiety among chronically ill heart patients: Age differences in risk and predictors. *Research in Nursing & Health, 13,* 87-97.

Numbers of nurses certified in gerontology on the rise. (1990). *Oasis, 7,* 2, 5.

Oakley, D. (1986). Projecting the number of professional nurses required for in-hospital, direct care of older people, 1970-2050. *Western Journal of Nursing Research, 8,* 343-349.

Pallett, P. J. (1990). A conceptual framework for studying family caregiver burden in Alzheimer's type dementia. *Image: Journal of Nursing Scholarship, 22,* 52-58.

Pasquale, D. K. (1987). A basis for prospective payment for home care. *Image: Journal of Nursing Scholarship, 19,* 186-191.

Phelan, J. Y. (1990, September 14). Telephone communication. Washington, DC: Gerontological Society of America.

Phillips, L. R. (1989a). Age: A truly confounding variable. *Western Journal of Nursing Research, 11,* 181-195.

Phillips, L. R. (1989b). Elder-family caregiver relationships: Determining appropriate nursing interventions. *Nursing Clinics of North America, 24,* 795-807.

Phillips, L. R. (1989c, April). *Research-based elder care: The future is now.* Paper presented at the Elder Care: Today's Research, Tomorrow's Practice Symposium, Boston, MA.

Phillips, L. R., & Rempusheski, V. F. (1985). A decision-making model for diagnosing and intervening in elder abuse and neglect. *Nursing Research, 34,* 134-139.

Phillips, L. R., & Rempusheski, V. F. (1986a). Caring for the frail elderly at home: Toward a theoretical explanation of the dynamics of poor quality family caregiving. *Advances in Nursing Science, 8,* 4, 62-84.

Phillips, L. R., & Rempusheski, V. F. (1986b). Making decisions about elder abuse. *Social Casework, 67,* 3, 131-140.

Phillips, L. R., Rempusheski, V. F., & Morrison, E. (1989). Developing and testing the beliefs about caregiving scale. *Research in Nursing & Health, 12,* 207-220.

Pieper, B., Cleland, V., Johnson, D. E., & O'Reilly, J. L. (1989). Inventing urine incontinence devices for women. *Image: Journal of Nursing Scholarship, 21,* 203-209.

Reed, P. G. (1986a). Developmental resources and depression in the elderly. *Nursing Research, 35,* 368-374.

Reed, P. G. (1986b). Religiousness among terminally ill and health adults. *Research in Nursing & Health, 9,* 35-41.

Reed, P. G. (1987). Spirituality and well-being in terminally ill hospitalized adults. *Research in Nursing & Health, 10,* 335-344.

Reed, P. G., (1989). Mental health of older adults. *Western Journal of Nursing Research, 11,* 143-163.

Rempusheski, V. F. (1988a). Caring for self and others: Second generation Polish American elders in an ethnic club. *Journal of Cross-Cultural Gerontology, 3,* 4, 223-271.

Rempusheski, V. F. (1988b). Nursing administrators: What are their research needs? How can they support critical care research? *Heart & Lung, 17,* 456-457.

Rempusheski, V. F. (1990a). The gerontological nursing program. *Nursing Administration Quarterly, 14,* 2, 7-10.

Rempusheski, V. F. (1990b). Role of the extended family in parenting: A focus on grandparents of preterm infants. *Journal of Perinatal and Neonatal Nursing, 4,* 2, 43-55.

Rempusheski, V. F., & Phillips, L. R. (1988). Elders versus caregivers: Games they play. *Geriatric Nursing, 9,* 1, 30-34.

Robb, S. S. (1985). Urinary incontinence verification in elderly men. *Nursing Research, 34,* 278-282.

Robb, S. S., Stegman, C. E., & Wolanin, M. O. (1986). No research versus research with compromised results: A study of validation therapy. *Nursing Research, 35,* 113-118.

Roberts, B. L., & Lincoln, R. E. (1988). Cognitive disturbance in hospitalized and institutionalized elders. *Research in Nursing & Health, 11,* 309-319.

Robinson, K. M. (1989). Predictors of depression among wife caregivers. *Nursing Research, 38,* 359-363.

Robinson, L. D. (1981). Gerontological nursing research. In I. M. Burnside (Ed.), *Nursing and the aged* (2nd ed.) (pp. 654-666). New York: McGraw-Hill.

Ryan, M. C., & Austin, A. G. (1989). Social supports and social networks in the aged. *Image: Journal of Nursing Scholarship, 21,* 176-180.

Ryden, M. B. (1984). Morale and perceived control in institutionalized elderly. *Nursing Research, 33,* 130-136.

Shamansky, S. L., & St. Germain, L. (1987). The elderly market for nurse practitioner services. *Western Journal of Nursing Research, 9,* 87-106.

Shelley, S. I., Zahorchak, R. M., & Gambrill, C. D. S. (1987). Aggressiveness of nursing care for older patients and those with do-not-resuscitate orders. *Nursing Research, 36,* 157-162.

Small, N. R., & Walsh, M. B. (Eds.). (1988). *Teaching nursing homes: The nursing perspective.* Owings Mills, MD: National Health Publishing.

Speake, D. L., Cowart, M. E., & Pellet, K. (1989). Health perceptions and lifestyles of the elderly. *Research in Nursing & Health, 12,* 93-100.

Steinke, E. E., (1988). Older adults' knowledge and attitudes about sexuality and aging. *Image: Journal of Nursing Scholarship, 20,* 93-95.

Stevenson, J. S., & Topp, R. (1990). Effect of moderate and low intensity long-term exercise by older adults. *Research in Nursing & Health, 13,* 209-218.

Stone, R. I., & Kemper, P. (1989). *Spouses and children of disabled elders: Potential and active caregivers.* Rockville, MD: National Center for Health Services Research and Health Care Technology Assessment.

Stokes, S. A., & Gordon, S. E. (1988). Development of an instrument to measure stress in the older adult. *Nursing Research, 37,* 16-19.

Strumpf, N. E., & Evans, L. K. (1988). Physical restraint of the hospitalized elderly: Perceptions of patients and nurses. *Nursing Research, 37,* 132-137.

Travis, S. S. (1988). Observer-rated functional assessments for institutionalized elders. *Nursing Research, 37,* 138-143.

U.S. Bureau of the Census. (1990). *Statistical abstract of the United States* (100th ed.). Washington, DC: Government Printing Office.

U.S. Department of Health, Education and Welfare. (1979). *Healthy people: The Surgeon General's report on health promotion and disease prevention* (DHEW publication No. PHS 79-55071). Washington, DC: Government Printing Office.

Whedon, M. B., & Shedd, P. (1989). Prediction and prevention of patient falls. *Image: Journal of Nursing Scholarship, 21,* 108-114.

White, H. E., Thurston, N. E., Blackmore, K. A., Green, S. E., & Hannah, K. J. (1987). Body temperature in elderly surgical patients. *Research in Nursing & Health, 10,* 317-321.

Wilson, H. S. (1989). Family caregiving for a relative with Alzheimer's dementia: Coping with negative choices. *Nursing Research, 38,* 94-98.

Wolanin, M. O. (1983). Clinical geriatric nursing research. In H. H. Werley & J. J. Fitzpatrick (Eds.), *Annual review of nursing research* (pp. 77-99). New York: Springer.

2

Building Theory for Gerontological Nursing

JOANNE E. RYAN

Objectives:

(1) Appreciates criteria of aging as clinical conceptual tools and theoretical constructs for research
(2) Realizes power of analytic thinking flowing from clinical observations in congruence with existing knowledge, concepts, hypotheses, and theory for explication of nursing research
(3) Analyzes components of theory building for development of theoretical models in gerontological nursing
(4) Integrates gerontological nursing concepts in curricular processes

INTRODUCTION

In *Precepts* (c. 450 B.C.) found in the Hippocratic collection (Hippocrates, 1962), physicians and medical students were warned that if theorizing arises from plausible fiction rather than from a clear foundation of fact, it will be patients who suffer and not practitioners. From the beginning of the Hippocratic health care model adopted by the Western world, knowledge has been linked to theory and theory to practice with practice as the learning ground to discover facts which then could lead on to theory. This basic scientific model contained elements of recorded observations from history taking, physical examination, diagnoses, prognoses, prescription of therapeutic regimes and determination of patient progress, recovery, or adverse reaction to the regimes. The similarity to the nursing process today is remarkable.

Table 2.1
Theory Construction

Explication of assumptions
Delineating concepts
Identifying linkages among phenomena
Definition of terms
Stating hypotheses
Testing hypotheses

In gerontological nursing, existing knowledge, concepts, and theories of aging in scientific fields are important to know and consider in building blocks of nursing knowledge, concepts, and theory.

Theory construction consists of the following processes: explication of assumptions, delineating concepts, identifying linkages among phenomena, definition of terms, stating hypotheses, and testing hypotheses (see Table 2.1 for an outline of these elements).

Key factors in aging knowledge, concepts, and theory are criteria of aging, biophysical/psychosocial factors, theories of aging, and nursing. These factors will be evaluated in the following sections.

CRITERIA OF AGING

Strehler (1977) has identified four criteria of aging. He argues that aging is universal, intrinsic, progressive, and deleterious. All four criteria must be met before a phenomenon can be identified as normal aging. There have not been counterarguments to these criteria, although deleterious is the least used criterion in efforts to distinguish normal aging from pathological processes and in differentiation of normal and dysfunctional states. These criteria also have become guidelines to critique theories of aging, and clinical tools to differentiate aging from pathology.

If these criteria are accepted, then it is immediately apparent that there is a sharp demarcation between the continuation of normal aging and the external attempts to mask aging. Whether or not cosmetics, plastic surgery, and fashion are used to appear younger in an age of youth, the intrinsic process of aging will progress for all and eventually will lead to death because all species are time limited.

Using these criteria in nursing assessment provides strong intellectual tools. For example, in normal aging the skin will become less elastic, lose some collagen structuring, have decreased oil excretion, lose adipose padding under the skin, and will discolor to some extent (see Table 2.2 for a brief overview

Table 2.2
Brief Overview of Selected Normal Aging Changes

Vision	yellowing cornea (Carter, 1982) increased density, rigidity, opaqueness of lens (Leighton, 1973) sclerosing of iris (Bell, Wolf, & Bernholz, 1972; Leighton, 1973) stiffening of ciliary muscles (Carter, 1982) atrophy of photoreceptor cells (Carter, 1982) changes in depth perception (Bell et al., 1972)
Hearing	ossification of bone (Timiras, 1978)
Muscle	decrease in number and strength of fibers (Schimke & Agneil, 1983)
Bone	decrease in density and mass (Jacobs, 1981)
Cardiovascular	decrease in elasticity, pumping ability, reaction time (Lipsitz, 1989)
Gastrointestinal	probable decrease in muscle tone and digestive enzymes (Schneider, 1983)
Renal & Bladder	decrease in number of nephrons, elasticity and strength of muscular tone (Shock et al., 1984)
Cognitive	maintenance or some decrease of intelligence but decreasing ability to solve problems after 60 (Botwinick, 1977)
Skin	decreasing elasticity and decreasing underlying adipose tissue and collagen support (Grove & Kingman, 1983).
Immune System	decreasing response to bacterial antigen and beginning to produce autoantibodies to make immune response to own tissue (Weksler, 1990; Harvard, 1981; Gershwin, Beach, & Hurley, 1983; Kay & MacKinodon, 1976).
Body Composition	fat percentage increases 16% from 25% to 75% and water decreases 8% (Jacobs, 1981)
Metabolism of Drugs	absorption is achieved but liver detoxification is impaired and delayed (Ritschel, 1978) prolonged renal clearance (Cuny, 1979)

of normal physiological aging changes). Observation of dryness of the skin, wrinkles, lines, an appearance of skin thinness, and some skin discolorations are expected with aging. In contrast, bruising, lacerations, and neoplasms are not to be considered as intrinsic, universal aging because these are not found on all aging people and in the case of bruising and lacerations, these are not intrinsic normal aging but external trauma. Growths and marked skin changes of pigment can be noted by the nurse for medical referral. These may be pathologies triggered by sun radiation or other external environmental toxins but need medical attention.

These criteria can also be used in broader clinical nursing contexts. For example, if a record is made in assessment of an elderly person such as pain or unsteadiness of gait the nurse must look further because these traits may be progressing and deleterious, but they are not universal. Again, any factor in an elderly person must meet all four criteria before it can be identified as normal aging. These criteria then allow us to take the myth out of aging. Clearly, acceptance of confusion, immobility, and disease as normal aging is an error of knowledge and lack of conceptual use of accepted aging criteria.

A main assumption flowing from this discussion of criteria of aging is that aging is a normal process of life. This assumption is in direct contrast to any assumption that aging is a disease process that should be treated.

THEORIES OF AGING

Serious research into the aging process itself has been expanding within the last 20 years. In such a short time, large banks of data are not readily available and perhaps theories of aging have not been grounded in the amount of research that would give a high probability of certitude. Hayflick (1985) has categorized theories of aging into organ theories (immune system, neuroendocrine), physiological theories (free radical), and Genome based theories (genetic). The theories of aging are found throughout literature on aging. These include genetic theory research (Abbot, Abbey, Bolling, & Murphy, 1978; Morin, 1985; Rothstein, 1986; Sohal, Birnham, & Cutler, 1985); physiological research of aging (Cerami, Dassara, & Brownlee, 1987; Colett, Griffith, & Zil, 1984; Finch & Hayflick, 1977; Havard, 1981; Morin, 1985); and organ theories (Everitt & Meites, 1989; Finch & Hayflick, 1977; Gershwin, Beach, & Hurley, 1983; Havard, 1981; Hayflick, 1976; Weksler, 1981; Weksler, 1990).

Although these theories are not mutually exclusive and thereby cannot be categorized, the theories do shed light on observations, facts, and functions of the aging process (see Table 2.3). These theories also raise questions as to whether aging is multifactional across systems and perhaps whether even more fundamental factors are involved in aging than have been identified. An open mind must be kept. For example, a research report by Rudman et al. (1990) concluded that "diminished secretion of growth hormone is responsible in part for decreased lean body mass, increased adipose tissue and thinning of skin" (p. 1). These factors were reversed by giving synthetic human growth hormone. Although the study was small (21 men, 61 to 81 years) and falls under the neuroendocrine theory of aging, it raises the old argument of whether aging itself is a disease process rather than a normal process.

Table 2.3
Criteria and Theories of Aging Changes

Universality	Progressiveness		Intrinsicality	Deleteriousness
		- and -		
CAN BE USED TO CRITIQUE THEORIES OF AGING			*CAN BE USED TO DIFFERENTIATE NORMAL AGING FROM PATHOLOGY, e.g.:*	
Genetic			alert	confused
Autoimmune			yellowing of cornea	glaucoma
Neuroendocrine			thin skin	skin neoplasms
Free radical			diminished muscle strength	extreme weakness/ paralysis
			teeth in good repair	dentures

Source: Criteria: Strehler (1977)

Weksler (1990) speculates that, "it is possible that the damaging agent in Alzheimer's, whatever that might be, may be potentiated by a subsequent auto-immune attack on brain cells by the immune system" (p. 75). Such speculation is congruent with hypotheses related to an autoimmune theory of the aging process.

PSYCHOSOCIAL THEORIES OF AGING

Psychosocial theories of aging have not been well accepted. Many psychosocial theories of aging have been investigated, however, including research by Abbot et al., 1978; Avon, 1983; Beattie, 1970; Birren & Schaie, 1977; Botwinick, 1977; Havighurst, 1975; Neugarten, 1977; Nowlin, 1973; Peck, 1968; Thomae, 1980; Weinstock, 1974).

Psychosocial theorists of aging include Erickson (1959), who described eight stages of life leading to integrity versus disgust in old age and Havighurst (1968), who described disengagement and patterns of personalities found in the aged. Birren and Renner (1980) argue that the model of stages of life "has not been researched or with credibility . . ." (p. 8). Thomae (1980) criticized

Havighurst's eight personality types (Havighurst, 1968) because Havighurst "believes that patterns of aging are consequences of individual choices rather than outcomes of social, biological, and biographical constellations" (p. 302).

The basic determinants in psychological theories of aging and development according to Baltes and Willis (1977) are biological, environmental, and interactional. These lead to major process constructs such as maturational, ecological, and learning. These concepts are more comprehensive in scope than are trait or pattern lists and allow for a wider scope of research into psychological aging across cultures and in a holistic approach.

Neugarten (1977, after review of longitudinal and follow-up studies concluded that personality is maintained over time. This is widely accepted and should alert nurses that when a change in personality occurs, possible underlying pathology may be occurring and referral to a medical practitioner should be made.

Evans et al. (1989) find evidence in a literature review that an association exists between stress and lowered immunity and between lowered immunity and depression. This approach to knowledge is both biophysical and psychosocial.

Woodruff (1983) found that performance on cognitive tests can be improved in old age with interventions (see Chapter 7, Health Education of the Older Client.) It is becoming more clear that it is problematic to separate the human being into psychosocial and biophysical components. As knowledge and research advance, we see that each area is affected by the other and both have genetic, intrinsic, universal foundations. Conceptually, it can be useful to use these two categories to study phenomena but only if the interface of the other category is not ignored.

NURSING

Curriculum Construction

The educational, research, and practice components of gerontological nursing are becoming important contributions to the richness of the profession. These can be built into curriculum, research, and practice.

The needs of society are important concerns when developing a nursing curriculum. Demographic data in this century provide overwhelming evidence of the aging of our society in ever growing numbers (Fries, 1980; Gaitz & Samorajski, 1985). These statistics and projections indicate that nursing students must be prepared in knowledge of aging and nursing care of the elderly and their families. Knowledge of community resources and federal policies are also helpful in assisting aging clients. The usual vertical threads in most nursing curricula flowing through each year of nursing education are: human beings, nursing, health, and society. Gerontological knowledge can be placed along this framework in such areas as growth and development, human needs, health behaviors, clinical areas of nursing practice, and impact on society of an aging population. The horizontal curricular thread at each learning level is the nursing process. This includes rich opportunity to assist students to build knowledge about aging clients, their families, their community, and their culture. As students learn careful collection of data from nursing history, physical and psychosocial assessment, nursing diagnoses, interaction with clients to establish goals or begin a therapeutic regime, and measurement of client outcome, gerontological knowledge from many fields as well as nursing can be incorporated.

If the basic assumption is made that aging is a normal process, then health teaching can be instituted throughout the life cycle. The National Institute on Aging in "Research Advances in Aging" (1987) has reported that the "vast majority of older persons show little decline . . . until they reach their eighties." Compliance to health teaching can increase the probability of healthful aging. Such teaching would include adequate calcium intake throughout life but particularly before age 30. Avoidance of extreme tanning and sunburns in younger years is desirable to prevent skin neoplasms in later years. Prevention or cessation of tobacco use is advocated.

Balanced nutrition (Gambert & Guansing, 1980), adequate rest and sleep (Krehl, 1974; Mann, 1973), and exercise are all positive influences on health throughout life. Developing many interests, friends, and good family relationships pays a large dividend for the elderly in quality of life.

As aging progresses and systems decline in function wherein the body no longer can make physiological adaptations as in youth, technological and environmental changes can be made in order for the aged person to function adequately. Such innovations include light control for illumination and elimination of glare, eye glasses or new lenses, hearing enhancers such as hearing aids, telephone technology for those with hearing impairments, home arrangement for safety and ease of access within the home, and use of personal and community support systems for transportation and social events.

Nursing Research

Research settings are available wherever nurses are caring for elderly clients. These include adult day-care centers, geriatric health screening clinics, community nursing in homes, acute care agencies, rehabilitation centers, any long-term care unit, and nursing homes. Graduate nursing students and faculty have done research in all of these settings and have been made welcome by staffs, clients, and families. The agencies have appreciated student-faculty clinical practice as well as findings from research. The feedback of new knowledge and ways of conceptualizing aged individuals has affected nursing practice. These processes interconnect education, practice, and research with linkages among all three. A prototype for this type of research has been in the teaching nursing home (Schneider, Wendland, Zimmer, List, & Ory, 1985) and can be adapted to all areas of care (see Chapter 1).

Kim (1983) proposed that three domains of theory development in nursing are client, environment, and nursing action. In gerontological nursing, these three domains are easily identified with access to all three domains. Both quantitative and qualitative studies are needed as well as longitudinal and one-time research. Theories and models of nursing can be used as conceptual frameworks. Nursing research studies also can be performed to test these theories and models for gerontological nursing. Review of literature as it pertains to aging, aging people, and health care is becoming more extensive, more instructive, and extremely important for nursing research, education, and practice. Gerontological nursing research is of interest to the National Institute on Aging and the Center for Nursing at the National Institutes of Health.

Areas for nursing research in gerontological nursing including the following.

> *Nursing assessment:* valid tools to be used in assessment, effectiveness of interdisciplinary approach in assessment, key information from nursing histories, determination of changes in health status
> *Nursing health teaching:* effectiveness of health teaching, readiness to learn by aged clients, effective and ineffective outcomes of compliance to teaching
> *Direct nursing interventions:* effectiveness on outcome of activity, exercises, diet changes, decrease in polypharmacy, strategies for sleep improvement, changes in lighting and safety factors in environment, bladder and bowel control. These outcomes could be tested in areas such as life satisfaction, self esteem, or increased activity.
> *Development of additional nursing diagnoses:* older clients may have many discreet phenomena not yet identified.

For possible questions for nursing research, see Table 2.4.

Within these broad areas of nursing research in gerontological nursing, a solid base of knowledge can be established. From such a base, an intellectual environment would be created for theory development and testing that would feed into clinical practice for the benefit of the older person.

Clinical Practice

Declines in function of aging clients brings forth nursing creativity in adapting environments and obtaining technology to assist older people in adjusting to age related changes. These include more light but less glare, more safety awareness with elimination of safety hazards such as scatter rugs and

Table 2.4
Possible Nursing Research Questions in Clinical Practice Flowing From

Criteria of Aging, *Theories of Aging,* *Process of Aging*		*Clinical Gerontological Practice*	
Concepts			
Time	Does time taken to achieve cognitive or motor tasks increase with age?	Time	Do frail elderly who are given wide time allotments achieve more tasks as in ADL?
Space	Do space requirements change with age?	Space	Does placing chairs every 20 feet in long-term care facilities allow frail elderly to walk farther?
Color Vision	Does yellowing of cornea affect color knowledge?	Color	Do elderly (75+) perceive correct colors of medications and tape strips or urine testing?

extension cords, and clear traffic areas in homes and institutions. Assisting the elderly to obtain technologies to assist vision, hearing, dentition, and mobility safety devices (canes, walkers) is necessary following careful assessment. A focus on maintaining all possible function is important (Ward, 1984). Seeing is a function that can be assisted by environmental changes and technology, as are hearing and mobility. If the nurse can assist clients to achieve more normal patterns of sleep (Colling, 1983), exercise, and diet (Mann, 1973; Young, 1986) then these too can give the elderly more strength to maintain function. Listening with attention and respect to older people is crucial while planning with them ways and means to change environment, add technology, and assisting them to adjust and cope (McRae, 1989) to daily and life changes.

SUMMARY

Just as in 450 B.C., theory must be built and tested. In gerontological nursing, literature review of many fields yields facts, hypotheses, and tentative theories. These are helpful in building knowledge and identifying assumptions and concepts. In nursing practice, careful recording of data can build knowledge, observation of phenomenon can provide clues to statements of hypotheses. Research studies can be designed to test these hypotheses. All of this provides a rich milieu for nursing students and faculty to learn, discover, test, analyze, and implement gerontological nursing practice in field trials of final testing of hypotheses. In this way, theory in gerontological nursing can be built.

REFERENCES

Abbot, M. H., Abbey, H., Bolling, D., & Murphy, E. (1978). The familial component in longevity—a study of offspring of nonagenarians: III. Intrafamilial studies. *American Journal of Human Genetics, 2,* 105-120.

Avon, J. (1983). Biomedical and social determinants of cognitive impairment in the elderly. *Journal of the American Geriatric Society, 31,* 137-143.

Baltes, P. B., & Willis, S. L. (1977). Toward psychological theories of aging and development. In J. Birren & K. Schaie, (eds.), *Handbook of the psychology of aging.* New York: Van Nostrand Reinhold.

Beattie, W. M. (1970). The design of supportive environments for the life span. *Gerontologist, 10,* Part 1.

Bell, B., Wolf, E., & Bernholz, C. D. (1972). Depth perception as a function of age. *Aging and Human Development, 3,* 77-81.

Birren, J. E., & Schaie, K. W. (Eds.). (1977). *Handbook of the psychology of aging.* New York: Van Nostrand Reinhold.

Birren, J. E., & Renner, V. J. (1980). Concepts and issues of mental health and aging. In J. Birren and R. B. Sloane (Eds.), *Handbook of Mental Health and Aging.* Englewood Cliffs, NJ: Prentice-Hall.

Botwinick, J. (1977). Intellectual abilities. In J. Birren & K. W. Schaie (Eds.), *Handbook of the psychology of aging.* New York: Van Nostrand Reinhold.

Carter, J. H. (1982). The effects of aging upon selected visual functions: Color vision, glare insensitivity, field of vision and accommodation. In R. Sekuler, D. Line, & K Dismukes (Eds.), *Aging and human visual function* (pp. 121-130). New York: Alan R. Liss.

Cerami, A. H., Dassara, H., & Brownlee, M. (1987). Glucose and aging. *Scientific American, 256,* 90-97.

Colett, I., Griffith, S. R., & Zil, J. (1984). Some problems with the concept of normal aging. *Journal of Operational Psychiatry, 15,* 51-54.

Colling, J. (1983). Sleep disturbances in aging: A theoretic and empiric analysis. *Advances in Nursing Science, 6,* 36-44.

Cuny, G. (1979). Pharmacokinetics of salicylates in elderly. *The Gerontologist, 25,* 49.

Erickson, E. (1959). Identity and the life cycle. *Psychological Issues, Monograph I.* New York: International University Press.

Evans, D. L., Leserman, J., Pedersen, C. A., Golden, R. N., Lewis, M. H., Folds, J. A., & Ozer, H. (1989). Immune correlates of stress and depression. *Psychopharmacology Bulletin, 25,* 319-324.

Everitt, A., & Meites, J. (1989). Mini review: Aging and anti-aging effects of hormones. *Journal of Gerontology, 44,* B 139-147.

Finch, C. E., & Hayflick, L., (Eds.), (1977). *Handbook of the biology of aging.* New York: Plenum.

Fries, J. F. (1980). Aging, natural death and the compression of morbidity. *New England Journal of Medicine, 303*:130.

Gaitz, C. M., & Samorajski, T. (1985). *Aging 2000: Our health care destiny. Volume I: Biomedical issues.* New York: Springer.

Gambert, S. R., & Guansing, A. R. (1980). Protein-calorie malnutrition in the elderly. *Journal of the American Geriatric Society, 27*, 272-275.

Gershwin, M. E., Beach, R., & Hurley, L. (1983). Trace metals, aging and immunity. *Journal of the American Geriatric Society, 31*, 374-377.

Grove, G. L., & Kingman, A. (1983). Age associated changes in human epidermal cell renewal. *Journal of Gerontology, 38*, 137.

Havard, C. W. H. (1981). The thyroid and aging. *Clinics in Endocrinology and Metabolism, 10*, 162.

Havighurst, R. (1968). Personality and patterns of aging. *The Gerontologist, 8*, 23.

Havighurst, R. J. (1975). *Life-styles transitions related to personality after age fifty.* Paper presented at International Society for Study of Behavioral Development Symposium, Israel.

Hayflick, L. (1976). The cellular biology of human aging. *New England Journal of Medicine, 295*, 1302.

Hayflick, L. (1985). *The aging process: Current Theories.* New York: Alan R. Liss.

Hippocrates. (1962). *Hippocrates.* (T. E. Page et al., eds.) (Translated by W. H. S. Jones.) Volume I. *Precepts.* Cambridge, UK: Harvard University Press.

Jacobs. R. (1981). Physical changes in the aged. In M. O. Devereaux, (Ed.), *Elder care: A guide to clinical geriatrics.* New York: Grune & Stratton.

Kay, M. M. B., & MacKinodon, T. (1976). Immunobiology of aging: Evaluation of current status. *Clinical Immunological Immunopathology, 6*, 394-413.

Kim, H. S. (1983). *The nature of theoretical thinking in nursing.* East Norwalk, CT: Appleton & Lange.

Krehl, W. (1974). The influence of nutritional environment on aging. *Geriatrics*, pp. 29-65.

Leighton, D. A. (1973). Special senses: Aging of the eye. In J. C. Brocklehurse (Ed.), *Textbook of geriatric medicine and gerontology* (pp. 254-264). New York: Churchill Livingstone.

Lipsitz, L. A. (1989). Mini review: Altered blood pressure homeostasis in advanced age: Clinical and research implications. *Journal of Gerontology, 44*, 179-183.

McRae, R. R. (1989). Age differences and changes in the use of coping mechanisms. *Journal of Gerontology, 44*, 161-169.

Mann, G. V. (1973). Relationship of age to nutrient requirements. *American Journal of Clinical Nutrition, 26*, 1096-1097.

Morin, R. J. (1985). *Frontiers in longevity research.* Springfield, IL: Charles C Thomas.

National Institute on Aging. (1987). Research advances in aging 1984-1986. Bethesda, MD: Author.

Neugarten, B. L. (1977). Personality and aging. In J. Birren & K. W. Schaie, (Eds.), *Handbook of the psychology of aging.* New York: Van Nostrand Reinhold.

Nowlin, J. B. (1973). Physical changes in later life and their relationship to mental functioning. In E. W. Busse & E. Pfeiffer (Eds.), *Mental illness in later life*, pp. 147-152. Washington, DC: American Psychiatric Association.

Peck, R. C. (1968). Psychological development in the second half of life. In B. L. Neugarten (Ed.), *Middle age and aging*, pp. 89-91. Chicago: University of Chicago Press.

Ritschel, W. A. (1978). Age dependent disposition of amobarbital: Analog computer evaluation. *Journal of North America Geriatric Study, 26*, 540.

Rothstein, M. (1986). Biochemical studies of aging. *Chemical & Engineering News, 64*, 26-39.

Rudman, D., Feller, A., Hoskote, S. M., Gergans, G. A., Lalitha, P. Y., Goldberg, A. F., Schlenker, R. A., Cohn, L., Rudman, I. W., & Mattson, D. E. (1990). Effects of human growth hormone in men over 60 years old. *New England Journal of Medicine, 323,* 1-6.

Schimke, R. T., & Agneil, M. (1983). Biologic mechanisms in aging: Summary of conference proceedings. *Journal of the American Geriatric Society, 31,* 404.

Schneider, E. L. (1983). Correspondence from Washington: Biomarkers of aging. *Journal of the American Geriatric Society, 31.*

Schneider, E., Wendland, C., Zimmer, A., List, N., & Ory, M. (Eds.). (1985). *The teaching nursing home.* New York: Raven Press.

Shock, N. W., Greulich, R. C., Andres, R., Arenberg, D., Costa, P. T., Jr., Lakatta, E. G., & Tobin, J. D. (1984). *Normal human aging: The Baltimore longitudinal study of aging* (NIH Publication No. 84-2450). Bethesda, MD: National Institutes of Health.

Sohal, R. S., Birnbaum, L. & Cutler, R. (Eds). (1985). *Molecular biology of aging: Gene stability and gene expression.* New York: Raven Press.

Strehler, B. (1977). *Time, cells and aging.* New York: Academic Press.

Timiras, P. (1978). Biological perspectives on aging. *American Scientist, 66,* 605-613.

Thomae, H. (1980). Personality and adjustment to aging. In J. Birren & R. B. Sloane, (Eds.), *Handbook of mental health and aging.* Englewood Cliffs, NJ: Prentice-Hall.

Ward, R. (1984). The marginality and salience of being old: When is age relevant? *The gerontologist, 24,* 227-232.

Weinstock, C. (1974). Successful aging: A psychological point of view. *Aging: Its challenge to the individual and to society.* New York: Fordham University Press.

Weksler, M. (1981). The senescence of the immune system. *Hospital Practice, 16,* 53.

Weksler, M. E. (1990). Protecting the aging immune system to prolong quality of life. *Geriatrics, 45,* 74-76.

Woodruff, D. S. (1983). A review of aging and cognitive processes. *Research on Aging, 5*(2), 139-153.

Young, E. A. (Ed.). (1986). *Nutrition, aging, and health.* New York: Alan R. Liss.

DEVELOPMENTAL PERSPECTIVES IN AGING

3

Wellness and Aging

SUSAN NOBLE WALKER

Objectives:

(1) Evaluate older adults' perception of their health status.
(2) Analyze the meaning of health for older adults.
(3) Respect older adults' ability to accept responsibility for informed decision making about their health and life-style behaviors.
(4) Integrate assistance with behavior change to achieve a wellness life-style in nursing interactions with older clients in all settings.

INTRODUCTION

The U.S. Surgeon General has described three complementary components of an effective national health strategy for people of all ages:

Medical care begins with the sick and seeks to keep them alive, make them well, or minimize their disability. *Illness prevention* begins with a threat to health—a disease or environmental hazard—and seeks to protect as many people as possible from the harmful consequences of that threat. *Health promotion* begins with people who are basically healthy and seeks the development of community and individual measures which can help them to develop lifestyles that can maintain and enhance their state of well-being. (U.S. Department of Health, Education and Welfare [HEW], 1979, p. 119)

Although illness, functional dependency, and death may result from basic human biology or genetics as well as from past and present environmental exposures and life-style behaviors, it has been estimated that at least 50% of deaths in the United States each year are due to unhealthy life-styles (HEW, 1979). Functional status and quality of life are also influenced by life-style behaviors. The vast majority of older people live in the community, function effectively, and retain the capacity to make decisions and to implement changes in health behavior. Yet, until recently, the health care system for older adults was heavily weighted toward medical care, with some attention paid to illness prevention. Older adults generally were not viewed as appropriate targets of health promotion efforts.

In 1983, Gelein reviewed the literature on health in old age and concluded that although extensive research had been reported on the disease processes and chronic illnesses associated with aging, little was known about health in old age or about the practices in which older adults engage to protect or enhance their health. Fortunately, this situation is beginning to change. For a variety of compelling scientific, political, and economic reasons, the attention of health care professionals during the past few years has increasingly been focused on health promotion and illness prevention among older adults.

This chapter will address the potential for wellness in old age, the perception of health status and the meaning of health for older adults, the value and components of a health-promoting life-style and some resources that gerontological nurses may use to assist older adults in modifying their life-styles to enhance wellness and promote healthy aging.

AGING AND HEALTH

The later years of life are not destined to be accompanied by unavoidably declining health, despite the fact that older adults are the greatest consumers of medical care today. Although Americans 65 and older comprise only a little more than 11% of the population, they account for more than 25% of drug prescriptions written, 33% of hospital beds occupied, and 30% of health care bills paid (American Hospital Association, 1985). Data from the National Health Interview Survey, however, indicates that the health of noninstitutionalized adults 65 and older showed consistent and substantial improvement from 1961 to 1981 (Palmore, 1986). Days of restricted activity and bed disability were reduced by 10% and 12%, injuries and acute illnesses declined by 13% and 15%, and various types of visual and hearing impairments declined by 10%-18%. Palmore suggests that sanitation, health care, and life-styles have improved and caused both life expectancy increases and improved health and functional status for the average older person. It seems reasonable to project a scenario in which future cohorts of older adults are even healthier as they enjoy the benefits of a lifetime of healthy life-style practices that are now becoming more widespread. Fries and Crapo (1981) have described a rectangularization of the survival curve, in which nearly all individuals survive to advanced age relatively free of the effects of disease until shortly before death and in which premature death and disability from chronic disease is eliminated by the removal of behavioral and environmental risk factors.

The informed gerontological nurse is in a position to promote healthy aging by dispelling myths and stereotypes about aging held by the general public, serving as an advocate by fostering activated consumerism on the part of older adults as they interact with the health care system, and emphasizing health promotion and life-style change in professional interactions with older adults. Such goals can be accomplished more effectively when nurses understand how their older clients evaluate their health, what health means to them, and the particular life-style behaviors that can be adopted and maintained to enhance wellness.

THE PERCEPTION OF HEALTH BY OLDER ADULTS

Perceived Health Status

How do older adults assess their own health? Perceived health status or self-rated health has been studied extensively and has been found to include such components as perception of recent changes in health (Tissue, 1972), perception of health status in comparison to age peers (Cockerham, Sharp, & Wilcox, 1983; Maddox, 1962; Shanas, Townsend, Wedderburn, Friis, & Stehouwer, 1968), and perception of disruption of one's life by health problems (Myles, 1978). Perceived health status can be measured both by single item self-ratings of overall health status along a 3-, 4-, or 5-point continuum from "excellent" to "poor" (George & Bearon, 1980) and by multiple item scales such as the self-rated health subindex of the physical health domain on the Philadelphia Geriatric Center Multilevel Assessment Instrument (Lawton, Moss, Fulcomer, & Kleban, 1982) or the 32-item Health Perceptions Questionnaire (HPQ), developed for use with adults of all ages in the Rand Health Insurance Study (Ware, Davies-Avery, & Donald, 1978). The HPQ has six subscales (prior health, current health, health outlook, health worry/concern, resistance-susceptibility, and sickness orientation) that can be used comprehensively or selectively.

Perceived Health Status and Mortality

Several large scale longitudinal studies have found perceived health status to be a significant predictor of mortality in subsequent years (Kaplan & Camacho, 1983; Mossey & Shapiro, 1982; Singer, Garfinkel, Cohen, & Srole, 1976). A number of reasons have been postulated to explain why health self-ratings are so predictive of future death. First, self-rated health reports may reflect the person's ability to detect subtle physiological changes or occult disease that has not yet manifested itself in signs or symptoms. Kaplan and Camacho (1983) point to recent work in the field of psychoneuroimmunology that suggests that individuals may be able to access and use information about interactions among these systems to arrive at judgments of perceived health. Second, the optimism evidenced by high self-ratings of health may in itself be protective of health by engaging psychophysiological mechanisms that increase host resistance. Conversely, low ratings may reflect an underlying state of depression or other emotional disturbance that adversely affects health. Finally, high self-rated health may be associated with more positive health habits, which themselves are associated with a reduction in mortality risk. Whatever the mechanism operating to link perceived health with mortality, it would seem prudent to listen carefully to what older adults say about their health and to consider that information to be as significant as more objective data.

Influences on Perceived Health

Self-ratings of health are significantly related to a number of demographic and socioeconomic variables. When differences in perceived health status were found in empirical studies of older adults, those with more education (Cockerham et al., 1983; Ferraro, 1980; Markides & Martin, 1979; Osborn, 1973), higher family income (Markides & Martin, 1979; Osborn, 1973), and higher socioeconomic status (Maddox, 1962; Osborn, 1973) tended to rate their health more favorably than others. The relationship of economic status to perceptions of health is particularly noteworthy. Self-assessment of health varies dramatically with income; data presented to the U.S. Senate Special Committee on Aging (1986) indicated that twice as many older adults with incomes above $35,000 rated their health as excellent as did those with incomes under $10,000, and three times as many with incomes under $10,000 rated their health as poor as did those with incomes above $35,000. Although the number of older people living in poverty is declining, older minorities and women still tend to have lower incomes, suggesting them as important targets for health promotion efforts.

Perceived health status also is positively correlated with older age. When adults aged 18 to 93 were asked to rate their health in comparison to others of the same age, persons more than the age of 60 were twice as likely as those less than 60 to feel that their health was much better than others of their age (Cockerham et al., 1983). Using data from a national survey, Ferraro (1980) found that those 75+ reported more illnesses and greater disability than those 65-74 but had a more positive view of their own health, and suggested that stereotypical views of advanced old age as a time of poor health may lead the old-old to see themselves as more exceptional than they really are and to overestimate their health in relation to others their age. Linn and Linn (1980) found no difference in number of diagnoses or extent of disability between the old and the very old groups, although more of those 75+ than those 65-74 still assessed their health as good or very good, and suggested, alternatively, that persons who live into extreme old age are a biologically elite group exempted from the major diseases that kill others at an earlier age. Both studies found that disability or impairment of functional status explained more variance in health self-ratings among older adults than did number of illness conditions. This finding has particular relevance for understanding what older adults may be evaluating when they rate their own health.

Definition of Health

Objective health status as measured by clinical examination of the older adult and perceived health status as reflected in self report, although correlated, at times may yield quite different results. It is possible that such discrepancies may be explained by the fact that assessments by clinicians and clients are based on different definitions of health or conceptualizations of what it means to be healthy. The objective findings of a clinical examination may provide information only about a single dimension of health as the absence of symptoms or of illness. The individual's self-evaluation of health status may include additional aspects of health such as feeling good, being able to do things that are important, coping with life's demands, and achieving one's potential.

Smith (1983) reviewed the extensive literature on health from a variety of disciplinary perspectives and categorized the definitions of health that she found into four models. In the *clinical model,* health is viewed as the absence of disease or disability and is characterized by the absence of signs and symptoms. This view of health is reflected in much of traditional medical practice and writing. In the *role performance model,* health is viewed as maximal performance of socially defined roles such as worker or parent. This view of health is reflected in the writings of Parsons (1972), the sociologist who defines health with reference to the individual's participation in the social system. In the *adaptive model,* health is viewed as flexible adjustment to changing circumstances. This view of health is reflected in the work of Dubos (1965, 1979), the microbiologist and pathologist who defines health in terms of the ability to adapt both biologically and socially to varying environmental circumstances. In the *eudaimonistic model,* health is viewed as exuberant well-being or high-level wellness. This view of health is reflected in the writings of Maslow (1961, 1970), the psychologist who defines health as the actualization or realization of one's intrinsic potential for fulfillment and complete development.

Walker and Volkan (1990) studied the meaning of health to community-living adults aged 55 to 91, using the *Laffrey Health Conception Scale* (Laffrey, 1986) that contains four subscales to measure the models of health definition described by Smith. Older adults agreed in descending order with the functional, eudaimonistic, adaptive, and clinical definitions of health. On the basis of findings that the eudaimonistic, adaptive, and role performance subscales were highly correlated and related to an underlying wellness dimension, and that the clinical subscale alone was related to a second underlying absence of illness dimension of health conception, the researchers proposed a model of health conception depicted in Figure 3.1.

The clinical definition of health as the absence of illness alone is clearly inappropriate for the majority of older adults for whom chronic illness is a fact of life. Such a view of health implies that if chronic disease cannot be reduced or eliminated, the person can never experience higher levels of health. The three more positive, growth-oriented components of the wellness dimension of health conception—described as role performance, adaptive, and eudaimonistic models—may have greater relevance for older adults, since they allow for movement toward health despite the presence of disease or symptoms.

In an editorial in the *Journal of Gerontological Nursing,* Schraff (1981) speculated about the true meaning of health for the elderly as she recalled a statement made by John Quincy Adams on his 80th birthday, in response to an inquiry about his health:

> John Quincy Adams is well, but the house in which he lives at present is becoming dilapidated. It is tottering upon its foundation. Time and seasons have nearly destroyed it. Its roof is pretty well worn out. Its walls are much shattered and it trembles with every wind. I think John Quincy Adams will have to move out soon. But he himself is quite well, quite well. (p. 331)

Schraff wonders whether health professionals would agree with Mr. Adams's assessment of his own health status, and whether others with similar problems would perceive themselves as well. She suggests that:

> Mr. Adams is trying to tell us that being well has nothing to do with the presence or absence of pathology. He seems to be saying that well-being depends on one's own awareness of the meaning of life and one's ability to grow in consciousness as life unfolds. I believe that Mr. Adams was well because he had developed a pattern of living that was in harmony with his

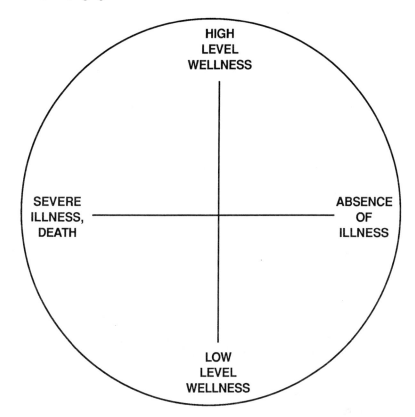

Figure 3.1. A Multidimensional Model of Health Conception Among Older Adults

body and with his surroundings. . . . If human beings can be well in spite of physical and mental frailties, ought we not also to look at ways to foster well-being of the whole person? (p. 331)

Based on years of clinical experience with older people, she calls for a multidimensional and holistic view of health and well-being and an approach to health promotion that takes into account the person-environment relationship rather than intercession in disease processes alone. Such a multidimensional conceptualization is consistent with the often quoted World Health Organization's (WHO) definition of health as "a state of complete physical, mental and social well-being, not just the absence of disease or infirmity."

Defining health is of more than academic interest. Health psychologists suggest that health conception is one motivating factor influencing health-seeking behavior and there is evidence for an association between individuals' definitions of health and their involvement in health-promoting life-styles (Walker, Pender, Sechrist, Frank-Stromborg, & Volkan, 1990). Interventions to alter or expand health conception therefore may be an effective approach to increasing healthy life-style behaviors. In designing health promotion programs for older adults, it seems essential to define what "health" means, to understand clearly what the program will be designed to promote. There are different implications for program content when health is defined as absence of illness and when it is defined as high level wellness.

HEALTH-PROMOTING OR WELLNESS-ENHANCING LIFE-STYLES

The Value of Healthy Life-Style Practices

Knowles (1972, 1977) and Farquhar (1978) cited the mounting evidence of the extent to which people's life-style choices and behaviors influence their health in calling for individuals to accept responsibility for health and for health care providers to acknowledge and encourage client's self-responsibility. A series of cross-sectional and longitudinal studies in the Human Population Laboratory of Alameda County, California since 1965 have provided support for the association between life-style and current health status (Belloc & Breslow, 1972), future health status (Wiley & Camacho, 1980), and mortality (Belloc, 1973; Berkman & Syme, 1979). Life-style components examined in these studies were social ties or networks and personal habits of sleeping, eating, physical activity, alcoholic beverage consumption, and smoking. The association between healthy life-style practices and health outcomes also has been supported in studies of other general adult populations (Kaplan, Cassel, & Gore, 1977; Reed, 1983; Wilson & Elinson, 1981) and of aged populations (McGlone & Kick, 1978; Palmore, 1970; Stenback, Kumpulainen, & Vauhkonen, 1978). The association between healthy life-style practices and good health in later adulthood found in these studies suggests that life-style indeed may influence both the quality and length of life.

Components of a Healthy Life-Style

Pender (1987) suggests that health-protecting (illness-preventing) behavior and health-promoting behavior should be viewed as complementary components of a healthy life-style, and that "their integrated manifestation in person-environment interactions is critical to health enhancement throughout the life span" (p. 5). Health-protecting behavior is directed toward decreasing the individual's probability of encountering illness or injury and is disease-specific. It involves activities to reduce threats to health, including adherence to self-care regimens for chronic illness to minimize the likelihood of experiencing complications. The concept of prevention actually extends beyond life-style behaviors to include preventive health services provided by health care professionals, including immunizations for protection against influenza and pneumonia, and screening tests such as mammograms and stool occult blood studies for early detection of breast and colon cancers. Because these are services offered to essentially healthy people who may not otherwise be in contact with the health care system, the responsibility for obtaining preventive services still rests with the individual.

In contrast, the health-promoting component of life-style, which is the focus in this chapter, is "a multidimensional pattern of self-initiated actions and perceptions that serve to maintain or enhance the level of wellness, self-actualization and fulfillment of the individual" (Walker, Sechrist, & Pender, 1987, p. 77). It is a positive approach to living that is joy-motivated and leads individuals toward realization of their highest potential for well-being. A wellness-enhancing life-style is pursued because it is satisfying and enjoyable, and not because of a wish to avoid disease (Ardell, 1979).

Dunn (1961) wrote in *High Level Wellness* of the value of life-style in promoting not only longevity, but wellness. Building upon these ideas, Travis (1977) and Ardell (1979) described the dimensions of a wellness life-style as self-responsibility, nutritional awareness, stress management or control, physical fitness, and environmental sensitivity. Walker et al. (1987) found empirical support for classifying 48 actions and perceptions into six dimensions of a health-promoting life-style: self-actualization, health responsibility, exercise, nutrition, interpersonal support, and stress management; and developed the *Health-Promoting Lifestyle Profile* to measure them.

Health-Promoting Life-Style Patterns of Older Adults

The prevalence of many health-promoting life-style practices has been found to be greater among older people than younger age groups in a number of studies (Belloc & Breslow, 1972; Brown & McCreedy, 1986; Harris & Guten, 1979; Prohaska, Leventhal, Leventhal, & Keller, 1985; Walker, Volkan, Sechrist, & Pender; 1988). The greater prevalence of healthy behaviors among older people may be explained by the fact that those members of the cohort who followed deleterious life-styles died at earlier ages or by an increasing sense of vulnerability, greater wisdom and prudence, and an increasing acceptance of self-responsibility that occurs with maturity, or by some combination of these factors.

Older adults are clearly able to identify intentional behaviors to enhance wellness. Brody (1985) asked adults aged 62 and older what they did to improve or maintain their health and reported that 59% identified from two to six purposeful health promotion activities, 29% identified one activity, and only 12% could think of nothing they did to promote health. Activities included exercise (84%), diet/nutrition (48%), keeping busy (25%), socializing (23%), avoiding worry (18%), and visits to health professionals (only 9%). Respondents gave both specific illness-preventive and more general health-promotive reasons for these behaviors, and about half said their regimens were self-prescribed, one-third said they had been advised by their physicians, and the remainder said they were recommended by the media, relatives, or friends. Maloney, Fallon, and Wittenberg (1984), in a study described more fully below, asked 90 older adults participating in focus groups to discuss what they do to maintain or improve their own health. The most prominent themes among responses were the needs to keep busy and involved with people and to maintain a positive outlook on life and activities within the categories of exercise and nutrition were frequently mentioned as ways to keep healthy. Other beneficial activities identified were monitoring blood pressure, exercising self-discipline to do things in moderation, having regular health check-ups, and getting rest and relaxation.

More comprehensive data concerning health-promoting behavior of older adults will be available in the future, because items about individual health behaviors and knowledge of health practices were included in the 1985 and 1990 National Health Interview Survey. Responses broken down by four age groups make it possible to compare knowledge and behavior of adults over 65 with younger groups (Thornberry, Wilson, & Golden, 1986).

HEALTH PROMOTION PROGRAMS
FOR OLDER ADULTS

Older Adults: Suitable Targets for
Health Promotion Programs?

The potential of health promotion and illness prevention activities to save lives, improve the quality of life and, eventually, to reduce health care expenditures already has been recognized (HEW, 1979). The proportion of persons over age 65, the greatest consumers of health care in this country, has been increasing and will continue to increase. Yet, until recently, older adults have not been viewed by health care providers, health educators, or fitness experts as a suitable target for health promotion programs.

There are a number of reasons for the omission of older adults from health promotion efforts, many of them related to the widespread acceptance of negative stereotypes and myths about aging both by the general public and by health care providers. Older people who believe those misconceptions may consider activities such as exercise or meditation to be age-inappropriate and so are less likely to initiate such efforts or to demand access to suitable programs. Erroneous beliefs that older people are "set in their ways" and unable or unwilling to change or that a lifetime of "bad health habits" has resulted in irreversible damage and it is too late to change also serve as deterrents. Somers, Kleinman, and Clark (1982) observe that the public and professionals who hold these beliefs assume the posture that older people should be left alone to enjoy the time they have left without any outside intervention to change their life-style behaviors.

Minkler and Fullarton (1980) have described some characteristics of health promotion programs themselves that further explain their exclusion of older adults. Preventive medicine focuses on reducing the risks of premature morbidity and mortality, whereas older people are seen as already having achieved or exceeded their expected life expectancy. They are seen as chronically ill people for whom the goal of disease prevention would not be relevant and as people without a future for whom the goal of life extension would be inappropriate. Another objective of many health and fitness programs has seemingly been the pursuit of perennial youthfulness, the achievement of the perfect body and the prevention of aging, which surely would lead them to dissociate themselves from those who had "failed"—the already aged. In reality, health promotion is relevant to anyone of any age or condition. If understood in its broader sense of facilitating movement toward wellness through the processes of learning and development of human potential, health promotion is as relevant for older adults as for younger—perhaps more so. Older adults continue to be able to learn, although they may require more time to do so; in the absence of pathology, intellectual abilities are maintained, and may even be improved, with advancing years. Certainly old age is a time not only to review the accomplishments of one's past life, but also to reevaluate and progress with life.

Are Older Adults Interested in Health Promotion?

Although some are certainly more interested than others, the answer appears to be a resounding yes! Older adults are very interested in their health and are willing and able to make life-style changes to improve their health status. In fact, their willingness to adopt healthy behaviors may actually exceed that of other age groups. Such were the conclusions of a market research study undertaken by the U.S. Public Health Service's Office of Disease Prevention and Health Promotion, National Institute on Aging and National Cancer Institute, and by the Administration on Aging to determine the interest of older people in acquiring health information and their ability and desire to make life-style changes, if necessary, to improve their health (Maloney et al., 1984).

The authors of that study reviewed relevant literature and collected qualitative data from discussions held with 15 focus groups of older adults in the Washington, D.C. and Los Angeles areas. Within the groups, two concerns were evident that contribute to understanding the greater interest of older adults in health and health promotion:

> A significant concern and dread over health care costs was expressed as either the first or second issue in each group conducted . . . respondents were most vocal about the cost of hospitalization, nursing home costs, and insurance issues. Also expressed was some concern over the possibility that Social Security and Medicare payments might soon be either reduced or terminated, further limiting the elderly person's ability to cope if serious illness strikes. . . . Related to the issue of health care costs were concerns about being incapacitated and alone . . . concern about maintaining their independence and not becoming a burden to others. (p. 7)

Discussions within the focus groups revealed that, beyond the fear of becoming sick, older people have an orientation toward staying well and functional, and that they recognize the need and accept responsibility for working toward those goals. The authors concluded that:

> it was clear . . . that the participants were active, vigorous, and health oriented. Health was a top-of-the-mind issue for them, as evidenced by their enthusiasm and interest in discussing it. Furthermore, participants were not just sickness or problem oriented; they were very much concerned with the notion of staying well. (p. 9)

Haggerty (1977) has enumerated the difficulties involved in achieving a change in life-style behaviors to improve health for persons of any age and Pender (1987) has described nursing strategies for assisting clients with the process of life-style modification. Anyone who has attempted to modify his or her own life-style behaviors recognizes the magnitude of the task involved. There is no reason, however, to think that the task is too difficult for older adults to accomplish or that it would not be beneficial. Maloney et al. (1984) reported that the evaluation of a public education campaign in California found that "respondents 65 and older showed greater gains in knowledge and changes in behavior than did younger age groups" (p. 5). Maddox (1985) also concluded after reviewing the literature that "unhealthful behavior *is* modifiable" and that "the beneficial effects of healthful behavior and lifestyles can be observed among older adults (it is never too late to benefit)" (p. 1025).

Little is yet known about the incidence and success of older adults' life-style change initiatives. In one study of the efforts of older adults to change their health practices, Allen (1986) interviewed residents of a small rural town who were 65 years old and over, about life-style change efforts during the previous year. He found that 83% reported having made at least one effort to change health practices, with the number of changes ranging from one to nine. A variety of life-style modification attempts were reported, with the most common being concerned with balanced diet (attempted by 38% of elders), weight control (35%), regular exercise (35%), community service (26%), stress reduction (22%), muscle flexibility (19%), improved social life (19%), and smoking cessation (18%). Further, 45% of the reported life-style change initiatives were sustained for a period of 6 months or more, the duration after which it is generally accepted that a change is likely to be incorporated permanently into one's life-style patterns.

Resources for Program Development

There have been a number of successful efforts to offer comprehensive health promotion programs for older adults and many have developed manuals and source books that are valuable resources. Such programs include the Senior Actualization & Growth Explorations (SAGE) Project in Berkeley, California (Information can be obtained from SAGE, 1713A Grove Street, Berkeley, CA 94709.), the Wallingford Wellness Project in Seattle, Washington (Fallcreek & Mettler, 1984), the Healthy Lifestyles for Seniors Project in Santa Monica, California (Warner-Reitz & Grothe, 1981), the Dartmouth Self-Care for Senior Citizens Program in Hanover, New Hampshire (Simmons, Roberts, & Nelson, 1986), the GROWING YOUNGER and GROWING WISER programs in Boise, Idaho (Kemper, 1986), and STAY WELL in New York City (Sainer & Freedman, 1988). The Brookdale Foundation Group recently has established an on-line national computerized data base of innovative direct service programs for older adults, entitled AGE BASE. Information about wellness programs designed to serve the well or frail elderly is indexed and retrievable as a free service of the Foundation, 126 East 56th Street, New York, NY 10022. These resources are representative of the number available for those wishing specific guidance in developing health promotion services for individuals or groups of older adults.

Health Promotion With Older Adults in Broader Context

This chapter has intentionally addressed health promotion with older adults only in the context of facilitating life-style behavior change to achieve wellness, yet such a focus on individual responsibility for health ignores the social context within which health-related decisions are made. Minkler (1983) calls for a broader system-centered approach to health promotion for the elderly that includes interventions to achieve both individual and environmental change that may involve providing advocacy training and legislation that protects the rights of older persons, and a comprehensive continuum of community-based health and social services as well as helping older individuals gain access to knowledge, skills, and other resources for meeting personal health goals and objectives.

Such a system-centered approach was reflected at the 1988 Workshop on Health Promotion and Aging convened by the U.S. Surgeon General to assess what was known about health promotion with older adults in nine areas concerned with illness prevention and wellness promotion (medication, alcohol, dental health, mental health, preventive health services, exercise, smoking cessation, nutrition, and injury prevention) and to make recommendations for policy, service, education, and research in these areas (U.S. Department of Health and Human Services, 1988).

Health promotion in its broadest context must address social and environmental influences such as those addressed in Unit 3 of this book, and the reader is reminded that they are indeed essential components of comprehensive health promotion programming for older people. The following section describes the role of the Clinical Nurse Specialist (CNS) in providing health enhancing programs for older adults.

IMPLICATIONS FOR THE
CLINICAL NURSE SPECIALIST

The following nursing interventions are among those needed to improve wellness programs among older adults: (1) Initiate wellness interventions in all nursing plans for older adults in all settings, (2) Provide health education programs for older adult consumers and for both formal and informal caregivers of elderly persons, (3) Conduct research to determine the outcomes of nursing interventions designed to promote wellness in aging in all settings where elders reside, (4) Dispel myths and stereotypes about aging held by the general public, health care providers and older adults, that suggest because the elderly have failed in preventing aging and in maintaining a perfect body, they are not acceptable targets of health promotion programs, and (5) Promote legislation that provides health promotion programs for older adults, thereby decreasing health care costs and increasing life satisfaction for the elderly.

SUMMARY

Older adults in general have an accurate perception of their health status and are interested in health promotion activities. They can benefit from health promotion activities at any age, in any setting. The elderly, like other age groups, prefer to make decisions involving their health status and to participate actively in programs that can improve their lives and reduce the financial and human cost of acute and long-term care. Research is limited concerning the outcomes of health promotion programs among the elderly, although some theoretical approaches have been proposed. The CNS has a major role in promoting health and providing wellness programs for older adults in a variety of settings.

REFERENCES

Allen, J. (1986). New lives for old: Lifestyle change initiatives among older adults. *Health Values, 10* (6), 8-18.

American Hospital Association. (1985). *Health promotion for older adults: Planning for action.* Chicago: Center for Health Promotion.

Ardell, D. B. (1979). The nature and implications of high level wellness, or why "normal health" is a rather sorry state of existence. *Health Values: Achieving High Level Wellness, 3* (1), 17-24.

Belloc, N. B. (1973). Relationship of health practices and mortality. *Preventive Medicine, 3,* 67-81.

Belloc, N. B., & Breslow, L. (1972). Relationship of physical health status and health practices. *Preventive Medicine, 1,* 409-421.

Berkman, L. F., & Syme, L. (1979). Social networks, host resistance, and mortality: A nine-year follow-up study of Alameda County residents. *American Journal of Epidemiology, 109* (2), 186-204.

Brody, E. M. (1985). *Mental and physical health practices of older people.* New York: Springer.

Brown, J. S., & McCreedy, M. (1986). The hale elderly: Health behavior and its correlates. *Research in Nursing and Health, 9,* 317-329.

Cockerham, W. C., Sharp, K., & Wilcox, J. A. (1983). Aging and perceived health status. *Journal of Gerontology, 38,* 349-355.

Dubos, R. (1965). *Man adapting.* New Haven, CT: Yale University Press.

Dubos, R. (1979). *Mirage of health.* (reprint ed.). Garden City, NY: Doubleday Anchor.

Dunn, H. L. (1961). *High level wellness.* Arlington, VA: R. W. Beatty.

Fallcreek, S., & Mettler, M. (1984). *A healthy old age.* New York: Haworth.

Farquhar, J. (1978). *The American way of life need not be hazardous to your health.* New York: Norton.

Ferraro, K. F. (1980). Self-ratings of health among the old and the old-old. *Journal of Health and Social Behavior, 21,* 377-383.

Fries, J. F., & Crapo, L. M. (1981). *Vitality and aging.* San Francisco: Freeman.

Gelein, J. G. (1983). Aging women and health. *Topics in Clinical Nursing, 4*(4), 56-58.

George, L. K., & Bearon, L. B. (1980). *Quality of life in older persons.* New York: Human Sciences Press.

Haggerty, R. J. (1977). Changing lifestyles to improve health. *Preventive Medicine, 6,* 276-289.

Harris, D. M., & Guten, S. (1979). Health-protective behavior: An exploratory study. *Journal of Health and Social Behavior, 20* (1), 17-29.

Kaplan, B. H., Cassel, J. C., & Gore, S. (1977). Social support and health. *Medical Care, 15,* 47-58.

Kaplan, G. A., & Camacho, T. (1983). Perceived health and mortality: A nine-year follow-up of the human population laboratory cohort. *American Journal of Epidemiology, 117*(3), 292-304.

Kemper, D. (1986). The Healthwise program: GROWING YOUNGER. In K. Dychtwald (Ed.), *Wellness and health promotion for the elderly* (pp. 263-274). Rockville, MD: Aspen Systems Corporation.

Knowles, J. H. (1972). The responsibility of the individual. *Daedalus, 106,* 57.

Knowles, J. H. (1977). The responsibility of the individual. In J. H. Knowles (Ed.), *Doing better and feeling worse: Health in the United States.* New York: Norton.

Laffrey, S. C. (1986). Development of a health conception scale. *Research in Nursing and Health, 9,* 107-113.

Lawton, M. P., Moss, M., Fulcomer, M., & Kleban, M. H. (1982). A research and service oriented Multilevel Assessment Instrument. *Journal of Gerontology, 37* (1), 91-99.

Linn, B. S., & Linn, M. W. (1980). Objective and self-assessed health in the old and very old. *Social Science and Medicine, 14A,* 311-315.

McGlone, F. B., & Kick, E. (1978). Health habits in relation to aging. *Journal of the American Geriatrics Society, 26* (11), 481-488.

Maddox, G. L. (1962). Some correlates of differences in self-assessment of health status among the elderly. *Journal of Gerontology, 17,* 180-185.

Maddox, G. L. (1985). Intervention strategies to enhance well-being in later life: The status and prospect of guided change. *Health Services Research, 19* (6), 1007-1032.

Maloney, S. K., Fallon, B., & Wittenberg, C. K. (1984, May). *Aging and health promotion: Market research for public education* [Executive summary]. Washington, DC: Public Health Service, Office of Disease Prevention and Health Promotion.

Markides, K., & Martin, H. (1979). Predicting self-rated health among the aged. *Research on Aging, 1,* 97-112.

Maslow, A. H. (1961). Health as transcendence of environment. *Journal of Humanistic Psychology, 1,* 1-7.

Maslow, A. H. (1970). *Motivation and personality* (2nd ed.). New York: Harper & Row.

Minkler, M. (1983). Health promotion and elders: A critique. *Generations, 7*(3), 13-15, 67.

Minkler, M., & Fullarton, J. (1980). *Health promotion, health maintenance and disease prevention for the elderly.* (Background paper for the 1981 White House Conference on Aging prepared for the Office of Health Information, Health Promotion, Physical Fitness and Sports Medicine, Department of Health and Human Services, Public Health Service, Washington, DC).

Mossey, J. M., & Shapiro, E. (1982). Self-rated health: A predictor of mortality among the elderly. *American Journal of Public Health, 72,* 800-808.

Myles, J. F. (1978). Institutionalization and sick role identification among the elderly. *American Sociological Review, 43,* 508-521.

Osborn, R. W. (1973). Social rank and self-health evaluation of older urban males. *Social Science and Medicine, 7,* 209-218.

Palmore, E. (1970). Health practices and illness among the aged. *The Gerontologist, 10,* 313-316.

Palmore, E. B. (1986). Trends in the health of the aged. *The Gerontologist, 26* (3), 298-302.

Parsons, T. (1972). Definitions of health and illness in the light of American values and social structure. In E. G. Jaco (Ed.), *Patients, physicians and illness.* New York: Free Press.

Pender, N. J. (1987). *Health promotion in nursing practice* (2nd ed.). East Norwalk, CT: Appleton & Lange.

Prohaska, T. R., Leventhal, E. A., Leventhal, H., & Keller, M. L. (1985). Health practices and illness cognition in young, middle aged, and elderly adults. *Journal of Gerontology, 40* (5), 569-578.

Reed, W. L. (1983). Physical health status as a consequence of health practices. *Journal of Community Health, 8,* 217-228.

Sainer, J. S., & Freedman, F. (1988). *STAY WELL: A health promotion program for older adults.* New York: New York City Department for the Aging, Health Promotion Services.

Schraff, S. (1981). Perception of health by the elderly. *Journal of Gerontological Nursing, 7* (6), 331.

Shanas, E., Townsend, P., Wedderburn, D., Friis, H., & Stehouwer, J. (1968). *Older people in three industrial societies.* New York: Atherton Press.

Simmons, J. J., Roberts, E., & Nelson, E. C. (1986). The Dartmouth self-care for senior citizens program: Tools, strategies, and methods. In K. Dychtwald (Ed.), *Wellness and health promotion for the elderly,* (pp. 235-246). Rockville, MD: Aspen Systems Corporation.

Singer, E., Garfinkel, R., Cohen, S. M., & Srole, L. (1976). Mortality and mental health: Evidence from the Midtown Manhattan restudy. *Social Science and Medicine, 10,* 517-525.

Smith, J. A. (1983). *The idea of health.* New York: Teachers College Press.

Somers, A. R., Kleinman, L., & Clark, W. (1982). Preventive health services for the elderly: The Rutgers Medical School project. *Inquiry, 19,* 190-221.

Stenback, A., Kumpulainen, M., & Vauhkonen, M. (1978). Illness and health behavior in septuagenarians. *Journal of Gerontology, 33* (1), 57-61.

Tissue, T. (1972). Another look at self-rated health among the elderly. *Journal of Gerontology, 27* (1), 91-94.

Thornberry, O. T., Wilson, R. W., & Golden, P. M. (1986). Health promotion data for the 1990 objectives, Estimates from the National Health Interview Survey of Health Promotion and Disease Prevention, United States, 1985. *Advance Data From Vital and Health Statistics,* No. 126. (DHHS Publication No. PHS 86-1250). Hyattsville, MD: Public Health Service, National Center for Health Statistics.

Travis, J. W. (1977). *Wellness workbook for health professionals.* Mill Valley, CA: Wellness Resource Center.

U.S. Department of Health, Education and Welfare. Public Health Service. (1979). *Healthy people: The Surgeon General's report on health promotion and disease prevention.* (DHEW Publication No. PHS 79-55071). Washington, DC: Government Printing Office.

U.S. Department of Health and Human Services. Public Health Service. (1988). *Proceedings of the Surgeon General's workshop, Health promotion and aging.* Washington, DC: Government Printing Office.

U.S. Senate Special Committee on Aging (1986, November). *The health status and health care needs of older Americans* (Senate Committee Publication No. 87-6635). Washington, DC: Government Printing Office.

Walker, S. N., Pender, N. J., Sechrist, K. R., Frank-Stromborg, M., & Volkan, K. (1990). *Cognitive/perceptual factors and other characteristics associated with health-promoting lifestyles among community-dwelling older adults.* Manuscript submitted for publication.

Walker, S. N., Sechrist, K. R., & Pender, N. J. (1987). The Health-Promoting Lifestyle Profile: Development and psychometric characteristics. *Nursing Research, 36* (2), 76-81.

Walker, S. N., & Volkan, K. (1990). *Health conception among older adults.* Manuscript submitted for publication.

Walker, S. N., Volkan, K., Sechrist, K. R., & Pender, N. J. (1988). Health-promoting lifestyle of older adults: Comparisons with young and middle-aged adults, correlates and patterns. *Advances in Nursing Science, 11* (1), 76-90.

Ware, J. E., Davies-Avery, A., & Donald, C. A. (1978). *Conceptualization and measurement of health for adults in the health insurance study. Vol. 5: General health perceptions.* Santa Monica, CA: Rand Corporation.

Warner-Reitz, A., & Grothe, C. (1981). *Healthy lifestyle for seniors.* New York: Meals for Millions/Freedom from Hunger Foundation.

Wiley, J. A., & Camacho, T. C. (1980). Life-style and future health: Evidence from the Alameda County study. *Preventive Medicine, 9,* 1-21.

Wilson, R. W., & Elinson, J. (1981). National survey of personal health practices and consequences: Background, conceptual issues, and selected findings. *Public Health Reports, 96,* 218-225.

4

Sleep in Old Age

CAROLYN C. HOCH

Objectives: At the completion of this chapter, the reader will be able to:

(1) Critique physiological parameters of sleep in aging persons.
(2) Analyze the impact of normal aging on sleep.
(3) Analyze the effect of pathology during aging on sleep.
(4) Evaluate sleep disturbances in the elderly.
(5) Evaluate assessment tools and methods of measuring the sleep of older adults.
(6) Apply nursing care strategies to assist the elderly in coping with sleep disturbances.

INTRODUCTION

Over the past 15 years, biological, clinical, and epidemiological research has provided evidence that sleep is affected by the aging process. Sleep disturbances represent a major problem among elderly individuals, with up to 35% of persons over the age of 65 having sleep related problems (National Institute of Health [NIH], 1990). Changes in sleep are also the source of frequent concern among the elderly and their caregivers. In view of these facts, it is vitally important for nurses to implement plans that include helping older persons achieve satisfaction in sleep.

AUTHOR'S NOTE: Supported in part by National Institute of Mental Health Grant No. MH00792.

The demographics of the United States are changing as the population is living longer. An estimated 27 million people are currently over the age of 65 with projections that by the year 2000 there will be more than 5 million persons in the "old-old" 85+ year age group (U.S. Bureau of the Census, 1986). The elderly spend an average of 20% of their annual income on health care costs, with this expected to continue to rise over the next decade (Rabin, 1985). Many of the illnesses that elders experience, or their treatments, have a negative impact on the ability of the elderly individual to achieve long uninterrupted periods of sleep or an adequate depth of sleep, thus compounding the distress associated with chronic illness. Moreover, many daytime complaints and health problems seen in late life may be related to specific sleep disorders. The elderly are the age group most severely affected by disorders of initiating and maintaining sleep, resulting in the consumption of disproportionate quantities of sleeping pills and tranquilizers. Nighttime insomnia and/or the medication used to relieve it leads to deterioration in daytime alertness and functioning resulting in a significant amount of distress (Carskadon & Dement, 1981; Dement, Miles, & Carskadon, 1982). Because the elderly are at the extreme end of the life span, studying their sleep provides information about sleep and aging effects in general as well as clues to improving the health and quality of life among all late life age groups.

Studies have suggested that sleep-related behaviors very often precipitate a family's decision to institutionalize an elderly relative (Rabins, Mace, & Lucas, 1982; Sanford, 1975). Sleep-related behavioral disturbances, including nocturnal wandering, confusion, and agitated behavior, are not well tolerated by caregivers and may trigger a family's decision to institutionalize an older, demented relative (Pollak & Perlick, 1987). Any understanding of how the aging system might be contributing to deteriorations in the sleep and health of the elderly would have an impact on the elderly themselves and on society as a whole. Any reduction in the institutionalization rate, even by just a single point, would surely pay for itself many times over (Reynolds, Hoch, & Monk, 1989). In the various primary, secondary, and tertiary care settings where nurses work with older adults, there are numerous opportunities to observe changes in sleep behavior or to hear elders and their caregivers describe their sleep. Knowledge of physiological and behavioral sleep characteristics and of the sleep disturbances that occur with normal and pathologic aging provide the basis for assessment and subsequent intervention (Hoch & Reynolds, 1986).

The purpose of this chapter is to review knowledge of several sleep related areas: (1) sleep and the measurement of sleep, (2) sleep and healthy aging, (3) sleep and pathology in aging, (4) sleep disturbances and aging, (5) sleep problems in the nursing home, (6) sleep and mortality, (7) assessment and intervention for sleep disturbances, and (8) future directions.

SLEEP AND THE MEASUREMENT OF SLEEP

Sleep Physiology

Sleep is a set of complete physiological processes involving a predictable sequence of operating states within the central nervous system identified by electroencephalographic (EEG) patterns and by specific behaviors (Hoch & Reynolds, 1986; Hoch, Reynolds, & Houck, 1988). There are two kinds of sleep: non-rapid-eye-movement (NREM) and rapid-eye-movement (REM) (see Table 4.1). NREM sleep is composed of four distinct stages. Stage 1 is a transition period between wakefulness and sleep lasting only a few minutes. The individual is relaxed and drowsy but still somewhat aware of the environment. EEG recordings show low-voltage waves of three to seven cycles per second. Stage 2 is true sleep and lasts from 5 to 20 minutes. The individual is unaware of surroundings but can be easily awakened, thus Stage 2 is also called "light sleep." The EEG recording shows sleep spindles with bursts of waves shaped like the letter K. Stage 3 is the first component of "deep" sleep and consists of slow EEG delta waves of one to four cycles per second. During Stage 3, an individual's muscles relax, pulse rate slows, and temperature decreases. From here, the individual moves into the deepest NREM sleep, Stage 4. There is little body movement and arousal is difficult. Stages 3 and 4 combined last from 15 to 30 minutes and are thought to be a restorative and relaxing period (Hauri, 1982; Hoch & Reynolds, 1986).

Each sleep cycle takes approximately 90 minutes. The individual moves through the four NREM sleep stages, then gradually returns up through light (Stage 2) sleep. Instead of reentering Stage 1 and awakening, the individual enters REM sleep or "dream" sleep. During REM sleep, EEG and biological activity appear similar to wakefulness. However, the individual is even more difficult to arouse than in NREM deep sleep Stage 3 and 4. During REM sleep, the pulse, respiration, blood pressure, and basal metabolic rate increase although muscle tone and deep tendon reflexes decrease. In addition, vivid dreams are frequently reported following arousal from REM sleep. REM sleep lasts 10 to 15 minutes and is thought to be important to learning, memory, and adaptation (Hauri, 1982; Hoch & Reynolds, 1986).

Cycles of NREM and REM sleep are determined by the total time spent asleep. Individuals usually have four or five complete cycles per night. Sleep cycles in the earlier half of the night are dominated by NREM Stages 3 and 4. As the night progresses, NREM time decreases and REM time increases. About 20% of total nocturnal sleep time is spent in REM sleep (Hauri, 1982; Hoch & Reynolds, 1986).

Table 4.1
NREM[a] AND REM[b] Sleep Stages

NREM	
Stage 1	NREM sleep with low voltage activity waves 3 to 7 cycles per seconds; a transition between wakefulness and sleep.
Stage 2	NREM sleep marked by the appearance of sleep spindles and/or K-complexes.
Stage 3	NREM sleep with delta waves occupying 20%-50% of EEG activity.
Stage 4	Deepest NREM sleep, with delta waves occupying more than 50% of EEG activity.
REM	EEG and biological activity appear similar to wakefulness; arousal very difficult; lasts an average of 10 minutes.

a. Non-Rapid-Eye-Movement
b. Rapid-Eye-Movement

Sleep Measurement

Sleep is measured objectively by EEG recordings and observational methods, and subjectively through self-reports (see Table 4.2). Electroencephalographic recordings of sleep are typically obtained in a laboratory during nocturnal and/or daytime sleep periods and requires a minimum of at least one full night of recording. Often, however, a series of three consecutive nights are recorded to allow for night one to serve as an adaptation period to recording procedures and a different sleep milieu. Measurement of EEG sleep variables is based on data from nights two and three. The major advantage of laboratory study is objective and accurate biological data measurement about sleep variables. These studies are limiting, however, because of the necessity for expensive equipment and technical proficiency in obtaining and interpreting results and because the person is removed from the normal sleep milieu. Portable recording methodologies are also available for use in community settings. Portable technologies provide accurate data but are restricted in number and type of EEG variables that can be recorded. Electroencephalographic sleep recordings can be scored by hand or by automated computer analysis. Sleep variables are grouped as measures of sleep continuity and REM sleep (see Table 4.3). Sleep architecture is composed of the NREM sleep Stages 1 through 4.

Sleep continuity measures include:

total recording period;
sleep latency which is time from lights out until the appearance of 10 minutes of
    Stage 2 sleep interrupted by no more than 2 minutes of wake;

Table 4.2
Sleep Measurement Methods

Objective Methods

Electroencephalographic (EEG) Recording
  Sleep Laboratory
  Portable Monitoring

Observation
  Direct
  Video

Subjective Methods

Questionnaires
Interviews

---

awake or time after sleep onset and before the final morning awakening;
time spent asleep is time asleep less awake time during the night after sleep onset;
arousal or period of wakefulness lasting 30 seconds or longer;
sleep efficiency or ratio of time spent asleep to total recording period; and
sleep maintenance or ratio of time spent asleep to total recording period after
    sleep onset.

Measures of REM Sleep are:

REM latency which is the number of minutes of sleep until the first REM period;
REM time or the total number of minutes of REM sleep;
REM activity which is the sum of rapid eye movements throughout the night;
REM density as ratio of total REM activity to total REM time;
REM intensity as ratio of REM activity to time spent asleep; and
REM period which is the time from one REM period to another (Reynolds, &
    Hoch, 1988).

Additional sleep variables involving nocturnal leg movements and breathing are generally recorded during EEG monitoring. Nocturnal myoclonus is the number of periodic leg movements during sleep that are associated with arousal. Measures of breathing include: apneas, hypopneas, and oxygen desaturations. Apnea is cessation of airflow during sleep for 10 seconds or longer. Hypopnea is a decrease in airflow during sleep to less than one third of baseline for at least 10 seconds. Oxygen desaturation is decrease in oxyhemoglobin during the night, usually associated with apnea or hypopnea events.

    Observational methods for measuring sleep are utilized in institutional settings. Periodic or continuous monitoring of sleep behaviors is done via direct

Table 4.3
Sleep Continuity and REM Sleep Variables

Sleep Continuity Variables

Total Recording	total number of minutes from initial plug-in to the end of the recording.
Sleep Latency	Time from lights out until the appearance of 10 minutes of Stage 2 sleep interrupted by no more than 2 minutes of wake or Stage 1.
Awake	Time spent awake after sleep onset and before the end of the recording period.
Time Spent Asleep	Time spent asleep, less any awake during the night after sleep onset.
Arousal	Period of wakefulness lasting 30 seconds or longer.
Sleep Efficiency	Ratio of time spent asleep to total recording period.
Sleep Maintenance	Ratio of time spent asleep to total recording period after sleep onset.

REM Sleep Measures

REM Latency	Number of minutes of sleep onset until the first REM period.
REM Time	Total number of minutes of REM Sleep.
REM Activity	Each minute of REM Sleep is scored on a 9-point scale (0-8) for number of rapid eye movements, the sum for the whole night providing REM activity.
REM Density	Ratio of total REM Activity to total REM time.
REM Intensity	Ratio of REM Activity to time spent asleep.
REM Period	Occurrence of at least 3 consecutive minutes of REM sleep separated by no less than 20 minutes NREM sleep from the next occurrence of REM sleep.

personal observations or through video recordings of subjects. Observations are recorded on data forms developed prior to the study and are typically categorical and descriptive. Observational study is less expensive than EEG recordings but yields less precise data and introduces questions of rater reliability and bias as well as validity as compared with EEG data.

Subjective self-report data are collected through post-sleep questionnaires, interviews, and sleep quality surveys and are recorded on forms such as sleep logs. Self-reports are valuable sources of information because they reflect an individual's attitudes, beliefs, and perceptions about his or her sleep and indicate problem areas; data are, however, estimates.

SLEEP AND HEALTHY AGING

Electrophysiological sleep studies of healthy elders have documented a set of altered sleep patterns associated with the healthy aging process, including fragmented sleep, increased NREM Stages 1 and 2 (light) sleep, decreased NREM Stage 4 (deep) sleep, decreased absolute amounts of REM sleep and numerous transient arousals of 3 to 15 seconds (Feinberg, 1974; Feinberg, Koresko, & Haller, 1967; Hayashi & Endo, 1982; Hoch, Reynolds, Kupfer, & Berman, 1988; Kales, Wilson, & Kales, 1967; Miles & Dement, 1980a; Prinz, 1977; Reynolds, Kupfer, Taska, Hoch, Sewitch, & Spiker, 1985. These characteristics demonstrate the brittleness and shallowness of the nocturnal sleep of older people. In addition, circadian rhythm disturbances are manifested by redistribution of sleep across the 24-hour day. Many elderly report retiring earlier and earlier at night as they become older, reflecting a phase advance of their major sleep period. Some elders develop multiple, shorter sleep-wake periods over a 24-hour day called polyphasic sleep-wake cycle.

Another important characteristic of sleep in late life is daytime napping. Evidence exists that daytime sleepiness among elders may be a compensatory response to fragmented nocturnal sleep (Carskadon, Brown, & Dement, 1982; Carskadon, van den Hoed, & Dement, 1980). In addition, social factors such as boredom, custom, and socioeconomic pressures may enforce and reinforce napping behavior in the elderly (Kupfer & Reynolds, 1983).

The ability to sleep versus need for sleep is another issue in sleep and healthy aging. The question often posed is, do older people sleep less because they need less sleep or because they cannot sleep as well as younger adults? Over an adult lifetime, the actual total amount of time spent asleep (including nocturnal sleep and daytime naps) during a 24-hour period only decreases by about one hour. Age-related EEG sleep patterns support the view that the elderly have less ability to sleep rather than less need for sleep because the ability to have slow-wave sleep and long uninterrupted sleep periods declines with age. Therefore, the occurrence of daytime sleepiness in many elderly may be a manifestation of unmet sleep need. Recent research, however, also suggests that some aspects of age-related sleep alterations may be reversible. For example, following a period of sleep deprivation or a sleep restriction pattern of progressively and systematically spending less time in bed, the elderly responded with recovery sleep having increased amount of delta sleep and improved sleep continuity (Reynolds et al., 1986; Spielman, Raskin, & Thorpy, 1983).

Gender-related differences have been noted in the sleep of the healthy elderly with men showing more impaired sleep maintenance and less delta sleep than women (Hoch, Reynolds, Kupfer, & Berman, 1988; Kahn & Fischer, 1969; Kahn, Fischer, & Lieberman, 1970; Reynolds, Kupfer, Taska, Hoch, Sewitch, & Spiker, 1985). It is interesting to note, however, that older women are more likely than men to complain of sleep disturbance and to receive sleeping pills (Miles & Dement, 1980b). A possible explanation may be the gender-related differences in sleep perception and effects of sleep disruption on mood. Elderly women show higher and more stable correlations between estimates of sleep quality and objective laboratory measures of sleep (Reynolds, Kupfer, Berman et al., 1987) and elderly women find sleep deprivation to be a more mood-disturbing experience than elderly men (Reynolds et al., 1986). Thus it is possible that elderly women may be more sensitive to sleep quality and sleep loss than elderly men.

The effects of advancing age on the stability of sleep structure and subjective reports of sleep quality have been examined over time (Hoch, Reynolds, Kupfer, & Berman, 1988). Most EEG sleep variables and perceptions of sleep quality were stable over a time period. Elderly men and women both showed significantly more awakenings during the second recording series. Gender-dependent sleep changes were noted only in phasic REM measures; and REM activity, density, and intensity increased in men over time and decreased in the women. Finally, subjective estimates of sleep quality, although stable over time, showed gender-dependent differences with women reporting a lower sleep quality than men.

SLEEP AND PATHOLOGY IN AGING

In addition to the sleep changes associated with the normal aging process are the sleep disturbances related to specific pathological factors including physical illness, depression, dementia, medications, transient situational disorders, and sleep habits. Each of these factors will be analyzed in the following sections.

Physical Illness

It has been estimated that two thirds of the individuals age 65 and older have one or more chronic medial illness (Miles & Dement, 1980a). Illnesses producing chronic pain contribute significantly to sleep alterations (Hoch & Reynolds,

1986). As arthritic joints stiffen during the inactivity of sleep, pain may awaken the person. Angina pain resulting from coronary artery vasoconstriction at the onset of REM sleep may disturb sleep (Hauri, 1982; Orem & Barnes, 1981). Epigastric pain that causes arousal from sleep can result from reflux of gastric acid into the esophagus or from the increase in gastric secretion that is associated with exacerbation of peptic and duodenal ulceration during periods of REM sleep (Kales & Kales, 1974). In chronic obstructive pulmonary disease (COPD), lack of oxygen saturation may be the result of inadequate ventilatory exchanges during sleep resulting in frequent nocturnal arousals that represent a physiologically adaptive response to improve ventilation (Hauri, 1982). Fluid accumulation in the lungs of elderly individuals who have congestive heart failure produces labored breathing and resultant sleeplessness (Lerner, 1982). In addition, benign prostatic enlargement, prostatic disease, diabetes mellitus, and urethritis (especially in elderly women) may all produce nocturnal awakening during the night to urinate and disrupt sleep (Hoch & Reynolds, 1986).

Depression

Sleep research has demonstrated electroencephalographic sleep changes associated with late life depressive illness. The sleep of depressed elderly is characterized by high REM sleep percentage, long first REM periods, greater density of phasic rapid eye movements, shorter REM latency, and extreme sleep maintenance difficulty (Hoch, Buysse, & Reynolds, 1989). It is noteworthy that several of the sleep changes that occur in late-life depression also occur, although to a lesser extent, during the course of normal aging (Hoch, Reynolds, Nebes et al., 1989). An age-dependent increase in wakefulness after sleep onset and decrease in slow-wave sleep occur in both normal aging and depression. REM sleep shortens considerably in depression and may also be a component of normal aging (Kupfer, Frank, & Ehlers, 1989). The capacity to sustain REM sleep inhibition during the first half of the night is diminished by advancing age as well as by depressive illness. Additionally, the shortening of REM sleep latency and alteration of intranight temporal distribution of REM sleep with greater early REM sleep density specifically characterizes the sleep of elders with major depressive disorders (Reynolds, Kupfer, Taska, Hoch, Spiker et al., 1985). Sleep maintenance difficulties of depressed elders also correlates significantly with the severity of depression, as measured by Hamilton depression ratings (Hamilton, 1967).

An interactive relationship between sleep regulation and depression has also been supported through self-report measures of sleep disturbances and depressed feelings in community resident elders (Rodin, McAvay, & Timko, 1988). Frequency of depressed mood has been associated with reports of difficulty falling asleep, waking up frequently in the night, early morning awakening, and not feeling rested in the morning. This finding is consistent with EEG sleep studies that have suggested the importance of early morning awakening as a significant finding among depressed elders (Kupfer, Reynolds, Ulrich, Shaw, & Coble, 1982; Kupfer et al., 1989).

Dementia

Elderly individuals with probable Alzheimer's disease frequently have disturbances in nocturnal sleep and sleep-wake cycles such as insomnia, wandering, and sundowning. These sleep-related disturbances may result from degenerative changes in the Alzheimer's disease process such as loss of or damage to the neuronal pathways that initiate and maintain sleep and that control respiration (Hirano & Zimmerman, 1962; Smallwood, Vitiello, Giblin, & Prinz, 1973; see Chapter 16 on Alzheimer's disease).

Sleep research has demonstrated EEG sleep changes among Alzheimer's patients in varying stages of the disease. The sleep of elderly individuals with probable Alzheimer's dementia compared with that of healthy elderly controls has been characterized by greater disruption of sleep continuity, decreased REM sleep time and activity, decreased amounts of NREM Stages 3 and 4 sleep, and frequent daytime naps with nighttime periods of wakefulness (Prinz et al., 1982; Reynolds, Kupfer, Taska, Hoch, Spiker et al., 1985). Concurrent with advancing dementia, Alzheimer's patients show a gradual but progressive loss of phasic activity, both of rapid eye movements in dream sleep and of spindles and K-complexes in NREM sleep. Finally, Alzheimer's patients have significantly more sleep-disordered breathing (Ancoli-Israel, Parker, & Butters, 1985; Billiard, Touchen, & Passarent, 1980; Frommlet, Prinz, Vitiello, Ries, & Williams, 1986; Hoch, Reynolds, Kupfer, Houck et al., 1987; Hoch, Reynolds, Nebes et al., 1989; Reynolds, Kupfer, Taska, Hoch, Sewitch, Restifo et al., 1985; Smirne et al., 1981; Vitiello et al., 1984). These sleep variables have been explored as potential biological markers for Alzheimer's disease. However definitive markers in early or mild dementia have not yet been isolated.

Medications

Medications such as stimulants, depressants, and other drugs or their side effects may contribute to sleep disturbances. The elderly are at particular risk because chronic illness and home medication usage increase with age. Age-dependant changes in pharmacokinetics, especially in the distribution, metabolism, and excretion of drugs, tend to interfere with the sleep-wake cycle in elderly persons (Fielo & Rizzolo, 1985; Hollister, 1977).

Sleep is also disturbed by alcohol, caffeine, and nicotine. Initially alcohol is a depressant and may have hypnotic effects but it soon fragments sleep and contributes to disturbed, restless sleep.

Transient Situational Disorders

Transient situational factors such as the loss of a loved one can precipitate sleep disturbances among the elderly. Persons with sleep disorders resulting from transient situational factors are those individuals who have slept normally prior to a clearly stressful event and who develop insomnia lasting three weeks or less.

Sleep Habits

Poor sleep habits are common correlates of sleep disorders among the elderly. Examples include irregular sleep-wake schedule; excessive environmental temperature or noise; evening use of alcohol, nicotine, or caffeinated beverages. Other factors such as obsessive worry about sleep or use of the sleep setting for activities not conducive to sleep may also impair sleep (Hauri, 1982; Reynolds, Kupfer, Hoch, & Sewitch, 1985).

SLEEP DISTURBANCES AND AGING

Several sleep disturbances have been studied in relation to advancing age: sleep-disordered breathing, nocturnal myoclonus, excessive daytime sleepiness, and insomnia. Each disturbance can be the result of pathology or may precipitate other significant sequelae among the elderly. These disturbances will be examined in the following sections.

Sleep-Disordered Breathing

Sleep-disordered breathing (apnea, hypopnea, oxygen desaturation) and its relation to advancing age is detected during nocturnal polysomnographic recordings with oral and nasal thermistors to measure airflow and bellows to monitor respiratory effort. Sleep apnea occurs when at least five apneas or hypopneas occur per hour of sleep, with each apnea or hypopnea event lasting a minimum of 10 seconds. Apnea index (AI) is the number of apneas per hour of sleep; apnea-hypopnea index (AHI) is the number of apneas and hypopneas per hour of sleep. Apneic events are usually followed by an awakening or arousal and can be associated with many symptoms including decreased blood oxygen levels, cardiac arrhythmias, nocturnal hypertension, nighttime confusion, and neuropsychiatric impairment.

The prevalence of sleep-disordered breathing has been examined in healthy elders as well as in randomly selected, community resident elders. Results consistently demonstrate age-related increases in the prevalence of sleep-disordered breathing (AncoliIsrael, 1989; Ancoli-Israel & Kripke, in press; Hoch, Reynolds, Kupfer, Houch et al., 1987; Hoch, Reynolds, Nebes et al., 1989). Estimates of AI and/or AHI of five or greater have been reported on one fourth to one third of the elderly studied. Gender differences have also been noted with increased prevalence of sleep apnea in elderly men versus elderly women. However, the significance of the condition is not clear.

The impact of sleep-disordered breathing may be greater in medically compromised elders. Higher rates of sleep apneas have been found among nursing home residents (Ancoli-Israel & Kripke, in press) and in randomly selected elderly medical ward patients with congestive heart failure (Ancoli-Israel, 1989). Studies have also reported significant associations between sleep-disordered breathing, pulmonary and cardiovascular disease (Guilleminault, Connolly, & Winkle, 1983; Kales, Bixler, & Cadieux, 1984; Lavie, Rachamin, & Rubin, 1984).

Nocturnal Myoclonus Disturbances

Nocturnal myoclonus or periodic leg movements in sleep is a sleep disturbance in which people kick or jerk their legs every 20 to 40 seconds periodically throughout the night. It is measured by polysomnographic recordings of anterior tibialis muscle activity. Myoclonus index (MI) is the ratio of periodic leg movements associated with arousals to total sleep time in hours. Among elderly with sleep complaints, the rates of nocturnal myoclonus range from 4% to 31% (Ancoli-Israel, Kripke, Mason, & Messin, 1981; Reynolds et al., 1980). However, in studies with healthy elderly people, rates of myoclonus range from 25% to 60% (Dickel, Sassin, & Mosko, 1986; Okudaira et al., 1983).

Excessive Daytime Sleepiness

A reduction of or disturbance during nighttime sleep results in increased sleepiness the next day. Excessive daytime sleepiness in the elderly may, therefore, be indicative of an underlying sleep problem that causes deterioration in the continuity of nocturnal sleep. Investigations have also shown that the elderly take more naps than younger people (Carskadon et al., 1982; Tune, 1968; Webb & Swinburne, 1971). Daytime sleepiness is measured objectively by the multiple sleep latency test (MSLT) using polysomnography during four or five daytime naps lasting 20 minutes each. The MSLT measures how long it takes an individual to fall asleep and whether REM sleep occurs. Research has demonstrated that elderly consistently fall asleep in less than 15 minutes, more quickly than other comparative age groups (Richardson, Carskadon, & Flagg, 1978). When elders are asked to describe their sleep and daytime functioning subjectively, most report that their sleep is satisfactory but they also report daytime sleepiness (Ancoli-Israel, Kripke, & Mason, 1984). MSLT data in conjunction with nocturnal sleep studies would be useful to determine the extent and severity of daytime sleepiness and to explore relations with the nocturnal sleep variables of elders.

Insomnia

Studies suggest that the elderly are the largest age group affected by disorders of initiating and maintaining sleep (Carskadon & Dement, 1981; Dement et al., 1982; Miles & Dement, 1980a). Insomnia is a perception by an individual that his or her sleep is inadequate or abnormal. Generally included are nocturnal symptoms of difficulty initiating sleep, frequent awakenings from sleep, a short sleep time, and "nonrestorative" sleep. Daytime symptoms resulting from poor sleep include the following: fatigue, sleepiness, depression, anxiety, and other mood changes. These symptoms are similar to those complaints most frequently offered by elders about their sleep: spending more time in bed, taking longer to fall asleep, awakening more often, being sleepy in the daytime, and needing longer to adjust to changes in the usual sleep-wake schedule. Medication is generally an acceptable treatment for transient insomnia among the elderly, lasting for three to four weeks and resulting from situational causes. For prolonged or chronic geriatric insomnia, however, nonpharmacologic interventions are warranted. Research protocols for geriatric insomnia using sleep restriction and relaxation training methods have had only limited success (Bliwise, Friedman, & Yesavage, 1988).

SLEEP PROBLEMS IN THE NURSING HOME

Disturbed sleep with nighttime wandering is one of the most frequent reasons why elderly individuals are institutionalized (Pollak & Perlick, 1987; Sanford, 1975). Sleep disturbances and related behaviors and complaints are common among nursing home populations. Studies have estimated that 35% of nursing home residents receive tranquilizing medications (James, 1985; U.S. Public Health Service, 1976).

Observations, interviews, and questionnaire measures are the most frequent methodologies used in studies of sleep in nursing home settings. Sleep patterns around the clock have been observed with increasing amounts of sleep in a

24-hour period usually resulting from increased daytime sleep rather than an increase in nocturnal sleep (Regestein & Morris, 1987). Investigations have also demonstrated large amounts of individual variability in the sleep patterns of nursing home patients (Bliwise, Bevier, Bliwise, & Dement, 1987; Jacobs, Ancoli-Israel, & Parker, in press). Objectively recorded sleep via portable nocturnal polysomnography was utilized in a randomly selected group of elderly nursing home patients (Jacobs et al., in press). These patients averaged only 39.5 minutes of sleep per hour in any hour of the night and 50% woke up at least two times per hour. When a subgroup of these nursing home residents were observed for 24 hours, patients spent some portion of every hour asleep. In addition, their sleep was so fragmented that they rarely experienced a single hour of consolidated sleep (Ancoli-Israel, Parker, Sinall, Mason, & Kripke, 1989). As previously described, sleep-disordered breathing is also more prevalent among nursing home residents than community residing elders (Ancoli-Israel & Kripke, in press).

SLEEP AND MORTALITY

Mortality rates during various times at night have been studied. Mortality rates from all causes are estimated to increase 30% during sleep (Smolensky, Halberg, & Sargent, 1972). Excessive death between 2:00 A.M. and 8:00 A.M. has been found, with the peak being relatively specific to ischemic heart disease in persons over the age of 65 years (Mitler, Hajdukovic, & Shafor, 1987). Studies have shown that people who report either sleeping less than seven hours or more than eight hours have a higher mortality rate, with 86% of deaths among individuals older than 60 years of age (Belloc, 1973; Kripke, Simons, Garfinkel, & Hammond, 1979). It has been hypothesized that sleep apnea may be one cause of increased mortality (Kripke, Ancoli-Israel, Mason, & Messin, 1983; Kripke et al., 1979).

ASSESSMENT AND INTERVENTION

The biological changes that occur in sleep with both normal aging and disease in old adults can explain many sleep-wake disturbances. For example, frequent daytime sleepiness may be related to the following EEG sleep findings: prolonged sleep onset; decreased sleep maintenance, especially during the last two hours of sleep; less deep (Stages 3 and 4) sleep; and increased light sleep (Stage 2). Diminished sleep efficiency, impaired sleep maintenance, and alterations in Stage 2 predispose the Alzheimer's victim to be a light sleeper who awakens frequently but does return to sleep. The sleep of depressed elderly includes disturbances reported in general by individuals with depression: difficulty falling asleep, staying asleep, and early morning awakening (Hoch, Reynolds, & Houck, 1988).

Sleep assessment, as an integral part of general health assessment, focuses on the type of sleep disturbance, its duration, its probable causes, and its effects upon the person. Nursing assessment should determine whether a sleep disturbance requires medical referral or if it can be relieved through nursing intervention. Research data in themselves are not an adequate basis upon which to build a specific intervention protocol. They do suggest areas in which sleep hygiene interventions can be helpful in reducing the effect of sleep alteration on elderly. These interventions should be directed at strengthening the sleep-wake cycle of the elderly in order to combat the changes in sleep continuity, efficiency, or maintenance. Elderly persons and their families need to know that some sleep disturbances may be an unavoidable consequence of aging. It is not that less sleep is needed, but rather the ability to sleep seems to diminish with age. The elderly person should work toward a consistent bedtime, get up at the same time each morning, and shorten or eliminate naps. If sleep does not come or is interrupted during the night, the person may get out of bed but should remain inactive in order to preserve the 24-hour rest-activity period (Hoch, Reynolds, & Houck, 1988; Hoch & Reynolds, 1986).

FUTURE DIRECTIONS

Perhaps one of the most salient issues facing nurses who work with both healthy and ill elders is to recognize the delicate and complex interaction among aging, illness, and sleep. A priority for future research is the identification of multidimensional correlates (psychobiological, neurophysiological, neuropharmacological, metabolic, and chronobiological) of late life sleep disorders. It also remains to be determined if electrographic sleep data can be used to validate the subjective sleep changes frequently expressed by the elderly. Once these investigations are complete, a specific framework for nursing interventions for late life sleep disorders can be developed.

REFERENCES

Ancoli-Israel, S. (1989). Epidemiology of sleep disorders. In T. Roth & T. Roehrs (Eds.), *Clinics in geriatric medicine*. Philadelphia: W. B. Saunders.

Ancoli-Israel, S., & Kripke, D. (in press). Epidemiology of sleep apnea in the elderly. *Sleep*.

Ancoli-Israel, S., Kripke, D., & Mason W. (1984). Obstructive sleep apnea in a senior population. *Sleep Research, 13,* 130.

Ancoli-Israel, S., Kripke, D. F., Mason, W., & Messin, S. (1981). Sleep apnea and nocturnal myoclonus in a senior population. *Sleep, 4,* 349-358.

Ancoli-Israel, S., Parker, L., & Butters, N. (1985). Respiratory disturbances during sleep and mental status: Preliminary results from a TNH. *The Gerontologist, 25,* 6-11.

Ancoli-Israel, S., Parker, L., Sinall, R., Mason, W., & Kripke, D. (1989). Sleep fragmentation in patients from a nursing home. *Journal of Gerontology, 44,* M18-21.

Belloc, N. B. (1973). Relationship of health practices and mortality. *Preventative Medicine, 2,* 67-81.

Billiard, M., Touchen, M., & Passarent, P. (1980). Sleep apneas and mental deterioration in elderly subjects. In W. P. Koella (Ed.). *Sleep: 5th European congress on sleep research* (pp. 400-402). Amsterdam: Karger, Basel.

Bliwise, D. L., Bevier, W. C., Bliwise, N. G., & Dement, W. C. (1987). Systematic behavioral observation of sleep/wakefulness in skilled care nursing home. *Sleep Research, 16,* 170.

Bliwise, D. L., Friedman, L., & Yesavage, J. A. (1988). A pilot study comparing sleep restriction therapy and relaxation training in geriatric insomniacs. *Sleep Research, 17,* 148.

Carskadon, M., Brown, E., & Dement, W. (1982). Sleep fragmentation in the elderly: Relationship to daytime sleep tendency. *Neurobiology of Aging, 3,* 321-327.

Carskadon, M., & Dement, W. (1981). Cumulative effects of sleep restriction on daytime sleepiness. *Psychophysiology, 18,* 107-122.

Carskadon, M., van den Hoed, J., & Dement, W. C. (1980). Insomnia and sleep disturbance in the aged: Sleep and daytime sleepiness in the elderly. *Journal of Geriatric Psychiatry, 13,* 135-151.

Dement, W., Miles, L., & Carskadon, M. (1982). "White paper" on sleep and aging. *Journal of the American Geriatric Society, 30,* 25-50.

Dickel, M. J., Sassin, J., & Mosko, S. (1986). Sleep disorders in an aged population: Preliminary findings of a longitudinal study. *Sleep Research, 15,* 116.

Feinberg, I. (1974). Changes in sleep cycle pattern with age. *Journal of Psychiatric Research, 10,* 283-306.

Feinberg, I., Koresko, R. L., & Haller, N. (1967). EEG sleep patterns as a function of normal and pathological aging in men. *Journal of Psychiatric Research, 5,* 107-144.

Fielo, S., & Rizzolo, M. A. (1985). The effects of age on pharmacokinetics. *Geriatric Nursing, 6,* 332-337.

Frommlet, M., Prinz, P., Vitiello, M. V., Ries, R., & Williams, D. (1986). Sleep hypoxemia and apnea are elevated in females with mild Alzheimer's disease. *Sleep Research, 15,* 189.

Guilleminault, C., Connolly, S. J., & Winkle, R. A. (1983). Cardiac arrhythmia and conduction disturbances during sleep in 400 patients with sleep apnea syndrome. *American Journal of Cardiology, 52,* 490-494.

Hamilton, M. (1967). Development of a rating scale for primary depressive illness. *British Journal of Social Clinical Psychology, 6,* 278-296.

Hauri, P. (1982). *Current concepts: The sleep disorders.* Kalamazoo, MI: Upjohn.

Hayashi, Y., & Endo, S. (1982). All-night sleep polygraphic recording of healthy aged persons: REM and slow wave sleep. *Sleep, 5,* 277-283.

Hirano, A., & Zimmerman, H. M. (1962). Alzheimer's neurofibrillary changes. *Archives of Neurology, 7,* 227-242.

Hoch, C. C., Buysse, D., & Reynolds, C. (1989). Sleep and depression in late life. *Clinics in Geriatric Medicine, 5,* 259-274.

Hoch, C. C., & Reynolds, C. F. (1986). Sleep disturbances and what to do about them. *Geriatric Nursing, 7,* 24-27.

Hoch, C. C., Reynolds, C., & Houck, P. (1988). Sleep patterns in Alzheimer's depressed and healthy elderly: Implications for nursing assessment and intervention. *Western Journal of Nursing Research, 10,* 239-256.

Hoch, C. C., Reynolds, C., Kupfer, D., & Berman, S. (1988). Laboratory note: Stability of EEG sleep and sleep quality in healthy seniors. *Sleep, 11,* 521-527.

Hock, C. C., Reynolds, C. F., Kupfer, D. J., Berman, S. R., Houck, P. R., & Stack, J. (1987). Empirical note: Self-report versus recorded sleep in healthy seniors. *Psychophysiology, 24,* 293-299.

Hock, C. D., Reynolds, C. F., Kupfer, D. J., Houck, P. R., Berman, S. R., & Stack, J. A. (1987). Sleep-disordered breathing in normal and pathologic aging. *Journal of Clinical Psychiatry, 47,* 499-503.

Hoch, C. C., Reynolds, C. F., Nebes, R. D., Kupfer, D. J., Berman, S. R., & Campbell, D. (1989). Clinical significance of sleep-disordered breathing in Alzheimer's disease: Preliminary data. *Journal of the American Geriatric Society, 37,* 138-144.

Hollister, L. E. (1977). Prescribing drugs for the elderly. *Geriatrics, 32, 71-73.*

Jacobs, D., Ancoli-Israel, S., & Parker, L. (in press). Twenty-four hour sleep/wake patterns in a nursing home population. *Psychological Aging.*

James, D. S., (1985). Survey of hypnotic drug use in nursing homes. *Journal of American Geriatrics Society, 33,* 436-439.

Kahn, E., & Fischer, C. (1969). The sleep characteristics of the normal aged male. *Journal of Nervous and Mental Disorders, 148,* 477-494.

Kahn, E., Fischer, C., & Lieberman, L. (1970). Sleep characteristics of the normal aged female. *Comprehensive Psychiatry, 11,* 274-278.

Kales, A., Bixler, E., & Cadieux, D. (1984). Sleep apnea in a hypertensive population. *Lancet, ii,* 1005-1008.

Kales, A., & Kales, J. D. (1974). Sleep disorders: Recent findings in the diagnosis and treatment of disturbed sleep. *New England Journal of Medicine, 290,* 487-499.

Kales, A., Wilson, T., & Kales, J. D. (1967). Measurement of all-night sleep in normal elderly persons: Effect of aging. *Journal of American Geriatric Association, 15,* 405-410.

Kripke, D. F., Ancoli-Israel, S., Mason, W., & Messin, S. (1983). Sleep-related mortality and morbidity in the aged. In M. H. Chase & E. D. Weitzman (Eds.). *Sleep disorders: Basic and clinical research* (pp. 415-429). New York: Spectrum.

Kripke, D., Simons, R., Garfinkel, L., & Hammond, E. (1979). Short and long sleep and sleeping pills: Is increased mortality associated? *Archives of General Psychiatry, 36,* 103-106.

Kupfer, D. J., Frank, E., & Ehlers, C. L. (1989). EEG sleep in young depressives: First and second night effects. *Biological Psychiatry, 25,* 87-97.

Kupfer, D., & Reynolds, C. (1983). A critical review of sleep and its disorders from a developmental perspective. *Psychiatric Development, 4,* 367-386.

Kupfer, D., Reynolds, C., Ulrich, R., Shaw, D., & Coble, P. (1982). Sleep, depression and aging. *Neurobiology of Aging: Experimental and Clinical Research, 3,* 351-360.

Lavie, P., Rachamin, B., & Rubin, A. E. (1984). Prevalence of sleep apnea syndrome among patients with essential hypertension. *American Heart Journal, 108, 373-376.*

Lerner, R. (1982). Sleep loss in the aged: Implications for nursing practice. *Journal of Gerontological Nursing, 8,* 323-326.

Miles, L. E., & Dement, W. (1980a). Sleep and aging. *Sleep, 3,* 119-220.

Miles, L. E., & Dement, W. (1980b). Sleep-wake complaints of elderly men and women. *Sleep, 3,* 121-129.

Mitler, M. M., Hajdukovic, R. M., & Shafor, R. (1987). When people die, cause of death versus time of death. *American Journal of Medicine, 82,* 266-274.

National Institute of Health (NIA). (1990). *The treatment of sleep disorders of older people.* Washington, DC: National Institute of Health.

Okudaira, N., Fukuda, H., Nishihara, K., Ohtani, K., Endo, S., & Torii, S. (1983). Sleep apnea and nocturnal myoclonus in elderly persons in Vilcabamba, Ecuador. *Journal of Gerontology, 38,* 436-438.

Orem, J., & Barnes, C. D. (1981). *Physiology in sleep.* New York: Academic Press.

Pollak, C. P., & Perlick, D. (1987). Sleep problems and institutionalization of the elderly. *Sleep Research, 16,* 407.

Prinz, P. (1977). Sleep patterns in the healthy aged: Relationships with intellectual functions. *Journal of Gerontology, 32,* 179-180.

Prinz, P. N., Peskind, E. R., Vitaliano, P. P., Raskin, M. A., Eisdorfer, C., Zemcuznikov, N., & Gerber, C. J. (1982). Changes in the sleep and waking EEGs of nondemented and demented elderly subjects. *Journal of the American Geriatrics Society, 30,* 86-93.

Rabin, D. I. (1985). *Waxing of the gray, waning of the green in American's aging older society.* Washington, DC: National Academy Press.

Rabins, P. V., Mace, N. L., & Lucas, M. J. (1982). The impact of dementia on the family. *Journal of the American Medical Association, 248,* 333-335.

Regestein, Q. R., & Morris, J. (1987). Daily sleep patterns observed among institutionalized elderly. *Journal of the American Geriatrics Society, 35,* 767-772.

Reynolds, C. F., Coble, P. A., Black, R. S., Holzer, B., Carroll, R., & Kupfer, J. (1980). Sleep disturbances in a series of elderly patients: Polysomnographic findings. *Journal of the American Geriatrics Society, 23, 164-170.*

Reynolds, C. Hoch, C., & Monk, T. (1989). Sleep and chronobiologic disturbances in late life. In E. W. Busse & D. Balzer (Eds.). *Geriatric Psychiatry* (pp. 475-488). Washington, DC: American Psychiatric Press.

Reynolds, C., Kupfer, D., Hoch, C., & Sewitch, D. (1985). Sleeping pills for the elderly: Are they ever justified? *Journal of Clinical Psychiatry, 46,* 9-12.

Reynolds, C., Kupfer, D., Hoch, C., Stack, J., Houck, P., & Berman, S. (1986). Sleep deprivation in healthy elderly men and women: Effects on mood and on sleep during recovery. *Sleep, 9,* 492-501.

Reynolds, C. F., Kupfer, D. J., Taska, L. S., Hoch, C. C., Sewitch, D. E., Restifo, K., Spiker, D. G., Zimmer, B., Marin, R. S., Nelson, J., Martin, D., & Morcyz, R. (1985). Sleep apnea in Alzheimer's dementia: Correlation with mental deterioration. *Journal of Clinical Psychiatry, 46,* 257-261.

Reynolds, C. F., Kupfer, D. J., Taska, L. S., Hoch, C. C., Sewitch, D. E., & Spiker, D. G. (1985). Sleep of healthy seniors: A revisit. *Sleep, 1,* 20-29.

Reynolds, C. F., Kupfer, D. J., Taska, L. S., Hoch, C. D., Spiker, D. G., Sewitch, D. E., Zimmer, B., Marin, R. S., Nelson, J. P., Martin, D., & Morycz, R. (1985). EEG sleep in elderly depressed, demented and healthy subjects. *Biological Psychiatry, 20,* 431-442.

Richardson, G. S., Carskadon, M. A., & Flagg, W. (1978). Excessive daytime sleepiness in man: Multiple sleep latency measurement in narcoleptic and control subjects. *Electroencephalography and Clinical Neurophysiology, 45,* 621-627.

Rodin, J., McAvay, G., & Timko, C. (1988). A longitudinal study of depressed mood and sleep disturbances in elderly adults. *Journal of Psychological Science, 43,* 45.

Sanford, J. R. A. (1975). Tolerance of debility in elderly dependents by supporter at home: Its significance for hospital practice. *British Medical Journal, 3,* 471-473.

Smallwood, R. G., Vitiello, M. V., Giblin, E. C., & Prinz, P. (1973). Sleep apnea: Relationship to age, sex and Alzheimer's dementia. *Sleep, 6,* 16-22.

Smirne, S., Francescki, M., Bareggi, S. R., Comi, G., Mariani, E., & Mastrangelo, M. (1981). Sleep apneas in Alzheimer's disease. In S. K. Basel (Ed.), *Sleep: 1980 European congress sleep research* (pp. 433-444). Amsterdam: Karger, Basel.

Smolensky, M., Halberg, F., Sargent, F. L. (1972). Chronobiology of the life sequence. In I. S. Tokyo, (Ed.), *Advances in Climatic Physiology* (pp. 281-318).

Spielman, A., Raskin, P., & Thorpy, M. (1983). Sleep restriction treatment for insomnia. *Sleep Research, 12,* 286.

Tune, G. S. (1968). Sleep and wakefulness in normal adults. *British Medical Journal, 2,* 269-271.

U.S. Bureau of the Census. (1986). *Age structures of the U.S. population in the 21st century.* (SB-1-86). Washington, DC: Government Printing Office.

U.S. Public Health Service. (1976). Physician's drug prescribing patterns in skilled nursing facilities (DHEW Publication No. US 76-50050, pp. 1-60). Washington, DC: Government Printing Office.

Vitiello, M. V., Bokan, J. A., Kukull, W. A., Muniz, R. L., Smallwood, R. G., & Prinz, P. N. (1984). Rapid eye movement sleep measures of Alzheimer's dementia patients and optimally healthy individuals. *Biological Psychiatry, 19.* 721-734.

Webb, W. B., & Swinburne, H. (1971). An observational study of sleep in the aged. *Perceptive Motor Skills, 32,* 895-898.

5

Sexuality in Aging

ELAINE E. STEINKE

Objectives: The learner will:

(1) Apply knowledge of stereotypes, myths, and attitudes about sexuality in aging to client interactions.
(2) Analyze research findings on sexuality in aging and apply the information to client care situations.
(3) Evaluate a plan of care for older adults with sexual needs and/or problems, incorporating physical, psychosocial, and sociocultural perspectives.
(4) Analyze a teaching plan for clients with sexual dysfunction related to chronic conditions.

INTRODUCTION

Sexuality is a topic that has often been neglected by health professionals. Health professionals usually incorporate teaching on physical and occupational changes necessitated by a disease process but totally neglect sexual counseling. This can be a serious injustice to clients who have sexual concerns, either expressed or unexpressed.

Efforts made at sexual counseling are sometimes half-hearted attempts that either skirt the issue or present vague general information. Researchers have noted that inadequate instruction can lead to increased fear of sexuality in cardiac patients (Papadopoulos, Larrimore, Cardin, & Shelly, 1980). A study by Shuman and Bohanchich (1987) found that most nurses were aware of the need to provide sexual information after myocardial infarction. On the variables of comfort, preparedness, and execution of teaching, however, most of the subjects rated these as either "usually" or "rarely." This indicated that nurses may understand the importance of teaching on sexual matters, but following through with actual teaching may vary from nurse to nurse and client to client. It is likely that only those patients posing a question receive sexual counseling.

The elderly in particular are assumed to have little need of sexual information. If health professionals are reluctant to talk about sex in general, would they begin by addressing sexuality for the older adult? This is not likely given the general negative societal attitudes toward sexuality in aging. A number of studies, however, have demonstrated that older adults show sexual interest and activity (Brecher, 1984; Starr & Weiner, 1981; White & Catania, 1982). The growing number of older adults in the population suggests that sexuality is an area that will increase in importance.

This chapter will explore myths, attitudes, and definitions of sexuality in aging. It will include an analysis of research related to physical and psychosocial concerns. Assessment and application of research findings by the clinical nurse specialist is examined.

STEREOTYPES, MYTHS, AND ATTITUDES

America is a youth-oriented society. This fact is particularly evident in the area of sexuality. We are continually bombarded with media portrayals of sex and sexuality. Popular magazines have advertisements with sexual meanings. Cartoons have shown mostly negative views of sexuality with age. Even bumper stickers tout sexual messages. These are just a few examples of ways that sexuality is brought to our attention. In most instances, a positive portrayal of sexuality relates to youth.

Kuhn (1976) identified five myths of sexuality and aging that are widely accepted by society: (1) Sex is not important for older persons, (2) an interest in sexual activity for an older person is abnormal, (3) remarriage of an older person should be discouraged, (4) it is appropriate for an older man to seek a younger woman, but an older woman should not get involved with a younger man, and (5) older people in long-term care institutions should be separated by gender. The general population, health professionals, and young, middle-aged, and older adults continue to believe these myths.

These beliefs lead to stereotyping and generally negative societal attitudes toward sexuality in aging. Other attitudes suggest that aging leads to impotence, sexually active older persons are morally perverse, older persons are sexually undesirable, or too fragile to make love, even if they so desired (Butler

& Lewis, 1976). Any signs of interest in sexuality or open discussions of sex by older persons often lead to a label of being lecherous. Sexual interest that would make a man a "playboy" at age 30, at 70 makes him a "dirty old man" (Eliopoulos, 1987). Older persons are therefore viewed as being asexual, incapable of sexual expression. Sviland (1975, p. 98) states that the elderly are "forced into mandatory retirement from sexual activity." Because many older adults believe these myths, the stereotyping of the elderly has become a self-fulfilling prophecy. Older adults, believing they are asexual, behave accordingly; however, there are a number of elderly who actively continue to express their sexuality (Brecher, 1984; Starr & Weiner, 1981).

DEFINITIONS OF SEXUALITY

The myths and stereotypes tend to present sex and sexuality as being the same, when in fact sexuality is a broad term that encompasses all types of sexual feelings as well as behaviors. Sexuality has been defined in various ways. It is the love, warmth, touching, and sharing between people (Ebersole & Hess, 1990). It is the "quality of the person, an energy force that is expressed in every aspect of the person's being" (Starr & Weiner, 1981, p. 12). Sexuality is a reflection of our sexual identity, our maleness or femaleness (Moran, 1979). Berlin (1978) indicated that sexuality involves anything that gives pleasure, sexual or emotional; excitement or comfort. In essence, sexuality is a basic human need that encompasses psychosocial, sociocultural, and physical dimensions. This is depicted in the model in Figure 5.1. It provides a framework for viewing sexuality from a holistic perspective, including the multifaceted dimensions explored in this chapter. Each of the components of the model should be considered by the clinical nurse specialist when evaluating sexuality in older clients.

PHYSIOLOGIC CHANGES WITH AGE

Researchers have been studying physiologic changes in sexuality with age since the pioneering studies of Kinsey and associates (Kinsey, Pomeroy, & Martin, 1948, 1953). The studies of Christenson and Gagnon (1965), Christenson and Johnson (1973), Newman and Nichols (1960), and Pfeiffer (1969, 1977) indicate that older adults are physically capable of sexual expression. In general, the research findings show a decline in sexual activity over time for both men and women, with less sexual activity noted in older women. Pfeiffer (1977), however, made two general conclusions from longitudinal data: Sexual interest and activity beyond the age of 60 is not a rare phenomenon, and

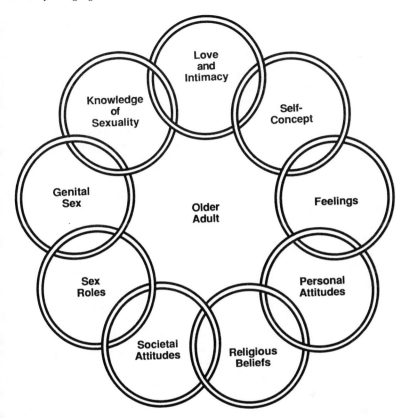

Figure 5.1. A Framework for Viewing Sexuality from a Holistic Perspective

patterns of sexual interest and activity vary for men and women of the same age. These findings are supported by other researchers (Bretschneider & McCoy, 1988; Weizman & Hart, 1987). It should be noted that those persons who are interested in sex and were sexually active in their younger years will likely continue this pattern in their later years.

Masters and Johnson's (1966, 1970) research findings on the normal physiologic changes of aging support the ability of older adults to remain sexually active. Sixty-one women and 39 men were studied to obtain data on the normal physiologic changes that affect sexuality in aging. Physical changes affecting sexual function in the aging female include decreased vaginal lubrication, and reduced length, width, and expansive ability of the vagina. The intensity of sexual tensions is diminished. However, the clitoris maintains a similar response as in younger women. Regardless of these physiologic changes, the female is fully capable of sexual expression in the presence of regular, effective sexual stimulation.

Studies in the aging male demonstrate changes in erection and ejaculation (Masters & Johnson, 1966, 1970). Penile erection time is tripled or doubled. Once an erection is achieved, it can be maintained for extended periods of time without ejaculation. Full erection may not occur until just prior to ejaculation. Orgasmic response is similar to younger males, although there is decreased force and sensation of the ejaculate that may appear as seminal fluid seepage. Ejaculation may be a single stage rather than a two stage process. Orgasm may not occur with every intercourse if it is frequent. There is a longer refractory period as compared to younger males.

In summary, these normal changes with age do not inhibit sexual activity in older adults. The problem of vaginal dryness can be relieved with the use of a water soluble jelly prior to intercourse. A positive benefit of the longer erection time in males is that it gives more time to pleasure the female partner in achieving orgasm. An understanding of these normal physical changes provides a basis for understanding the sociocultural and psychologic variables that impact sexuality in aging.

SOCIOCULTURAL AND PSYCHOLOGICAL ASPECTS

The attitudes and stereotypes about sexuality in aging affect the older person's view of the aging process. Lack of knowledge about the physical changes associated with age can create fear and frustration in older adults. Changing social relationships and friendship patterns also play a role.

Social variables include the stereotypes of the aged, partner availability, and other obstacles to sexual expression. The stereotype of the sexless older years has had damaging effects on the elderly. As mentioned previously, for some older adults this stereotype has led to a self-fulfilling prophecy, inhibiting sexual expression. Those older adults who do experience sexual desires often feel guilty and ashamed (Barash, 1977).

Partner availability is a significant problem for the older adult. Older women especially have difficulty in finding sexual companionship because there are fewer older men available. On the other hand, older men have much greater choice in choosing an older woman for a partner. Society has rejected sexual activity outside of marriage, especially for the older adult. This poses a dilemma for the older adult. Should persons engage in sexual relationships outside of marriage and risk the ridicule of family and friends? Should they remarry? Should they withdraw from heterosexual activity? Older adults may choose to masturbate to relieve sexual tension; however, this activity can induce guilt reactions in the individual.

Additional obstacles to sexual expression include health, economics, and family disapproval. A large proportion of the aged decline in health with advancing years. Some alterations in health are a result of physiologic changes, whereas others result from disease. An understanding of the normal changes of age can alleviate some of the older person's fears. Alternate approaches to sexual expression can be devised as necessary to minimize the effect of chronic illness on sexuality.

Economics can be a problem in that an older couple wanting to remarry may not be financially able to do so. Frequently, remarriage means a reduction in social security benefits or pensions. Therefore, it may not be financially feasible for a couple to remarry.

Family disapproval of the selected mate can provide a difficult situation for the older adult. Children may express concerns about the parent's mental status, the selected mate's intentions and inheritance issues. These children also tend to have the same negative stereotypes as the rest of society in regard to sexuality in aging, which impacts the older family member.

Psychologic variables affecting the aged are interest, religious attitudes, beliefs, and self-esteem. Ebersole and Hess (1990, p. 486) stated that "sexual health is individually defined and wholesome if it leads to intimacy (not necessarily coitus) and enriches the involved parties." Sexual interest can be a lifelong process, showing varying levels of progression throughout life.

Religious attitudes of aged persons are generally reflected in their views of sexuality. Many religions teach that sex is for the sole purpose of procreation and beyond this activity, there is no further purpose for sex. Masturbation may also be discouraged. A widowed older person seeking expression of sexual needs may very well be hampered by these religious beliefs that reinforce the concept of the aged as being asexual.

Altered self-esteem can have a pronounced effect on the sexual relationship. Findings of a study by Stimson, Wase, and Stimson (1981) suggested that sexuality is an important component of self-esteem for the older man. Women tended to use youthful standards to judge themselves and related feelings of attractiveness to self-worth. The study suggested that views of sexuality are different for older men and women, and individual values, beliefs, and attitudes play a significant role in self-perception.

Other psychologic factors affecting sexuality are guilt, depression, monotony, anger, performance anxiety, unresolved grief, and self-doubt (Ebersole & Hess, 1990). These can negatively affect sexual interest and activity. Monotony is a factor mentioned by couples in long-standing marriages.

Two studies using large samples provide further evidence of the viability of sexuality with age (Brecher, 1984; Starr & Weiner, 1981). These studies examined both physical and psychosocial aspects of sexuality in aging. Results demonstrated that many older adults are both interested in sexuality and engage in sexual behaviors. There is some controversy about the sampling method used in the Starr & Weiner (1981) report (Morgan & Phillips, 1983). The large sample size, however, adds some credibility to the results.

The research presented represents a broad and sometimes diverse view of sexuality in aging. It is important to note that although sexual activity does decrease with age, a large percentage of the older population is sexually active. This pattern would seem to be a reflection of the person's attitudes and values towards themselves as a person. Therefore, the physical, psychosocial, and sociocultural dimensions of sexuality are intertwined in a way that makes sexuality individually defined.

ANALYSIS OF RESEARCH

Research on sexuality and aging is somewhat limited. There are very few studies cited in the nursing literature, with most information coming from the social sciences (Steinke & Bergen, 1986). Much of the research is not recent and some was conducted with relatively small samples. For these reasons, it can be questioned whether these studies accurately reflect today's older adults (Travis, 1987). It is this author's opinion, however, that sexual attitudes have not changed a great deal in reference to the elderly. Open discussions about sexuality continue generally to focus on the young. The negative societal stereotyping of sexuality in aging does continue although its impact on the aged may be lessened to a small extent. Health professionals, although still reluctant to talk about sexuality, tend to have a generally more positive view of sexuality in aging. It is anticipated that in the future older adults will assert themselves and help others recognize that sexuality is a viable need regardless of age.

Some general conclusions can be made based on the research presented. Although sexual activity may decline with age, other forms of sexual expression continue, for example touching, caressing, sexual fantasies. Persons who are sexually active in younger years will likely continue this pattern of activity into older years. Physically, most older adults are capable of sexual activity. Contrary to popular beliefs, older adults are accepting of masturbation, oral sex, and nudity. Social and psychological barriers prove to be the most confounding in relationship to sexual expression. Sexual interest is generally maintained even though sexual opportunities may decline. Partner availability is a major hindrance for the older female. Other barriers such as diminished self-esteem, depression, monotony, financial concerns, health, and religious attitudes were discussed previously. Although the desire for sexual expression is alive and well in most older adults, confounding factors may prove prohibitive in carrying out sexual behaviors.

Because many older adults have internalized negative stereotyping and have withdrawn from sexual behaviors, believing they are asexual, education could provide one avenue for correcting these beliefs. Few research studies have focused on this area. White and Catania (1982) reported on a study using a psychoeducational intervention to evaluate sexuality in aging. The sample included 30 each of elderly, nursing home staff, and adult family members of older persons. The purpose of the study was to assess the effects of an older age oriented program on the three groups of subjects. Methodology included the use of the Aging Sexual Knowledge and Attitudes Scale (ASKAS) developed by White and Catania (1982) as a pretest, education sessions, and the ASKAS as a posttest, with experimental and control groups. The education sessions included information on physical, social, and psychological aspects of sexuality and aging. Mean scores for the experimental groups for the aged, staff, and family showed significant increases in knowledge and significantly more permissive attitudes from pre-test to post-test. Other significant results for the aged experimental group were increased sexual satisfaction, rated importance of sexual activity, and incidence of sexual intercourse and masturbation. These results indicate that the use of an educational intervention can have a significant impact on the older adult's view and practice of sexuality and aging.

Brower and Tanner (1979) conducted a study examining sexual knowledge and attitudes using a two-session education program and two questionnaires. Results showed no change from pretest to posttest on the study variable. However, the pretest sample size was 30, but at the posttest only 7 and 4 subjects took each of the two posttests. The small sample size possibly affected the results of this study.

In a study of 102 men and women between the ages of 60 and 85 years of age, quantitative and qualitative aspects of sexuality and aging were investigated by Adams (1980). Subjects utilized a self-administered questionnaire to rate activities and attitudes toward sexual experience at the present time as contrasted to their 20s and 30s. The author indicated that although some decline in sexual functioning does occur with age, this belief has been over emphasized by researchers. Findings indicated that when sexual activity was defined to include activities other than heterosexual intercourse, an increase in sexual functioning occurred.

Another study sought to determine older adults' knowledge and attitudes about sexuality and aging (Steinke, 1988). Twenty-four subjects were pretested using an interview format with the ASKAS. In addition, demographic information and data on sexual behaviors and sexual satisfaction were collected. Experimental subjects received one hour education sessions once a week for four consecutive weeks. Four to six weeks after completion of the educational intervention, subjects for both experimental and control groups were posttested using the same measure as in the pretest. Results showed increased knowledge from pre-test to posttest for the experimental group. Attitudes, however, remained unchanged. The experimental group did not show significant changes on the variables of frequency of sexual behaviors and sexual satisfaction. The relatively short time period of the study may have precluded these changes. The small sample size was also a factor.

Several conclusions can be drawn from the research studies cited. Education seems to be a viable way of addressing the myths and stereotypes of sexuality in aging, particularly if there are several education sessions over an extended period of time. Attitudes about sexuality change more slowly, therefore testing of subjects should be extended to allow changes in attitudes to occur. Nurses and other health professionals need to identify knowledge level and attitudes about sexuality and aging, and provide the necessary educational programs. Longitudinal studies with a middle-aged population designed to measure knowledge and attitudes about sexuality in aging from middle age through old age would enhance knowledge in this area. All adults need to be taught the facts about sexuality in aging so that they have informed and realistic expectations as they age.

In summary, the limited research available does lend support to the need for education of all adults about sexuality and aging. Armed with knowledge, perhaps some of the myths, stereotypes, and inaccurate information can be changed.

Assessment, Diagnoses, and Application

Assessment of sexual function should occur as part of the general nursing assessment. In this way, it is not as threatening to the client. Sometimes it is helpful to initiate a discussion of sexuality and aging by making a statement about the normality of the topic. For example, the nurse might say, "Many older adults continue to be sexually active into their later years, while others are not. How would you describe your present level of sexual activity?" This acknowledges the person as a sexual being and gives him or her permission to talk about sexuality. In another example, the nurse says, "Many older persons have concerns about resuming sexual activity after a heart attack. What concerns do you have?" Expressing the universality of the topic provides a good way of introducing the sensitive area of sexuality. The nurse may elicit a great deal of assessment data from these simple questions. It also allows clients the option to state that they have not been sexually active or have no concerns about sexuality.

The nursing assessment begins with a general assessment that examines usual sexual patterns, marital status, living arrangements, general concerns about sexuality, and knowledge of sexuality in aging. Physical assessment involves determining if chronic health problems have impacted on the individual's sexual function; degree of sexual activity; changes in erection or ejaculation; difficulties with arousal, vaginal lubrication, or orgasm; or pain with intercourse. A psychosocial assessment should determine sexual interest, partner availability, degree of sexual satisfaction, attitudes and beliefs, and the presence of psychological variables. A more formalized method of sexual assessment can be used, such as the Permission, Limited Information, Specific Suggestion and intensive therapy (P-LI-SS-IT) model by Annon (1976) (MacElveen-Hoehn, 1985).

Sexual assessment is an important and necessary component of the nursing assessment. The data gained from such an assessment is essential in providing comprehensive care to the client. We do a tremendous disservice to our clients by neglecting this area.

There are two North American Nursing Diagnoses Association (NANDA) approved nursing diagnoses for sexual concerns: altered sexuality patterns and sexual dysfunction. Altered sexuality patterns may include reported changes in sexual functioning, lack of knowledge of the sexual changes with age, and any of the psychosocial factors discussed previously. Steinke (1991) provides an example of a nursing care plan for an older adult with the diagnosis of altered sexual patterns.

The nursing diagnosis of sexual dysfunction relates to sexual problems incurred by chronic illnesses or their treatments, changes in sexual relationships, performance anxiety, and dissatisfaction with the sex role. If the contributing factor to sexual dysfunction is a chronic illness, then interventions should be aimed at improving sexual function or helping the client adapt to the changes in function. A thorough assessment is paramount in this situation. In addition to the assessment criteria previously mentioned, the nurse needs to determine the onset of the sexual dysfunction. Was it present before the onset of the medical problem? To what extent has it impacted sexual function? What is the client's perception of the problem? Answers to these questions aid in developing approaches to deal with the sexual dysfunction. Each approach will vary somewhat depending on the underlying problem.

CHRONIC ILLNESS AND SEXUAL FUNCTION

Selected chronic illnesses are presented in the following section for which clients commonly express sexual concerns. Strategies are provided for teaching and intervention.

Cardiovascular Disease

Many older adults with cardiovascular disease are fearful of returning to sexual activity, particularly after a myocardial infarction (MI). Generally, if clients can climb two flights of stairs or walk a few blocks briskly, they can resume sexual activity. However, the client should be assessed considering such factors as general health, overall recovery from the MI, present level of physical activity, fatiguability, and the emotional and physical impact of sexual activity on the heart (Hogan, 1985).

There are additional factors that influence the decision to return to sexual activity after experiencing heart disease. Baggs and Karch (1987) studied sexual counseling of females with coronary artery disease. Sixty-three percent of the 58 women were sexually active. Reasons for sexual inactivity in the remaining subjects were partner availability, choice of the partner, partner impotence, lack of interest, fear, age, depression, and dyspareunia. Subjects were questioned about the information they received on returning to sexual information, and of these, 29% read a brief statement from the rehabilitation booklet or protocol sheet. Two clients had spoken to a health care provider about sexual concerns. This study supports the need for sexual counseling for all cardiac clients regardless of age, sex, or marital status. Sexual activity can be resumed post-Myocardial Infarction (MI) in 6 to 14 weeks. The time variance relates to consideration of client factors mentioned previously. Fear and anxiety are major factors in delaying or ceasing sexual activity. The client or partner may fear further incidences of chest pain or an MI. Walz and Blum (1987) report that MIs have occurred during intercourse when circumstances included sex with a new partner, a younger partner, or unfamiliar surroundings.

In these circumstances, psychic stress related to the situation enhanced the chance of chest pain and MI. Client teaching should include the following points: (1) the client should be well rested; (2) avoid heavy meals or alcohol consumption prior to intercourse; (3) choose a position comfortable for both partners—recent research shows that position does not greatly increase physical demands on the body for the MI client (Walz & Blum, 1987); (4) nitroglycerine is sometimes used before sexual activity, particularly if chest pain is experienced with intercourse; (5) the use of sexual pleasuring (touching, fondling, etc.) before intercourse allows a gradual rise in vital signs and helps to decrease strain on the heart; and (6) open communication and consideration by both partners is important.

Changes in sexual function of the hypertensive client usually occur in the later stages of hypertension and are often related to drug therapy. Untreated hypertension causes damage to blood vessels, leading to erectile dysfunction in the male. Treatment with sympathetic blockers, peripheral vasodilators, and diuretics may cause changes in libido, difficulty in maintaining an erection, delayed or missed ejaculation, or impotence. Emotional stress related to these problems may tend to exacerbate the hypertension. It is important to counsel clients that drug effects are individualized; a drug may not have the same impact on sexual function from one person to another. There are also new drugs on the market that might be chosen that would not cause as many adverse effects on sexual function. In general, as the blood pressure becomes normalized, there is noted improvement in sexual function. However, the side effect of sexual dysfunction from drug therapy for cardiovascular conditions, continues to be a problem.

The client who experiences a cerebrovascular accident (CVA) has many changes in emotions. This combined with the physical disabilities has a pronounced effect on body image. They fear that they are no longer sexually inviting. The CVA client may experience rejection from a partner. Once again, open communication is extremely important. The couple can jointly discover new erotic areas. Position changes can aid in sexual intercourse (McCormick, Riffer, & Thompson, 1986). Those clients with good upper body strength may assume the superior position. A wheelchair with removable arms can be used for sexual intercourse. Couples might lie perpendicular to each other in bed which tends to increase sexual satisfaction. A male CVA patient who is able to stand and balance, might stand with the female leaning forward across an elevated bed or table. These are just a few examples of position changes that help to minimize the physical impairments of the client who has experienced a CVA.

Teaching the client who has cardiovascular conditions should be individualized and based on a comprehensive assessment. For best results, teaching should include the client's partner, either individually or in group instruction. The nurse should emphasize that tachycardia, tachypnea, and tiredness are usual reactions during intercourse. Abnormal symptoms include prolonged chest pain, shortness of breath, palpitations lasting more than 15 minutes after intercourse, and prolonged exhaustion. This as well as the specific information noted previously should be taught.

Diabetes Mellitus

The client with diabetes faces a challenge in that a return to the pre-illness state is not possible. It is a disease that has a pronounced effect on body function as well as body image. In addition, the client may be challenged to find new ways of approaching sexual relationships.

Type I diabetics have greater changes in sexual function related to diabetic neuropathies. Few studies have focused on sexual function in the female diabetic. Reported changes in sexual function, however, include vaginal dryness and delayed orgasm related to decreased flexibility and tightness of the vagina. Strategies for teaching the female with diabetes include the following: strict diabetic control to help maintain sexual interest and function; prompt treatment of candidal vaginitis; sexual stimulation before intercourse or use of a water soluble jelly to prevent vaginal dryness; and an emphasis on sexuality as a whole, including other forms of sexual expression.

Diabetes has a pronounced effect on the male. Physical changes include erectile impotence with a flaccid penis and retrograde ejaculation. Anxiety and depression are common psychologic causes of impotence. If the male has severe erectile dysfunction in the presence of good diabetic control, the prognosis for recovery of sexual function is poor. Although the severity of erectile dysfunction varies, there is no cure for impotence related to diabetic neuropathy. Sexual counseling includes helping the client deal with feelings of guilt, anger, depression, and low self-esteem; exploring other methods of sexual expression; and the possible use of penile prosthetic devices. There are several types of devices to choose from. A urologist can help the client decide if and what type of device might be appropriate. One complication of these devices is infection, which can be a problem because wound healing is slowed in the diabetic.

Arthritis

Most older Americans suffer from some form of arthritis. They exhibit varying degrees of disability that can impact sexual expression. Teaching is aimed at finding positions of comfort, having sexual activity at a time of day when there is least discomfort, and taking pain relieving and anti-inflammatory medications as prescribed. Although the effects of arthritis on sexual function are not as devastating as in other chronic illnesses, changes in sexual function can occur.

Cancer

Many people have the mistaken belief that clients with cancer have no interest in sexuality. Although it is true that libido may be diminished during acute stages of illness, the client may show sexual interest during other less critical times. Sexual intimacy continues to be a viable need for the client with cancer. One example is the older woman with breast cancer. She may experience feelings of loss, denial, anger, guilt, and depression. There may be chronic grief related to metastases and progression of the disease and treatment. For these reasons body image is also threatened. The woman may only focus on the loss of the breast rather than recognizing other ways of meeting sexual needs. Self-esteem reflects our worth and value as a person. Sharing intimacy is a source of establishing personal value. Communication remains a fundamentally important concern.

Nursing strategies for assisting the female facing a mastectomy include exploring the degree of importance of the breasts to the client's sexual self-concept; discussing other areas of sexual eroticism; allowing the person to grieve; assessing readiness to look at the incision and discuss breast prostheses;

exploring fears; role-playing situations likely to be encountered with a sexual partner; and changing position to decrease pain in the surgical arm, if applicable. These position changes are: (1) male astride with small pillow over the incision, (2) female astride with incision and arm supported with a pillow, (3) side lying with affected arm down, and (4) rear entry with the woman lying on pillows to minimize pressure on the affected area (Schwarz-Appelbaum, Dedrich, Jusenius, & Kirchner, 1984).

Other gynecological cancers and treatments such as radical vulvectomy, cancer of the uterine corpus, and pelvic exteneration can have pronounced effects on sexuality. The psychological variables previously mentioned apply here as well. A good baseline sexual history that considers previous patterns of sexual enjoyment and orgasm are important as it impacts on the decision to retain the clitoris (e.g., radical vulvectomy). The nurse needs to provide factual information in a sensitive and caring manner.

The older male who experiences prostatic cancer may receive treatment involving surgery and radiotherapy. Males having a transurethral prostatic resection generally have no loss of potency or erection, although retrograde ejaculation does occur. Clients should be told that this is not harmful and that they can expect cloudy urine after ejaculation. If a suprapubic or retropubic prostatectomy is performed, problems include retrograde ejaculation and physiologic or psychogenic erectile dysfunction. Treatment with radiotherapy may cause erectile dysfunction in some males, genital edema, urinary stress incontinence, urethral stricture, and diarrhea. These may impact on sexuality. Hormonal manipulation might also be employed by means of a bilateral orchidectomy and the use of estrogens. This may cause decreased libido, impotence, phallic atrophy, gynecomastia, and depression. Penile implants as previously mentioned are also a treatment option.

Cancer, whatever the type, has varied yet pronounced effects on sexuality. As with all of the chronic conditions described, client counseling is paramount to the psychosexual well-being of the older adult facing these problems.

SUMMARY

This chapter has presented sexuality in aging as a multifaceted phenomenon involving physical, psychosocial, and sociocultural dimensions. Sexuality is individually defined, meaning that handholding, caressing, or just being with a friend may be as important or more important than more physical sexual behaviors for some older adults. Although education for the purpose of negating the myths and stereotypes is important, the client's needs and wishes must also be respected. We cannot force this new knowledge on unsuspecting older adults. We must recognize them as unique individuals with special needs.

Health professionals must address sexual needs within the context of the general physical and psychosocial assessment and incorporate this information into the plan of care, considering both the normal sexual changes with age and problems associated with chronic conditions. Health professionals must set aside their own biases and beliefs, and educate themselves about sexuality in aging, to provide holistic care to the older adult.

REFERENCES

Adams, C. (1980). Sexuality and the older adult. Unpublished doctoral dissertation, University of Massachusetts.

Annon, J. (1976). *Behavioral treatment of sexual problems: Brief therapy* (Vol. 1). New York: Harper & Row.

Baggs, J., & Karch, A. (1987). Sexual counseling of women with coronary artery disease. *Heart & Lung, 16,* 154-159.

Barash, D. (1977). Sexuality in the aging: is there life after sixty? *Meninger Perspective, 8,* 5-11.

Berlin, H. (1978). Your doctor discusses: Sexuality in mature/late life. *Planning for Health, 21,* 2.

Brecher, E. (1984). *Love, sex, and aging.* Boston: Little, Brown.

Bretschneider, J., & McCoy, N. (1988). Sexual interest and behavior in healthy 80-to 102-year-olds. *Archives of Sexual Behavior, 17,* 109-29.

Brower, H., & Tanner, L. (1979). A pilot study of older adults attending a program on human sexuality. *Nursing Research, 28,* 36-39.

Butler, R., & Lewis, M. (1976). *Sex after sixty.* New York: Harper & Row.

Christenson, C., & Gagnon, J. (1965). Sexual behavior in a group of older women. *Journal of Gerontology, 20,* 351-356.

Christenson, C., & Johnson, A. (1973). Sexual patterns in a group of older never-married women. *Journal of Geriatric Psychiatry, 7,* 88-98.

Ebersole, P., & Hess. P. (1990). *Toward healthy aging: Human needs and nursing response.* St. Louis: C.V. Mosby.

Eliopoulos, C. (1987). *Gerontological nursing* (2nd ed.). Philadelphia: J. B. Lippincott.

Hogan, R. (1985). *Human sexuality, a nursing perspective.* (2nd ed.). East Norwalk, CT: Appleton & Lange.

Kinsey, A., Pomeroy, W., & Martin, C. (1948). *Sexual behavior in the human male.* Philadelphia: W. B. Saunders.

Kinsey, A., Pomeroy, W., & Martin, C. (1953). *Sexual behavior in the human female.* Philadelphia: W. B. Saunders.

Kuhn, M. (1976). Sexual myths surrounding aging. In W. Oakes, G. Melchivide, & I. Fischer (Eds.). *Sex and the lifecycle* (pp. 117-124). New York: Grune & Stratton.

MacElveen-Hoehn, P. (1985). Sexual assessment and counseling. *Seminars in Oncology Nursing, 1,* 69-75.

Masters, W., & Johnson, V. (1970). *Human sexual inadequacy.* Boston: Little, Brown.

Masters, W. & Johnson, V. (1966). *Human sexuality.* Boston: Little, Brown.

McCormick, G., Riffer, D., & Thompson, M. (1986). Coital positioning for stroke afflicted couples. *Rehabilitation Nursing, 11,* 17-19.

Moran, J. (1979). Sexuality: An ageless quality, a basic need. *Journal of Gerontologic Nursing, 5,* 13-16.

Morgan, D., & Phillips, D. (1983). *Dubious data on sexuality: The Starr-Weiner report.* Paper presented at the annual meeting of the Gerontological Society, San Francisco, CA.

Newman, G., & Nichols, C. (1960). Sexual activities and attitudes in older persons. *Journal of the American Medical Association, 173,* 33-35.

Papadopoulos, C., Larrimore, P., Cardin, S., & Shelley, S. (1980). Sexual concerns and needs of postcoronary patient's wives. *Archives of Internal Medicine, 140,* 38-41.

Pfeiffer, E. (1969). Geriatric sex behavior. *Medical Aspects of Human Sexuality, 3,* 19-29.

Pfeiffer, E. (1977). Sexual behavior in old age. In E. Busse & E. Pfeiffer (Eds.), *Behavior and adaptation in late life* (2nd ed.), (pp. 130-141). Boston: Little, Brown.

Schwarz-Appelbaum, J., Dedrich, J., Jusenius, K., & Kirchner, C. (1984). Nursing care plans: Sexuality and treatment of breast cancer. *Oncology Nurses' Forum, 11,* 16-24.

Shuman, N., Bohanchich, P. (1987). Nurses' attitudes towards sexual counseling. *Dimensions of Critical Care Nursing, 6,* 75-81.

Starr, B., & Weiner, M. (1981). *The Starr-Weiner report on sexuality in the mature years.* New York: McGraw-Hill.

Steinke, E. (1988). Older adults' knowledge and attitudes about sexuality and aging. *Image: Journal of Nursing Scholarship, 20,* 93-95.

Steinke, E. (1991). Nursing care plan for altered sexuality patterns. In F. Rogers-Seidl (Ed.), *Geriatric nursing care plans.* St. Louis: MO: C.V. Mosby.

Steinke, E., & Bergen, M. (1986). Sexuality and aging: A review of the literature from a nursing perspective. *Journal of Gerontologic Nursing, 12,* 6-10.

Stimson, A., Wase, J., & Stimson, J. (1981). Sexuality and self-esteem among the aged. *Research on Aging, 3,* 228-239.

Sviland, M. (1975). A program of sexual liberation and growth in the elderly. In R. Solnick (Ed.), *Sexuality and aging* (pp. 96-115). Los Angeles: University of Southern California Press.

Travis, S. (1987). Older adults' sexuality and remarriage. *Journal of Gerontologic Nursing, 13,* 8-14.

Walz, T., & Blum, N. (1987). *Sexual health in later life.* Lexington, MA: D.C. Heath.

Weizman, R., & Hart, J. (1987). Sexual behavior in healthy married elderly men. *Archives of Sexual Behavior, 16,* 39-44.

White, C., & Catania, J. (1982). Psychoeducational intervention for sexuality with the aged, family members of the aged, and people who work with the aged. *International Journal of Aging and Human Development, 15,* 121-138.

6

Leisure in Later Life

FRANCIS A. McGUIRE
ROSANGELA BOYD

Objectives: Upon completing this chapter, the reader will be able to:

(1) Critique the relationship between continuity and change to leisure in the later years;
(2) Evaluate potential benefits of leisure involvement;
(3) Identify factors shaping and limiting leisure involvement;
(4) Evaluate age related differences in leisure involvement;
(5) Analyze the therapeutic benefits of recreation involvement.

INTRODUCTION

Advances in public health measures and medical technology have added years to the lifetime of the American population. Quantity of years, however, does not necessarily coincide with quality of life, as Havighurst cautiously suggested (1961). Quality of life is defined by George and Bearon (1980) in terms of four underlying dimensions, subdivided into subjective and objective. Life satisfaction and self-esteem are classified as subjective whereas general health/functional status and socioeconomic status are labeled objective.

For many years, a major concern regarding the successful maintenance of quality of life in old age was adjustment to retirement. Miller (1965) vehemently claimed that retirement resulted in an identity crisis. Loss of working status, according to Miller, represented a degrading role loss, which leisure could not replace. More recently, it has been found that the mere withdrawal from the working role is not what accounts for loss of self-esteem among older adults. Better predictors to adjustment are: (a) retirement income, and (b) availability of friends with whom to socialize (Teaff, 1985).

Atchley (1977) has challenged Miller's identity crisis theory with his continuity theory. Finding no evidence that retirement per se negatively influenced quality of life, Atchley proposed that continuity in other roles, such as those related to family, friends, and community can minimize identity loss. The author went further to suggest that leisure could effectively provide the opportunity for continued positive self-identity in old age.

In fact, the examination of the meanings attributed to work clearly shows close relationships to those meanings derived from leisure. Havighurst's (1977) list of meanings included: a basis for self-worth, a locus of social participation, a source of prestige, a chance to create, an opportunity to be of service to others, and a way of passing time.

THE ROLE AND MEANING OF LEISURE IN LATER LIFE

Leisure at any period of life is more than merely filling time with activities. In fact, leisure has a role in personal welfare. According to Kelly (1982), it provides a wide range of benefits to individuals. These include: self-expression, physical health, companionship, rest and relaxation, a chance to try something new, building social relationships, getting in touch with nature, testing oneself in risk or competitive situations, and a chance to meet the expectations of others. Leisure can provide opportunities to meet most human needs. As Kelly indicated in a later publication (1987), leisure is an integral part of the process of becoming a person with a satisfying life marked by continuity of meaning and identification rather than merely a series of experiences. Leisure is not a "time out" from this pursuit of identification but rather an integral part of the process. To view leisure as anything less than primary in the lives of individuals is to lessen its potential. This may be particularly true in the lives of older individuals whose opportunities to find meaning and identification may be reduced as a result of the role loss that frequently accompanies the aging process. The last period of the life course, identified as the "culmination" period by Kelly, is typified by a seeking of continued competence and autonomy in leisure as well as an interior integration of meaning and continued social integration.

A necessary starting point in discussing leisure in the later years is a brief clarification of what is meant by the term leisure. A simple definition was offered by Kelly (1982) who stated: "Leisure is activity that is chosen primarily for its own sake" (p. 23). It is marked by relative freedom and intrinsic satis-faction. This definition results in several conclusions about leisure. The first is that it is personal and therefore difficult to identify. Individuals bring their own history, physical and mental state, emotional needs, intellectual perspec-tive, and personality to an activity and these influence the meaning of that activity. Participation in a yoga class may mean five different things to five different participants. One person may do it for relaxation, another for status, another because a family member asked to participate, another for health ben-efits, and another for spiritual reasons. The difficulty of attaching meanings and motivations to activities is that they not only vary across individuals but may also vary within an individual. A person may jog one day for health and fitness related reasons and for social reasons the next day. As Kelly indicated after summarizing the career of one activity, dancing, "In the end it is the meaning to the participant that is crucial. It is that meaning, that definition of the activity for a time and place, which determines whether doing the activity is primarily expressive leisure, social leisure, or activity that is required by social or professional roles" (p. 25).

Leisure is also a complex phenomenon and therefore one that is neither easily understood nor explained. It is simplistic to identify older individuals as members of a "leisure class" because they typically have large periods of unobligated time, and identify leisure as a panacea that will replace what has been lost as a result of aging. It is also impossible to dismiss the potential value of leisure, however, by identifying it as something secondary to other realms of behavior such as work. Leisure can be a primary factor in an individual's life if that is the individual's choice. The key to understanding leisure is to recognize it as an individual and personal factor in people's lives.

In spite of the difficulties in understanding leisure and its meaning, the examination of the work in the area, and some of the generalities gleaned from the research will provide insight into leisure in the later years. The remainder of this chapter will attempt to do that.

THE NATURE OF LEISURE IN LATER LIFE

Obviously, one should not expect that a 65-year-old who has been raised to honor the work ethic will suddenly replace an occupation of 40 years with new recreational pursuits. Leisure has the potential to preserve and enhance self-identity, but it cannot be imposed. Its efficacy greatly depends on the develop-ment of interests and habits that begin prior to retirement and extend into postretirement years.

Continuity theory represents an alternative to the preceding disengagement theory (Cumming & Henry, 1961) and activity theory (Havighurst, Neugarten,

& Tobin, 1968). Advocates of the disengagement theory would suggest that as a silent pact between the older individual and a society, the former would withdraw from active involvement, accepting a more passive role as part of the "natural" aging process. Studies finding a decrease in leisure participation would be used to support such point of view. Developed as a reaction to the disengagement theory, the activity theory postulates the need to replace old roles through substitution of new activities for those dropped or no longer feasible. The greater the activity, the more satisfied the individual would be. A number of studies were generated to investigate the relationship between activity and life satisfaction in old age (Teaff, 1985), with mixed results. Clearly the relationship between leisure and adjustment cannot be explained solely in terms of disengagement or activity.

As Sessoms (1985) stated, "The theory of continuity assumes an integrated and holistic approach, an evolutionary process, which moves people from one stage of life to the next, with no radical departure from previous activity patterns" (p. 238). Decreases in certain activity pursuits do not represent withdrawal, but rather a natural tendency of life development. Patterns of participation remain sufficiently stable so that radical substitution is not necessary for life satisfaction, either. Indeed, continuity in valued activity pursuits may be considered more fulfilling than high activity levels. Quality of involvement rather than quantity of activities is the key to life satisfaction.

Gordon, Gaitz, and Scott (1976) found that although participation tended to decline with age in activities characterized as highly active, external to the home, and physically demanding, it remained stable for activities pursued indoors with family or friends, or involving the media. Because most research into activity patterns has used cross-sectional designs, it is not absolutely safe to assume that changes are due to the aging process rather than differences between age cohorts. The patterns found appear to support the existence of a shared core of activities, which suggests a commonality in adult leisure (Kelly, 1985). Activities that seem to constitute a common ground in adult leisure involvement are precisely those retained by older individuals. Examples identified by Kelly from a national survey were: (a) watching television (engaged in by 88% of the respondents), (b) reading (71%), (c) listening to the radio (62%), and (d) spending the evening with relatives (83%). A possible conclusion is that those activities forming the core of adult leisure are carried on into old age because they are easily accessed and gratifying to their participants.

The notion of continuity and core, however, should not overshadow the existence of change and balance in the leisure behavior of the older adult. New skills and activities are constantly learned, even after age 65. Data from the 1983 Nationwide Recreation Survey indicate that some outdoor activities such as horseback riding, backpacking, and birdwatching were first tried after age 65 by many of the respondents. A study by McGuire, Dottavio, and O'Leary (1987) identified a large group of older individuals who exhibited a lifelong model of leisure involvement. These individuals, labeled "expanders," were in contrast to another group, labeled "contractors," who exhibited a childhood determination approach to leisure. The expanders added leisure activities to their repertoire throughout life. The contractors learned most of the leisure activities in which they engaged throughout life prior to reaching 20 years of age. Contractors reduced the activities they did as life progressed whereas the expanders were continually adding activities. The attempt to uncover general patterns of participation cannot neglect the immense variability existent within age groups. There is as much diversity between the young and old as there is among the elderly themselves.

This realization of diversity within commonality supports Kelly's proposal of a "core plus balance" model (1985). Balance stands for variety in leisure. As individuals move along their life course, the balance is likely to change. As identities and social roles are shaped, new experiences are sought for different purposes. Although the core of leisure behavior may be touched by development, it is the balance part of the model that is most likely to change, giving people their ever evolving uniqueness.

BARRIERS TO LEISURE INVOLVEMENT

MacNeil and Teague (1987) emphasize the importance of lifelong leisure learning in allowing individuals the opportunity to choose freely how to spend their unobligated time. Programs focusing on leisure education are beneficial in enabling older individuals to overcome barriers associated with the aging process.

Many older individuals experience obstacles that restrict their leisure choices. These constraints result in a latent demand for leisure that cannot be met until they are removed. Examples of leisure constraints identified in the past are: lack of time, fear of disapproval, lack of skills, health impediments, resource limitations, and lack of companionship (McGuire, 1984). Although constraints may not be totally eliminated by individual efforts, they may be minimized through leisure education. Leisure education programs are usually designed to address issues such as attitude clarification, information seeking, and skill development. Often barriers such as lack of money, equipment, or facilities are a result of poor knowledge of community resources available to the individual. The time factor and the approval concern may be dealt with by examining one's priorities and perceptions of benefits regarding leisure involvement as well as values placed on it by society in general.

Health limitations may be overcome by creative adaptations in activities. Just as there is diversity in activity preferences and participation among older individuals, there are differences in factors constraining leisure involvement.

Factors such as personality, experience, environment, and resources will influence the nature and impact of constraints. A common problem faced by the elderly is the underestimation of their abilities, by themselves as well as others. Programs may be geared toward low functioning levels of activity because of stereotypes regarding the elderly's ability to learn new skills, their lack of motivation, or their health and physical limitations. Although it is true that some physical losses are associated with old age, these do not necessarily restrict leisure involvement and the ability to enjoy an independent leisure life-style. More than 90% of all American elderly live in the community, requiring only some supportive services to continue their participation in the mainstream of society.

A key issue in facilitating leisure involvement may be attracting the older individual to the agencies equipped to run such activity programs. The challenge in captivating and maintaining the interest of the older individual may depend on the ability of recreation providers to offer as much variety as possible in a prosthetic environment, where the attitudes of staff reflect openness and respect for the participant's dignity. Instead of limiting the elderly to tedious segregated programs that carry the negative stigma of serving those who are no longer able to enjoy normal life, programmers and administrators should develop integrated programs focusing on interest and not age.

Kelly in a recent position paper (undated) raised a simple but often neglected issue concerning the aging process: the fact that it is indeed a process. Frequently there appears to be a belief that only two types of older individuals exist: those who are alert and active and those who are impaired and dependent. It is often forgotten that a transition takes place from one stage into the next. The "in-betweeners," as Kelly calls those traveling through the aging path, are more the rule than the exception. It is the responsibility of helping professionals to create enabling conditions to extend the capable years, delaying deterioration, as well as the impact of losses, as much as possible. Kelly suggests that individual continuity and social integration represent major avenues to prolong the "good years." In leisure, he proposes to detach age labels from programs, gearing them to activity categories instead. An example would be not to concentrate all efforts into creating all sorts of options in centers exclusively directed at senior citizens, but to motivate the elderly to remain involved in specific leisure-oriented groups such as bowling leagues, golf clubs, or cultural associations.

Although such efforts are admirable, they cannot change the reality of an aging population, many of whom may need external assistance to lead satisfying lives. As it is now, the proportion of those 65 years old or older who live in institutions such as nursing homes is rather small—only 5%. This percentage, nevertheless, is known to increase with age. Twenty-three percent of persons older than age 85 are institutionalized (AARP, 1989). Considering that the 85+ group is the fastest growing group among the older population, it is expected that placement in long-term care facilities will become more common in the years to come.

THE ROLE OF LEISURE IN LONG-TERM CARE FACILITIES

It is quite clear that Americans are still reluctant to place dear ones or to seek voluntary admission in nursing homes. Past horror stories about isolation and decay have created a general phobic reaction, which has generated the impression that nursing homes are the last resort for those too sick and/or impaired to live elsewhere. To erase such negative perceptions, professionals in long-term care need to deal with objective problems that arise with the relocation of older individuals from their homes to an institutional environment.

Often, admission into a long-term care institution is accompanied by a number of losses affecting identity, independence, and control. The loss of social groups of reference is one of the problems faced by those who leave their home in the community to become one of many patients in an institutional setting. From being head of a household, the older individual moves into a closed, structured, and restrictive environment, given a space limited area, often to be shared with a complete stranger, and discouraged from keeping more than the most essential goods. A lifetime of belongings and memories are left behind. For some, it may be the first time in several decades that they even have had to sleep on a different bed. Individuals who might have been in positions of power before are now in the "patient" position. The concern for falls and wandering behavior may lead staff to use restraints and restrict patients from free ambulation. The fragility shown in the older body arouses the need to protect and help even at times when this is only reinforcing the "sick" role. Perceiving the low expectations of those surrounding them, many elderly persons may settle for dependency, only confirming old stereotypes. This vicious cycle of increasing incompetence has been described as the social breakdown syndrome by Kuypers and Bengton (1973) (see Chapter 21 concerning ethics and the use of restraints in nursing homes).

Placement in a long-term care facility may also result in increased feelings of helplessness (Baltes & Baltes, 1986; Langer, 1983; Langer & Rodin, 1976; Mercer & Kane, 1979; Voelkl, 1986). Control, defined by feelings of efficacy and ability to accomplish desired goals, is drastically reduced when one is not encouraged to participate in decision making and engage in autonomous behavior. As a result of not perceiving opportunities to exercise control, an individual may recoil into the world of indifference and passivity.

Although the picture painted above appears quite gloomy, it does not represent the inescapable destiny of older persons. The social breakdown syndrome and negative consequences of helplessness can be fought off by presenting the elderly with opportunities for control, self expression, and autonomy. Interventions such as those described by Langer and Rodin (1976) are effective in reversing the deleterious effects of loss of choice and control.

THERAPEUTIC RECREATION IN LONG-TERM CARE FACILITIES

An area where nurses are most likely to come into contact with providers of leisure services to older individuals is in working with therapeutic recreators. Therapeutic recreation is the use of recreation activities to facilitate the development, maintenance, and expression of an appropriate leisure life-style. This is accomplished through treatment, leisure education, and recreation participation. Therapeutic recreators focusing on the treatment function will typically be members of the treatment team and focus on treatment and rehabilitation. In this situation therapeutic recreators follow a process marked by assessment, problem identification, identification of treatment goals, design of a treatment plan, implementation, progress reporting, and decision making related to termination or further treatment (Peterson & Gunn, 1984). When therapeutic recreation is focused on treatment, the intent is to reduce functional limitations experienced by individuals. For example, if an older individual is experiencing a limitation resulting from physical decline and at least partly from disuse, the therapeutic recreator might develop a program to increase strength and endurance through a regimen of aerobics and swimming. The focus is not on leisure as it was earlier defined but rather on the use of recreational activities to achieve a therapeutic purpose. This prescriptive approach is often used by activity directors in long-term care facilities in order to achieve therapeutic benefits.

McCormick (1990) provided an extensive literature review that examined the therapeutic benefits of recreation to older individuals. She indicated, "The objectives of recreational therapy program . . . have as a primary concern the enhancement of the resident's quality of life" (p. 6). McCormick cites a variety of benefits of recreation to residents of long-term care facilities. These include: structuring time; providing continuity between pre and post institutional experience; stimulating interest; preserving skills; preventing physical and mental deterioration; restoring physical, emotional, cognitive, and social functioning; providing stimulation; reducing stress; and adjusting to the long-term care facility environment.

A major factor in maximizing the benefits of leisure involvement is the opportunity to exercise choice and control. For individuals to be able to exercise choice, though, they need to be oriented to their environment and be introduced to the available options within it.

Engagement in recreational activities may function as a stress relieving mechanism because it distracts the attention of participants, sometimes to the point that concentration and absorption in the task blocks out external stimuli (Csziksentmihali, 1975). In situations of chronic pain, this alteration in awareness may prove quite beneficial.

ASSESSMENT OF
LEISURE INTERESTS AND ABILITIES

To ensure therapeutic benefits, recreation programs require extensive planning. Planning should involve residents so that interests, skills, and needs are taken into consideration. Knowing past leisure life-style, unique abilities, functional limitations, and other relevant characteristics of residents not only allows for better selection of activities, but also enhances the chances for bringing about successful experiences and building upon old talents, eventually increasing self-esteem.

As Witt, Connolly, and Compton (1980) stated, "assessment should be viewed as a tool to providing quality services through acquisition, interpretation and use of relevant and reliable information on client service needs" (p. 7). In the field of therapeutic recreation, assessments are conducted to meet one of two goals: (a) to explore client leisure knowledge, interests, and skills, and (b) to gather baseline data related to leisure activities, such as motor skills, communication abilities, and social behavior (Joswiak, 1980).

At the conclusion of the assessment, the therapeutic recreation professional should: (a) be aware of client's baseline knowledge and skills, (b) have the necessary elements to identify long- and short-term objectives with the client, (c) be able to design relevant teaching strategies and therapeutic interventions, (d) be capable of judging and documenting progress made in relation to objectives and interventions formulated throughout the continuum of services provided (Joswiak, 1980).

Some of the most popular leisure assessment instruments available at this time are:

- Mirenda Leisure Interest Finder (Wilson, Mirenda, & Rutwouski, 1975);
- Leisure Activity Blank (LAB) (McKechnie, 1975);
- State Technical Institute Leisure Activities Profile (STILAP) (Navar, 1979);
- Leisure Diagnostic Battery (LDB) (Ellis & Witt, 1986).

LEISURE AND THE LIVING ENVIRONMENT

In any type of intervention, it is crucial to look at the total environment. Factors in the living environment may either inhibit or facilitate involvement in activities. An environment that is designed to compensate for physical losses associated with the aging process will allow involvement in programs. Three dimensions must be considered in creating an open, prosthetic environment for the elderly: environmental cues, environmental stimulation, and environmental support (Schwartz, 1975).

Cues are important in facilitating freedom of movement, sense of orientation, and feelings of safety. They assist in locating key areas or staff members and warn against possible hazards. Large-print signs, raised textures, auditory devices, lights, and brightly painted doors are some examples of cues (Schwartz, 1975).

Environmental stimulation can be used to promote the use of the five senses through introduction of variety and challenge into the routine of residents. Some suggestions include the use of bright contrasting colors, mood enhancing music, decorations hanging on walls or from ceilings; exciting foods and beverages; living creatures such as plants, fish, pets, and other soft objects for holding and stroking; changeable materials such as calendars and pictures; and multimedia programs for entertainment, discussion, or information (Schwartz, 1975).

Environmental support is a complement to the previous two. Just as it is not sufficient to remove architectural barriers in order to encourage the elderly to engage in recreation, it is not enough, either, to modify the physical environment without creating an awareness of its openness and possibilities. Orientation programs that explore opportunities available, formation of committees to greet new members, advise staff or plan activities, and the introduction of innovative programs to bring about positive change are all illustrations of the environmental support concept. Attempts such as those reported by Langer and Rodin (1976) and Schultz (1976) can be easily reproduced. Langer and Rodin gave a group of residents of nursing homes the opportunity to make meaningful choices concerning activities in which to participate and what plant to keep and care for. Responsibility was also enhanced by encouraging participants to voice concerns and suggestions to staff members. The results included increases in activity level, sociability, and alertness. Lower mortality and slower health decline were also found in a follow-up study conducted a year later (Rodin & Langer, 1977).

Schultz used visitations as the object of predictability and control for residents of a private retirement home. Residents who were allowed to select the schedule for visitations were found to have greater physical and psychological gains at the end of the study than those who were only informed about the schedule, and even greater gains over those who were visited on a totally unpredictable schedule. Long-term results of this study were not as encouraging as those in Langer and Rodin's (Schultz & Hanusa, 1978). The explanation for this contrast lies in the fact that once the project was terminated, opportunities for exercising control were extinguished. On the other hand, participants in Langer and Rodin's study were given the message that they were the ones responsible for their environment and actively encouraged to act on this belief on a daily basis. This type of intervention is more likely to last because it affects the perception and practice of control in a more comprehensive and consistent way.

Recreation has an enormous potential to introduce diversity, excitement, and challenge into the lives of older adults. In settings where the elderly come in contact with a variety of staff members, it is necessary that all helping professionals share the same attitude and commitment regarding the principles of independence, individuality, and growth.

CONCLUSION

This chapter has provided a brief overview of the area of leisure in the later years. No single chapter can fully explore the richness and diversity of this area; however, several key issues have been discussed.

The potential value of leisure to individuals in the later stages of life is clear. It can be a vehicle for meeting a variety of needs. The role losses that accompany events such as retirement, the dispersal of the family as children become adults, and the death of a spouse, alter an individual's life-style. Part of this alteration is available outlets for meaning and identity in life. Leisure is one potential replacement for these lost outlets. The ability to use leisure as a force in increasing the quality of life, depends on the capabilities of the individual to do so. The role of leisure service providers is to enhance this capability.

REFERENCES

American Association of Retired Persons. (1989). *A profile of older Americans.* Washington, DC: American Association of Retired Persons.

Atchley, R. (1977). *The social forces in later life* (2nd ed.). Belmont, CA: Wadsworth.

Baltes, M. M., & Baltes, P. B. (1986). *The psychology of control and aging.* Hillsdale, NJ: Lawrence Erlbaum.

Csziksentmihali, M. (1975). *Beyond boredom and anxiety.* San Francisco: Jossey-Bass.

Cumming, E., & Henry, W. E. (1961). *Growing old: The process of disengagement.* New York: Basic Books.

Ellis, G. D., & Witt, P. A. (1986). The Leisure Diagnostic Battery: Past, present and future. *Therapeutic Recreation Journal, 20*(4), 31-47.

George, L. K., & Bearon, L. B. (1980). *Quality of life in older persons: Meaning and measurements.* New York: Human Sciences Press.

Gordon, C., Gaitz, C., & Scott, J. (1976). Leisure and lives: Personal expressivity across the life span. In R. Binstock & E. Shanas (Eds.), *Handbook of aging and the social sciences.* New York: Van Nostrand Reinhold.

Havighurst, R. J. (1961). The nature and values of meaningful free-time activity. In R. Kleemeier (Ed.) *Aging and leisure: A research perspective into the meaning of time.* New York: Oxford University Press.

Havighurst, R. J. (1977). Life-style and leisure patterns. In R. A. Kalish (Ed.), *The later years: Social applications of gerontology.* Berkeley, CA: Brooks/Cole.

Havighurst, R. J., Neugarten, B., & Tobin, S. (1968). Disengagement and patterns of aging. In B. Neugarten (Ed.), *Middle age and aging.* Chicago: University of Chicago Press.

Joswiak, E. (1980). Recreation therapy assessment with developmentally disabled persons. *Therapeutic Recreation Journal, 14*(4), 29-38.

Kelly, J. R. (1982). *Leisure.* Englewood Cliffs, NJ: Prentice-Hall.

Kelly, J. R. (1985). Sources of leisure styles. In T. L. Goodale & P. A. Witt (Eds.). *Recreation and leisure: Issues in an era of change.* State College, PA: Venture Publishing.

Kelly, J. R. (1987). *Freedom to be: A new sociology of leisure.* New York: Macmillan.

Kelly, J. R. (undated). Life in-between: Continuity and constriction. Unpublished manuscript.

Kuypers, J. A., & Bengton, V. L. (1973). Social breakdown and competence: A model of normal aging. *Human Development. 16,* 181-201.

Langer, E. J. (1983). *The psychology of control.* Beverly Hills, CA: Sage.

Langer, E. J., & Rodin, J. (1976). The effects of choice and enhanced personal responsibility for the aged: A field experiment in an institutional setting. *Journal of Personality and Social Psychology, 34*(2), 423-431.

MacNeil, R. D., & Teague, M. L. (1987). *Leisure and aging: Vitality in later life.* Englewood Cliffs, NJ: Prentice-Hall.

McCormick, A. (1990). *Benefits of an outdoor setting on the quality of life of nursing home residents involved in an activities program.* Unpublished master's thesis, Clemson University.

McGuire, F. (1984). A factor analytic study of leisure constraints in advanced adulthood. *Leisure Sciences, 6*(3), 313-326.

McGuire, F. A., Dottavio, F.D., & O'Leary, J. T. (1987). The relationship of early life experiences to later life leisure involvement. *Leisure Sciences, 9,* 251-258.

McKechnie, G. E. (1975). *Manual for the leisure activity blank.* Palo Alto, CA: Counseling Psychologists Press.

Mercer, S., & Kane, R. A. (1979). Helplessness and hopelessness among the institutionalized aged: An experiment. *Health and Social Work, 4*(1), 91-116.

Miller, S. (1965). The social dilemma of the aging leisure participant. In A. M. Rose & W. Peterson (Eds.). *Older people and their social worlds.* Philadelphia: F. A. Davis Co.

Navar, N. (1979). Leisure skill assessment process in leisure counseling. In D. J. Szymanski & G. L. Hitzhusen (Eds.). *Expanding horizons in therapeutic recreation VI,* Columbia: Curators University of Missouri.

Peterson, C.A., & Gunn, S. L. (1984). *Therapeutic recreation program design: Principles and procedures.* Englewood Cliffs, NJ: Prentice-Hall.

Rodin, J., & Langer, E. J. (1977). Long-term effects of a control relevant intervention with the institutionalized aged. *Journal of Personality and Social Psychology, 35*(12), 897-902.

Schultz, R. (1976). Effects of control and predictability on the physical and psychological well-being of the institutionalized aged. *Journal of Personality and Social Psychology, 33*(5), 563-573.

Schultz, R., & Hanusa, B. H. (1978). Long-term effects of control and predictability-enhancing interventions: Findings and ethical issues. *Journal of Personality and Social Psychology, 36,* 1194-1201.

Schwartz, P. A. (1975) Planning micro-environments for the aged. In D. S. Woodruff & J. E. Birren (Eds.), *Aging: Scientific perspectives and social issues.* New York: D. Van Nostrand.

Sessoms, H. D. (1985). Lifestyles and life cycles: A recreation programming approach. In T. L. Goodale & P. A. Witt (Eds.), *Recreation and leisure: Issues in an era of change.* State College, PA: Venture Publishing.

Teaff, J. D. (1985). *Leisure services with the elderly.* St. Louis, MO: Times Mirror/Mosby.

Voelkl, J. E. (1986). Effects of institutionalization upon residents of extended care facilities. *Activities, Adaptation and Aging, 8*(3-4) 37-45.

Wilson, G. T., Mirenda, T. J., & Rutwouski, B. A. (1975). Milwaukee leisure counseling model. *Leisurability, 2*(3), 11-17.

Witt, P. A., Connolly, P., & Compton, D. M. (1980). Assessment: A plea for sophistication. *Therapeutic Recreation Journal, 14*(4), 5-8.

7

Health Education of the Older Client

MARTHA J. FOXALL

Objectives: At the completion of this chapter, the reader will be able to:

(1) Critique selected research on cognitive and noncognitive factors that can influence learning, especially in older adults.
(2) Analyze the impact of learning deficits on health education outcomes of older clients.
(3) Apply teaching strategies in health education situations with older clients designed to minimize learning deficits associated with cognitive and noncognitive factors.

INTRODUCTION

By the year 2000, older adults will constitute 15% of the population of the United States (Hentges, 1980). Although being old does not necessarily mean being ill, there is evidence that with increasing age comes an increase in the incidence of health problems, especially cumulative chronic diseases (U.S. Department of Health and Human Services, 1987). For example, it has been estimated that 80% of all persons 65 years and older have at least one chronic disease (California Nurses' Association, 1985) and that approximately 50% of all noninstitutionalized persons older than 65 are so affected (U.S. Bureau of the Census, 1980). Thus older adults with health problems make up an increasing proportion of the population of persons to whom nurses provide care.

A significant aspect of the nursing care of older clients is health education. Positive health education outcomes depend, in part, on accurate interpretation of sensory information and efficient coordination of motor activities (Roberts & Lincoln, 1988). Both of these depend on cognitive processing as a means of knowing and responding to the learning situation (Roberts & Lincoln, 1988). Various factors may result in sufficient cognitive impairment to interfere with knowing and responding. The nursing literature contains little information about the impact of these problems on learning of older clients. Nevertheless, if nurses are to effect positive health education outcomes with older clients, they must be knowledgeable about factors that can influence learning and must recognize the implications for the teaching process.

The following sections will analyze the cognitive and noncognitive factors shown to have an impact on the learning of older clients. Cognitive factors to be discussed include intelligence, memory, and problem-solving. Noncognitive factors include education level, loss of speed, meaningfulness, interference, organization, and sensory and health impairment. In addition, the research on effect of medications on learning will be examined. These factors were selected primarily because they are the focus of most of the existing research. In this chapter, *older adult, older client,* and *older learner* all refer to the individual 65 years of age or older.

COGNITIVE FACTORS AFFECTING LEARNING

Intelligence

Intelligence has been defined as the actual ability as well as the potential ability to behave appropriately when coping with and solving problems (Botwinick, 1967). Consideration of intelligence is important, because it deals with cognitive abilities closely related to any learning endeavor. In general, a higher level of intelligence is considered advantageous because it should allow a person to learn more quickly and efficiently (Peterson, 1983).

Research on the intellectual abilities of older adults is abundant. The literature reflects the changing views on the topic over time. Early studies (H. Jones & Conrad, 1933; Miles & Miles, 1932; Wechsler, 1939, 1955) consistently demonstrated a prominent decrement in performance with advancing age, presumably indicative of a decline in intelligence of higher order cognitive functioning. Research in the last 30 years, however, has demonstrated that intelligence and learning ability do not necessarily decline with age (Baltes & Labouvie, 1973; Birren & Woodruff, 1973; Eisdorfer, 1968; Granick & Friedman, 1973; Labouvie-Vief & Gonda, 1976). Rather, many older people maintain a high level of intellectual functioning into very old age.

A classic aging pattern has been described by Botwinick (1978). Verbal abilities are generally stable from 20 to 50 years of age, whereas psychomotor abilities decline from the late 20s on. After age 65 to 70, verbal ability declines slowly, and after age 60 performance ability declines more rapidly. Neither decline, however, takes the individual to the level of incompetence. Botwinick's aging pattern is consistent with the concept of crystallized and fluid intelligence (Cattell, 1963). Crystallized intelligence, which depends on sociocultural influences, grows slowly over the life span, whereas fluid intelligence, which is more dependent on genetic influences, declines gradually (Knox, 1978).

The discrepancy between past and present studies of intellectual ability of older adults may be due, in part, to differences in types of studies (Huppert, 1982). For example, longitudinal studies show very little decline or improvement in mental ability during a person's lifetime, compared to cross-sectional studies of groups at a single point in time. In cross-sectional studies there are important generational as well as age differences between groups. The education, life experiences, culture, and nutrition of older groups are very different from those of younger groups. Such generational or cohort differences account for much of the variation in mental test performance between age groups. In other words, it is not so much that mental ability deteriorates with aging as that succeeding generations are becoming brighter (Huppert, 1982). This fact was demonstrated by Schaie (1975) using a longitudinal and cross-sectional research design. Schaie found that intelligence was maintained throughout adulthood, with little decline before age 60 to 70. However, intelligence scores of each generation were slightly higher than those of the preceding generation. In other words, each generation maintained its own level of intelligence, but the level of the following generation was slightly higher.

Memory

Another important area of particular concern to the nurse in learning situations is the possibility of memory impairment that may be associated with the aging process. Memory has been defined as "the mental registration, retention, and recall of past experiences, knowledge, ideas, sensations, and thoughts" (Taber, 1989, p. 1103). Memory performance is essential to successful learning (C. Greenberg & Powers, 1987). Information that is presented cannot be retrieved if it has not been committed to memory. Memory studies generally involve some classification of the time between presentation and retrieval, such as very short-term, which involves retrieval after a few seconds; short-term, a few seconds to several minutes; and long-term, a period of minutes to several years (E. B. Bolton, 1978).

There has been considerable research in memory of older adults. The general consensus is that the aging process does affect memory to some degree (Craik, 1977; Erber, 1982; Huppert & Kopelman, 1989; Perlmutter, 1980;

Smith, 1980; Zarit, Gallagher, & Kramer, 1981). Most studies have reported little age-related memory loss on tasks that do not exceed the span of immediate or very short-term memory (Bromley, 1958). Tasks requiring a longer span, however, have usually revealed a decrement in performance with increasing age (Taub, 1966). Even though the decline in very short-term memory may be small, it has the potential for affecting short-term retrieval (E. B. Bolton, 1978).

Interestingly, older adults may not perceive themselves as having memory problems. Using data from a national survey (National Center for Health Statistics, 1986), Cutler and Grams (1988) examined the prevalence of self-reported memory problems in a sample aged 55 and older ($N = 14,783$). Fifteen percent of the respondents indicated they had had difficulty remembering events frequently during the previous year, while 26% reported having no trouble. Of those reporting memory problems, only 18% said the problem was happening with increasing frequency. It was suggested that the results may have resulted from denial, effects of social desirability on responses to the memory items, and a reluctance of some respondents to acknowledge the existence of a condition that might associate negatively with being old.

Several explanations have been offered for age-related memory loss. In laboratory studies, the finding that memory of verbal material after a delay is poorer in older persons than in younger persons has usually been attributed to an "acquisition" deficit, rather than to faster forgetting (Craik, 1977; Gounard & Hulicka, 1977; Hulicka & Weiss, 1965; Huppert, 1982; Moenster, 1972). Huppert and Kopelman (1989) found that when the same stimulus was given to 74 subjects aged 16 to 83 years, older respondents performed significantly more poorly than younger respondents. Increasing the duration of stimulus exposure for the older respondents resulted in comparable performances for older and younger respondents. The investigators concluded that normal aging produced a mild acquisition deficit as well as a significant increase in the forgetting rate.

Problem Solving

The results of most research on age differences in problem-solving abilities consistently indicate that significantly more time is needed to solve problems with increasing age (Arenberg, 1968; Hayslip & Sterns, 1979; Lee & Pollack, 1978). The difference, however, may be more of a perceptual than a cognitive problem. Examining the effects of age on perceptual problem-solving strategies, Lee and Pollack found that time needed to solve problems increased significantly between 40 and 50. A significant age-related decline in the number of problems solved was also found. Regardless of age, all respondents used an active global approach. The discrepancy between the age groups was felt to imply that the decline in problem-solving ability with age was due to a decline in perceptual field independence rather than a deficit in higher order cognitive processes.

There is also evidence that the difference in problem-solving ability between young and older adults is dependent upon the problem to be solved. Denney and Palmer (1981) investigated differences in ability to solve two types of problems in a group of 84 adults between 20 and 70 years of age. Performance on traditional problem-solving tasks decreased linearly across age, although performance on practical or real-life problems increased to a peak in the 40-and-50-year-old group and decreased with increasing age thereafter. The researchers suggested that the developmental function obtained for problem-solving during the adult years depended upon the type of problems.

NONCOGNITIVE FACTORS INFLUENCING LEARNING

Education Level

There is evidence that level of education influences cognitive ability of the aged (Birren & Morrison, 1961; Gonda, Quayhagen, & Schaie, 1981; Kesler, Denney, & Whitely, 1976). Blum and Jarvik (1974) found that, on a battery of cognitive tests, both men and women who were initially classified as more able showed less decline with age than did those initially classified as less able. When classification was based on level of education rather than initial ability, the better educated showed the lesser decline. Higher ability was also significantly associated with higher educational level. Similarly, Kim (1986), in a clinical study of response time and health care learning of older clients, found that the patient's prior knowledge had a significant impact on the post-test learning performance.

Education level has also been related to everyday memory problems. Cutler and Grams (1988), in their analysis of survey data, found that the prevalence of having had frequent problems remembering things during the previous year was significantly greater for respondents with less education.

Stone and Schaie (1980), however, found no significant relationship between educational level and decline in cognitive functioning. Education does appear to play an interactive role in the maintenance of intellectual functioning (Willis, 1985). For example, several studies have shown prior level of educational attainment to be the most significant predictor of participation in adult education in midlife (Cross, 1981; Johnstone & Rivera, 1965).

The significance of these findings to nurses in learning situations is that approximately half of older adults are undereducated and nearly three million are categorized as functionally illiterate (Peterson, 1974).

Loss of Speed

Another explanation for memory deficits in older adults may be related to a major cognitive deficit that results in a general slowing of behavior or reduction in processing speed as the result of altered central nervous system functioning (Birren, 1974; Birren, Woods, & Williams, 1980; Botwinick, 1978; Salthouse, 1982; Welford, 1977, 1980). Studies of response time and paced learning have shown slowing of both psychomotor behavior and cognitive functioning. For example, B. Greenberg (1973) observed some slowing in psychomotor tasks among older patients in an extended care facility.

With respect to cognitive functioning, laboratory studies of learning have shown that older adults performed more slowly than younger adults when required response time was short (Calhoun & Gounard, 1979; Canestrari, 1963; Hulicka, Sterns, & Grossman, 1967; Schaie & Strother, 1968). When response time was lengthened, both the older and the younger adults benefited, but the older adults utilized significantly more time than the younger (Arenberg, 1965; Canestrari, 1963; Eisdorfer, Axelrod, & Wilkie, 1963; Monge & Hultsch, 1971). In an interesting study of effects of speech rate, linguistic structure, and processing time on speed of processing in normal aging, Wingfield, Poon, Lombardi, and Lowe (1985) found speech rate and segment length related significantly to a decline in recall among older respondents.

Slowness of response time of older adults, however, does not necessarily mean intellectual decline. Several studies (Levine, 1971; Sakata & Fendt, 1981) have shown that, when speed was not a factor in testing, the intellectual abilities of older adults showed much less decline and even in some instances showed an increase or no significant difference between younger and older respondents.

Storandt (1977), however, reported that older adults exhibited poorer performance than younger adults on the Wechsler Adult Intelligence Scale (WAIS) measure of intelligence, even when a bonus for rapid performance was eliminated. Although the scores of older adults improved without the bonus, they were not raised to levels achieved by the young. Storandt suggested that factors other than reduced speed of performance contributed to the decline of the older adult on measures of intelligence.

Self-paced response conditions have also been found to facilitate learning in older adults (Calhoun & Gounard, 1979; Canestrari, 1963; Hulicka et al., 1967). Similar findings were reported by Kim (1986) in a study to determine if older patients performed better in health care learning when provided slower or self-paced response conditions. Kim randomly assigned 105 patients to three response conditions: fast-paced, slow-paced, and self-paced. Learning performance under fast and slow pacing did not differ; learning under self-pacing was superior to the two experimenter-paced conditions. Canestrari (1963), however, noted that although the older persons in his study performed more efficiently in the self-paced situation, their performance was slower than that of the younger persons. Other studies have yielded different results. For example, Panicucci, Paul, Symonds, and Tambellini (1968) noted that a self-paced response condition did not help older persons in learning health care information. Their subjects were patients, however, and other factors, such as their health problems, may have influenced the results.

Meaningfulness

Several studies have suggested that memory (or retention) is very closely related to the meaningfulness of the information to be learned. Meaningfulness or relevancy of material can affect motivation and learning of the older adult (Denney & Palmer, 1981; Joiner, 1981; Knox, 1978; Roumani, 1978). If the learner perceives the materials as irrelevant or not sensible, the materials will not be processed. Recognition skills of older adults are reduced in the presence of irrelevant cues in comparison to younger adults (Erber, 1974; Kausler & Klein, 1978; Rabbitt, 1965). Further, Rabbitt (1965) suggested that it is more difficult for older persons to refrain from attending to irrelevant information; thus they take longer to inspect and react to a stimulus. Hulicka (1967) found an 80% attrition with subjects age 65 to 80 years on learning tasks that were meaningless or had little or no interest for them. When Hulicka changed the tasks and made them more meaningful, the older subjects carried out the tasks willingly, although their performance was still inferior to that of the younger comparison group.

On the other hand, Craik (1968) and Hanley-Dunn and McIntosh (1984) found older adults to be no worse than younger adults at recalling meaningless material. Hanley-Dunn and McIntosh examined the relationship between meaningfulness and recall of names by 56 young and 56 old adults. The older adults performed as well as the younger adults and recalled significantly more meaningful material than did the younger adults. Despite the equal or better levels of recall, however, the older adults rated their own perceived performance lower than did the younger adults. It was also noted that both groups of subjects found the nonmeaningful material very frustrating. Craik noted that the older adults in his study exhibited an increasing deficit as the material became more amenable to organization. More recently, others, using familiar materials, some specifically designed to be cohort-relevant, indicated much less and in some cases no age decline on many tasks similar to those encountered in everyday life (Barrett & Wright, 1981; Erber, Galt & Botwinick, 1985).

Interference

Research has also shown that interference can impede learning. Arenberg and Robertson (1974) delineated several kinds of interference that appeared to have a particular influence on older adults during the memory and learning process: interference from prior events, current events, or subsequent events. Interference from prior events such as previous learning, although helpful in some situations, can be detrimental in learning new material if the new material involves unlearning the old. Interference from concurrent events or distractions during learning include fast pacing, dividing attention, and response interference. Interference from subsequent events refers to the effects of learning a second task on the recall of the first task.

Organization

Craik and Masani (1967) suggested that part of the memory deficit found in older adults may result from their inability to utilize structure in information to organize material. Craik and Masani found that although both young and old subjects showed better learning and recall with more grammatically structured lists, the aged performed more poorly relative to the young as lists containing more structure were introduced. The inability to utilize list structures was found only for aged subjects with low verbal ability however.

Similarly, a study by Hultsch (1969) indicated that the memory of older adults may be enhanced by measures designed to help them organize material and that older adults with high verbal ability performed as well as the young. In another study, Hultsch (1971) provided both younger and older subjects with word lists and required half of the sample to organize the words into categories of their own design and half merely to look at the words. Although the younger subjects outperformed the older subjects under both conditions, the performance of the older group was significantly better when they were required to organize than it was in the neutral condition. Other studies have shown that the organization of material into categories and the use of category names can enhance recall (Bower, Clark, Lesgold, & Winzenz, 1969; Tulving & Pearlstone, 1966). Tulving and associates found that when subjects were taught the categories before presentation of the material to be learned, recall was increased. Ausubel (1960) also found that use of advanced organizers improved recall. Further, Ley, Bradshaw, Eaves, and Walker (1973) found that recall of medical information increased with use of advanced organizers or explicit categorizations such as "what is wrong," "tests," "what will happen," "treatment," and "what you must do."

In a study by Hultsch (1971), half of the subjects were instructed to learn word lists using category labels provided by the experimenter. The other half were given neutral instructions to learn. Memory performance of the older subjects was superior with organizational instructions. In a later study, Hultsch (1974) found that with repeated exposure to the memory task, older subjects improved their performance on word lists. In other words, in the absence of both instructions to organize and organizational aids, the amount of organization demonstrated by the older group spontaneously increased. Based on this finding, Hultsch (1974) suggested that training the older person to organize and merely providing opportunity to practice a task may be ineffective in enhancing memory.

Motivational factors such as interest and personal meaning have been shown to be associated with task relevance (Alpaugh, Renner, & Birren, 1976; Taub, 1980). Other personality factors such as cautiousness, fear of failure, self-doubt, and cognitive style preference seem to affect older adults to a greater extent than young (Alpaugh & Birren, 1977; Botwinick, 1966; Klein, 1972; Okun & diVesta, 1976; Peterson & Eden, 1981).

Hess and Markson (1980) have suggested that what earlier studies had interpreted as a decline in learning capacity is now being seen as cohort differences in test-taking behavior. For example, older adults have been shown to be reluctant to engage in risk-taking behavior. The possibility that "fear of failure" replaces "need to achieve" as a motivating force in older individuals cannot be ignored.

Sensory Impairment

Sensory impairments have also been identified as factors that interfere with cognitive processing (Libow, 1973; Roberts & Lincoln, 1988; Snyder, Pyrek, & Smith, 1976; Verwoerdt, 1976).

Vision

The National Center for Health Statistics (1983) provided the following estimates of the numbers of persons with visual impairments in the United States in 1977. Severe visual impairments—inability to read newspaper print with conventional correction—were estimated to affect 1.4 million persons, including 990,000 over age 65. Legal blindness, defined as 20/200 or worse visual acuity and/or less than 20 degrees of visual field, was estimated for 550,000 persons, including 230,000 over age 65. By the year 2000, approximately 376,000 older adults are expected to be legally blind, and 1,760,000 to experience severe visual impairment (Lowman & Kirchener, 1979). These figures reflect the substantial increase in visual impairment that occurs with age.

For most older adults, visual impairment is not severe enough to interfere with normal functioning. Generally the effects of aging on vision are gradual and in most cases can be compensated for to some degree (Kline & Schieber, 1981). Several common gradual changes, however, may create problems for the older adult in learning situations.

The common visual problems associated with normal aging that are most relevant to learning situations include alterations in the lens and the size of the pupil of the eye (Carter, 1982; Corso, 1971; Pitts, 1982; Reading, 1966). Alterations in the lens include loss of elasticity and increased opacity and yellowing. These conditions result in increased sensitivity to glare and screening out some of the dark green, blue, and violet light rays (Corso, 1971); decreased focusing power (Hamasaki, Ong, & Marg, 1956), farsightedness, or the inability to focus on close objects (Kline & Schieber, 1981; Pitts, 1982); decreased visual processing speed (Kline & Schieber, 1981; Kosnik, Winslow, Kline, Rasinski, & Sekuler, 1988; Walsh, 1976); decreased image formation (Birren, 1964; Comalli, 1970; Corso, 1971; Reading, 1966; Wolf, 1960). Distance acuity (Weale, 1978), and pattern recognition (Walsh, 1976) are also affected. Increased contrast sensitivity results in an inability to adjust to extremes of light and dark (Owsley, Sekuler, & Siemsen, 1983). Pupil size is reduced and becomes less flexible, resulting in reduced light transmission through the eye (Carter, 1982; Pitts, 1982; Reading, 1966).

In addition to age-related visual impairment, the prevalence of diseases of the eye, such as cataracts and macular degeneration, increases with age (Kline & Schieber, 1985; DHHS, 1987).

There is evidence of possible effects of visual impairment on educational endeavors. Kosnik and associates (1988), in a pair of surveys of 415 adults aged 18 to 100, found that older adults had trouble reading small print, took longer carrying out visual tasks, and had more trouble with glare and dim illumination. Further, a relationship between impaired vision and cognitive functioning has also been suggested. Snyder and associates (1976) placed 295 older persons with a mean age of 85.2 years into one of three groups based on acuity: adequate vision, low vision, and legally blind. The group with adequate vision scored the highest on a mental function test; the group of legally blind persons scored the lowest.

Based on self-reports by respondents, Cutler and Grams (1988) found that persons having memory problems during the past year included 12% of those with no vision problems but 31% of those reporting a lot of trouble with vision. Approximately 40% of respondents with a lot of trouble seeing reported an increase in memory problems, compared to 14% without vision problems.

Hearing

Hearing sensitivity, particularly for high frequency sounds, also decreases in many older adults as the result of physiological changes in the auditory system (Peterson, 1983). The prevalence of hearing loss in older adults has been estimated to be 261 per 1,000 in the age range of 65 to 74 and 387 per 1,000 among people 75 and older; after age 55, men tend to show more hearing loss than women (DHHS, 1987).

Granick, Kleban, and Weiss (1976) compared older people (mean age 75.9 years) who had experienced some hearing loss to determine the relationship between mild hearing loss and cognitive functioning as measured by the WAIS. The results revealed substantial association between hearing losses and scores on the intellectual measures. Verbal measures, such as recall of stored information, defining concepts, and describing abstract relationships, showed these relationships much more extensively than did performance tests. This was true even when the respondents were able to hear and understand verbally presented directions, and to give appropriate oral responses and grasp abstract relationships. Findings are significant because the two WAIS subtests (Information and Vocabulary) that are generally associated with retained cognitive effectiveness by the aged (Botwinick, 1973), demonstrated the greatest extent of decline in relation to hearing loss. Granick and associates (1976) suggested that their findings imply that older adults may be more intellectually capable than their test performances suggest and that hearing is an important variable in the measurement of cognitive functioning.

Memory problems increased from 12% of respondents with no hearing problems to 35% of those who reported a lot of hearing problems in the study by Cutler and Grams (1988). Increasing frequency of problems remembering was also associated with more severe impairments. Approximately 38% of respondents experiencing a lot of trouble hearing reported increased memory problems, compared to approximately 14% of respondents who did not experience hearing problems.

Hearing impairments in the older adult resulting from pathological conditions may also be significant in learning situations. Decker (1974), for example, found that more than 70% of patients over 50 years of age admitted to a rehabilitation department of a large hospital had hearing loss sufficient to prevent them from interacting in a satisfactory manner with those around them.

The basic changes in vision and hearing identified in the research suggest that a significant number of older adults will have difficulty processing visual and verbal information. The significance of vision and hearing impairments in learning is that the senses are needed to obtain information from the environment; therefore, sensory deficits reduce the accessibility of necessary information. Thus sensory deprivation may prevent the older adult from fully participating in the health education experience by decreasing informational inputs (Decker, 1974; Granick et al., 1976; Kosnik et al., 1988; Snyder et al., 1976). In health education situations, appropriate behavior depends upon interpreting and understanding the stimuli in one's environment. Impaired vision and hearing reduce the availability of stimuli that are necessary to elicit appropriate behavior (Locke, 1971). The most critical factor for cognitive processing from an information-processing point of view, involves first registering information peripherally and then passing it into the central processing system. Therefore, nurses must be concerned with vision and hearing impairments among older adults and the impact of these impairments in limiting input of information. If information is not perceived, it is not available for the cognitive processes in which nurses are interested.

Health Impairment

The relationship between health factors and learning performance in older adults has received little attention in the nursing literature (Roberts & Lincoln, 1988; Roslaniec & Fitzpatrick, 1979). Also, relatively few studies in the general literature have been directly concerned with health and cognitive behavior of any age group. Even though researchers recognize the potentially confounding effects of health factors on behavior, controlling for these variables is difficult (Elias, 1980).

Based on the findings of Craik (1968) and Hanley-Dunn and McIntosh (1984), it could be speculated that older adults would recall health information as well as young adults, since health information is assumed to be meaningful material. Evidence in this area, however, is inconsistent. Ley and Spelman (1967) found that older patients recalled more information than younger patients; others have found that older patients recalled less (Anderson, Dodman, Kopelman, & Fleming, 1979). Another study found that, although there was no significant association between age and recall, with increasing age patients recalled less information (Joyce, Caple, Mason, Reynolds, & Mathews, 1969). An interesting finding in the study by Anderson and associates was that only 40% of the information given was recalled correctly by a sample of 151 rheumatology patients ranging in age from 15 to 82 years, with a mean age of 52.

Physical Health

While research is limited, there is increasing evidence to suggest that physical factors are associated with and determine changes in cognitive functioning of older adults (Abrahams, 1976; Arbuckle, Gold, & Andres, 1986; Botwinick & Birren, 1963; Craik, Byrd, & Swanson, 1987; Field, Schaie, & Leino, 1988; Morris, Wolf, & Klerman, 1975; Perlmutter & Nyquist, 1990; Rust, 1965). A precise understanding of the specific mechanisms by which health may affect intellectual performance is unknown (Perlmutter & Nyquist, 1990). It is known, however, that physiological alterations interfere with the availability and transport of oxygen, nutrients, and neurochemicals required for neural function (Roberts & Lincoln, 1988). Such alterations include electrolyte imbalance, toxic substances, and abnormal functioning of enzymes that regulate neural metabolism (Libow, 1973; National Institute on Aging Task Force [NIA], 1980).

In the general population, perceived current health status and perceived changes in health have been related to memory problems. Using national survey data, Cutler and Grams (1988) found that among older persons, memory problems increased from 10.7% of those reporting excellent current health to 30.4% of those reporting poor health. Respondents who believed that their health was worse than it had been the previous year were also significantly more likely to report frequent problems remembering things than were those whose health had remained the same or improved. Similarly, 43% of those who perceived their health as being worsened noted increased memory problems, compared to 16% who reported improved health. Supportive findings were reported in a recent study by Perlmutter and Nyquist (1990). Studying self-reported health and several kinds of intelligence performance in 127 adults between 20 and 90 years, Perlmutter and Nyquist found that both physical and mental health accounted for significant variance in intelligence performance, particularly in older adults.

Hulicka (1967) designed a study in which 60 healthy and 120 hospitalized persons aged 17 to 85 were tested on four learning-memory tasks. The health status of each patient was estimated from the number of diagnoses and months of hospitalization during the preceding 5 years. The patients demonstrated the typical decline in performance as a function of age. When the effects of health status were cancelled out by analysis of covarience, however, the significant negative relationship between age and performance scores disappeared. In the same study, healthy groups outperformed like-aged hospitalized groups on all tasks, and the performance of healthy 60-year-olds compared favorably with that of healthy college students on three of the four tasks. The most interesting comparison was between hospitalized 20-year-olds and healthy 60-year-olds in the community. The healthy 60-year-olds actually outperformed the hospitalized 20-year-olds on three of the tasks. Hulicka concluded that comparisons between healthy young adults and older persons of dubious health are an inappropriate basis for conclusions about the effects of aging on learning and memory.

Activity limitations associated with impaired motor function also have been related to interference with cognitive processing. Immobility resulting from hip fracture was a significant predictor of cognitive disturbance in 91 hospitalized older adults (Williams et al., 1979) Further, Zubek (1963) demonstrated that 5 minutes of physical exercise four times a day minimized or eradicated cognitive disturbance in persons subject to sensory deprivation.

Although relatively few diseases have been studied and results are inconsistent, there is increasing evidence that suggests that some diseases, particularly chronic diseases, affect cognitive behavior and that the effect is more pronounced for older than younger adults (Manton, Siegler, & Woodbury, 1986). Diseases that affect cortical integrity, particularly those resulting in local cell loss, and interfere with circulation in the brain are related to slow response

(Eisdorfer & Wilkie, 1977; Obrist, 1972). The chronic diseases that have been the most thoroughly examined are diseases of the cardiovascular system, such as coronary artery disease, cerebrovascular disorders, and hypertension (Willis, 1985).

Cardiovascular diseases. Diseases of the cardiovascular system have been shown to influence intellectual functioning and psychomotor performance. Several studies have reported that cardiovascular disorders (Botwinick & Storandt, 1974; Eisdorfer & Wilkie, 1977; Goldman, Kleinman, Snow, Bidus, & Koral, 1974; Spieth, 1964, 1965) and cerebrovascular disorders (Light, 1978) have a positive association with cognitive decline and slow response. In general, individuals with cardiovascular disease appear to be most impaired on the speed of psychomotor performance and on highly speeded tests of cognitive ability (Botwinick & Storandt; Spieth, 1964, 1965). Credited as the first to report declines in reaction time associated with cardiovascular disorders, Spieth studied the psychomotor and self-paced performance of more than 600 men aged 23 to 59 years. Respondents with cardiovascular and cerebrovascular disorders (except for medicated hypertensives) performed significantly more poorly on both psychomotor and self-paced tasks than did healthy respondents of the same age. Slow responses in persons with cardiovascular disorders may not be related to heart or blood pressure problems, but rather to concomitant cerebrovascular problems, mainly a poor oxygen supply to the brain (Birren et al., 1980). Abrahams and Birren (1973) found that men who demonstrated coronary-prone behavior had significantly longer response times than men of the same age who did not demonstrate coronary-prone behavior. In addition, Botwinick and Storandt (1974) reported a correlation between self-report of cardiovascular symptoms and reaction time in elderly respondents.

Other studies, however, have reported a negative relationship between intellectual functioning and cardiovascular disorders. For example, L. Thompson, Eisdorfer, and Estes (1966) found that the association between cardiovascular disease and cognitive performance disappeared when socioeconomic status was considered. Further, Hertzog, Gribbin, and Schaie (1975) also failed to find a significant influence of cardiovascular disorders on measures of intelligence in older adults. Similar results were reported by Schaie (1980) after an analysis of 155 subjects followed over 14 months. Initially cardiovascular disease resulted in lowered function on all variables monitored. When age was controlled, however, the effect was no longer significant for either Space or Word Fluency. When socioeconomic status was controlled, lowered function was found only for Number and the composite Index of Intellectual Ability. These findings were interpreted to mean that cardiovascular disease was more prevalent in members of older cohorts and those of lower socioeconomic status, who also performed lower on the Primary Mental Abilities Test. It was suggested that although cardiovascular disease did contribute to cognitive decline, the variance accounted for was not large, and there were likely to be indirect rather than specific causal effects. For example, cardiovascular disease may lead to changes in life-style that more directly affect cognitive function (Hertzog, Schaie, & Gribbin, 1978). Less healthy life-styles among persons of low education and intellectual ability may have modest causal effects upon the development of cardiovascular disease (Sprott, 1980).

In the study by Hertzog et al. (1978), results were consistent with the findings of others (Spieth, 1965; Wilkie & Eisdorfer, 1971), suggesting a negative relationship between CVD and performance on psychometric tests of intelligence and speeded psychomotor tasks (Botwinick & Storandt, 1974; Spieth, 1965). The findings were consistent with the hypothesis that CVD may accelerate the decline in performance on speed tasks seen in normal aging (Botwinick, 1973; Botwinick & Birren, 1963). Although heart disease has been associated with cognitive changes on composite measures of intellectual abilities, it has been difficult to identify the particular cognitive abilities that are the most susceptible to the effects of heart problems (Willis, 1985).

Hypertension. Hypertension also appears to influence intellectual functioning of older adults. Using the WAIS as a measure of cognitive functioning, Wilkie and Eisdorfer (1971) investigated the relationship between intellectual decline and elevated blood pressure in three groups of older adults: normotensive, moderately elevated, and hypertensive. WAIS scores of the hypertensive respondents were found to be lower initially. The group showing the greatest stability of intellectual function during the study, however, were respondents 60 to 69 years old whose blood pressure was moderately elevated initially. Later, Wilkie, Eisdorfer, and Nowlin (1976) found that hypertension exacerbated age-related memory deficit over a 6.5-year period. Wilkie and Eisdorfer (1971) also reported a decline in verbal memory and WAIS scores over a 6.5-year follow-up period for hypertensives.

Elias, Robbins, Schultz, and Streeten (1986) compared hypertensives and normotensives and found that hypertensives performed more poorly. Neither group, however, exhibited decline over the 5- to 6-year test-retest interval. Similar results were reported in a later study by Elias, Schultz, Robbins, and Elias (1989). Other studies have reported accelerated change over time (Hertzog et. al., 1978; Wilkie & Eisdorfer, 1971).

Manton and associates (1986) examined the relationship between cognitive ability and physical health using a rating of functional health, diastolic blood pressure, and self-rated health in community-dwelling adults aged 60 and older. Excellent cognitive performance was maintained in persons who retained their physical and mental health. Significant diastolic blood pressure hypertension (i.e., greater than 120) was related to the lowest levels of cognitive functioning. Similarly, Huppert (1982) reported that in a 10 year prospective study, older persons with hypertension (diastolic B.P. > 95 mm Hg) showed a marked drop in I.Q. and a deterioration in memory, whereas the performance of the older persons with normal blood pressure remained stable. In addition, hypertensives also performed more poorly for a measure of learning set information (categories test) and two tests of memory for forms experienced by touch only. Untreated hypertensive subjects performed almost as slowly as subjects with cardiovascular disease, whereas those whose blood pressure had been brought within normal limits by medications performed similarly to normotensive subjects. The researchers concluded that reduction in blood pressure improves cognitive function in aged. Conversely, Elias et al. (1989) found no significant differences in performance between medicated and nonmedicated hypertensive groups.

Psychological Health

The incidence of affective disorders has been found to range from 10% to 65% for both hospitalized and community dwelling older adults (Busse & Pfeiffer, 1973). A growing body of evidence suggests that mental health problems may also reduce learning in older adults. The nurse needs to be concerned with problems of depression, confusion, specific neurological disorders, and effects of medications.

Depression. Estimates are that about 20% to 25% percent of older adults experience occasional depression. The high frequency among older adults of events such as loss of spouse, loss of physical health, loss of accustomed living arrangements, and loss of job through retirement predispose them to depression (Gounard & Hulicka, 1977). Conditions associated with depression include sleeplessness, anxiety, low self-esteem, and fatigue (Schaie & Schaie, 1979; Schaie & Willis, 1978). These conditions contribute more to inability of the older client to fully participate in the learning process than to lowered cognitive and intellectual functioning (Manton et al., 1986).

Several investigators have reported that the predominance of negative affect in depression is associated with cognitive disturbance (Jarvik & Perl, 1981; Kahn & Miller, 1978; Libow, 1973; Poe & Holloway, 1980). Roslaniec and Fitzpatrick (1979) examined changes in the mental status of 25 clients aged 65 to 89 during 4 days of hospitalization in an acute care setting. The results showed no significant difference for attention/concentration; significant deterioration in levels of consciousness, orientation, and abstract reasoning; and significant improvement on Day 4 in performance of memory tasks. It was noted, however, that scores on memory tasks the fourth day were lower than those achieved on admission day, except for one recall test. The investigators suggested that the improved scores on that test may have resulted from using the same Story Recall Test for both Day 1 and Day 4 assessments.

Confusion. Acute confusional states (rapid onset confusion) have been documented, especially in older hospitalized patients. The incidence in all patients admitted to general hospital units has been estimated at 10% to 50% (Butler &Lewis, 1973; Garner, 1970; Gehi, Strain, Weltz, & Jacobs, 1980; Liston, 1982). In patients aged 70 or older, estimated rates are 41% to 50%

(Seymour, Henschke, Cape, & Campbell, 1980; Warshaw et al., 1982). Lipowski (1980) estimated that nearly one half of patients 60 years or older admitted to general hospitals were likely to exhibit symptoms of confusion. Chisholm, Deniston, Igrisan, and Barbus (1982), studying 99 hospitalized patients over 60, found that 55 had acute confusion. Only 5 of the 55 patients had been labeled confused on admission.

Further support for the finding that hospitalization contributes to impaired mental status of older adults was provided in a comparison of hospitalized and nonhospitalized older persons by Comalli, Krus, and Wapner (1965). Both groups of patients were ambulatory, in relatively good health, and comparable in education, occupation, socioeconomic status, and age. The groups were compared on four tests of cognitive functioning. Results revealed that the hospitalized group showed greater regression than the community group. Hospitalization was thus seen as a condition that either induced or was symptomatic of formal developmental regression in cognitive performance.

Although confusion is not well understood, physiological and medication causes have been documented (Ahronhein, 1982: Libow, 1973; Lipowski, 1980: NIA, 1980: Portnoi, 1981). Factors suggested as contributing to the confusion of older hospitalized patients, include physiological and drug-induced changes (Ahronhein, 1982; Libow, 1973; Lipowski, 1980; NIA, 1980; Portnoi, 1981) and environmental changes, such as disruption in the pattern and meaning of life experiences (Wolanin & Phillips, 1981); hospital routines, unfamiliar technological devices, and constantly changing personnel (Williams, Campbell, Raynor, Mlynarczyk, & Ward, 1985); alteration in sensory input (Bolin, 1974; Chodil & Williams, 1970; Jackson & Ellis, 1971; Roberts, 1973; Wolanin & Phillips); social isolation (Ziskind, 1964); and decreased motor activity (Ziskind, 1964; Zubek & MacNeil, 1966; Zubek & Wilgosh, 1963).

Confusion among older hospitalized patients has also been linked to hip fracture. Examining 170 hip-fractured patients more than 60 years of age, Williams and associates (1985) found that 51.5% experienced confusion within the first 5 days following surgery. These patients had had no previous history of mental impairment. The investigators suggested that the suddenness of the injury, rapid sequence of hospitalization surgery, and lack of time to work through the events of the potential outcome contributed to the patients' confusion.

Neurological Disorders. There is also evidence that specific neurological disorders are associated with decreased cognitive functioning in older adults. For example, Canavan et al. (1989) assessed 19 patients in the early stages of Parkinson's disease (ages 32 to 74 years) on three tests of problem solving: patients had to use feedback from the experimenter. Only one patient had been treated with L-dopa and treatment had begun only recently. Comparisons between the Parkinson group and a control group of patients with frontal or temporal lobe lesions showed no significant difference between the groups. Patients in the early stages of Parkinson's disease were not impaired at all on the three difficult learning tasks. However, Parkinson's patients who were impaired tended to be older than those who were not. The researchers concluded that pathology associated with Parkinson's disease has greater effect on learning behavior in older than in younger people.

Patients with Alzheimer-type dementia (AD), even in the early stages, have been found impaired in the acquisition of new information (Kaszniak, Garron, & Fox, 1979; Miller, 1974; Moscovitch, 1982). Based on the results of their study to determine the relationship between normal aging and dementia, Huppert and Kopelman (1989) suggested that the magnitude of the acquisition defect in Alzheimer patients appears to be much greater than that found in normal aging.

Effects of Medications. Along with their greater incidence of chronic diseases, older adults are more likely to use multiple prescription and over-the-counter drugs that contribute to cognitive disturbance and reduce intellectual activity. More medications are prescribed for older adults than for any other age category. Estimates are that older adults account for 30% of the prescription drugs used in this country, while representing only 12% of the population (American Association of Retired Persons, 1984). A 1982 survey showed that the average number of prescriptions was 7.5 per person in the general population, but 14.2 per person among older adults (Kasper, 1982). Multiple problems may complicate drug therapy in older adults. Aging affects absorption, distribution, metabolism, and excretion of medications (Garnett & Barr, 1984), increased number of drugs used, and decreased compliance with drug regimes. These problems can lead to such negative outcomes as decreased cognitive and psychomotor function. Among the side-effects of psychoactive drugs are confusional states and changes in cognitive status (Beers et al., 1988; Kane, Ouslander, & Abrass, 1989).

Alterations in pharmacokinetic action with aging and multiple drug use or misuse have been found to increase the possibility of drug reaction and drug interaction associated with cognitive processing (Jarvik & Perl, 1981; Libow, 1973; Liston, 1982; Poe & Holloway, 1980). Other researchers, however, have reported different results. In a study of 94 hospitalized and 78 institutionalized older persons, Roberts and Lincoln (1988) found that drugs did not significantly influence cognitive disturbance in either group. This finding was felt to be due in part to the inadequacy of the measurement of drugs used in the study. The investigators indicated that the only valid assumption is that increasing the number of drugs related to cognitive disturbance increases the probability that an effect will occur.

In addition to contributing to decline in cognitive functioning, medications may also reduce the energy level of the older client. The reduced level may be manifested as listless behavior, lack of interest, or unwillingness to participate in the learning situation. Thus the older client may be less likely to benefit from the learning situation (Peterson, 1983).

TEACHING STRATEGIES

To improve the quality of learning and maximize the outcomes of health education for the older client, the nurse needs to acknowledge factors that influence learning and to use teaching strategies to minimize these factors. Several issues should be of particular concern.

(1) While the research on cognitive and noncognitive factors of aging implies some negative effect on learning, very little research is available to quide the selection of teaching strategies.

(2) Research on the factors mentioned above has been conducted largely in laboratory situations.

(3) The factors may act alone or in combination to influence learning of the older client, making the selection of which strategies to promote learning even more difficult.

(4) Although some research has evaluated the validity of teaching strategies developed for students of all ages, results are still inconclusive (C. R. Bolton, 1978).

(5) The desired outcomes of health learning range from the acquisition of simple psychomotor skills to comprehension of fairly complex information, depending on the client and the situation.

When these issues are taken into account, it is difficult to draw general conclusions about educational situations involving older clients.

Until teaching strategies have been tested in clinical situations, however, it may be useful for nurses to modify the teaching strategies inferred by laboratory studies. Often these strategies can facilitate learning for all age groups but require specific and magnified attention for the older client. In other situations, modifications are specific for the older client. Some authorities have suggested that because no specific teaching strategies can guarantee success for the older adult, an eclectic approach is needed (DeCrow, n.d.; Hedge, McEvoy-Tamil, & Woodall, 1984). A continuum from the intensely concentrated to the casual should be considered as teaching strategies are selected (Peterson, 1974). The approach used in this paper is based on inferences from laboratory and clinical studies, suggestions from authorities in educational gerontology, and the experience of the writer.

With respect to teaching strategies in general, there is some evidence that lecture is better for assuring immediate recall, whereas discussion results in better problem solving and promotes more favorable attitudes toward the material (Nolan, 1974; R. Thompson, 1974; Wooley, 1974). Hooper and March (1978), however, found that when 99 older adults enrolled in a university class were asked whether they preferred lecture, seminar, discussion, or laboratory or workshop-type classes, only 41% preferred lecture, 14.4% preferred lecture and discussion, 14.4% liked seminar or discussion, 10.8% preferred laboratory or workshop, 2.9% preferred lecture and lab, and 9.4% had no preference. Of those who preferred lecture, 59% said they felt safer in a lecture class, and 29% said they enjoyed listening to the expert (the lecturer). Of those who preferred some discussion classes, 70.5% commented that the preference was based on a desire for stimulation and involvement.

Others have reported that many older adults do not necessarily like working in discussion classes (Brandle, 1977; Joiner, 1981). This may be due to feeling insecure about the value of their contributions, being ignored by others, or not receiving the respect they feel is due from others in the group. Frequently, health education is conducted in discussion classes, such as those for diabetic teaching and stroke rehabilitation. The nurse should be sensitive to the feelings of older clients with respect to group classes.

Strategies Related to Cognitive Factors

The literature on intelligence implies that older clients can continue to learn and to change their behavior. Even beyond age 70, few people are so restricted in neurological function that they cannot learn when they choose to (Peterson, 1983). In addition, intelligence level is of little value in determining the learning capacity of older adults, because predictive studies that indicate the chance of success in learning situations based on intelligence level are unavailable (Schaie & Parr, 1981).

In teaching older clients, the nurse must assume that they will differ greatly in intelligence. Although innate ability should be considered, assessment of noncognitive factors may be more relevant than relying on the level of intelligence (Peterson, 1983). Little can be done about innate ability, but the nurse can be more influential with noncognitive factors. Older clients can best be assisted by determining their particular needs with respect to both cognitive and noncognitive factors and tailoring the learning situation to these needs.

Research on the impact of aging on memory shows conflicting findings. Strategies such as frequent review and building on previous material, however, may help the older client overcome the problem of long-term memory (Joiner, 1981). Another type of review can involve including some parts of previously presented material when new material is presented. These two strategies will also help older clients build self-confidence as successful learners.

Another possibility for enhancing memory is use of a multisensory approach. Arenberg (1968, 1977) found that a combined visual and auditory presentation resulted in better performance on a memory task than did visual presentation alone. Reading visually presented material aloud also resulted in better retention than reading silently. Arenberg concluded that using more than one sense modality may help insure that information enters the cognitive processing system and is available for use when it needs to be retrieved.

On the other hand, visual presentation may be less facilitative for remembering than verbal, because verbal abilities are maintained better in older adults than nonverbal abilities. The nurse again should also be sensitive to individual differences. As with any age group, it would be useful for the older client to analyze the modality that is most facilitative to him or her.

The use of cues has been found to be particularly effective in aiding retrieval from memory (E. B. Bolton, 1978). When the material necessitates some type of memorization, a cue indicating the nature of what is to be recalled is especially helpful to older clients. Visual cues such as cards have been helpful in psychomotor tasks involving a series of steps. Verbal and written cues aid in recalling written or spoken responses (E. B. Bolton, 1978). It is also important to determine memory effectiveness and to be sure that the information presented is being perceived.

Finally, the nurse should consider carefully what the older client should remember. The nurse may encourage the client to write down essential information and check that it is accurate.

Strategies Related to Noncognitive Factors

Since self-paced experienced conditions are advantageous for some older adults, older clients should be allowed to learn at their own pace when possible. More time should be allowed both to take information in and to get response out (Gounard & Hulicka, 1977). When possible, the older client should be given the opportunity to set the pace of the task. Without adequate time to learn, the health education outcome may be poor, because learning may be incomplete or inaccurate (Kim, 1986). Self-pacing may also allow older clients to use their experience in problem solving and therefore demonstrate as much competence as or more than their younger counterparts (Boss, 1984).

Use of programmed instruction and other self-directed learning materials that allow total self-pacing without time constraints are suggested strategies (Woodruff & Walsh, 1975). Older adults have shown a preference for self-directed teaching strategies (Brandle, 1977; Brown & Hill, 1984). Such strategies also encourage older adults to draw upon their own experiences and needs to fulfill a learning task, making a class more learner-centered and more meaningful. It should be kept in mind, however, that self-directed learning strategies require the learner to have a high degree of autonomy, a requirement that can prove difficult for learners unfamiliar with the strategy (C. R. Bolton,

1978). C. R. Bolton suggested that for self-directed learning to succeed, the older adult must understand the practical steps involved in the preparation of the program.

Others have supported the need to make learning material meaningful to the needs of the older adult. The nurse should relate the material to learning goals (Woodruff & Walsh, 1975), keeping in mind why the client is learning the health information and what he or she is expected to do with it outside of the learning situation. The nurse should also remember that older clients bring to any learning situation a variety of backgrounds and experiences. They can be taught to relate newly learned information to information they already know. By drawing upon their own experience with the health problem, the nurse can make learning more meaningful, thus providing a good environment for acquisition. Minimizing time requirements and removing stressful evaluation techniques can also contribute to the meaningfulness of the learning situation. Older clients may also benefit from intensive efforts to enhance and emphasize meaningfulness of material through overviews and summaries.

Another method of increasing meaningfulness is presentation of material in ways that are as concrete as possible, because research has indicated a decline in abstract thinking with aging (Arenberg, 1968). It may not always be possible to increase the concreteness or familiarity of information. The older client can, however, be encouraged to use concrete and meaningful examples of new material, to identify familiar aspects of new material, and to work gradually with new material in order to increase familiarity (C. Greenberg & Powers, 1987).

Results from the literature show that recall of information can be enhanced by organization of the material to be learned. The nurse may present information in an organized manner pointing out the organization categories, providing organization cues such as category labels, and providing advanced organizers (C. Greenberg & Powers, 1987).

To reduce interference, Ley and Spelman (1967) suggested that information should be given in a sequence with the most important item first, and that essential information should be written down. Measures should be taken to prevent or reduce the influence of counterinformation. Conflict between sources can be minimized by presenting complete information from a single source, rather than several sources. The exception would be situations where several resources are used as a method of reinforcement. Even then, care should be taken to assure that information from all sources is consistent.

According to several studies, learning may have to be broken up into small bits for the older adult, especially new material (Botwinick, Brinley, & Robbin, 1966; J. Jones, 1976; Ross, 1968). Health-related information is frequently difficult to learn. The nurse may help the client deal with new material by setting up small tasks with few components, and leading a discussion on a few areas at a time. Use of review, visual association, and verbal association may also enhance learning of material perceived to be complex (Arenberg & Robertson-Tchabo, 1980). The nurse may also have the older client review information and repeat use of skills at every opportunity.

Several inferences can be drawn from research on vision and hearing impairments in older adults. First, the nurse should be aware of cues that the older client is not seeing or hearing properly. Older adults may be unwilling to admit to vision or hearing problems. Cues may be behaviors such as squinting to see the board, holding small print material closer, talking unusually loud, failing to respond, and asking that a statement be repeated.

Strategies that may be helpful for older clients with vision and hearing problems include seating them closer to the front of the room or to the presenter and using visual aids. Visual aids can also help with difficulty in understanding unfamiliar material. Visuals allow the older client to see an image and relate that to the new sound that he or she must associate with that image. Visuals are also helpful in the retention of information for a longer period of time.

Additional help for older clients with vision problems includes writing on the chalkboard and providing materials with larger print. Materials may be made more legible by providing a high contrast between the background and the writing, such as the use of red, yellow, or orange colors on a dark chalkboard (Peterson, 1983).

Because older clients may also be particularly sensitive to room lighting, (Zemke & Zemke, 1981), they should be encouraged to control their own lighting whenever possible (Peterson, 1983). If clients are unable to do this themselves, the nurse should do it for them. Lighting can be controlled by opening or closing blinds or shades or adjusting artificial lighting. The older client can also be seated away from a window with bright light. Sometimes older clients may need more light. Lighting should be adjusted to reduce glare, and should come from behind and above the older client in order to optimize vision (Peterson, 1983). Light-dark adaptation can be facilitated by waiting a short time after turning off the lights before beginning to show a film or slides (Peterson, 1983).

Other strategies that can facilitate learning in older clients with hearing problems include speaking slowly, speaking a little louder, lowering the voice pitch, and speaking as clearly as possible (Peterson, 1983). It should also be helpful to reduce interference from outside noise and to elicit continual feedback to ensure that the older client understands what is being said.

The nurse should also be sensitive to the inability of the older client to tolerate very hot or very cold room temperatures. If the older client is uncomfortable, he or she is not likely to be attentive to the material to be learned. Temperatures in the mid to upper 70s have been found most comfortable for the older client (Peterson, 1983).

Because fatigue and health state may create some degree of interference with learning, health education sessions should be as brief as possible, but meaningful. With respect to hospitalized older clients, Williams et al. (1985) suggested that confusion may be reduced by conscious attention to interpersonal and environmental nursing approaches such as continuity of care, weaving orientation into conversation, giving rationale for treatments and procedures, and correcting vision and hearing impairments when possible with glasses and a hearing aid (Kim, 1986). Self-pacing may also allow older clients to use their experience in problem solving and therefore demonstrate as much or more competence than their younger counterparts (Boss, 1984). Confusion states and depression are important in explaining variances in learning performances of older adults. Therefore, information on older clients' cognitive function may help nurses identify those who have special learning needs (Kim, 1986). Careful assessment of the older clients' physical and mental status would assist in identifying those with the highest probability of developing confusional episodes. Special attention should be given to needs for repeated instruction.

Finally, attention to affective factors is important for all learners; however, given the older adult's increased cautiousness and tendency to omit responses (Botwinick, 1984), a supportive environment in which stress and pressure to perform are reduced is particularly facilitative for the older learner (Ross, 1968).

In summary, an attempt has been made in this chapter to examine selected research on cognitive and noncognitive factors that may influence learning in older adults and in light of the impact of learning deficits on health education outcomes, and to suggest teaching strategies for nurses whose responsibility it is to facilitate learning of older clients.

REFERENCES

Abrahams, J. P. (1976). Psychological correlates of cardiovascular diseases. In M. F. Elias & B. E. Eleftheriow (Eds.), *Special review of experimental aging research: Program in biology* (pp. 330-350). Bar Harbor, ME: EAR, Inc.

Abrahams, J. P., & Birren, J. E. (1973). Reaction time as a function of age and behavioral predisposition to coronary heart disease. *Journal of Gerontology, 28,* 471-478.

Ahronhein, J. C. (1982). Acute confusional states in the elderly. *Seminars in Family Medicine, 3,* 20-25.

Alpaugh, P. K., & Birren, J. E. (1977). Variables affecting creative contributions across the adult life span. *Human Development, 20,* 240-248.

Alpaugh, P. K., Renner, V. J., & Birren, J. E. (1976). Age and creativity: Implications for education and teachers. *Educational Gerontology, 1,* 17-40.

American Association of Retired persons (1984). *Prescription drugs: A survey of consumer use, attitudes and behavior.* Washington, DC: American Association of Retired Persons.

Anderson, J. L., Dodman, S., Kopelman, M., & Fleming, A. (1979). Patient information recall in a rheumatology clinic. *Rheumatology and Rehabilitation, 18,* 18-22.

Arbuckle, T. Y., Gold, D., & Andres, D. (1986). Cognitive functioning of older people in relation to social and personality variables. *Psychology and Aging, 1,* 55-62.

Arenberg, D. (1965). Anticipation interval and age differences in verbal learning. *Journal of Abnormal Psychology, 70,* 419-425.

Arenberg, D. (1968). Concept problem solving in young and old adults. *Journal of Gerontology, 23,* 279-282.

Arenberg, D. (1977). The effects of auditory augmentation on visual retention for young and old adults. *Journal of Gerontology, 32,* 192-195.

Arenberg, D. L., & Robertson, E. A. (1974). The older individual as a learner. In S. Grabowski & W. D. Mason (Eds.), *Learning for aging* (pp. 2-39). Washington DC: Adult Education Association of the U.S.A.

Arenberg, D., & Robertson-Tchabo, E. A. (1980). Age differences and age changes in cognitive performance: New "old" perspectives. In R. L. Sprott (Ed.), *Age, learning ability and intelligence* (pp. 139-157). New York: Van Nostrand Reinhold.

Ausubel, D. P. (1960). The use of advanced organizers in the learning and retention of meaningful verbal material. *Journal of Educational Psychology, 51, 267-272.*

Baltes, P. B., & Labouvie, G. V. (1973). Adult development of intellectual performance: Description, explanation and modification. In C. Eisdorfer & M. P. Lawton (Eds.), *The psychology of adult development and aging* (pp. 157-217). Washington, DC: American Psychological Association.

Barrett, T. R., & Wright, M. (1981). Age-related facilitation in recall following semantic processing. *Journal of Gerontology, 36,* 194-199.

Beers, M., Avorn, J., Soumerai, S. B., Everitt, D. D., Sherman, D. S., Salem, S. (1988). Psychoactive medication use in intermediate facility residents. *Journal of the American Medical Association, 260,* 3016-3020.

Birren, J. E. (1974). Translations on gerontology—from lab to life: Psychophysiology and speed of response. *American Psychologist, 29,* 808-815.

Birren, J. E. (1964). *The psychology of aging.* Englewood Cliffs, NJ: Prentice-Hall.

Birren, J. E., & Morrison, D. F. (1961). Analysis of the WAIS subtests in relation to age and education. *Journal of Gerontology, 16,* 363-369.

Birren, J. E., & Woodruff, D. W. (1973). Human development over the life span through education. In P. B. Baltes & K. W. Schaie (Eds.), *Life-span developmental psychology: Personality and socialization* (pp. 305-337). New York: Academic Press.

Birren, J. E., Wood, A. M., & William, M. V. (1980). Behavioral slowing with age: Causes, organization, and consequences. In L. W. Poon (Ed.), *Aging in the 1980's: Psychological issues* (pp. 293-308). Washington, DC: American Psychological Association.

Blum, J. E., & Jarvik, L. F. (1974). Intellectual performance of octogenarians as a function of education and initial ability. *Human Development, 17,* 364-375.

Bolin, R. H. (1974). Sensory deprivation: An overview. *Nursing Forum, 3,* 241-258.

Bolton, C. R. (1978). Alternative instructional strategies for older learners. In R. H. Sherron, D. B. Lumsden, & R. K. Loring (Eds.), *Introduction to educational gerontology* (pp. 105-129). Washington, DC: Hemisphere Publishing.

Bolton, E. B. (1978). Cognitive and non-cognitive factors that affect learning in older adults and their implications for instruction. *Educational Gerontology: An International Quarterly, 3,* 331-344.

Boss, R. S. (1984). *Inevitable decline: Exploding the senility myth: A positive paper.* Washington, DC: U. S. Department of Education, National Institute of Education.

Botwinick, J. (1966). Cautiousness in advanced age. *Journal of Gerontology, 21,* 347-353.

Botwinick, J. (1967). *Cognitive processes in maturity and old age.* New York: Springer.

Botwinick, J. (1973). *Aging and behavior.* New York: Springer.

Botwinick, J. (1978). *Aging and behavior* (2nd ed.). New York: Springer.

Botwinick, J. (1984). *Aging and behavior* (3rd ed.). New York: Springer.

Botwinick, J., Birren, J. E. (1963). Cognitive processes: Mental abilities and psychomotor responses in healthy aged men. In J. E. Birren, R. M. Butler, S. W. Greenhouse, L. Sokoloff, & M. R. Yarrow (Eds.), *Human aging: A biological and behavioral study* Publication No. 986, (pp. 97-108). Washington, DC: Government Printing Office.

Botwinick, J., Brinley, J. F., & Robbin, J. S. (1962). Learning a position discrimination and position reversals by Sprague-Dawley rats of different ages. *Journal of Gerontology, 17,* 315-319.

Botwinick, J., & Storandt, M. (1974). Cardiovascular status, depressive affect, and other factors in reaction time. *Journal of Gerontology, 29,* 543-548.

Bower, G. H., Clark, M. C., Lesgold, A. M., & Winzenz, D. (1969). Hierarchial retrieval schemes in recall of categorized word lists. *Journal of Verbal Learning on Verbal Behavior, 8,* 323-343.

Brandle, M. (1977). Language education for aging students. *Australian Review of Applied Linguistics, 1,* 62-68.

Bromley, D. (1958). Some effects of age on short term learning and remembering. *Journal of Gerontology, 13,* 398-406.

Brown, C., & Hill, E. (1984). *Producing a successful language learning program for older adults.* Paper presented at the annual meeting of Teachers of English to Speakers of Other Languages, Houston, TX.

Busse, E. W., & Pfeiffer, E. (1973). *Mental illness in later life.* Washington DC: American Psychiatric Association.

Butler, R. N., & Lewis, M. I. (1973). *Aging and mental health.* St. Louis: C. V. Mosby.

Calhoun, R. O., & Gounard, B. R. (1979). Meaningfulness, presentation rate, list length, and age in elderly adults' paired-associate learning. *Educational Gerontology: An International Quarterly, 4,* 49-56.

California Nurses' Association. (1985). *The preparation, utilization and regulation of nursing personnel.* San Francisco: California Nurses' Association.

Canavan, A. G. M., Passingham, C. D., Marsden, C. D., Quinn, N., Wyke, M., & Polkey, E. E. (1989). The performance of learning tasks of patients in the early stages of Parkinson's disease. *Neuropsychologia, 27,* 141-156.

Canestrari, R. E. (1963). Pace and self-paced learning in young and elderly adults. *Journal of Gerontology, 18,* 165-168.

Carter, J. H. (1982). The effects of aging upon selected visual functions: Color vision, glare sensitivity, field of vision and accommodation. In R. Sekuler, D. Kline, & K. Dismukes, *Aging and human visual function* (pp. 121-130). New York: Alan R. Liss.

Cattell, R. B. (1963). Theory of fluid and crystallized intelligence: A clinical experiment. *Journal of Educational Psychology, 54, 1-22.*

Chisholm, S. E., Denistoń, O. L., Igrisan, R. M., & Barbus, A. J. (1982). Prevalence of confusion in elderly hospitalized patients. *Journal of Gerontological Nursing, 8,* 87-96.

Chodil, J., & Williams, B. (1970). The concept of sensory deprivation. *Nursing Clinics of North America, 5,* 453-465.

Comalli, P. E. (1970). Life-span changes in visual perception. In L. R. Goulet & P. B. Baltes (Eds.), *Life-span development psychology: Research and theory* (pp. 211-226). New York: Academic Press.

Comalli, P. E., Krus, D. M., & Wapner, S. (1965). Cognitive functioning in two groups of aged: One institutionalized, the other living in the community. *Journal of Gerontology, 20,* 9-13.

Corso, J. F. (1971). Sensory processes and age effects in normal adults. *Journal of Gerontology, 26,* 90-105.

Craik, F. I. M. (1968). Short term memory and the aging process. In G. A. Talland (Ed.), *Human aging and behavior* (pp. 131-168). New York: Academic Press.

Craik, F. I. M. (1977). Age differences in human memory. In J. E. Birren & K. W. Schaie (Eds.), *Handbook of the psychology of aging* (pp. 384-420). New York: Van Nostrand Reinhold.

Craik, F. I., Byrd, M., & Swanson, J. M. (1987). Patterns of memory loss in three elderly samples. *Psychology and Aging, 2,* 79-86.

Craik, F. I. M., & Masani, P. A. (1967). Age differences in the temporal integration of language. *British Journal of Psychology, 58,* 291-299.

Cross, K. P. (1981). *Adults as learners.* San Francisco: Jossey-Bass.

Cutler, S. J., & Grams, A. E. (1988). Correlates of self-reported everyday memory problems. *Journal of Gerontology, 43,* 582-590.

Decker, T. N. (1974) A survey of hearing loss in older age population. *The Gerontologist, 14,* 402-403.

DeCrow, R. (n.d.). *New learning for older Americans: An overview of national effort* Washington, DC: Adult Education Association of the U.S.A.

Denney, N. W., & Palmer, A. M. (1981). Adult age differences on traditional and practical problem-solving measures. *Journal of Gerontology, 36,* 323-328.

Eisdorfer, C. (1968). Arousal and performance: Experiments in verbal learning and a tentative theory. In G. A. Talland (Ed.), *Human aging and behavior: Recent advances in research and theory* (pp. 189-216). New York: Academic Press.

Eisdorfer, C., Axelrod, S., & Wilkie, F. I. (1963). Stimulus exposure timed as a factor in serial learning in an aged sample. *Journal of Abnormal and Social Psychology, 67,* 594-600.

Eisdorfer C., & Wilkie, F. (1977). Stress, disease, aging, and behavior. In J. E. Birren & K. W. Schaie (Eds.), *Handbook of the psychology of aging* (pp. 251-275). New York: Van Nostrand Reinhold.

Elias, M. F. (1980). Disease, aging and cognition: Relationships between essential hypertension and performance. In R. L. Sprott, (Ed.), *Age, learning ability, and intelligence* (pp. 78-113). New York: Van Nostrand Reinhold.

Elias, M. F., Robbins, M. A., Schultz, N. R., & Streeten, D. H. P. (1986). A longitudinal study of neuropsychological test performance for hypertensive and normotensive adults: Initial findings. *Journal of Gerontology, 41,* 503-505.

Elias, M. F., Schultz, N. R., Robbins, M. A., & Elias, P. K. (1989). A longitudinal study of neuropsychological performance for hypertensives and normotensives: A third measurement point. *Journal of Gerontology, 44,* 25-28.

Erber, J. T. (1974). Age difference in recognition memory. *Journal of Gerontology, 29,* 177-181.

Erber, J. T. (1982). Memory and age. In T. M. Field, A. Huston, H. C. Quay, L. Troll, & G. E. Finley (Eds.), *Review of human development* (pp. 569-584). New York: John Wiley.

Erber, J. T., Galt, D., & Botwinick, J. (1985). Age differences in the effects of contextual framework and word-familiarity on episodic memory. *Experimental Aging Research, 11,* 101-103.

Field, D., Schaie, K. W., & Leino, E. V. (1988). Continuity in intellectual functioning: The role of self-reported health. *Psychology and Aging, 4,* 385-392.

Garner, H. H. (1970). Confrontation techniques applied to delirium and confusional states. *Illinois Medical Journal, 137,* 71-73.

Garnett, W. R., & Barr, W. H. (1984). *Geriatric pharmacokinetics.* Kalamazoo, MI: Upjohn Company.

Gehi, M., Strain, J. J., Weltz, N., & Jacobs, J. (1980). Is there a need for admission and discharge cognitive screening for the medically ill? *General Hospital Psychiatry, 2,* 186-191.

Goldman, H., Kleinman, K., Snow, M., Bidus, D., & Koral, B. (1974). Correlations of diastolic blood pressure and cognitive dysfunction in essential hypertension. *Diseases of the Nervous System, 35,* 571-572.

Gonda, J., Quayhagen, M., & Schaie, K. W. (1981). Education, task meaningfulness, and cognitive performance in young-old and old-old adults. *Educational Gerontology; An International Quarterly, 7,* 151-158.

Gounard, B. R., & Hulicka, I. M. 1977). Maximizing learning efficiency in later adulthood: A cognitive problem-solving approach. *Educational Gerontology: An International Quarterly, 2,* 417-427.

Granick, S., & Friedman, A. S. (1973). Educational experience and maintenance of intellectual functioning by the aged: An overview. In L. F. Jarvik, C. Eisdorfer, & J. E. Blum (Eds.), *Intellectual functioning in adults* (pp. 59-64). New York: Springer.

Granick, S., Kleban, M. H., & Weiss, A. D. (1976). Relationships between hearing loss and cognition in normally hearing aged persons. *Journal of Gerontology, 31,* 434-440.

Greenberg, B. (1973). Reaction time in the elderly. *American Journal of Nursing, 73,* 2056-2058.

Greenberg, C., & Powers, S. M. (1987). Memory improvement among adult learners. *Educational Gerontology; An International Quarterly, 13,* 263-280.

Hanley-Dunn, P., & McIntosh, J. L. (1984). Meaningfulness and recall of names by young and old adults. *Journal of Gerontology, 39,* 583-585.

Hamasaki, D., Ong, J., & Marg, E. (1956). The amplitude of accommodation in presbyopia. *American Journal of Optometry and Archives of American Academy of Optometry, 33,* 3-14.

Hayslip, B., & Sterns, H. L. (1979). Age differences in relationship between crystallized and fluid intelligence and problem-solving. *Journal of Gerontology, 34,* 404-414.

Hedge, D., McEvoy-Tamil, P., & Woodall, T. P. (1984). *Helping the older adult to succeed in the ESL classroom.* Paper presented at the annual meeting of the California Association of Teachers of English to Speakers of Other Languages. San Jose, CA.

Hentges, K. (1980). Education for successful aging. *Lifelong Learning: The Adult Years, 3,* 20-22, 26.

Hertzog, C., Gribbin, K., & Schaie, K. W. (1975). *The influence of cardiovascular disease and hypertension on intellectual stability.* Paper presented at the 28th annual meeting of the Gerontology Society, Louisville, KY.

Hertzog, C. Schaie, K. W., & Gribbin, K. (1978). Cardiovascular disease and changes in intellectual functioning from middle to old age. *Journal of Gerontology, 33,* 872-833.

Hess, B. B., & Markson, E. W., (1980). *Aging and old age.* New York: Macmillan.

Hooper, J. O., & March, G. B. (1978). A study of older adults attending university class. *Educational Gerontology: An International Quarterly, 3,* 321-330.

Hulicka, I. M. (1967). Age differences in retention as a function of interference. *Journal of Gerontology, 22,* 180-184.

Hulicka, I. M., Sterns, H., & Grossman, J. (1967). Age-group comparisons of paired-associate learning as a function of paced and self-paced association and response times. *Journal of Gerontology, 22,* 274-280.

Hulicka, I. M., & Weiss, R. L. (1965). Age differences in retention as a function of learning. *Journal of Consulting Psychology, 29,* 125-129.

Hultsch, D. F. (1969). Adult age differences in the organization of free recall. *Developmental Psychology, 1,* 637-638.

Hultsch, D. F. (1971). Adult age differences in free classification and free recall. *Developmental Psychology, 4,* 338-342.

Hultsch, D. F. (1974). Learning to learn in adulthood. *Journal of Gerontology, 29,* 302-308.

Huppert, F. A. (1982). Does mental function decline with age? *Geriatric Medicine, 12,* 32-37.

Huppert, F. A., & Kopelman, M. D. (1989). Rates of forgetting in normal ageing: A comparison with dementia. *Neuropsychologia, 27,* 849-860.

Jackson, C. W., & Ellis, R. (1971). Sensory deprivation as a field of study. *Nursing Research, 20, 46-54.*

Jarvik, L., & Perl, M. (1981). Overview of physiologic dysfunctions related to psychiatric problems in the elderly. In A. J. Levenson & R. C. W. Hall (Eds.), *Aging: Vol. 14. Neuropsychiatric manifestations of physical disease in the elderly* (pp. 1-15). New York: Raven Press.

Johnstone, J. W. C., & Rivera, R. J. (1965). *Volunteers for learning.* Chicago: Aldine.

Joiner, E. G. (1981). *The older foreign language learner: A challenge for colleges and universities.* Washington, DC: Center for Applied Linguistics.

Jones, H. E., & Conrad, H. W. (1933). The growth and decline of intelligence: A study of homogeneous population between the ages of ten and sixty. *Genetic Psychology Monograph, 13,* 233-298.

Jones, J. E. A. (1976). A descriptive study of elderly art students and implications for art education (Doctoral dissertation, University of Oregon, 1976). *Dissertation Abstracts International, 37,* 941.

Joyce, C. R. B., Caple, G., Mason, M., Reynolds, E., & Mathews, J. A. (1969). Quantitative study of doctor-patient communication. *Quarterly Journal of Medicine, 38, 183-194.*

Kahn, R. L., & Miller, N. E. (1978). Adaptational factors in memory function in the aged. *Experimental Aging Research, 4,* 273-289.

Kane, R. L., Ouslander, J. G., & Abrass, I. B. (1989). *Essentials of clinical geriatrics.* New York: McGraw-Hill.

Kasper, J. A. (1982). *Prescribed medicines: Use, expenditures, and sources of payment, data preview 9, National Health Care Expenditure study* (DHHS Publication No. PHS 82-3320, April). Washington, DC: Government Printing Office.

Kaszniak, A., Garron, D., & Fox, J. (1979). Differential effects of age and cerebral atrophy upon span of immediate recall and paired association learning in older patients suspected of dementia. *Cortex, 14,* 285-294.

Kausler, D. H., & Klein, D. M. (1978). Age differences in processing relevant versus irrelevant stimuli in multiple-item recognition learning. *Journal of Gerontology, 33, 87-93.*

Kesler, M. S., Denney, N. W., & Whitley, S. E. (1976). Factors influencing problem solving in middle-aged and elderly adults. *Human Development, 19,* 310-320.

Kim, K. K. (1986). Response time and health care learning of elderly patients. *Research in Nursing and Health, 9,* 233-239.

Klein, R. L. (1972). Age, sex and task difficulty as predictors of social conformity. *Journal of Gerontology, 27,* 229-236.

Kline, D. W., & Schieber, F. (1981). What are the age differences on visual sensory memory? *Journal of Gerontology, 36,* 86-89.

Kline, D. W., & Schieber, F. (1985). Vision and aging. In J. E. Birren & K. W. Schaie (Eds.), *Handbook of the psychology of aging* (pp. 296-331). New York: Van Nostrand Reinhold.

Knox, A. B. (1978). *Adult development and learning.* San Francisco: Jossey-Bass.

Kosnik, W. Winslow, L., Kline, D., Rasinski, K., & Sekuler, R. (1988). Visual changes in daily life throughout adulthood. *Journal of Gerontology: Psychological Sciences, 43,* 63-70.

Labouvie-Vief, G., & Gonda, J. N. (1976). Cognitive strategy training and intellectual performance in the elderly. *Journal of Gerontology, 31,* 327-332.

Lee, J. A., & Pollack, R. H. (1978). The effects of age on perceptual problem-solving strategies. *Experimental Aging Research, 4,* 37-54.

Levine, N. R. (1971). Validation of the Quick Test of intelligence screening of the elderly. *Psychological Reports, 29,* 167-172.

Ley, P., Bradshaw, P. W., Eaves, D., & Walker, C. M. (1973). A method for increasing patients' recall of information presented by doctors. *Psychological Medicine, 3,* 217-220.

Ley, P., & Spelman, M. S. (1967). *Communicating with the patient.* London: Staples Press.

Libow, L. S. (1973). Pseudo-senility: Acute and reversible organic brain syndrome. *Journal of the American Geriatric Society, 21,* 112-120.

Light, K. C. (1978). Effects of mild cardiovascular and cerebrovascular disorders on serial reaction time performance. *Experimental Aging Research, 4,* 3-22.

Lipowski, Z. (1980). Organic mental disorders: Introduction and review of syndromes. In H. Kaplan, A. Freedman, & B. Sudock (Eds.), *Comprehensive textbook of psychiatry* (pp. 1359-1391). Baltimore, MD: Williams and Wilkins.

Liston, E. H. (1982). Delirium in the aged. *Psychiatric Clinics of North America, 5,* 49-86.

Locke, S. (1971). Neurological disorders of the elderly. In A. Chinn (Ed.), *Working with older people: Vol. IV, Clinical aspects of aging* (pp. 45-49). Washington, DC: Government Printing Office.

Lowman, C., & Kirchener, C. (1979). Elderly blind and visually impaired persons: Projected numbers in the year 2000. *Journal of Visual Impairment and Blindness, 73,* 73-74.

Manton, K. G., Siegler, I. E., & Woodbury, M. A. (1986). Pattern of intellectual development in later life. *Journal of Gerontology, 41,* 486-499.

Miles, C. C., & Miles, W. R. (1932). The correlation of intelligence scores and chronological age from early to later maturity. *American Journal of Psychology, 44,* 44-78.

Miller, E. (1974). Dementia as an accelerated ageing of the nervous system: Some psychological and methodological considerations. *Age and Ageing, 3,* 197-202.

Moenster, P. A. (1972). Learning and memory in relation to age. *Journal of Gerontology, 27,* 361-363.

Monge, R., & Hultsch, D. (1971). Paired-associates learning as a function of adult age and the length of the anticipation and inspection intervals. *Journal of Gerontology, 26,* 157-162.

Morris, J. N., Wolf, R. S., & Klerman, L. V. (1975). Common themes among morale and depression scales. *Journal of Gerontology, 30,* 209-215.

Moscovitch, M. (1982). A neuropsychological approach to perception and memory in normal and pathological aging. In F. I. M. Craik & S. Trehub (Eds.) *Advances in the study of communication and affect: Aging and cognitive process* (Vol. 8, pp. 55-78). New York: Plenum.

National Center for Health Statistics. (1983). *Eye conditions and related need for medical care among persons 1-74 years of age, United States, 1971-72.* (DHHS Publication No. PHS 83-1678). Washington, DC: Government Printing Office. [Vital and Health Statistics, Series 11, No. 228].

National Center for Health Statistics. (1986). Aging in the eighties: Preliminary data from the supplement on aging to the National Health Interview Survey, United States, January-June 1984. *Advance Data from Vital and Health Statistics, 115,* 1-8.

National Institute on Aging Task Force. (1980). Senility reconsidered: Treatment possibilities for mental impairment in the elderly. *Journal of the American Medical Association, 244,* 259-263.

Nolan, J. D. (1974). Are lectures necessary? *Science Education, 4,* 253-256.

Obrist, W. (1972). Cerebral physiology of the aged: Influence of circulatory disorders. In N. C. Gaitz (Ed.), *Aging and the brain* (pp. 117-133). New York: Plenum.

Okun, M. A., & diVesta, F. J. (1976). Cautiousness in adulthood as a function of age and instructions. *Journal of Gerontology, 31,* 571-576.

Owsley, C., Sekuler, R., & Siemsen, D. (1983). Contrast sensitivity throughout adulthood. *Vision Research, 23,* 689-699.

Panicucci, C. L., Paul, P. B., Symonds, J. M., & Tambellini, J. L. (1968). Expanded speech and self-pacing in communication with the aged. *ANA Clinical Sessions.* New York: Appleton-Century-Croft.

Perlmutter, M. (1980). An apparent paradox about memory aging. In L. W. Poon, J. L. Fozard, L. S. Cermak, D. Arenberg, & L. W. Thompson (Eds.), *New directions in memory and aging* (pp. 345-354). Hillsdale, NJ: Lawrence Erlbaum.

Perlmutter, M., & Nyquist, L. (1990). Relationships between self-reported physical and mental health and intelligence performance across adulthood. *Journal of Gerontology, 45,* 145-144.

Peterson, D. A., (1974). The role of gerontology in adult education. In S. M. Grabowski & W. D. Mason (Eds.), *Learning for aging* (pp. 41-60). Washington, DC: Adult Education Association of the U.S.A.

Peterson, D. A. (1983). *Facilitating education for older learners.* San Francisco: Jossey-Bass.

Peterson, D. A., & Eden, D. Z. (1981). Cognitive style and the older learner. *Educational Gerontology; An International Quarterly, 7,* 57-66.

Pitts, D. G. (1982). The effects of aging on selected visual functions: Dark adaptation, visual acuity, stereopsis and brightness contrast. In R. Sekuler, D. W. Line, & K. Dismukes (Eds.), *Aging and human visual functions* (pp. 131-159). New York: Alan R. Liss.

Poe, W., & Holloway, D. (1980). *Drugs and the aged.* New York: McGraw-Hill.

Portnoi, V. A. (1981). Diagnostic dilemma of the aged. *Archives of Internal Medicine, 141,* 734-737.

Rabbitt, P. M. (1965). An age decrement in the ability to ignore irrelevant information. *Journal of Gerontology, 20,* 233-238.

Reading, V., (1966). Yellow and white headlamps glare and age. *Transactions of Illuminating Engineering Society, 31,* 108-121.

Roberts, S. (1973). Territoriality: Space and the aged patient in intensive care units. In I. Burnside (Ed.), *Psychosocial nursing care of the aged* (pp. 195-210). New York: McGraw-Hill.

Roberts, S. L., & Lincoln, R. E. (1988). Cognitive disturbance in hospitalized and institutionalized elders. *Research in Nursing & Health, 11,* 309-319.

Roslaniec, A., & Fitzpatrick, J. J. (1979). Changes in mental status in older adults with four days of hospitalization. *Research in Nursing and Health, 2*, 177-187.

Ross, E. (1968). Effects of challenging and supportive instructions on verbal learning in older persons. *Journal of Educational Psychology, 59, 261-266.*

Roumani, J. (1978). *Foreign language learning for older learners: Problems and approaches.* Washington, DC: Peace Corps.

Rust, L. D. (1965). Differences in strength of mediated-interference responses among minimally arteriosclerotic and non-arteriosclerotic subjects. (Doctoral dissertation, State University of New York at Buffalo, 1965). *Dissertation Abstracts International, 265, 6189.*

Sakata, R., & Fendt, P. F. (1981). Learning capacity and the older adult: Implications for lifelong learning. *Lifelong Learning, 4,* 10-13.

Salthouse, T. A. (1982). *Adult cognition: An experimental psychology of human aging.* New York: Springer.

Schaie, K. W. (1980). Age changes in intelligence. In R. L. Sprott (Ed.), *Age, learning ability, and intelligence* (pp. 41-77). New York: Van Nostrand Reinhold.

Schaie, K. W. (1975). Age changes in adult intelligence. In D. S. Woodruff & J. E. Birren (Eds.), *Aging: Scientific perspectives and social issues* (pp. 137-148). New York: Van Nostrand Reinhold.

Schaie, K. W., & Parr, J. (1981). Intelligence. In A. W. Chickering and Associates. *The modern American college: Responding to the new realities of diverse students and a changing society* (pp. 114-138). San Francisco: Jossey-Bass.

Schaie, K. W., & Schaie, T. P. (1979). Clinical assessment and aging. In J. E. Birren & K. W. Schaie (Eds.), *Handbook of the psychology of aging* (pp. 692-723). New York: Van Nostrand Reinhold.

Schaie, K. W., & Strother, C. R. (1968). A cross-sequential study of age changes in cognitive behavior. *Psychological Bulletin, 70,* 671-680.

Schaie, K. W., & Willis, S. L. (1978). Life-span development: Implications for education. *Review of Research in Education, 6,* 120-156.

Schmitt, F., Murphy, M., & Saunders, R. E. (1981). Training older adult free recall rehearsals strategies. *Journal of Gerontology, 36,* 329-337.

Seymour, D. G., Henschke, P. J., Cape, R. D. T., & Campbell, A. J. (1980). Acute confusional state and dementia in the elderly: The role of dehydration/volume depletion, physical illness and age. *Age and Aging, 9,* 137-146.

Smith, A. D. (1980). Age differences in encoding, storage, and retrieval. In L. W. Poon, J. L. Fozard, L. S. Cermak, D. Arenberg, & L. W. Thompson (Eds.), *New directions in memory and aging* (pp. 345-354). Hillsdale, NJ: Lawrence Erlbaum.

Snyder, L. H., Pyrek, J., & Smith, K. C. (1976). Vision and mental function of the elderly. *The Gerontologist, 16,* 491-95.

Spieth, W. (1964). Cardiovascular health status, age, and psychological performance. *Journal of Gerontology, 19,* 277-284.

Spieth, W. (1965). Slowness of task performance and cardiovascular diseases. In A. T. Welford & J. E. Birren (Eds.), *Behavior, aging, and the nervous system* (pp. 266-400). Springfield, IL: Charles C Thomas.

Sprott, R. (1980). *Age, learning ability and intelligence.* New York: Van Nostrand Reinhold.

Stone, V., & Schaie, K. W. (1980). *Intelligence. Life, stress, and health: A LISREL analysis.* Paper presented at annual meeting of the Gerontological Society, San Diego, CA.

Storandt, M. (1977). Age, ability level, and method of administering and scoring the WAIS. *Journal of Gerontology, 2,* 175-178.

Taber, C. W. (1989). *Taber's cyclopedic medical dictionary* (5th ed.). Philadelphia: F. A. Davis.

Taub, H. A. (1966). Visual short-term memory as a function of age, rate of presentation, and schedule of presentation. *Journal of Gerontology, 21,* 388-391.

Taub, H. A. (1980). Life-span education: A need for research with meaningful prose. *Educational Gerontology: An International Quarterly, 5,* 175-187.

Thompson, R. (1974). Legitimate lecturing. *Improving College and University Teaching, 22,* 163-164.

Thompson, L. W., Eisdorfer, C., & Estes, E. H. (1966). Cardiovascular disease and behavior changes in the elderly. In E. Palmore (Ed.), *Normal aging* (pp. 227-231). Durham, NC: Duke University Press.

Tulving, E., & Pearlstone, Z. (1966). Availability versus accessibility of information in memory for words. *Journal of Verbal Behavior, 5,* 381-391.

U.S. Bureau of the Census (1980). *Statistical abstract of the United States* (101st ed. Series P-25, Nos. 802, 888). Washington, DC: Government Printing Office.

U.S. Department of Health and Human Services (1987). *Health statistics on older persons* (DHHS Publication No. PHS 87-1409). Hyattsville, MD: Public Health Service, National Center for Health Statistics. [United States, 1986. Series 3, No. 25].

Verwoerdt, A. (1976). *Clinical geropsychiatry.* Baltimore, MD: Williams & Wilkens.

Walsh, D. A. (1976). Age differences in central perceptual processing: A dichoptic backward masking investigation. *Journal of Gerontology, 31,* 178-185.

Warshaw, G. A., Moore, J. T., Friedman, W., Currie, C. T., Kennie, D. C., Kane, W. J., & Mears, P. A. (1982). Functional disability in the hospitalized elderly. *Journal of the American Medical Association, 248,* 847-850.

Weale, R. A. (1978). The eye and aging. In O. Hockivin (Ed.), *Interdisciplinary topics in gerontology.* Gerontological aspects of eye research, Vol. 13. New York: S. Karger.

Welford, A. T. (1977). Motor performance. In J. E. Birren & K. W. Schaie (Eds.), *Handbook of the psychology of aging* (pp. 450-496). New York: Van Nostrand Reinhold.

Wechsler, D. (1939). *The measurement of adult intelligence* (1st ed.). Baltimore, MD: Williams & Wilkins.

Wechsler, D. (1955). *Manual for the Wechsler adult intelligence scale.* New York: Psychological Corporation.

Wilkie, F. L., & Eisdorfer, C. (1971). Intelligence and blood pressure in the aged. *Science, 172,* 959-962.

Wilkie, F. L., Eisdorfer, C., & Nowlin, J. B. (1976). Memory and blood pressure in the aged. *Experimental Aging Research, 2,* 2-16.

Williams, M. A., Campbell, E. B., Raynor, W. J., Mlynarczyk, S. M., & Ward, S. E. (1985). Reducing acute confusional states in elderly patients with hip fractures. *Research in Nursing and Health, 8,* 329-337.

Williams, M. A., Holloway, J. R., Winn, M. C., Wolanin, M. O., Lawler, M. L., Westwick, C. R., & Chin, M. H. (1979). Nursing activities and acute confusional states in elderly hip-fractural patients. *Nursing Research, 28,* 25-35.

Willis, S. L. (1985). Towards an educational psychology of the older adult learner: Intellectual and cognitive skills. In J. E. Birren & K. W. Schaie (Eds.), *Handbook of the psychology of aging* (pp. 818-847). New York: Van Nostrand Reinhold.

Wingfield, A., Poon, L. W., Lombardi, L., & Lowe, D. (1985). Speed of processing in normal aging: Effects of speech rate, linguistic structure, and processing time. *Journal of Gerontology, 40,* 579-585.

Wolanin, M. O., & Phillips, L. R. F. (1981). *Confusion.* St. Louis: C. V. Mosby.

Wolf, E. (1960). Glare and age. *Archives of Ophthalmology, 60*, 502-514.

Woodruff, D. S., & Walsh, D. A. (1975). Research in adult learning: The individual. *The Gerontologist, 15*, 424-430.

Wooley, J. (1974). Improving the lecture. *Improving College and University Teaching, 22*, 183-185.

Zarit, S. H., Gallagher, D., & Kramer, N. (1981). Memory training in the community aged: Effects on depression, memory complaint, and memory performance. *Educational Gerontology; An International Quarterly, 6*, 11-27.

Zemke, R., & Zemke, S. (1981). 30 things we know for sure about adult learning. *Training, the Magazine of Human Resources Development*. Minneapolis, MN: Lakewood Publications.

Ziskind, E. (1964). A second look at sensory deprivation. *Journal of Nervous and Mental Disease, 138*, 223-232.

Zubek, J. P. (1963). Counteracting effects of physical exercises performed during prolonged perceptual deprivation. *Science, 142*, 504-506.

Zubek, J. P., & MacNeil, M. (1966). Effects of immobilization: Behavioral and EEG changes. *Canadian Journal of Psychology, 20*, 316-335.

Zubek, J. P., & Wilgosh, L. (1963). Prolonged immobilization of the body: Changes in performance and the electroencephalogram. *Science, 140*, 306-308.

8

Multiple Meanings of Death for Older Adults

JEANNE QUINT BENOLIEL

Objectives: At the completion of this chapter, the reader will be able to:

(1) Analyze the influence of loss and death on identity development and adaptations of older adults, including theoretical perspectives on death meanings in old age.

(2) Critique the variety of death-related experiences encountered as part of the aging process and how these different experiences affect the lives of older adults.

(3) Analyze the influence of context on the lived experience of older adults during their final years.

(4) Evaluate various assessment and intervention strategies for nurses to assist older persons to bring closure to life.

(5) Analyze the influence of social resources and decision-making policies on the death and dying of older people in the future.

INTRODUCTION

Death is one of the awesome parts of human existence. It marks the end of life and, across cultures, has been associated with aging. The meaning ascribed to death and its relationship to life has been central to cultural belief systems and has guided the development of group activities and practices associated

AUTHOR'S NOTE: Literature used in this analysis was gathered with the assistance of Linda Westbrook, University of Washington doctoral student in Nursing Science, and the Elizabeth Sterling Soule Professorship Fund.

with death-related events in all human societies. An explanation for the origin of humans and their relationship with the universe serves as a core for each belief system and generally becomes part of an organized religious tradition. Both beliefs and traditions vary across cultures and, historically, have contributed greatly to destructive human-to-human encounters and conflicts. In other words, all human beings interpret the meaning of death through socialization experiences under particular sociocultural and historical circumstances.

This chapter is concerned with the effects of death and death-related experiences on older adults and the implications of these changes for nursing services. The chapter begins with a review of the importance of loss experiences to identity development and the capacity to cope with adversity and change. Next comes discussion of death-related experiences associated with the aging process, followed by a section on the influence of context on opportunities to bring closure to life. Principles of assessment and assistance for clinical nurse specialists are reviewed in relation to various types of situations in which loss, death, or grief is a critical feature affecting the elderly person's ability to cope. The chapter ends with some thoughts about the influence of scarce resources and social policies on the deaths of older people in the future.

LOSS, IDENTITY, AND HUMAN ADAPTATION

Loss and separation are essential experiences in the process of developing an identity as a human being. Indeed, through experiencing attachments and separations with people and things individuals learn how to cope with adversity and change. Experiences with death in childhood can be critical influences on the coping mechanisms individuals use for responding to deaths and death-related events throughout their adult lives and into old age. Ironically, the process of developing a sense of autonomy is tied closely to life experiences in which an individual learns mastery through coping with separation and loss, including death (Benoliel, 1985a).

Sociocultural Influences

The meaning of death—the ultimate loss to humans—is learned through cultural socialization. Through this process individuals learn the values, beliefs, and social practices expected in relation to death—including rituals and rites associated with dying, grief expression, and bereavement (Eisenbruch, 1984; Palgi & Abramovitch, 1984). Of great importance is socialization into a religious belief system because, traditionally, it provides guidelines for the use of rituals marking the major human transitions of birth, puberty, marriage, and death.

Although religious traditions provide comfort for some older persons, they fail to do so for many others. In the twentieth century, society became secularized under the powerful influence of science and technology, and increasing numbers of people have doubts about the beliefs put forth in the name of religion. A major problem for many children in Western societies today is that the social norms governing proper behavior in relation to death have emphasized denial of its reality, thereby providing ambiguous guidelines for social conduct with the dying and the bereaved (Benoliel, 1985a). It is difficult for people to maintain a sense of symbolic immortality in a world characterized by mass death and victimization of the innocent. Yet as Rowe (1982) has noted, all individuals create for themselves metaphysical belief systems that incorporate ideas about life and death and provide a sense of security in an uncertain world.

The sociocultural environment of the family or kin network serves as the setting in which cultural socialization usually occurs. Yet it needs to be recognized that some older adults may have been brought up in institutions, refugee camps, or unstable and shifting living arrangements—experiences affecting their learned ways of responding to death. Of importance for nurses, an older person's identity has its origins in experiences during the formative years.

Personal Experience with Death

In addition to cultural socialization, direct experience with death during early life can have profound effects on the meaning of death to older adults. Particularly influential can be the loss of key adults during the formative years, the disorganizing effects of growing up in a country at war, or the massive losses associated with catastrophic events, such as floods, earthquakes, or tornados.

Other meanings older adults ascribe to death can derive from their shared cohort experiences with life events such as the Great Depression of the 1930s or military service during World War II. Large scale exposure to loss, suffering, and other distressing aspects of human existence can influence an individual's perceptions of life and death in important ways. Also important, these shared cohort experiences can interfere with the normal expected life course development of an entire generation of people (Meyer, 1988).

Particularly powerful are lived experiences that bring people into contact with mass death, such as happened to the survivors of Hiroshima (Lifton, 1967) and the American men and women who served in the Vietnam War (Lifton, 1973). Persons undergoing such catastrophic encounters with death are vulnerable to a persistent and long-lasting cluster of symptoms that has come to be known as post-traumatic stress disorder. Similar responses have been observed in family members and friends of someone who was murdered (Redmond, 1989).

Theoretical Perspectives on Death

Several theoretical perspectives provide different ways of thinking about the impact of death on human development and adaptations. Proponents of psychoanalytic theory emphasize reactions to loss and separation as an outcome of psychic conflict during infancy and childhood. Attachment theorists also acknowledge the power of early life experience on meanings of loss and death, but they emphasize the contribution of environment as well as intrapsychic influences on development. Whereas believers in the psychoanalytic tradition tend to view grief as illness, attachment theorists view it as an adaptive response (Benoliel, 1985a).

Several current theories provide explanations for how individuals construct death meanings out of their interactions with others and experiences in the world. Personal construct theorists believe that individuals have patterned ways of viewing the world, that is, screens through which events and experiences are interpreted and given meaning. In this view, experiences such as bereavement act to invalidate a person's construct system and create a need for a revision of the system (Woodfield & Viney, 1984-1985). Similarly Rowe (1982) observed that depressed persons had metaphysical belief systems that supported pessimistic and self-deprecating views of self, others, and the world.

In Marris's (1974) view people create structures of meaning through which they interpret and assimilate their experiences in the world. These structures consist of ideas, concepts, goals, and emotional attachments; and they provide a sense of continuity in living. When significant loss, such as death, is experienced, the structure of meaning no longer holds true. In this theory the process of grieving involves both emotional and cognitive work as part of transforming the structure of meaning into a new form, and suffering is part of that process of revision.

In Weenolsen's (1988) theory, human existence consists of an ongoing dialectic between losses of many kinds and efforts to overcome these losses through transcendence. The modes of transcendence can be situational (involvement in social activities), dispositional (use of psychologic defense mechanisms), and general (efforts to minimize or escape from the effects of loss). In this theory individuals' lives are characterized by *life themes* that reflect the meanings they attribute to their loss experiences and the ways used to transcend them. Out of their lived experiences individuals construct metaphorical systems through which they view the world and choose to behave. In loss-transcendence theory human responses to death are viewed as patterned modes of adaptation that reflect the inner guiding metaphorical systems.

DEATH AND THE AGING PROCESS

The aging process brings with it an increasing number of encounters with loss and death. For many people life changes produced by retirement, children leaving home, and physical deficits brought on by illness or simply getting old are forms of "social death." In addition, aging means increased exposure to loss of family and friends through death.

That death takes on new meanings for older people was demonstrated by Thorson and Powell (1988) who found that elders had lower death anxiety than younger age groups but, more importantly, the meanings of death were different. Older persons were concerned about being in control and life after death, whereas young people were focused on fear of pain, missing out, isolation, and decomposition of the body.

In a study of older women who used a senior center, Matthews (1979) found that discourse about death was ongoing with uncertainty about the how and when of death as a recurrent topic of discussion. Dying—not death—was a real concern, and fear of the dying process centered on "being a burden" and "suffering." To make potential loss of control less uncertain, the women used such strategies as monitoring warning signs that it was time to see the doctor, planning for distribution of key possessions, and planning for sudden physical malfunctions by making special arrangements—for example with a neighbor.

Kohn and Menon (1988) found that elderly persons talked about their concerns about suffering associated with the use of life-prolonging technology, but they did not talk openly about these matters with their physicians. For older people serious illness can serve as a critical turning point, bringing them closer to the end of life. Not uncommonly, older people with serious illness talk to nurses about their fears of needless suffering and the uncontrolled use of lifesaving technology to keep them alive. These conversations provide nurses opportunities to assist such older patients in making their wishes known to family members and physicians and to advocate for their wishes.

Illness and Dying

Although sudden death can end an older person's life, the more common pattern today is death at the end of a short or long experience of living with chronic illness. As Corbin and Strauss (1988) have described, the process of living with the social and physical losses brought on by progressive illness involves multiple adjustments by the dying person and family. These adjustments include rearranging priorities and goals, living with psychological ups and downs, preparing for death, and bringing closure to life. In reality, the deterioration and disability associated with dying brings new tensions into family relationships and may deplete both fiscal and social resources.

Particularly difficult for elders and their families is the diagnosis of Alzheimer's disease that brings social death long before biological death. Increasingly this disease as well as physically disabling ailments that prevent elders from self-care at home results in older persons being placed in nursing homes or other institutions for the remainder of their lives. Placement in a nursing home is a commonly expressed fear of older people. In a study of elderly residents in a Jewish nursing home, Kahn (1990) found that the ongoing threats to self were recognized by the elders in the phrase, "going downhill." Their adaptation to the demands of the environment was captured in the metaphor, "making the best of it." They maintained a sense of coherence and worth through the meaningfulness of their ties with personal history, family, and membership in the larger Jewish community.

The process of dying, whether at home or in an institution, brings with it multiple losses and increased reliance on others for assistance. Reed (1987) found that terminally ill adults indicated a greater spiritual perspective than either nonterminally ill or healthy adults. The experience of terminal illness makes great demands on the personal and social resources of elders and their families, including decisions about whether to die at home or in an institution. The adaptations of people living through this experience can be facilitated by nurses who are knowledgeable about the complex demands of terminal illness and the social dynamics that often come into play when families are faced with a stressful life situation (Benoliel, 1985b).

Dying often brings physical and psychological discomforts of many kinds as well as social withdrawal by family and friends. In the United States the largest number of dying patients in need of good palliative care services are older adults. According to recent mortality figures, 71% of the 2,141,000 estimated deaths in the United States in 1989 occurred in persons 65 years of age and older, with the death rate highest for those 85 years and older (National Center for Health Statistics, 1990, p. 9).

Widowhood and Bereavement

Widowhood long has been recognized as a critical experience for surviving spouses. Across disciplines, much research has been directed toward identifying risk factors capable of predicting unhealthy bereavement outcomes. There is a great deal of evidence that widowed persons of low socioeconomic status (SES) are less healthy than widowed with high SES, but it may be that social class rather than bereavement is the major contributing factor to these differences (Stroebe & Stroebe, 1987). Current evidence supports the premise that bereavement is a complex, multidimensional process involving physical, psychological, and social domains (Murphy, 1983). Among psychologists, risk factors associated with debilitating outcomes include sudden untimely death, multiple losses, high dependency on the deceased, perceived lack of support, and poor health prior to bereavement (Sanders, 1988).

In a longitudinal study of conjugal bereavement, Vachon et al. (1982) found that high and low distress scores of widows 2 years after spousal death could be predicted by a combination of 10 variables, including poor health pre-bereavement, low satisfaction with help, short terminal illness of husband, and high distress score 1 month after death. Searching for factors affecting the transition from wife to widow, Brock (1984) found widows 50 years and older at greater risk for decreased psychological well-being than young widows. Predictor variables included change postmarriage, life change in general, education, social participation, and life-style. In effect, these results show the lives of older widows constricted by limited education, fixed income, and fewer support resources.

Comparing widows and widowers on grief and the experience of widow-hood, Kirschling and McBride (1989) reported widows experiencing greater loss of vigor and more physical symptoms than widowers, whereas widowers experienced more denial. The women reported a high proportion of support from their ideas and beliefs, whereas the men did not (although this finding may reflect male difficulties in talking about such matters with a female interviewer). Despite differences in expressions of distress, widows and widowers used the same coping strategies. Similarly, Gass (1988) found that widows and widowers did not differ in appraisal, ways of coping, resource strength, and physical and psychosocial dysfunction. The findings did show that widowed persons who defined bereavement as a *harmful loss with other threats* were at greater risk for health dysfunctions than those who appraised bereavement as *harmful loss without threats* or as *a challenge* (Gass, 1988; Gass & Chang, 1989).

These studies provide evidence that older persons bring to the experience of widowhood established beliefs and adaptive patterns that guide their responses and behaviors in response to loss of a spouse. Wegmann (1987) reported that widows who had used hospice services and widows who had used hospital services for the spouse's terminal illness differed in religiosity and modes of preferred coping. Yet to be clarified is whether the coping preferences existed prior to the terminal illness and influenced choice of setting or were developed in response to the spouse's dying. That prior life experience is critical to a widow's beliefs about bereavement was demonstrated by Carter (1989) who found that the lived experience of bereavement was embedded in the meaning of the lost relationship to the survivor and the nature of the events that surrounded the death.

SOCIAL CONTEXT AND CLOSURE TO LIFE

Although older people bring to the experiences of dying and widowhood their predispositions and established modes of coping with life situations, their ways of adapting to them are influenced by factors in the sociocultural environment. For example, public reactions to the type of death can result in widows being labeled in particular kinds of ways. Calhoun, Selby, and Walton (1985-1986) compared adults' reported reactions to spousal death by suicide, motor vehicle accident, or leukemia. They found that the surviving spouse of suicide death was perceived as more to blame for the death, having had a greater chance to prevent death, and being more ashamed of the death; these widows faced a stressful event made even more stressful by perceptions of those around them.

Lifesaving as Cultural Imperative

In the United States after World War II the dominant orientation toward death has been lifesaving at all costs combined with a segregation of the dying into hospitals and nursing homes. Lifesaving as cultural imperative has evolved in tandem with the expansion of biomedical technology and is reflected in large medical centers that are oriented to offering specialized services and provide patients with fragmented and depersonalized experiences. At a time when older persons are faced with significant personal life events—such as terminal illness or widowhood—they not uncommonly find themselves in social systems that are not responsive to their personal goals, concerns, and needs.

Changes in the context of health care have caused nursing practice to become differentiated and specialized. Nurses encounter people (patients and families) who are facing death or death-related problems in five kinds of situations: intensive care, emergency care, recovery care, chronic care, and terminal care (Benoliel, 1977). Although nurses generally profess a concern for the well-being of the whole person, the structural conditions of many work settings support treatment-oriented activities and create obstacles to offering person-oriented services to patients and families.

The hospice movement appeared in the 1970s as part of a counterculture against impersonal death and dying (Benoliel, 1978; Stoddard, 1978). Across the years palliative care has developed as an area of specialized practice, and nurses have been major contributors to its conceptual and pragmatic development (Blues & Zerwekh, 1984; Dobratz, 1990) as well as to death counseling and death education as needed support services in a "death-denying" society (Benoliel, 1981). The development of bereavement support groups for elders was another manifestation of efforts to provide support services during a period of major transition (Lund, Dimond, & Juretich, 1985).

Closure to Life

Part of growing older includes preparation for death. This preparation occurs at the personal level through reflection and life review. It occurs at the social level through the establishment of wills, estate plans, and expressions of wishes about how and where death should occur. The reality of how much an elderly person can make his or her wishes known, can talk about personal dying, and can bring closure by completing unfinished business depends in great measure on other people and the extent to which they listen to those concerns and support the stated goals.

In many institutions there is a tendency for others—family members and providers—to take over decision making for elders "in their best interests." In a 1970 study of attitudes of nursing staff working in geriatric long-term care facilities, Jaeger and Simmons (1970) found the group split on the use of life sustaining measures until the end of life. Of some importance, about 50% viewed talking with patients about death as a taboo topic and about 15% were able to discuss such issues with patients in a meaningful way. It seems clear that elderly patients' opportunities to make choices and to participate in decisions about bringing closure to life depends on staff members able to converse with them about these matters of personal importance. In a later study of social factors influencing hospital dying, Martocchio (1982) noted that the very young and the very old had little power to negotiate for themselves. She reported that older people were relegated to passive roles by both providers and family members. Yet the issue of elders' opportunities to share in decisions has become something of a "right to die" movement. Concern about such participation has caused a convergence of biomedical ethics and the search for dignity in dying (Post, 1989).

ASSESSMENT AND ASSISTANCE PRINCIPLES

Helping older people to cope with death-related transitions requires a nursing framework oriented to the goals, needs, and concerns of persons undergoing a process of change. Such a framework is built on an assumption that major transitions—such as terminal illness, institutionalization, and widowhood—bring people face-to-face with new situations that require instrumental problem solving, adjustment to anxieties and threats, and confrontation with underlying existential concerns (Benoliel, 1985a).

Two concepts useful for creating a framework oriented toward person-centered care are *safe conduct* and *adaptation to loss as search for meaning*. Safe conduct is a principle of practice that incorporates two characteristics: individualization of care, and accessibility of the practitioner at times of maximum personal need (Benoliel, 1985b). Adaptation to loss as search for meaning is a principle of practice that attaches value to helping people achieve personal goals and find meaning while living through difficult life experiences. Gadow (1980) has referred to this principle as *existential advocacy.*

Assessment

Nursing practice oriented toward helping old people cope with death-related discontinuities and change requires thinking about assessment as an ongoing process of data gathering about the situation, the person, and the other people involved. It is a process based on a partnership model of practice achieved through the establishment of mutual goals, mutual agreement on ways and means of meeting goals, and mutual evaluation of both process and outcomes (Benoliel, 1985b). Interpersonal negotiation and contracting are critical features of the assessment process.

An important component of the process is risk assessment to determine the vulnerability of the persons involved to difficulties in coping and maladaptive outcomes. Factors observed to contribute to coping difficulties for older adults during bereavement include early feelings of wanting to die, confusion, and low self-esteem (Lund et al., 1985-1986); feelings of having contributed to the death in some way (Murphy, 1983); limited support resources (Kirschling & Austin, 1988; Remondet & Hansson, 1987; Warner, 1987); and pessimistic outlook on self and life in general (Rowe, 1982). In the case of terminal illness, risk factors can include differences in outcome goals of the dying patient and members of the family, problems in symptom management, and communication difficulties involving patient, family, and providers (Benoliel, 1985b; Martocchio, 1982).

Nurses also need guidelines for making judgments that an older person is adapting reasonably well or is moving toward a modification in meaning during the transition. Resolution of grief, for example, can be indicated by the person's recall of both positive and negative memories, ability to reach out to others, and new interests and activities (Garrett, 1987).

Assistance

Many guidelines exist to direct nurses in the technical problems associated with terminal illness and guidance of elders during bereavement. In most situations the key to helping elders achieve meaning through the lived experience of terminal illness, institutionalization, and widowhood as well as other losses lies in sensitivity to the personal views and wishes of the older individual, and communication strategies that promote positive coping and the achievement of personal goals. Knowledge about available community resources and support services is essential for helping elders find assistance suitable to their multiple needs. Developing a sense of when and when not to make referrals for specialized counseling is an attribute of some importance while assisting older persons to maximize their potential during their search for new meaning.

Research findings have shown that opportunities to talk about death concerns assist older people in their adaptations and responses. Following suicide of a nursing home resident, opportunities for elderly patients to discuss what has happened and what it means to them have been found helpful to their adaptations (Saul & Saul, 1988-1989). Sensitivity to differences in grief expression and mourning behaviors is vital when nurses are working with older people whose ethnic backgrounds are different from their own (Rosenblatt, 1988). Older widows and widowers were asked what advice they would give to persons just beginning the process of bereavement, and they had five suggestions: (a) keep busy, (b) be an individual, (c) talk with others, (d) have faith, and (e) give yourself time and take one day at a time (Rigdon, Clayton, & Dimond, 1987).

Communication is a central form of support for humans undergoing stressful periods of change. Much has been written about the value of having both a confidant and available social networks. Less recognition has been given to the importance of brief interactions with people *outside* a person's established kin and friendship network as providing an important social bridge between loss and reality (Rosenblatt, 1988). In their ongoing work nurses have many opportunities to engage in brief conversations with older persons about death-related matters of concern to them.

Helping older people achieve their personal goals is central to helping them construct meaning out of experiences of terminal illness, institutionalization, and widowhood. Of particular importance today are strategies by nurses to make sure that elderly persons' wishes *not* to be recipients of heroic medical measures be respected and entered into the multidisciplinary decision-making process (Youngner, 1987). Of equal importance are the many palliative care principles and practices that nurses can use to provide anticipatory guidance, manage distressing symptoms, and foster dignity of the person during the final weeks and days of life (Blues & Zerwekh, 1984).

ISSUES FOR THE FUTURE

Provision of services that support the concept of death with dignity is essential in a society with growing numbers of older persons. In the United States personal autonomy is a highly valued characteristic, and the concept of death with dignity likely should include the rights of older persons to participate in decisions about use or nonuse of life-sustaining medical treatments. Overall this goal probably has much to do with creating living environments in which dying is accepted as part of living and the aged themselves can decide that life-prolonging treatment is not in keeping with bringing closure to life in a dignified way.

Currently, do-not-resuscitate (DNR) orders are considered medical decisions, and consultation with others such as person or family is subject to the doctor's discretion (Ikuta, 1989). Shifting such decisions vis-à-vis older people toward a participatory model is a political matter that requires collaborative efforts by nurses, social workers, other providers, and the general public. Movement in this direction also depends on organized social efforts to shift the current negative meanings associated with suicide toward new ways of thinking about taking one's life as an acceptable option under certain conditions of living.

Another political issue relates to whether there will be limits placed on aged persons' access to health care resources—specifically, costly "high tech" procedures—compared to other age groups. Callahan (1987) has proposed consideration of the principle that medical care should no longer be oriented to resisting death after a person has lived out a natural life span. In contrast, Uddo (1986) has argued that withdrawal or refusal of food and hydration should not be based on age discrimination. Given the finiteness of health care resources, health care policy in the future will need to set limits on access to medical care. As Veatch (1988) has pointed out, new standards are needed to clarify the appropriate application of useless and marginally beneficial forms of treatment in light of the costs involved.

Nurses have the knowledge and skill essential to the creation of social environments that support the concept of "living while dying" for older people. To do so, they need to work together to develop person-oriented institutional care, family-centered home and hospice services (including respite for family providers), and political activities supportive of human needs for care as life draws to a close.

REFERENCES

Benoliel, J. Q. (1977). Nurses and the human experience of dying. In H. Feifel (Ed.), *New meanings of death* (pp. 124-142). New York: McGraw-Hill.

Benoliel, J. Q. (1978). The changing social context for life and death decisions. *Essence, 2* (2), 5-14.

Benoliel, J. Q. (1981). Death counseling and human development: Issues and intricacies. *Death Education, 4,* 337-353.

Benoliel, J. Q. (1985a). Loss and adaptation: Circumstances, contingencies, and consequences. *Death Studies, 9,* 217-233.

Benoliel, J. Q. (1985b). Loss and terminal illness. *Nursing Clinics of North America, 20,* 439-448.

Blues, A. G., & Zerwekh, J. V. (1984). *Hospice and palliative care nursing.* Orlando, FL: Grune & Stratton.

Brock, A. M. (1984). From wife to mother: A changing lifestyle. *Journal of Gerontological Nursing, 10*(4), 8-15.

Calhoun, L. G., Selby, J. W., & Walton, P. B. (1985-1986). Suicidal death of a spouse: The societal perception of the survivor. *Omega, 16,* 283-288.

Callahan, C. (1987). Terminating treatment: Age as a standard. *Hastings Center Report, 17*(5), 21-25.

Carter, S. (1989). Themes of grief. *Nursing Research, 38,* 354-358.

Corbin, J. M., & Strauss, L. (1988). *Unending work and care: Managing chronic illness at home.* San Francisco: Jossey-Bass.

Dobratz, M. C. (1990). Hospice nursing: Present perspectives and future directions. *Cancer Nursing, 13,* 116-122.

Eisenbruch, M. (1984). Cross-cultural aspects of bereavement. II: Ethnic and cultural variations in the development of bereavement practices. *Culture, Medicine, & Psychiatry, 8,* 315-347.

Gadow, S. (1980). Existential advocacy: Philosophical foundation of nursing. In S. F. Spicker & S. Gadow (Eds.), *Nursing: Images and ideals* (pp. 79-101). New York: Springer.

Garrett, J. E. (1987). Multiple losses in older adults. *Journal of Gerontological Nursing, 13*(8), 8-12.

Gass, K. A. (1988). Aged widows and widowers: Similarities and differences in appraisal, coping, resources, type of death, and health dysfunction. *Archives of Psychiatric Nursing, 2,* 200-210.

Gass, K. A., & Chang, A. S. (1989). Appraisals of bereavement, coping, resources, and psychosocial health dysfunction of widows and widowers. *Nursing Research, 38,* 31-36.

Ikuta, S. S. (1989). Dying at the right time: A critical legal theory approach to timing-of-death issues. *Issues in Law & Medicine, 5*(1), 3-66.

Jaeger, D., & Simmons, L. W. (1970). *The aged ill.* New York: Appleton-Century-Crofts.

Kahn, D. L. (1990). *Living in a nursing home: Experiences of suffering and meaning in old age.* Unpublished doctoral dissertation, University of Washington, Seattle.

Kirschling, J. M., & Austin, J. K. (1988). Assessing support—The recently widowed. *Archives of Psychiatric Nursing, 2,* 81-86.

Kirschling, J. M., & McBride, A. B. (1989). Effects of age and sex on the experience of widowhood. *Western Journal of Nursing Research, 11,* 207-218.

Kohn, M., & Menon, G. (1988). Life prolongation: Views of elderly outpatients and health care professionals. *Journal of American Geriatrics Society, 36,* 840-844.

Lifton, R. J. (1967). *Death in life: Survivors of Hiroshima.* New York: Random House.

Lifton, R. J. (1973). *Home from the war.* New York: Simon & Schuster.

Lund, D. A., Dimond, M. F., Caserta, M. S., Johnson, R. J., Poulton, J. L., & Connelly, J. R. (1985-1986). Identifying elderly with coping difficulties after two years of bereavement. *Omega, 16,* 213-224.

Lund, D. A., Dimond, M., & Juretich, M. (1985). Bereavement support groups for the elderly: Characteristics of potential participants. *Death Studies, 9,* 309-321.

Marris, P. (1974). *Loss and change.* London: Routledge & Kegan Paul.

Martocchio, B. C. (1982). *Living while dying.* Bowie, MD: Robert J. Brady.

Matthews, S. H. (1979). *The social world of old women.* Beverly Hills, CA: Sage.

Meyer, J. W. (1988). Levels of analysis: The life course as a cultural construction. In M. W. Riley, B. J. Huber, & B. B. Hess (Eds.), *Social structure and human lives* (pp. 49-62). Newbury Park, CA: Sage.

Murphy, S. A. (1983). Theoretical perspectives on bereavement. In P. L. Chinn (Ed.), *Advances in nursing theory development* (pp. 191-206). Rockville, MD: Aspen Systems Corporation.

National Center for Health Statistics. (1990). Births, marriages, divorces, and deaths for 1989. *Monthly Vital Statistics Report, 38*(12). Hyattsville, MD: Public Health Service.

Palgi, P., & Abramovitch, H. (1984). Death: A cross-cultural perspective. *Annual Review of Anthropology, 13*, 385-417.

Post, S. G. (1989). Biomedical ethics and the elderly: An emerging focus. *The Gerontologist, 29*, 568-570.

Redmond, L. M. (1989). *Surviving: When someone you love was murdered.* Clearwater, FL: Psychological Consultation and Education Services, Inc.

Reed, P. G. (1987). Spirituality and well-being in terminally ill hospitalized adults. *Research in Nursing & Health, 10*, 335-344.

Remondet, J. H., & Hansson, R. 0. (1987). Assessing a widow's grief—A short index. *Journal of Gerontological Nursing, 13*(4), 31-34.

Rigdon, I. S., Clayton, B. C., & Dimond, M. (1987). Toward a theory of helpfulness for the elderly bereaved: An invitation to a new life. *Advances in Nursing Science, 9*(2), 32-43.

Rosenblatt, P. C. (1988). Grief: The social context of private feelings. *Journal of Social Issues, 44*(3), 67-78.

Rowe, D. (1982). *The construction of life and death.* New York: John Wiley.

Sanders, C. M. (1988). Risk factors in bereavement outcome. *Journal of Social Issues, 44*(3), 97-111.

Saul, S. R., & Saul, S. (1988-1989). Old people talk about suicide: A discussion about suicide in a long-term care facility for frail and elderly people. *Omega, 19*, 237-251.

Stoddard, S. (1978). *The hospice movement.* New York: Random House.

Stroebe, W., & Stroebe, M. S. (1987). *Bereavement and health.* Cambridge, UK: Cambridge University Press.

Thorson, J. A., & Powell, F. C. (1988). Elements of death anxiety and meanings of death. *Journal of Clinical Psychology, 44*, 691-701.

Uddo, B. J. (1986). The withdrawal or refusal of food and hydration as age discrimination: Some possibilities. *Issues in Law & Medicine, 2*(1), 39-59.

Vachon, M. L. S., Rogers, J., Lyall, W. A., Lancee, W. J., Sheldon, A. R., & Freeman, S. J. J. (1982). Predictors and correlates of adaptation to conjugal bereavement. *American Journal of Psychiatry, 139*, 998-1002.

Veatch, R. M. (1988). Justice and the economics of health care. *Hastings Center Report, 18*(4), 34-40.

Warner, S. L. (1987). A comparative study of widows' and widowers' perceived social support during the first year of bereavement. *Archives of Psychiatric Nursing, 1*, 241-250.

Weenolsen, P. (1988). *Transcendence of loss over the life span.* New York: Hemisphere Publishing.

Wegmann, J. A. (1987). Hospice home death, hospital death, and coping abilities of widows. *Cancer Nursing, 10*, 148-155.

Woodfield, R. L., & Viney, L. L. (1984-1985). A personal construct approach to the conjugally bereaved woman. *Omega, 15*, 1-13.

Youngner, S. J. (1987). Do-not-resuscitate orders: No longer secret, but still a problem. *Hastings Center Report, 17*(1), 24-33.

SOCIOLOGICAL PERSPECTIVES AFFECTING THE NURSING OF OLDER ADULTS

9

Public Policy Impacting on Nursing Care of Older Adults

FAYE G. ABDELLAH

Objectives: At the completion of this chapter, the reader will be able to:

(1) Analyze historical and legislative events that have influenced public health policy for older adults;

(2) Synthesize concepts and facts related to public health policy for older adults, and

(3) Evaluate the role of the clinical nurse specialist (CNS) in providing nursing care to older adults within the constraints of public health policy.

INTRODUCTION

The purposes of this chapter are to analyze how public policy legislated in the past and currently evolving will affect the nursing care of older adults, how demographic patterns and health status factors assist in determining the focus of public policy, and what the importance is of economic resources in shaping public policy. The cost of health care services will continue to be a primary influence on health care policy in this decade and in the twenty-first century. The influence of emerging health care technology also will be examined in relation to public policy. The increasing involvement of state and local governments, as well as the role of business and industry in developing and implementing health care policy are considered. Strategies that can change public health policies in the future are proposed. In addition, the role of the CNS in gerontological nursing is reviewed in relation to the formulation and evaluation of public health policy.

WHAT IS PUBLIC HEALTH POLICY?

Public health policy formulation is viewed as the way issues are raised on the public agenda, the process by which laws are passed committing resources to programs that affect people, the development or withdrawal of rules and regulations that interpret laws, the process of program implementation, and the evaluation of the usefulness of the program (Aiken, 1982). Not only must the CNS know what constitutes public health policy, but also the nurse needs to be aware of major historic and legislative events that have influenced health care policy for older adults.

Past Events

Historically, parent caring and social concern for elder care has been rooted both in biblical teachings and in the legal system in the western world. The Christian Bible includes exhortations to "Honor thy Father and thy Mother that thy days may be long lived upon the land which the Lord thy God has given thee" (Exodus 20:12). These exhortations have been widely interpreted as meaning that adult children were morally responsible for elder parents.

Legal responsibility for relatives is based on Christian morality and eventually evolved in the English Poor Laws of 1601 that were passed to provide care for the destitute (Long, 1988). Some feared, however, that the provision of public funds or relief for the poor was likely to undermine family relationships. Consequently, payments were deliberately designed to maintain a state of destitution for those receiving public funds.

The nineteenth century brought an end to an agrarian society and the beginning of the industrial revolution. During this period of time, society placed 32% of its elderly in almshouses and on poor farms with the insane (Powell, 1977). All or most had substandard living conditions. Funds were supplied by county governments, were unequal in distribution, and were generated from property taxes.

By 1900, as a result of lobby by labor and fraternal organizations, old age pensions laws were passed in several states. They were subject to professional attacks and found difficult to administer (Long, 1988).

Following the election of Franklin Roosevelt as President of the United States, and during the Great Depression of the 1930s, legislation was passed creating the Social Security Act in 1935. This legislation, which was a part of Roosevelt's New Deal Program, was designed to reduce inequities in the state administered Older Americans Assistance Act.

In 1946, the Hill Burton Act was passed to assist in the construction of health care institutions. States receiving federal money to construct hospitals and nursing homes were required to meet minimum standards.

By 1950, the Social Security Administration paid for health care of welfare patients. States began developing standards for licensure of nursing homes (Chow, 1981).

In 1961, President Kennedy was instrumental in implementing the first White House Conference on Aging. Various sections of this conference made recommendations concerning the need for research and education in aging (Norman, 1982).

On July 14, 1965, President Johnson signed Public Law 89-73, creating the Older Americans Act (Norman, 1982). With the establishment of the Older Americans Act, the Administration on Aging (AOA) was formed at the national level to administer the act. The AOA is a part of the Department of Health and Human Services (DHHS). By 1966, all states had agencies for the aged as a prerequisite for participating in federal funding from the AOA. There are 10 DHHS regional offices that have jurisdiction over several states in each region.

The services provided by the Older Americans Act include: grants for research, training grants for people working in the aging field, and financial support for state agencies for the aged. The 10 national objectives of the AOA include the following: to provide for older adults an adequate income, the best possible health, suitable housing, restorative services, employment opportunities, retirement in dignity, pursuit of meaningful activity, efficient community services, benefit from research, and independence (Norman, 1986b).

Titles and amendments have been added to the Older Americans Act over the past several years (see Chapter 10). Some of the better known amendments include: the Nutritional Act, which provides for meals for older adults; legal services; transportation; and the Retired Senior Volunteer Program (RSVP). The Nutritional Act (Title VII) authorized a nutrition program for the elderly in 1972 (Norman, 1982). The purpose of the nutrition law was to provide hot meals and other nutritional services to persons over 60 years of age. Its enactment followed the White House Conference of 1971. The cost of the nutrition program is shared by the federal government and the states. In 1973, the federal government spent approximately $100,000 on this program and in 1986 about $668,000,000 (Norman, 1982, 1986b). The Older Americans Act is due for reapportionment in 1991 and various organizations will lobby to influence the outcome of this legislation (American Society on Aging Conference, 1990). The Older Americans Act is administered by the Commissioner on Aging (Older Americans Report, 1990).

In 1965, congress signed into law two titles under the Social Security Act: Title XVIII, establishing Medicare, and Title XIX to establish Medicaid. Information about these two National Health Insurance programs is included in Chapter 10 on economics in aging. Supplemental Security Income (SSI) was passed in 1974 and is also described in Chapter 10.

Another important legislative enactment related to aging was the creation of the National Institute on Aging (NIA) in 1974. A major purpose of the institute is the coordination and promotion of research in aging. NIA is one of 15 institutes at the National Institutes of Health, at Bethesda, MD.

In 1980, the Patient's Bill of Rights in Long-Term Care Facilities was passed (Chow, 1981). This bill of rights includes free association between residents and visitors, and establishes a residents' council, protects privacy and personal possessions, provides the right to obtain an itemized statement, and assures the performance of work only on a volunteer basis.

A different method of paying for hospital care for older adults was instituted in 1983, the Medicare Hospital Prospective Payment System (Business Week, 1983). This system is based on diagnosis-related groups (DRGs) that were designed to give hospitals an incentive to deliver services in a cost effective manner. Because hospitals are paid a fixed amount for each patient according to the medical diagnosis, it has lead to patients being discharged home earlier than in the past. Home health care support, however, has not increased significantly to meet this need.

Summary

The evolution of public health legislation in the United States is based on both Biblical sources and legislative events in England. As this nation began to have people living into old age, laws were enacted to care for the indigent. The Social Security Act of 1935 was a significant piece of legislation, enacted to provide some financial security to all older residents. President Kennedy recognized the need for a comprehensive program and initiated a White House Conference on Aging in 1961 to be conducted every 10 years. In 1965, major legislative measures created the Older Americans Act and the Administration on Aging. Medicare and Medicaid were enacted under the Social Security Act, to provide a national health insurance to a segment of the population. More recent legislation has included the Nutrition Act of 1972 and the National Institute on Aging in 1974. In 1983, DRGs were instituted as a method of controlling escalating health care costs. In the past, public policy evolved slowly over several years. Recently, however, it seems to change at a more rapid rate. Some reasons why public policy for older adults is currently the focus of debate among health care professionals and consumers will be discussed in the following section.

CURRENT PUBLIC POLICY

Why are we so concerned about public policy impacting on nursing care of older adults? A primary reason is because the cost of health care continues to rise three times as fast as the consumer price index. In spite of this enormous expenditure for health care, there still exists the absence of health care for millions, soaring medical costs, and the need to deal with the costs of long-term care for an aging population.

The following statistics indicate why public policy is of concern to both health care providers and consumers:

(1) Thirty-one million people in the United States have no health insurance, either private or government, and lack access to care;

(2) National health costs are expected to reach $661 billion in 1990—close to 12% of the U.S. gross national product;

(3) About 9 million people, particularly the aged, need long-term care;

(4) Only 5% of the elderly 65 and older live in institutions, yet they receive 80% of allocated federal funds through Medicare and Medicaid;

(5) Eight million of the 30 million elderly people in this country live alone, and 6 million are women over 65; and

(6) Fifty-six percent of those age 75 and older are limited in daily activities due to chronic conditions, and 86% of all elderly people suffer from one or more chronic condition (U.S. Department of Health and Human Services [DHHS], 1989).

As yet, there is no national consensus on how to handle these issues, how to control costs, or how to pay for needed services through the Government or the private sector. Current debate in both legislative and business groups tends to focus on who will pay for health care services. For the past several years the ANA has been on record supporting the rights of all persons to have equal access to health care (American Nurses' Association [ANA], 1980). In an edited text by Leader and Moon (1989) the majority of the authors support universal health care coverage, but differ on how the system can be financed.

ROLE OF FEDERAL GOVERNMENT

Nurses and other health care providers have become increasingly interested in public policy, particularly federal health policy. Perceptions are that professional activities of health providers are influenced by federal policies and programs. There are, however, potentials and limitations to what federal policy can do. We need to understand this to direct our energies toward implementing strategies that can be directed to helping older adults.

Health providers may overestimate the capacity of the federal government to affect practice. Many policy decisions made by industry have a greater impact on nursing practice than do the public health policy decisions of the federal government. Aiken (1982) suggests four ways in which federal health policies affect health care providers:

(1) The federal government pays for health care for the poor and the elderly;
(2) Federal health manpower programs support the training of health care providers to influence the supply, composition, or distribution of the work force;
(3) Federally supported research provides the source for new ideas and innovations; and
(4) Federal programs provide capital support for new and renovated health care facilities.

As advocates and service providers for at risk groups such as the poor and frail elder populations, the CNS is in a position not only to educate the public, but also to promote federal legislation that provides just and equitable access to adequate health care (ANA, 1980). Without federal guidelines and support, state and local government expenditures for health care and welfare services tends to be fragmented and uneven with some states providing excellent care and others unable or unwilling to provide the needed money and services.

PUBLIC POLICY GOALS

This is an appropriate time to identify the public policy issues impacting on nursing care of older adults that will greatly influence the nursing profession in the year 2000, and to assess recent developments in public health policy to determine the direction in which we will be, or ought to be, headed during the next decade. Any changes that might occur will require prior changes in public and private policies, and policy of both kinds will be determined by the political relationships and attitudes of the people.

There are three broad national goals for the nation that will impact on nursing care of older adults by the year 2000:

(1) increase life expectancy to at least 78 years;
(2) reduce disability caused by chronic conditions to a prevalence of no more than 7.0% of all people; and
(3) increase healthy years of life to at least 65 years (DHHS, 1989).

In the following sections each goal will be examined in relation to the effect it will have on health care for older adults.

Increase Life Expectancy

Life expectancy at birth, the average number of years an individual is expected to live, is an important measure of a nation's health. It is also a standard measure for international comparison. Life expectancy summarizes a population's current mortality experience in terms of average survival. This summary measure maintains some degree of continuity with the age-specific mortality reduction goals of the previous decade. In 1987, life expectancy at birth was 74.9 years, 71.5 for men and 78.3 for women. Life expectancy for whites was 75.5 compared to 69.7 for blacks (DHHS, 1989).

White females continue to have the longest life expectancy (78.8 years) followed by black females (73.8 years), white males (72.1 years), and black males (65.4 years) (DHHS, 1989). Reliable national estimates of life expectancy of other racial and ethnic minority groups are not available. Limited data, however, suggest that the life expectancy of American Indians may be about 3-6 years shorter than the average for men and women of all races (DHHS, 1989). Life expectancy for Hispanics in the southwest appears to be nearly the same as for whites in the same region. Asian Americans may actually have a longer life expectancy than the total population.

More than a full year's increase in life expectancy occurred between 1980 and 1986 (DHHS, 1989). Projection of the 1980 through 1986 life expectancy using a simple linear model suggests that life expectancy will be 77.7 in the year 2000. The target for this national health goal has been set slightly higher at 78 years. According to international rankings of life expectancy in 1986 (which was used in 1984 U.S. estimates), U.S. males ranked 18th at 71.3 years and U.S. females ranked 12th at 78.5 years. In contrast, top-ranked Japan reported life expectancies of 75.5 years for men and 81.6 years for women in 1986 (DHHS, 1989).

Reduce Disability Caused by Chronic Conditions

In 1987, the age-adjusted prevalence of limitation in major activity resulting from chronic conditions was 9.2% (DHHS, 1989). Disability caused by chronic conditions is defined as a limitation in major activity due to chronic conditions. Major activity refers to the usual activity for one's age-sex group whether it is working, keeping house, or living independently. Chronic conditions are defined as conditions that either (1) were first noticed 3 or more months ago, or (2) belong to a group of conditions such as heart disease and diabetes, which are considered chronic regardless of when they began. Knowing that life expectancy is high does not describe whether the population is predominantly well or is heavily burdened with chronic illness and disability.

In 1987, 8.9% of the population suffered a limitation in major activity due to chronic conditions (DHHS, 1989). About 3.7% were unable to carry on a major activity and an additional 5.2% were limited in the amount or kind of major activity they could perform (DHHS, 1989).

The age adjusted prevalence of limitation in major activity has been decreasing steadily, from 9.6% in 1983 to 8.9% in 1987. The target set for the year 2000 of 7.0% would represent more than a 20% reduction in disability due to chronic conditions between 1987 and the year 2000 (DHHS, 1989).

Increase Healthy Years of Life

In 1987, healthy years of life, also referred to as quality-adjusted life years (QALY), were estimated to be about 60. Given a life expectancy of 74.9 years, this means that about 60 years of life are spent in perfect health and about 15 years are spent in less than perfect health over the life span (DHHS, 1989).

Healthy years of life is defined as the duration of life discounted by some estimate of the quality of life. Healthy years of life is a summary measure of health that combines mortality (quantity of life) and morbidity (quality of life) into a single measure. Like life expectancy, it reflects the experience of all age groups.

In recent years, considerable research effort has been devoted to developing a health status index, a comprehensive measure of the health of a population. Although several approaches have been developed for combining mortality and morbidity, QALY has emerged as the most commonly used health status measure that includes both mortality and morbidity.

The goal for the year 2000 is to increase years of healthy life by 5 years, to 65 (DHHS, 1989). This increase in years of healthy life can be attained through a reduction in overall mortality, that is, by increasing life expectancy at birth from 74.9 to 80 years and reducing morbidity.

Although reliable national estimates of years of healthy life exist, they remain to be tested. The inclusion of this measure among the goals for the year 2000 represents a major advance.

Outcomes measurement is another emerging health policy movement—actually the next generation of DRGs (Geigole & Jones, 1990). The CNS is a key person to uncover or identify the health outcomes of treatment for the patient. At present, outcomes measurement is limited to mortality, morbidity, unnecessary hospital procedures, readmissions, and patient satisfaction. What is needed are data on outcomes related to the patient's quality of life—such measures as reduction of pain, improved mobility, improved mental state, and ability to return to work.

Long-Term Care Policy

The impact of public policies on health services delivery of care to the elderly is clearly evident today, as makers of public policy realize how difficult the problem of financing long-term care services will be in the future. According to Callahan (1981), long-term care (LTC) is likely to be the major public policy issue of the next decade.

There is an ever increasing demand for long-term care. Demand for publicly supported LTC services is already estimated to be three times greater than supply and was expected to increase by 40% by 1985 (Hudson, 1981). The importance of rethinking national health policies and programs for the elderly, with much more attention to ambulatory and long-term care, as well as more cost controls, is long overdue (Somers, 1980). Experience has indicated that long-term care regulation is cyclical in nature—disappointing provider performance resulting in new and tougher regulations, increased expectations, and disillusionment when expectations are not fulfilled. According to Christianson (1979), public health policy as it impacts on health care delivery to older adults will determine if this pattern can be altered.

One of the most dramatic changes occurring in our nation is the aging of our population. With the increase in numbers of older people come enormous opportunities and challenges for society. Today's older Americans, as a group, live longer, healthier, and financially more secure lives than previous generations. Certain segments of the older population, however, face serious health and financial problems.

By the year 2000, 13% of the population is expected to be age 65 and older, with the most rapid increases taking place among those age 75 and older (DHHS, 1989). Because health and mobility decline with advancing age, the chance of being limited in activity and in need of health and social services increases significantly for the oldest-old.

With the unprecedented gains in life expectancy for Americans made in this century has come the emergence of a population that is more likely to suffer from chronic health problems. Although the science based on the aging process is developing rapidly, each new insight brings with it many new questions. In the search for new ways to meet the health needs of older people, increased attention is being put on the role of disease prevention and health promotion.

Research is finding that many of the so-called signs of "old age" can better be identified as the combined effects of disease or the signs of abuse and disuse. The most prevalent of the diseases and chronic conditions for older people are those that derive from life-style and environmental factors, factors for which effective interventions oftentimes exist.

The study of long-term care, without question, is a high priority. This would include nursing in home care settings, as well as the complications related to long-term institutional care.

In 1988, the Office of the Surgeon General held the Ninth Surgeon General's Workshop on Health Promotion and Aging (Abdellah & Moore, 1988). The workshop focused on nine specific areas. These included: alcoholism, dental/oral health, physical fitness and exercise, injury prevention, medications, mental health, nutrition, preventive health services, and smoking cessation. Each of the work groups came up with specific recommendations regarding research, service, and education, and also included implications for health policy.

Palley and Oktay (1989) suggest that a sense of national direction is needed in developing an effective long-term care policy for the frail elderly. These authors suggest that the major issues include developing a family perspective that includes a balance between institutional and community based health care services, as well as implementing cost containment policies that can meet demands for health care services.

Clinical nurse specialists can be instrumental in effecting these changes by implementing only required services based on assessed need, promoting change, and evaluating progress. Defeat of the Catastrophic Long-Term Care Bill at the federal level in 1989 indicates that elder health care consumers are not willing to pay for services that they do not receive. This enactment would have been financed by all persons over 65 years of age even if they did not use or need the care. Lobbyists against the bill specified its inequity because all those 65 years of age and older eligible for Medicare would have to pay for the services even if they did not use them. It was pointed out that elementary and secondary education is financed by taxes from everyone, not just those who fit in this age group. The fact that the government had expected to pass this bill is evidenced by funds being deducted from Social Security payments after it was defeated. (See Table 9.1 for listing of selected legislative events related to public health policy for older adults.)

Emerging Medical Technology

Emerging medical technology is associated with about one third of the increase in total national health expenditures (Thompson, 1990). Many emerging technologies are moving the care of patients to their homes and community health centers. Patients are being discharged a lot sicker and take many devices with them; for example, ventilators, dialysis machines, pacemakers, and a variety of monitoring devices. These technologies must be evaluated in terms

Table 9.1
Selected Events Related to Public Health Policy for Older Adults

Legislation	Income	Employment	Health	Nutrition	Transportation	Housing	Research	Quality of Life
				Needs Addressed				
English Poor Laws (1601)	X					X		
Old Age Pension (1900)	X							
Social Security Act (1935)	X							
Hill Burton Act (1946)			X			X		
White House Conference on Aging (1961) (1971) (1981)	X	X	X	X	X	X	X	X
Older Americans Act (1965)	X	X	X	X	X	X	X	X
Social Security Amendment Medicare/Medicaid (1965)			X					
National Institute on Aging (1974)							X	
Supplemental Security Income (1974)	X							
Patient's Bill of Rights in LTC (1980)						X		X
DRGs (1983)			X					
Defeat of the Catastrophic LTC Bill (1989)			X					

Source: Adapted from Norman, J. W. (1986a). *A history of federal legislation relating to older Americans. A paper prepared by the National Clearing House on Aging Press, Washington, DC, pp. 1-3.*

of public policy to estimate future health manpower needs and supply requirements, the costs and effectiveness of health care, the dissemination of information, and the education of health professionals and consumers.

Molecular biology provides insight into the brain's functioning, providing a better understanding of Alzheimer's disease, stroke, and Parkinson's disease. Gene research has also changed the medical approach to a number of brain disorders, such as Huntington's disease. Mental illnesses, such as depression, are coming to be recognized as having genetic and biochemical components.

Emerging technologies affect public policies. The movement of machines into health care services resolves some problems and creates others—notably costs. An estimated $24.3 billion was spent in 1989 just for medical devices (Thompson, 1990).

EVALUATING PUBLIC HEALTH POLICY

We must recognize that many of the issues of greatest concern to us as nurses cannot be resolved by the federal government alone. Instead, public policy at the state level involving industry in collective bargaining and joint negotiations between nurses, physicians, and health care institutions represent strategies that may bring about solutions to these complex problems. There needs to be increased support of special projects to demonstrate the effectiveness and feasibility of new and innovative approaches.

The following are criteria for evaluating successful public health policy impacting on older adults:

(1) Personal health services are more evenly distributed throughout the country with an ample supply of health manpower and the availability of a variety of incentives for improving access;
(2) Major financial barriers to health services delivery have been removed or lowered for the most vulnerable group—older adults;
(3) State and local governments and portions of the private sector demonstrate readiness to provide for personal health services for older adults;
(4) A responsive health information system exists—one that is comprehensive and sensitive so as to permit effective monitoring and corrections; and
(5) Organizational and managerial capabilities of state and local governments and the private sector show steady improvement (Aiken, 1982).

Bold Strategies

Bold strategies that will change public health policies are necessary if the present system of health care delivery is to be changed. One such strategy is to reassess the role of hospitals. Today the technological base of modern medicine and the structure of health insurance payment makes the hospital the dominant institution in the health care delivery system. It is now necessary to reduce this dominance. Hospitals are expensive. Physician reimbursement practices encourage specialization and reliance on expensive technology. Finally, the hospital perpetuates the physician-centered medical model of cure rather than prevention, which results in the withholding of status and respect from other health professionals and in the loss of potential savings by denying the broader use of nonphysicians. Eighty percent of the hospital based health care delivery services now provided by hospitals could be shifted to alternative facilities, for example HMOs, other ambulatory care centers, community mental health centers, and home care programs. According to Weiner (1980), the strategy to change public health policy would involve the following:

(1) Changing the financial incentives to discourage overutilization of hospital based services and limit the growth of specialization;

(2) Restraining hospitals from deterring the development of nonhospital and community-based services, such as home care programs, and primary care health clinics;

(3) Enlarging hospital boards of trustees to include a majority of consumer representatives who are older adults;

(4) Shifting the base of training and education to nonhospital settings—the teaching nursing home concept is an excellent move in this direction;

(5) Enhancing the role of nonphysician health professionals, for example nurse practitioners and nurse gerontologists within the hospital setting to afford them a key role in decision making, hospital privileges, and access to patients;

(6) Encouraging hospital administrators and trustees to question whether it is necessary to maintain their hospital with its existing array of services; and

(7) Encouraging the development of economic incentives that will minimize regulation and place reliance on innovative approaches to other cost-containment methods that have proven to be effective.

Dychtwald and Zitter (1988) agree that elder care providers will be surprised by the changes during the next decade. These changes will include: a changing structure that will consist of an integrated system of all types of services and providers, complex financing with capitation removing incentives to overtreat, creating potentials for undertreatment, importance of quality, and delegating of duties from physicians to less expensive providers.

In addition, any proposal to manipulate incentives as a health policy device must be responsive to the following three questions:

(1) Who must be made subject to the incentives if the desired outcome is to occur;

(2) How do these individuals define rewards and penalties;

(3) How large must the inducement be to bring about the desired outcome?

SUMMARY

It is hoped that by the year 2000 we will have a public consensus emerge that provides a balance of federal, state, and local governments and private sector roles in health care delivery based on public health care policies that are equitable, cost-cutting, and coordinated to meet the health needs of older adults. The Clinical Nurse Specialist in gerontological nursing must be an informed participant in shaping public health care policy for older adults, because the role of the Clinical Nurse Specialist is to develop, implement, and evaluate nursing care that utilizes a holistic approach. Changes in public health care policy should be based on assessed need, not political expediency (Powell, 1977).

REFERENCES

Abdellah, F. G., & Moore, S. (Eds). (1988). *Surgeon General's Workshop on Health Promotion and Aging.* Washington, D.C: DHHS, PHS.

Aiken, L. H. (Ed.). (1982). *Nursing in the 1980's, crisis, opportunities, challenges.* Philadelphia: J. B. Lippincott.

American Nurses' Association. (1980). *Nursing, social* policy statement. Kansas City, MO: American Nurses' Association.

American Society on Aging Conference. (1990). Debate on Older Americans Act, Reapportionment, San Francisco, CA.

Business Week. (1983). The upheaval in health care, July 25. Cover story.

Callahan, J. J. (1981). The impact of federal programs on long-term care. In S. Altman & H. Sapolsky (Eds.), *Federal health programs: problems and prospects.* Lexington, MA: D. C. Heath.

Chow, R. (1981). Important legislative events: Past, present and future perspectives of long-term care and aging. *The Michigan Nurse,* October, 10-15.

Christianson, J. B. (1979). Long-term care standards: Enforcement and compliance. *Journal of Health Politics, Policy and Law, 4*(3), 414-422.

Dychtwald, K., & Zitter, M. (1988). Changes during the next decade will alter the way eldercare is provided, financed. *Modern Healthcare, 18* (16), 38.

Geigole, R., & Jones, S. (1990) Outcomes measurement: A report from the front. *Inquiry, 27* (1), 7-13.

Hudson, R. B. (1981). A block grant to the states for long-term care. *Journal of Health Politics, Policy and Law, 6* (1), 9-28.

Leader, S., & Moon, M. (Eds.). (1989). *Changing America's health care system.* Washington, DC: American Association of Retired Persons.

Long, C. (1988). Relative responsibility laws and the medicaid law. *Journal of Gerontological Nursing, 14* (7), 13-17.

Norman, J. W. (1982). The Older American's Act: Meeting the changing needs of the elderly. *Aging,* January/February. 2-10.

Norman, J. W. (1986a). A history of federal legislation relating to older Americans. Paper prepared by the National Clearing House on Aging Press, Washington, DC, pp. 1-3.

Norman, J. W. (1986b). *The Older Americans Act of 1965, as amended and its progress.* Washington, DC: National Clearing House on Aging.

Older Americans Report. (1990). Sample issue. Silver Spring, MD: Business Publishers.

Palley, H., & Oktay, J. (1989). Issues in setting the agenda for a long term care policy for the frail elderly. *Home Health Care Services, 10* (314), 15-43.

Powell, C. (1977). *Programs and services for the elderly, a survey.* Omaha, NE: University of Nebraska Press.

Somers, A. R. (1980). Rethinking health policy for the elderly: A six-point program. *Inquiry, 17* (Spring), 3-17.

Thompson, L. (1990, January 30). Medicine's new machines. *Washington Post,* p. 17.

U.S. Department of Health and Human Services. (1989). *Promoting health: Preventing disease. Year 2000 objectives for the nation* (PHS Draft Document). Washington, DC: Government Printing Office.

Weiner, S. M. (1980). Health care policy and politics: Does the past tell us anything about the future? *American Society of Law and Medicine, 5* (4), 331-341.

10

Economics of Aging

ANNA M. BROCK

Objectives: The purpose of this chapter is to examine major economic resources available to older persons in relation to housing, income, health, and social services. The objectives of this chapter include:

(1) Analyzing the importance of economics in aging and the role of the Clinical Nurse Specialist in providing nursing care to older adults in changing financial circumstances.
(2) Evaluating specific economic issues that affect older adults.
(3) Critiquing federal and community programs available to older adults.

INTRODUCTION

Part of the American dream is the notion of economic self-reliance. Most adults hope that throughout their life cycle they can provide for their own needs. One of the greatest fears of aging that many adults have is becoming destitute and dependent on family, friends, or society. Achievement of the self-sufficiency dream has not been realized successfully in recent years. According to the 1988 statistics from the U.S. Bureau of the Census (1987), 12.4% of persons older than 65 years are below the poverty level. Of women more than 65 years of age, 47% have less than $6,000 annual income, and the median income of all women older than 65 years is $6,313.

Most people expect financial resources in their retirement years to decline compared to their working years. They also expect, however, that the level of their expenditures will decline proportionately and this has not occurred. The inflation of the seventies and eighties reduced the value of financial assets. The elderly were especially hard hit because most rely on social security benefits or accumulated outside pension funds for the bulk of their income. These assets are usually fixed and cannot be changed by the individual. Therefore, most elders are unable to adjust their income to changing economic circumstances and hence are powerless to combat declining real income. Health care purchases are paid for in substantial part by private insurance, and federal health and social programs. Yet, the rising cost of these programs contributes substantially to rising government expenditures, size of government deficits, and more out-of-pocket costs to the aged health consumer.

Interest in the economics of elders and the way our nation deals with aging is a subject of interest to all nurses, especially those who care for the aged. Data from the U.S. Bureau of the Census (1988) indicates that as a nation we are growing older—more people are living longer. In 1988, approximately 12% of the American population, 29 million people, were 65 or older and 32,000 Americans are age 100 or older, with nearly 3 out of every 4 of these elder women. Those 85 or older comprise the fastest growing segment within the 65 and older cohort, and are projected to equal 5% of the population by the year 2040 (Longino, 1988). At the same time, because our society is gradually settling into zero population growth, the number of births is decreasing. Demographically this is significant because it means that the proportion of seniors in our population is mounting as wage earners decrease.

It is also clear that being old in America is not a homogeneous experience. There are now emerging two distinct groups of elders—the young-old (55-75 years) and the old-old (75+ years). As a group, the young-old are relatively healthy, independent, well-off, and active. The old-old, on the other hand, are ill, poorer, and dependent. Projections indicate that the old-old elderly is the fastest growing segment in our population.

With the rapid advances in medical technology and research, it is probable that in the near future death-causing diseases such as cardiovascular, pulmonary, and cancer will be overcome (Strumpf, 1988). This modern technology will result in added years for most citizens and also accrue to the senior population.

Yet, the fiscal resources necessary to meet tomorrow's needs of an aged America is decreasing. Every available economic prediction indicates that there is not enough money available to meet the needs of today's seniors, let alone tomorrow's. Our current policies for financial aid, health care, and social services for seniors are threatening to bust the budget. This has resulted in austerity, cutbacks, and limitations in services to seniors. The aging policy dilemma presents a serious challenge to elders who cannot manage without public support, to legislators who must cope with unbalanced budgets, and to those of us who want the American dream of economic self-reliance in our golden years.

FINANCIAL SITUATION OF THE AGED

Self-reliance and individualism have always been highly regarded American virtues. This is especially true for older persons and it is no less true today than it was 100 years ago. As always, the preponderance of responsibilities for economics, health, and life satisfaction rests with the individual. Sources in the literature identify real problems the elderly have with the realization of this dream and with the ways we as a nation deal with our elders. In most of what is written, the negative aspects of aging and our national response to the aged is overemphasized. There appears to be a misconception in our society that all elders are: victims of poverty, abandoned by their families in nursing homes, living in substandard housing, victims of inflation, and forced into a premature retirement.

Serious problems do exist. The drastically changed demographic composition of this nation has created financial difficulties. This situation presents a serious economic challenge. Yet, it should be emphasized that the great majority of today's elderly Americans are: the wealthiest, best fed, best housed, healthiest, most self-reliant population in our nation's history. Several demographic and health status factors have an economic impact on elders, however. These include: life expectancy, health, income, employment, and housing. Each factor will be analyzed separately in the following section.

LIFE EXPECTANCY

Life expectancy at birth in 1980 for American males was 70 years, for females 78 years; at the turn of the century the corresponding figures were 46 and 48 (Selkert & Broski, 1988). Today's child can expect to live nearly a quarter of a century longer than his or her great grandparents. Moreover, life expectancy has increased at every age level. Improved diet and exercise, along with better health care, will bring still further increases in life expectancy in the future. The 85 and older age group continually increases and is of great significance in economic, health, and social policy planning. The sex imbalance in this age group rises disproportionately in favor of female survival. In this group there are about 2.5 females to every male (Strumpf, 1988). Because most of that generation of females did not work outside the home, they are among the poorest and most frequently institutionalized segment of our population.

HEALTH

Many elderly do have some activity limitation, but severe decline reaches high prevalence only among those older than 85. Numerous studies show that chronological aging from 60 to 85 does not necessarily diminish interests and activities. The fact is that the overwhelming majority of old people in America are well and are living independently. On the average, older people spend less than 14 days a year in bed due to illness (Selkert & Broski, 1988). Only 5% of those 65 and older are institutionalized. A recent survey reported that 80% of the elderly have some chronic illness, but only 18% are limited in mobility by their impairments (Selkert & Broski, 1988). The same survey also shows that 80% of the noninstitutionalized elderly say their health is excellent, good, or fair.

Yet, the fact remains that more elders than younger cohorts are disabled and use health services more. Persons over 65 years of age see their physicians 50% more than younger people and have twice as many hospital stays for twice as long (U.S. Senate Special Committee on Aging, 1979).

The rising cost of health care is of major importance to elders. In 1963, before the advent of Medicare, the total per capita medical cost was $419 for people 65 years and older as compared to $4,202 in 1984 (U.S. Senate Special Committee on Aging, 1986). Even with federal funds, older people pay a considerable portion of their health care costs out of their own pockets. Direct out-of-pocket health costs for older adults averaged 15% of their income in 1984, averaging about $1,059 per person. The majority of these expenses were for physician services and health needs not covered by Medicare, Medicaid, or private insurance (U.S. Senate, 1986).

INCOME

The source of income for elderly persons has traditionally been their own accumulated savings, and private (e.g., from families) and public transfer payments. Social Security, which began as a basic pension for retirement, has grown over the years into the primary source of retirement income. Because a growing proportion of the population will be 65 and older in future decades and will have longer life expectancies, there is no doubt that the economy cannot afford real increases in Social Security benefits. The alternative is to rely on privately funded pensions, savings, and continued employment. With these alternatives come the issues surrounding what incentives can be offered to encourage growth of private pensions, savings plans, and delayed retirement. England (1987) concludes that the elderly are comparatively less poor than many other cohorts and in comparison to the elderly in preceding generations.

If home equity is not considered, the aged have a median net worth of $18,790 as compared to $7,783 for the general population. Yet, it is important to remember that the total net worth of these elders could be consumed by an 18 day hospitalization or 6 months in a nursing home. Furthermore, the elderly are particularly vulnerable to loss from inflation. They also suffer from price increases for particular items that weigh heavily on their budgets, such as paying for medications.

Poverty rates among certain groups of elders have remained high. Poverty rates among very old women living alone have remained high in the last three decades. The present cohort of aged blacks has been disadvantaged in education and income throughout their lives and thus are poor in old age. Older adults living in rural areas and in southeastern states also have increased poverty rates. In Mississippi, the poverty rate for older persons in 1979 was 34% (American Association of Retired Persons, 1988). Individuals more than 85 years of age are the poorest in our society.

EMPLOYMENT

Although it is now illegal to compel workers to retire at age 65, a trend of retirement before that age continues. In 1950 almost half of all elderly men were employed. The proportion fell to one-third by 1960 and to one-fifth by 1980. This decline is partially due to the attractiveness of the increasingly higher benefit available in the Social Security program and also to a drop in self-employment. In 1961 about 53% of the initial applicants for Social Security were less than 65 years of age. As of 1980, three-fourths sought reduced benefits available to those aged 62 to 64 (Older Americans Report, 1980).

It is questionable if this trend toward early retirement will continue. In the year 2000, full payment from Social Security will be increased to age 67 (Hendricks & Calasanti, 1986). The U.S. economy appears to be heading into a severe labor shortage, especially skilled labor (U.S. Senate, 1986). Almost all potential members of the labor force through the year 2000 have already been born. Even a dramatic increase in birth rate would not affect the labor force until after the turn of the century. In view of these trends, the most likely prospect for adding to the labor force is to increase the falling participation by elders. There appears to be widespread support for a policy that encourages able older workers to choose to continue working, while continuing to provide insurance against income loss at retirement for workers with health problems. But problems arise in attempting to design an acceptable and effective policy to extend working lifetimes. Some of the barriers that exist include age discrimination practices of employers and technological advance rendering the older worker less productive than the better educated young person. Other barriers exist because of health or displacement problems. Still others exist in law, such as the Social Security retirement income exclusion.

Nurses should also be aware of the psychological implications of early retirement, such as the desire to be free of the hassle of the workplace and to indulge in post retirement activities. In addition, older persons who are forced back into the workplace due to financial problems are frequently employed in semi-skilled occupations, such as clerks and waitresses. These jobs usually require long hours of standing and heavy work, for very low pay. These jobs may challenge younger workers, but they can be an excessive burden for an elderly person as well as a health hazard. Nurses can assist older employees by advocating for fair wages and healthful working conditions.

HOUSING

The popular conceptualization of the elderly as frail, dependent, senile individuals, living out their last years in an institution, has no factual basis. Many elders live in their own homes and have paid off mortgages (American Association of Retired Persons, 1987). Yet, living arrangements are a major problem for most individuals as they age.

It is a reality of modern times that rising energy and housing costs have joined the high costs of food and health care as necessities of life that contribute to the economic hardship of many aging persons. In addition to the financial difficulties, housing for the aged is problematic because of a lack of environmental support to assist them to remain residing and participating in the community.

Deterioration of housing, escalation of property taxes, and maintenance costs create many problems for elderly homeowners in keeping their homes. Elderly renters are extremely vulnerable to prohibitive rental fees, real estate speculation, and loss of living quarters because of removal of substandard, low rent apartment or hotel buildings. Physical impairments and a lack of available, affordable support services—such as homemakers, housekeepers, transportation, home health care, and meal service—keep many from being able to manage adequately in their homes.

The need for special housing for the aged has long been recognized. Numbers of governmental and privately funded experiments in alternative housing for the aged have been tested. These projects incorporated such variables as the availability of a comprehensive array of personal care services, special health and safety remedies, and recreational and leisure plans. Although most of these projects provide security, improve life satisfaction, and prove cost effective, there is no comprehensive plan for alternative living arrangements for the elderly at present.

In part, the reluctance to expand federal support of community-based services is due to a fear that such formal programs will substitute for informal programs and hence add immeasurably to the public burden. Far too little attention, however, has been given to the current incentives for substituting formal institutional care for informal care. Public programs pay for all living and personal care services in a nursing home, but there is little public subsidy of services in private homes that might enhance the ability of family and friends to meet the bulk of care needs.

FINANCIAL RESOURCES FOR THE ELDERLY

There is a broad range of benefits and services available from federal, state, and local resources to assist older people with problems related to health, income, or social services. It is essential that elders, their families, and health/social providers be aware of the types of services available to assist older people achieve a higher quality of life. Until recently, most of these benefits and services were felt to be the responsibility of the individual rather than society. Yet, because of economic crisis, the rapid increase in proportion of the aged, and the increased incidence of chronic morbidity, problems emerged that the individual elder's effort alone could not resolve. The CNS can not only educate the public concerning the financial needs of the elderly, but also assist the older adult to obtain available services. Gradually the government, in addition to providing income support and health care, has increased its involvement in education, crime prevention, nutrition, and other programs to assist the elderly.

Old Age, Survivors, and Disability Insurance (OASDI)

The Social Security Act was passed in 1935 in response to widespread economic hardship created by the Great Depression. The program started collecting payroll taxes in 1937 and first paid benefits in 1940. The program grew slowly: in 1950, only workers in commerce and industry were covered and the average monthly benefit for a retired couple was $72 (in 1986, average monthly benefit payments to recipients was $490) (Olson, 1986). In 1950, only 3.5 million persons received benefits as compared to 39 million beneficiaries in 1989 (U.S. Department of Health & Human Services [DHHS], 1989).

Amendments to the Social Security Act in 1950 expanded coverage and benefits levels. Disability insurance was added to the program in 1956, Medicare in 1965, and early retirement with actuarially reduced benefits in 1956 for women and in 1961 for men.

The last major revisions to the programs were in the seventies. In 1972, benefits were increased 20% and the law provided for automatic adjustment of benefits to reflect changes in the cost of living. This law was later modified to indicate how benefits are adjusted for inflation. In 1977, expanded eligibility as well as increased coverage and benefits in Medicare, Medicaid, and supplemental security income were made (Schiller & Snyder, 1981).

Coverage now extends to virtually all workers in the private sector of the economy. The largest uncovered group is among federal, state, and local governmental workers. Thus an estimated 90% of all workers turning 65 are entitled to benefits (U.S. Dept. of Health and Human Services [DHHS], 1988).

Old Age, Survivors, and Disability Insurance (OASDI) benefits were never meant to provide the total retirement income for an aged person. Yet, for many people this has in fact occurred. Benefits are based on average earnings over a period of years before retirement. Wives who have worked may receive their own benefits at 37.5% of the amount their husbands receive, whichever is the greater sum (DHHS, 1988). A widow more than 60 years old may collect her husband's benefits, prorated according to how long he collected them, or 100% of his benefits if he dies before retirement age (DHSS, 1988). If she has been getting her own benefits, she can continue to receive them if they are larger than the widow's benefit. Men who do not qualify on the basis of past employment, may also collect social security if their wife is eligible for benefits.

Those who want to continue in the workforce after retirement at age 65 may earn up to $8,400 without penalty (DHHS, 1988). This exclusionary amount increases annually, based on the cost of living. At age 70 an individual can return to full-time employment with no reduction in benefits.

The financing of OASDI is on a pay-as-you-go basis, with current benefits paid with current tax receipts. Thus benefits of retirees are paid by those in the work force, who in turn will have benefits paid by succeeding workers when they retire. Social Security is now building a reserve in trust funds to avoid later bankruptcy of the program. It remains to be seen if these reserves will be adequate to withstand prolonged or severe recessions or periods when earnings fail to grow as fast as prices. Some governmental reports include the reserve in the Social Security trust fund to mask the actual size of the federal deficit and others are suggesting reduction in Social Security payments because of possible depletion of the reserve funds (American Association of Retired Persons, 1990). There is little chance that this will take place but the American Association of Retired Persons suggests that it is beneficial that the situation is being discussed.

Supplemental Security Income (SSI)

Supplemental Security Income was initiated in 1974 to replace the federally reimbursed programs of aid to the aged, blind, and disabled administered by the states. It is a federally funded and administered program to provide a nationally uniform minimum income to aged, blind, and disabled persons. The major purpose of the program is to ensure a basic level of maintenance income for those not covered by Social Security as wage earners or dependents of wage earners, or those whose income is not sufficient to provide basic maintenance needs. This program is different than the Social Security Program and is administered by the Department of Health and Human Services (Baines, 1984). Despite the fact that many elderly qualify for this program, those on SSI live in poverty and destitution. However, recipients of SSI are eligible for Medicaid. The SSI program is also means or income tested. Therefore, persons must provide income information not required of those who receive Social Security, which is based on age and previous contributions. Consequently, the very wealthy as well as the poor receive Social Security payments, but only the very poor receive SSI.

Medicare

Medicare was enacted as part of the Social Security amendments of 1965 (Baines, 1984). This program was created to assist older people to meet the cost of health care. Despite its deficiencies, Medicare has provided a means to elders to obtain needed health care in times of escalating costs without decimating their total personal savings.

Medicare provides national health insurance to people 65 and older who are covered under the Social Security System, whether retired or not. People who are not part of the system can buy coverage for a monthly premium. In addition to the hospital insurance protection, each Medicare participant is also eligible to pay a monthly premium for medical insurance.

The hospital insurance plan covers the following, but is subject to certain deductibles and exclusions:

- unlimited hospitalization for approved care; paying a single annual deductible
- up to 150 days of care in a participating skilled nursing facility with no previous hospital stay
- unlimited home health care
- unlimited number of days of approved hospital care

The medical insurance plan covers, subject to deductibles, exclusions, and excessive charges:

- physician services
- outpatient care
- diagnostic tests procedures, x-rays
- home health aid services certified by physician as medically necessary

- physical and speech therapy
- expanded prescription drug benefits (DHHS, 1988, 1989)

Nurses should be aware that the deductible is approximately $500 each year for the hospital insurance, approximately $75 for medical insurance, and that the government pays only 80% of approved coverage. Many physicians refuse to participate, or collect more than allowed by Medicare, and the patient must pay or collect from supplemental insurance. The Medicare/Medicaid Handbook is published by the Health Care Financing Administration and can be obtained from the Social Security Administration. Changes occur frequently, therefore interested persons should review the latest edition of these booklets.

Medicaid

Medicaid is a joint federal and state program, administered by the states, that finances health services primarily for individuals, including the aged who are eligible to participate in the federally supported welfare programs: Aid to Families with Dependent Children and SSI. This program includes some health care services not included in the Medicare plan, such as dental and eye care.

Private Coverage and Out of Pocket Payments.

Private insurance covers a small percentage of health care expenses of the elderly. More than half of the elderly purchase private insurance to supplement Medicare coverage. The private health insurance coverage the elderly have purchased to supplement Medicare has frequently been duplicative, expensive, and has not provided adequate protection against extraordinary expenses.

Despite the availability of Medicare, Medicaid, and private insurance, the elderly still pay about 29% of their health care expenses directly out-of-pocket (Fischer, 1985). Nurses should encourage Medicare eligible elders to continue supplemental insurance despite the cost. It is necessary to have because of the noncovered costs in the Medicare programs. AARP has supplemental insurance, as do other agencies.

Housing Programs

Congress has passed a number of legislative acts designed to alleviate housing problems for older citizens. Among these programs is rental assistance for lower income families, the elderly, and the disabled. Direct loans at low interest are available to individuals to construct special rental housing facilities for the handicapped and the elderly. The federal government supports construction and rehabilitation of nursing homes. It subsidizes rental facilities that can be rented by the aged at rates below the existing market price. Information related to these housing programs can be obtained in most communities by contacting the local public housing authority, the Housing and Urban Development Area Office, or the Farmers Home Administration Office.

Social Services

The Older Americans Act of 1965 provided legislation for social services to the aged. Under this legislation, each state created an office to provide leadership in the coordination and development of services for the elderly. Some of the more significant programs and services carried out under this legislation are listed in Table 10.1.

Food Stamp Program

The food stamp program is a national program created to assist low income persons to obtain nutritious diets. The program is jointly administered by the Federal Department of Agriculture and by state or county social service departments. Special provisions set forth in this program address the needs of persons aged 60 or older. Food stamps issued to eligible elders can be used to purchase foodstuffs at authorized stores or to obtain meals at congregate nutrition programs and home delivered meal programs.

Research Agencies

The National Institute of Aging was established in 1974. The purpose is to conduct research on the biologic, demographic, and sociologic aspects of aging at its Gerontology Research Center in Baltimore, MD and to support research by others at universities and laboratories across the United States.

Within the National Institute for Mental Health, one division is devoted to problems of the aged: The Center for Studies of the Mental Health of the Aging. Its major role is to stimulate, coordinate, and support research training, and offer technical assistance relating to aging and mental health. Although it provides no monies for programs of service delivery to older people, it significantly affects the training of those working with elderly clients in community mental health centers and other service settings.

Community Resources

Over the years, it has become evident that governmental programs cannot provide all services needed by the aged. It has been demonstrated in many

Table 10.1
Social Services Provided by Older Americans Act of 1965

Senior Centers to meet the need for central place for older people to congregate, develop new interests, and socialize.

Nutrition Programs to provide nutritious means, in a centralized setting as well as to homebound elders. Recreational, educational, and health activities are incorporated in many sites as a regular part of the program.

Transportation Services have been provided to elders via special fares on existing public transportation systems and/or operation of specially equipped vehicles for the frail and handicapped.

Information and Referral Services were created to direct elders to the appropriate agency that provides needed services.

In-Home Services such as homemakers, telephone reassurance, chore maintenance, and home health aides were made available to enable older impaired individuals to remain living in the community.

arenas that private efforts can provide the same services at lower costs and without the involved "red tape" that some governmental programs have.

Transportation is an area in which the private sector, state and local governments, and federal government all have roles. Public ownership of mass transit has expanded over the past 30 years in both municipal and regional systems. The public systems have tried to restore the services dropped by the private companies, but economic problems at these levels of government have prevented implementation. In many urban areas, governments have provided Dial-A-Ride or similar services. These services should be continued and expanded where possible. The federal government has subsidized the development and operation of transit systems, but its aid has been focused mainly on high-use systems and routes.

For occasional travel, particularly in rural areas, the best solution is probably a friend or neighbor. Churches and community groups can help organize this approach by using sign-up sheets and recruiting volunteers to drive one day a week. A similar program, Neighborhood Watch, addresses the problem of crime prevention. Programs like Neighborhood Watch extend the capabilities of local police and provide a feeling of security for older people.

Education, recreation, and cultural activities are important for maintaining physical condition, mental alertness, and social contact. Education helps older people keep up with a rapidly changing world. Although advances in cable and satellite television systems promise a broad range of new educational experiences at home, the value of person-to-person discussion and the need to focus some educational activities on local issues mean that community discussion groups and other informal education will remain important.

Recreation and cultural activities are best managed on a local, nongovernmental basis because personal preference plays a large role in determining individual participation. A variety of activities run by different organizations or informal groups is likely to please more people than a large program run by government. For example, in the midwest, elders have formed square dance groups and chili gourmet groups that meet frequently for socialization, as well as to compete with similar local, regional, and state groups.

Churches serve the elderly in many ways. In addition to their primary role of providing organized worship, they sponsor many activities that bring elderly together with their peers as well as with younger people. Clergy are often excellent counselors and other members of the congregation are often willing to help older members in times of trouble.

Many communities have access to community resource books published by the United Way Fund. Area agencies on aging are excellent referral centers. Some of these agencies publish directories of services specifically for the elderly.

FUTURE TRENDS

Aging in America has changed what it means to be aged; the size of the elderly cohorts and even the process of aging itself have all undergone radical transformations. These changes are so rapid and pervasive that policy has not been able to keep pace. In fact, many critics maintain that present policies and programs have not kept up at all—that we deal with the aged's dilemmas in a fragmented way. Our current policies and programs are not thoughtfully planned out, creating a noncoherent policy on aging. Others believe our nation has responded to its seniors in a heroic way, unparalleled in any other country. They maintain that there exists a policy on aging, but its results have been so massive that our public policy for seniors is threatening to bust the budget.

Whatever view one takes, there is general agreement that the future policies for the aged will present a significant challenge to policymakers. Trends we see only vaguely today will present tremendous pressure on almost every social and economic structure in our nation in the near future. The future presents many unanswered questions. Will we be prepared to accommodate a populace that is more senior than junior? America will become more aged as the "baby boom generation becomes the senior boom." As medical technology eliminates the major causes of death, the "senior boom" could live to the venerable age of Methuselah.

Who will pay the bills? Can policymakers balance austerity and fiscal restraints and still meet the needs of the aged?

Such questions must be addressed with prudence and candor. What is needed is a foresighted approach to aging policy—a sober analysis of current trends, a realistic assessment of where these trends will lead, and development of a policy course that is compatible with the realities.

The following recommendations were made to address the financial constraints and budget problems of an aging population:

- In light of projected labor shortfalls in the upcoming decades, it is both desirable and necessary that elderly persons wishing to remain in the work force not be discouraged from doing so by government regulations. Toward this end, mandatory retirement should be eliminated.
- To improve the economic well-being of elderly Americans, high priority should be given to macroeconomic policies designed to control inflation.
- Private sector firms should allow all feasible restraint under existing circumstances to limit price increases.
- Governments at all levels should be wary of imposing any price, cost, or tax increases that would lead to increased inflation.
- Tax and economic policies must be pursued that increase the amount and improve the quality of productive capital available to the American worker.
- Steady monetary policy is needed to promote economic stability, reduce uncertainty, and facilitate retirement planning.
- The growth in federal budget outlays must be reduced to avoid neutralizing the positive effects of increased private saving.
- Regulations that unnecessarily inhibit the private sector's ability to meet society's needs should continue to be rescinded.
- To enhance increased labor force participation by older workers there should be a gradual elimination of disincentives in public and private retirement programs.
- Tax policy should be directed toward encouraging saving and investment in productive capital.
- A program of slow steady money growth, reduced marginal tax rates, and reductions in the growth of federal outlays is recommended for the control of inflation (Older Americans Report, 1989).

CONCLUSIONS

Gerontological nurses must be advocates of the people they serve. Future life-styles, well-being, and health for the aged will depend on more equal distribution of resources. The old saying "money isn't everything" may be true, but it certainly ensures security, power, and the ability to purchase health care and services. This chapter analyzed a wide variety of social, health, and income support programs available to elders. Many of these programs are fragmented, poorly distributed geographically, and difficult for the elder to understand.

Nurses have an important role in explaining benefits to elders and referring them and their families to services available. Some economists believe that the next decade in health care delivery will be one of consolidation and coordination of services with emphasis on determining priorities and making current programs more available. The nurse can be an important catalyst in seeing that the elderly benefit.

REFERENCES

American Association of Retired Persons. (1987). *Understanding senior housing.* Washington, DC: American Association of Retired persons.

American Association of Retired Persons. (1988). *A profile of older Americans.* Washington, DC: American Association of Retired Persons.

American Association of Retired Persons. (1990). *AARP Bulletin 31*(3), 10-12.

Baines, E. (1984). Medicare vs medicaid: Similarities and differences. *Journal of Gerontological Nursing, 70,* 36-37.

England, R. (1987). Greener era for gray America. *Insight, 3,* 7.

Fischer, C. (1985). Differences by age groups in health care spending. *Health Care Financing Review, 1,* 94.

Hendricks, J., & Calasanti, T. (1986). Social policy and ageing in the United States. In C. Phillipson & A. Walker (Eds.), *Aging and social policy.* Aldershot, UK: Gower.

Longino, C. (1988). Who are the oldest Americans? *The Gerontologist, 28*(4), 515-523.

Older Americans Report (1980, June, 24).

Older Americans Report (1989, December, 2).

Olson, L. (1986). *Policy for the elderly and the economy.* Paper presented at the Commission on Implications for the Economy of an Aging Population, White House Conference on Aging, Washington, DC.

Schiller, B. R., & Snyder, D. C. (1981, September). Linkages between private pensions and Social Security reforms. Study prepared for U.S. Senate, Special Committee on Aging, Washington, DC.

Selkert, L., & Broski, D. (1988). An aging society: Implications for health care needs. *Geriatrics & Gerontology, 8,* 197-148.

Strumpf, N. E. (1988). A new age for elderly care. *Nursing and Health Care, 8,* 445-448.

U.S. Bureau of the Census (1987). *Statistical abstract of the United States* (108th ed.). Washington, DC: Government Printing Office.

U.S. Department of Health and Human Services, Social Security Administration. (1988) *A message about medicare.* Baltimore, MD: Social Security Administration.

U.S. Department of Health and Human Services. (1989). *The medicare handbook* (No. HCFA 10050). Baltimore, MD: Health Care Financing Administration.

U.S. Senate Special Committee on Aging. (1979). *Part I, Developments in aging: 1978.* Washington, DC: Government Printing Office.

U.S. Senate Special Committee on Aging. (1986). Developments in aging: 1985. Vols. 1, 2, 3. Washington, DC: Government Printing Office.

11

Living Environments of Older Adults

FRANCES M. CARP

Objectives: At the completion of this chapter, the reader will be able to:

(1) Analyze the distribution of older adults in the variety of living environments within which they lead their lives.
(2) Empathize with the importance of independence to all older persons and for the large majority, the strong attachment to the ordinary homes and neighborhoods within which they live.
(3) Critique the merits of special housing for the elderly.
(4) Evaluate the causes and effects of institutionalization.
(5) Apply nursing strategies to maximize each individual's sense of competence and independence to the extent possible.

INTRODUCTION

The living environment (housing and neighborhood) is a vital influence on the well-being of older persons (Carp, 1987a). Only through transactions with the environment can an individual meet the basic needs necessary to life maintenance (e.g., food, health care). If life is to have acceptable quality and not be mere existence, the so-called "higher order" needs (e.g., interaction with other persons) must be met also. Autonomy is a fundamental human drive; for all normal adults the most central motive is to be able to meet their own needs independently (Maslow, 1954).

The crucial relationship seems to be the degree of congruence or "fit" of the individual's needs and capabilities with the demands and resources of the environmental context (Carp, 1987a). As human beings age, decrements in sensory-motor abilities occur and chronic health problems tend to accumulate, reducing the competence of the individual in efforts to cope with the environment. On the other hand, human needs—both life-maintenance and psychological—continue throughout the life span (e.g., persons do not cease needing companionship simply as a consequence of growing old). The problem of housing the older person is one of matching the demands of the living environment with the person's capabilities and matching the needs of the person with the environment's resources, in order that the individual is able to meet both life-maintenance and higher-order needs through his or her own efforts in transactions with the environment. If the individual is unable to achieve these goals, others will need to assist the person to obtain acceptable living arrangements.

Most older adults live in ordinary houses and apartments in their communities. For a long time both social programs and research focused on those in special housing and in institutions. As a result, generalizations about "the elderly" often were made on the basis of information about small and unrepresentative segments of that population. Recently attention has turned to the housing and living environments of the majority (Carp, 1987a). This chapter is organized to examine the living environments of the elderly, including special housing arrangements and the effect of institutionalization. It also includes nursing strategies that could assist older adults in meeting their housing needs.

HOUSING OF OLDER AMERICANS

Homes They Own

Most older citizens are homeowners. About 80% of persons 60 and older own their homes and almost two thirds of them are free of mortgages (Struyk & Soldo, 1980). More than a quarter of the nation's total number of homeowners are elderly. Seventy percent of elderly homeowners live in single-family houses and 30% live in other types of housing, mainly low-rise apartments, condominiums, and mobile homes.

Home ownership is a major economic asset (which many younger Americans are finding difficult to attain). In addition, for many elderly the home is seen as a major part of their legacy to their children. Home ownership has other important symbolic values (Csikszentmihalyi & Rochberg-Holton, 1981). One's own home is a place where personal and family treasures are stored, a milieu that brings back memories of important past events with family and friends.

Older homeowners are more likely than younger homeowners to live in houses that are themselves old and in need of repair. For example, they occupy 44% of the homeowner units in the United States that have multiple deficiencies as defined for the Annual Housing Survey conducted by the Bureau of the Census (Struyk & Soldo, 1980).

Rented Facilities

The quality of the housing of the smaller number of elderly renters is even less adequate than that of homeowners (Mayer & Lee, 1980). Although the renters look somewhat differently at specific physical qualities of their housing (O'Bryant & Wolf, 1983) (perhaps due to a difference in responsibility for upkeep, etc.), they too are loathe to leave it.

Attachment to Place by Homeowners and Renters

Despite the poorer quality of the housing of the elderly, the fact that they pay a higher proportion of their incomes for housing than do younger generations (Christensen & Carp, 1987), and other problems the elderly may encounter in the community, most older persons want to maintain an independent living situation as long as possible, preferably where they are (McAuley & Blieszner, 1985; Newman, Zais, & Struyk, 1984). This "attachment to place" is expressed in behavior: One study found that about two thirds of people 60 and older had lived in the same community for 21 or more years and 46% had lived in the same house during all of that time (American Association of Retired Persons, 1982).

Congregate Housing

Though much attention has been paid to public housing facilities for the elderly and to retirement residences, very small percentages of the older population live in them (Carp, 1987a) and in a real sense, their tenants are also "community residents." Such special housing arrangements are satisfactory for most individuals who choose and are selected to live in them and for whom, therefore, the person-environment fit is good (Carp, 1987b). The data indicate, however, that this type of housing is not suitable to all elderly persons and may be deleterious to some.

People go into congregate housing (facilities that provide services as well as shelter) of one type or another for various reasons (Streib, 1990). Declining health, reduced competence in coping with the former living environment in performing the tasks of daily living, constriction in the social network of family and friends (due to loss by death and to difficulties in getting together because of reductions in personal mobility and in transportation), and the increased risk of medical emergencies are factors that influence the decision to move to a new housing environment with supportive services, safety arrangements, and proximity to age peers. Usually the decision is influenced by other people. Most often, the older person moves in order to allay the worries of family members. Sometimes a physician or friend suggests or urges the advantages of such a milieu.

There are trade-offs, however, that make it more attractive to most people to grow old in their own apartments or houses. They may not want to be thrown together with persons not of their own choosing. Privacy would be jeopardized. Activities such as meals, scheduled by others, might not fit personal preferences. In general, some degree of autonomy would be lost.

Institutionalization

At any given time 4%-5% of persons aged 65 and older are in nursing homes, and this figure has remained the same in many studies using various sets of data over the past 20 years. With age, the chance of institutionalization increases from about 2% for those less than 75 years old to as much as 16% for those 85 and older.

Older persons are strongly averse to institutionalization and generally it is followed by their physical and cognitive decline (Pastalan, 1983). Some cases require care that can be provided only in a nursing home or similar facility. An unknown but probably significant percentage of elderly persons currently in these settings, however, are there primarily due to lack of other options, such as an available caregiver.

Some could no longer maintain independent living in the housing that was available to them and were unable to locate less demanding environments more congruent with their remaining abilities that would enable them to meet their own needs. The concept of "Smart Housing" (Lesnoff-Caravaglia, 1988) that takes advantage of human factors information and modern technology to design housing congruent with failing competencies and prosthetics for common problems in daily living could enable many elders to maintain independent community living, which they so greatly favor, for much longer.

For others currently institutionalized, the social support system could not meet the economic, physical, and emotional demands that would be involved by keeping the older person in the community. Often communities lack in-home services that would enable an older person to cope in her or his own home; often older persons and their social networks are not aware that such services exist, cannot afford to pay for them, or do not know how to make use of them.

As the population continues to age and retirement age creeps downward (U.S. Bureau of the Census, 1984), two generations in retirement are no longer novelties; in coming years they will be of more frequent occurrence. Because income is normally reduced significantly at retirement, adult children who are themselves retired may have difficulty in caring for their parents—physically, financially or both. Working-age children of the elderly often are members of two-job couples or are trying to cope as single, working parents. They are caught in the middle, with the needs of their parents on one side and the needs of their children on the other. This dual demand involves not only financial considerations but also those of time and energy. Priorities are difficult to set in such instances.

Usually it is not lack of love and concern that determine the failure of a child to take an aging parent into her or his own home. Much more often it is lack of space, time, and energy, and money for assistance in care of the older person. Currently, funds are available for the care of old people in nursing homes that are not available for their care in their children's homes. If these funding policies and practices could be altered, providing younger families the financial resources to purchase the help they need, it seems likely that some presently institutionalized elders could move out into the homes of relatives or at least into the community.

Adult Day Care

Day-care centers for the elderly may be as important as those for young children. Two-career couples and single, working parents cannot safely leave a frail and perhaps confused older person alone at home during working hours. Day care may solve this problem, enabling acceptance of the parent into the home. Even—or perhaps particularly—the family caregiver who is at home all day with the aged relative also needs the respite that day care of the older person can make possible. The emotional and psychological as well as physical drain of caregiving to an old person, particularly one who is cognitively impaired, is tremendous. Stress on the caregiver may jeopardize not only his or her own physical and mental health but also the well-being of the family.

In addition, the day care may benefit the older person, especially if she or he has been isolated and lacking in stimulation. Some elderly, confused persons can "graduate up" from day care focused at the level of reality-testing to normal senior-center participation after a period in the former, during which the person experienced both appropriate sensory-motor stimulation and interpersonal interactions (Zawadski & Ansak, 1983). The "senility" exhibited earlier stemmed at least in part from stimulus deprivation, loneliness, and perhaps depression rather than being due to irreversible decrements in central nervous system functioning.

Summary

Obviously it is also imperative to expand and publicize community-based programs to older persons in their relatives' homes or in their own. Institutionalization can be dramatically delayed and reduced by programs of nursing care, homemaking, shopping, personal service (e.g., supervising bathing) and friendly visiting into the homes of frail elderly persons. If the service-provider visits are scheduled ahead, they can also provide a period of respite for caregivers otherwise homebound by the elder.

It is difficult to fund such programs. Day care has been demonstrated cost-effective (Zawadski & Ansak, 1983). If Medicare policies, alone, were changed to allow payment for health care services in homes, this could result in a drastic reduction in the number of institutionalized elderly (Handler, 1981).

NURSING HOME SELECTION

Even with changes in fiscal policy, implementation and expansion of both day-care and in-home services along with public information about them, there will always be some elderly persons who require the type of long-term care that only an institution can provide.

In any decision, even this one, the older person should have as much participation as possible and she or he should have careful preparation for the move (Pastalan, 1983). The more frail the person, the more fraught with hazard is any move. The old are especially vulnerable to the move to a nursing home because they almost universally view it as "the beginning of the end". The more the patient-to-be can feel part of the decision-making process, the less will be the threat to his or her autonomy. In addition, the more the older adult can know about the new environment, prior to moving there permanently, the easier will be the transition.

Usually the person who needs nursing home placement is not capable of investigating the possibilities and weighing the pros and cons of each on his or her own. Some have made the decision for themselves by taking up residence, earlier, in a facility that includes all levels of residence and care. More commonly, relatives gather the information and assume responsibility for the decision. Most younger adults are not well versed concerning nursing homes and the crises that precipitate such placement of an older relative leave the younger persons in less than optimal emotional condition, so that professional assistance with information, advice, and thinking through the implications can be most helpful.

Ideally, the professional person assisting the family would be independent of any particular caregiving institution. It is important to place the well-being of the older person at the center, to consider her or his needs and capabilities and to figure out where they can best be met and accommodated. Nursing homes have their own selection standards, usually including space availability, the applicant's financial resources and the required level of care (often defined in terms of registered nurse and nurse aide hours) needed. Some homes do not admit persons with insufficient funds to pay full cost for as long as the person may live. Some will not take a patient who may run out of funds and become dependent on Medicaid. It is particularly difficult to find a bed for a person who must enter a nursing home on Medicaid payment alone and the quality of nursing homes that will accept the person who is dependent on Medicaid often have poor standards of care.

Placement cannot occur if the institution refuses, but willingness of the staff to admit an individual does not mean that this is the best place for the older person. This difference in emphasis or point-of-view is similar to that between a job-recruiter for a particular business and a career counselor at a college. Neither function is right or wrong; both are essential; they are simply different.

The "placement counselor" for the older person and family can help by providing information on institutions that are within the budget available and provide the necessary level of care. (Visiting the unaffordable only causes regret and guilt.) Certainly the professional person should have information on the basic considerations of cleanliness, health care, and accident hazards of any institution to be discussed. This should include not only knowledge about federal and state guidelines but also be based on inquiries through professional channels and personal visits at unscheduled times.

Although taste buds are less sensitive as we age, food takes on increasing importance as other sources of sensory gratification are lost. (Observe the gathering of wheelchairs at the door of the dining room well ahead of time.) The kitchen and food service are vitally important. Meals should be not only nutritionally adequate but also appropriately hot or cold, tasteful, and attractively presented.

The counselor can also bring to attention such matters as location and characteristics of management style and resident population. Easy access for family members and friends may (or may not) be of primary importance. A confused elder Catholic may find inscrutable the Passover observances at a predominantly Jewish institution. Programs available in a nursing home should be considered, in view of the proclivities of the particular prospective resident. Stimulus deprivation often mimics clinical depression (Holahan & Holahan, 1987) and a person will participate in or observe only those activities that are of interest to him or her.

On the Streets

No good estimates are available regarding the proportion of older persons among today's frightening numbers of homeless people. The success of the 1990 Census in counting them remains to be seen. Observation suggests that a significant percentage of the "bag ladies" and "street bums" are members of the elder population and among its members most at risk in every way.

Location of the Elderly in Today's Cities

Like other age groups, most of the elderly live in metropolitan areas. Three quarters of persons 60 and older live in urban areas (central cities and suburbs of them) (National Research Council, 1988).

Suburbanites

The suburbs are "graying," due more to "aging in place" than to recent moves. The tendency began after World War II and is expected to continue well into the next century (National Research Council, 1988). This flight to the suburbs may reflect "push" factors from central cities such as lack of low-cost housing, less attractive housing stock, undesired neighborhood alterations, and distance from family members, as well as "pull" factors from suburbs such as newer and more available housing, greater proximity to family members, less traffic congestion, and lower crime rate (Gutowsky & Field, 1979).

Once in the suburbs, people tended to remain there as they aged. One study showed that among suburban residents over age 75, 40% had bought their home more than 25 years earlier, compared to 14% of suburbanites aged 55-64 (Gutowsky & Field). About 60% of the "young-old" (55-75) and 45% of the "old-old" (75+) now live in the suburbs (National Research Council, 1988).

The suburban environment may present difficulties as people grow older (Carp, 1988). Facilities for shopping and meeting other needs necessary for maintaining independent living are sparse in suburban areas, usually incorporated into widely spaced malls or shopping centers. Physicians' offices usually are in central areas. Family and friends may live at some distance.

As long as suburban residents can drive their own automobiles, they can go wherever and whenever they choose in order to meet their subsistence, social, and emotional needs. With age, however, there is increasing likelihood that the driver's license will not be renewed, due largely to ocular changes (Bailey & Sheedy, 1988). Some older persons voluntarily give up driving at night even before their licenses are revoked, due to their own perception of visual difficulties, or limit their driving to the immediate area (Carp, 1988). For suburban residents, loss of automobile drivership sharply curtails the ability to obtain the resources requisite to continue independent living in the community, as well as social and psychological needs.

Public transportation is designed and scheduled for its primary consumer, the work commuter. Transit systems often do not meet the travel needs of retired suburbanites. Persons who have driven cars all their lives do not know how to use public transit. More important, older persons are more at risk of criminal victimization while on a trip by public transit (including the walk to the stop, the wait there, and the return walk back home); design features of vehicles and boarding areas pose difficult tasks and risks of accident for aging bodies; and the speed of operation is incongruent with a universal concomitant of aging— slowing of response (Carp, 1988).

Walking is becoming increasingly popular as a means of exercise appropriate to older persons but it is not useful as a means of transportation for elders in the suburbs. For example, shopping for food is a universal need for those living independently in the community. It is the rare suburban resident of any age who can fetch groceries on foot. The task is, of course, more daunting for the old (Carp, 1988).

Central City Residents

The old poor of the central cities are among those left behind as the more affluent and mobile flee urban decay for the safer and more attractive suburbs. The jury is not yet in regarding the suitability of central cities as residential areas for the elderly.

Some studies point to the negative characteristics of high crime rates, noise, traffic, and transiency as predominant. Others report that central-city elderly enjoy more active, autonomous, and satisfying use of their time, space, and social networks than do age peers in outer suburbs; and point to the important advantages of familiarity or "belongingness," availability of services and amenities, and the stimulation and vitality of the atmosphere (Carp, 1987a). As in most other instances, it probably is a matter of individual and environment congruence; and life in the central city is quite different for the tenant of an apartment in a new high-rise building than for the tenant of "skid row" accommodations or even for the tenant of a Single Room Occupancy (SRO) hotel. Only recently have the latter two been distinguished and SRO housing has been shown to be a viable alternative for marginal segments of the elderly population (Ehrlich, 1986). Nevertheless, SRO housing stock tends to be in poor repair and tenure is insecure because buildings are often torn down or rehabilitated for other uses (Weeden, Newcomer, & Byerts, 1986).

MIGRATION

Patterns of the Elderly

Older persons are less likely than younger ones to change their places of residence. For example, in the year 1983, about 5% of Americans older than 65 moved, compared to the national average of 17% for all ages (U.S. Senate Special Committee on Aging, 1985-1986). Most older persons who move do not go far; more than half stay in the same county; only 20% move to another state (National Research Council, 1988). Florida and California are the top two destination states, with Arizona a distant third (Rogers, 1989). Migration is more than a "numbers game": the needs and capabilities of movers vary. For example, the New York-to-Florida migration stream includes mostly retirement-age persons drawn by amenities, whereas the counter stream from Florida to New York is older and appears to be assistance-related (e.g., widows returning home after bereavement) (Rogers, 1989).

Patterns of the Younger Population

Migration patterns of younger people influence the living environments of the old. The movement of younger persons to metropolitan areas has left behind high concentrations of the elderly in 500 rural counties. The effects of this differential mobility have been felt most strongly in America's heartland. Of the 10 states with the highest percentages of elderly residents (Florida, Arkansas, Rhode Island, Iowa, Missouri, South Dakota, Nebraska, Kansas, Pennsylvania, and Massachusetts), 6 are agricultural midwestern states (National Research Council, 1988).

The Resulting Remnant of Rural Aged

Living environments of the rural old are objectively far inferior to those of their urban and suburban counterparts (Carp, 1987a). Housing is older, of lower value, in poorer physical condition, and more in need of repair, and is more likely to lack basic facilities such as plumbing.

The rural elderly tend to be in poorer health and to have less easy access to health care than do their age peers elsewhere. Transportation for shopping and other basic needs is poor. Facilities and services are too far from home for walking, roads tend to be narrow and poorly surfaced, and public transportation tends to be poor or absent (Bell & Revis, 1983). Services for the elderly are lacking or insufficient. Many rural elderly are spatially isolated from their children and other family members, and neighbors are distant, so meeting sociability needs is difficult. Loneliness, a problem among the old in general, is more pronounced among rural residents.

NURSING STRATEGIES

There is no one uniform role for nurses in regard to older persons. It depends upon the specific position in which the nurse is employed (e.g., internist's office, general hospital, long-term care, independent community practice) and the type of older persons who comprise the clientele that is served. One generalization can be made: Nurses—like all other persons in "helping" professions—are likely to form their conceptions of "the elderly" on the basis of atypical groups.

The problem of "agism" is now widely recognized as a problem both in gerontological service and research. Earlier, mention was made of how the misconceptions of "good" housing for the elderly, based on studies of select and not representative groups, led to incorrect assumptions about the majority. It is important to meet each older person with an open mind rather than with preconceptions based on his or her birth date. Competencies vary widely within any age group and there is considerable overlap between age groups.

In any relationship, a professional person does well to approach each older person as another human being with needs very similar to one's own. The most fundamental drive that we humans share is that for independence: awareness of this common trait is helpful. Because older persons are more likely to be suffering losses—in sensory-motor capacities, physical health, beloved persons, and social networks—they are perhaps especially sensitive to implied reductions in their status. This is sometimes done with the best of intentions. A common example is for a professional person a generation or two younger to address an older client or patient immediately by her or his first name. Cordiality is intended, but often this practice is perceived as a "put down" by the elder. Miss Manners or Emily Post might better be followed: Allow the senior person to determine the level of familiarity in address.

In the best of all possible worlds, there would be "housing counsel teams" available to all older persons that would work with each individual to define the parameters of the environment having the best "fit" to his or her capacities and preferences and, if a change is indicated, to locate and gain admission to a setting of that description. Such teams should include nurses as experts in providing nursing care services.

Meanwhile a goal that can guide each nurse in any setting, is to maximize the congruence between person and environment, either by suggesting or making alterations in the environment, or by suggesting and helping to locate a better one. As individual citizens and through professional organizations, nurses can significantly influence legislation and policy that expand and develop programs of service to enable oldsters to do what they most want—to remain in their community as long as possible.

SUMMARY

The living environment is highly important to older adults and is closely related to their well-being. The vital relationship between person and environment is the degree of congruence between them. For any individual, the crucial task is to match her or his needs and capabilities with the resources and demands of the environment. Older people strongly value their independence and want to remain in the community, preferably in their own homes. Life quality could be improved and premature institutionalization avoided by integrated systems of in-home services and care. For those who cannot meet their needs independently, living with children would be a more viable option if policies were changed to allow payment for their care to families, if day care were available and if respite were provided for caregivers. If institutionalization becomes necessary, care should be given to the continuing needs for person-environment congruence and for a sense of personal control. To the greatest extent possible the older person should be part of the relocation decision and she or he should be thoroughly prepared for a change in living environments.

REFERENCES

American Association of Retired Persons. (1982). *A profile of older Americans.* Washington, DC: American Association of Retired Persons.

Bailey, I. L., & Sheedy, J. E. (1988). Vision screening for driver licensure. In National Research Council, *Transportation in an aging society* (pp. 294-324). Washington, DC: National Research Council.

Bell, W. B., & Revis, J. S. (1983). *Transportation for older Americans.* Washington, DC: U.S. Department of Transportation.

Carp, F. M. (1987a). Environment and aging. In D. Stokols & I. Altman (Eds.), *Handbook of environmental psychology* (pp. 329-360). New York: John Wiley.

Carp, F. M. (1987b). The impact of planned housing. In V. Regnier & J. Pynoos (Eds.), *Housing the aged* (pp. 43-79). New York: Elsevier.

Carp, F. M. (1988). Significance of mobility for the well-being of the elderly. In National Research Council, *Transportation in an aging society: Vol. 2. Technical papers* (pp. 13-20. Washington, DC: National Research Council.

Christensen, D. L., & Carp, F. M. (1987). PEQI-based predictors of the residential satisfaction of older women. *Journal of Environmental Psychology, 7,* 45-64.

Csikszentmihalyi, M., & Rochberg-Holton, E. (1981). *The meaning of things: Domestic symbols and the self.* Cambridge, UK: Cambridge University Press.

Ehrlich, P. (1986). Hotels, rooming houses, shared housing, and other housing options for the marginal elderly. In R. Newcomer, M. Lawton, & T. Byerts (eds.), *Housing an aging society.* New York: Van Nostrand Reinhold.

Gutowsky, M., & Field, T. (1979). *The graying of suburbia.* Washington, DC: The Urban Institute.

Handler, B. (1981). *Housing needs of the elderly.* Ann Arbor: University of Michigan, National Policy Center on Housing and Living Arrangements for Older Americans.

Holahan, C. K., & Holahan, C. J. (1987). Self-efficacy, social support, and depression in aging. *Journal of Gerontology, 42,* 65-68.

Lesnoff-Caravaglia, G. (Ed.) (1988). Technology, environments, the process of aging [Special issue]. *International Journal of Technology and Aging, 1.*

Maslow, A. H. (1954). *Motivation and personality. New York: Harper.*

Mayer, N., & Lee, O. (1980). *The effectiveness of federal home repair and improvement programs in meeting elderly home-owner needs.* Washington, DC: The Urban Institute.

McAuley, W. J., & Blieszner, R. (1985). Selection of long-term care arrangements by older community residents. *The Gerontologist, 25,* 188-193.

National Research Council. (1988). *Transportation in an aging society.* Washington, DC: National Research Council.

Newman, S. J., Zais, J., & Struyk, R. (1984). Housing older America. In I. Altman, M. Lawton, & J. Wohlwill (Eds.), *Elderly people and their environments* (Vol. 7, pp. 17-55). New York: Plenum.

O'Bryant, S. L., & Wolf, S. M. (1983). Explanation of housing satisfaction of older home-owners and renters. *Research on Aging, 5,* 217-233.

Pastalan, L. A. (1983). Environmental displacement: A literature reflecting old person-environment transactions. In G. D. Rowles & R. J. Ohta (Eds.), *Aging and milieu: Environmental perspectives on growing old* (pp. 189-203). New York: Academic Press.

Rogers, A. (1989). Growth, concentration and temperature. *Research on Aging, 11,* 3-32.

Streib, G. F. (1990). Congregate housing: People, places, policies. In D. Tilson (Ed.), *Aging in place: Supporting the frail elderly in residential environments.* Glenview, IL: Scott, Foresman.

Struyk, R. J., & Soldo, B. J. (1980). *Improving the elderly's housing.* Cambridge, MA: Ballinger.

U.S. Bureau of the Census. (1984). *Projections of the population of the U.S. by age, sex, & race: 1983-2080.* Washington, DC: Government Printing Office.

U.S. Senate Special Committee on Aging (1985-1986). *Aging America.* Washington, DC: Government Printing Office.

Weeden, J. P., Newcomer, R. J., & Byerts, T. O. (1986). *Housing and shelter for frail and nonfrail elders.* In R. Newcomer, M. Lawton, & T. Byerts (Eds.). *Housing an Aging Society* (pp. 181-199). New York: Van Nostrand Reinhold.

Zawadski, R. T., & Ansak, M. L. (1983). Consolidating community-based long-term care, *The Gerontologist, 23,* 364-369.

12

Social Problems in Aging

ELIZABETH CLIPP

Objectives: Objectives for this chapter include the following:

(1) Evaluate demographic patterns associated with the older population, specifically, the "oldest-old" segment.
(2) Analyze the relationship between the shifting demography and
social problems in later life.
(3) Evaluate the impact of caregiving on the caregiver.
(4) Analyze the theoretical controversy in the elder abuse literature
surrounding the issue of dependency.
(5) Apply nursing care strategies in the process of treatment for
abused elders.

INTRODUCTION

All phases of life are marked by social changes that hold potential for adverse
health consequences. During later life, however, effective functioning is particularly challenged because older persons are at increased risk not only for
specific chronic conditions, but for multiple, interacting health conditions as
well. Factors contributing to social problems may stem from the individual, the
family, or the community and therefore require multidisciplinary approaches
to intervention. For example, the high incidence of role change and loss in later
life may decrease availability of social support. Although the majority of
elderly so affected do not qualify for psychiatric diagnoses, they may be more

AUTHOR'S NOTE: The author recognizes with gratitude the assistance of Linda K. George,
PhD, Duke University, Durham, NC, in writing this chapter.

vulnerable to the development of stress symptoms or stress-related disorders. Intervention efforts may need to target individual coping as well as formal and informal systems of support.

The impact of social problems in later life is directly related to the dramatically shifting age structure in our society. Nurse specialists committed to providing solutions to elderly clients should be aware that individuals over the age of 65 constitute the most rapidly growing segment in our society, currently about 11% of the American population. This is the largest percentage of elderly in United States history and is expected to increase to 26% in the next decade (Delafuente & Stewart, 1988; Matteson & McConnel, 1988). Older individuals are more likely than younger individuals to be poor, female, widowed, and suffering from several chronic diseases (Allan & Brotman, 1981). Moreover, by the end of this century, the greatest population increase will occur among the "oldest-old"; this has important implications for health care delivery because this group is more vulnerable than others to disability—physical, emotional, and social changes that necessitate care of the individual by family and society.

Some chapters in this text have emphasized the physiologic and psychologic changes that often accompany the aging process. This chapter is organized around two serious social problems in aging whose prevalence and impact are proportional to the changing demography: caregiver burden and elder abuse. These problems cause concern at any age but tend to be more severe in the elderly due to increased vulnerability and diminished adaptive reserve. Each problem will be discussed in terms of relevant research and implications for clinical practice. Psychotropic drug use among family caregivers will be examined as a potential coping method. Of special interest is information that will provide incentives to nurse specialists to target caregiver burden and elder abuse within a social component of geriatric assessment for the purpose of increasing the amount of tangible assistance and emotional support available to elderly patients. Other social problems such as attitudes, agism, poverty, dependency, and housing problems have been well described in this volume and elsewhere (Carnevali & Patrick, 1986; Gioiella & Bevil, 1985; Matteson & McConnell, 1988).

CAREGIVER BURDEN

Due to the graying of America, there are more elderly persons requiring varying levels of health care and assistance with activities of daily living. At the same time, changes in access to health care and increased labor force participation of women have placed great demands on the family and community to provide care for disabled elders. Although the notion of family caregiving is not new, demographic, social, and financial trends in our society create new concerns about the survival of caregivers. Currently, there are 7 million households caring for a disabled elderly person each year; females in this country can expect to spend 18 years of life caring for an aging parent; 80% of family caregivers to the elderly provide care 7 days a week; and, one out of five caregivers of elderly relatives has been providing care for more than 5 years (Select Committee on Aging, 1987). Compounding this growing social problem is the fact that federal funding for elder services in 1989 was less than half what it was in 1977 (Older Womens League, 1989).

The physical, emotional, economic, and social toll of providing care to a family member is usually quite high due to what has come to be called "caregiver burden" (Litman, 1971; Morycz, 1980; Robinson, 1983; Thompson & Doll, 1982; Zarit, Reever, & Bach-Peterson, 1980). Caregiver burden refers to the physical, psychological, financial, and emotional problems that can affect caregivers as they care for an impaired older person. Because of the diversity of issues implied by the notion of burden, definitions range from emotional overload (Thompson & Doll) to stress related to discontinuity of past habits and daily routine (Fatheringham, Skelton, & Haddinott, 1972).

Caregiver needs arise from feelings of competing demands and anticipatory bereavement, and from the strenuous physical labor required to care for an incompetent or bedbound patient. Many care recipients manifest aspects of their illness that have negative implications for caregivers' health, such as outbursts of hostility, wandering, and incontinence. These burdens are understandably worse for caregivers who are in poor health or struggling with financial problems. It is fairly common knowledge that many caregivers work without respite, often in virtual isolation. They struggle daily to manage the loneliness, exhaustion, and anguish of watching the physical or cognitive decline of a loved one. In the case of dementia, studies suggest that as a patient's health deteriorates, a crucial factor for caregiver well-being is adequate social support—namely, a supportive spouse or other household member (Cantor, 1983; Hanson, Sauer, & Seelbach, 1983). In fact, lack of a close confiding relationship has been identified as a factor that increases vulnerability to depression in the face of adversity (Lowenthal & Haven, 1968). As such, the corrosive effects of caregiving may be mediated or buffered (Dean & Lin, 1977; Ward, 1985) when supportive ties are available. Supported caregivers are provided with feelings of personal affection, opportunities to relate meaningfully to others, and tangible assistance during times of need or crisis. Although policymakers have begun to examine the problems caregivers face, they have virtually ignored the critical need of caregiver support.

CAREGIVING RESEARCH

Investigations of the caregiving experience are relatively new, with most studies emerging in the last decade. The majority of work has been cross-sectional and based on small samples. One line of research, however, conducted at Duke University, will be highlighted because of its substantive and methodological contributions to the understanding of the impact of caregiving upon the caregiver.

Since 1983 at Duke's Center for the Study of Aging and Human Development, longitudinal studies of caregiving have focused on the social and psychological problems associated with providing care to demented older adults (George, 1984). The studies are based on a sample of 510 caregivers, tested at two points in time, one year apart, using a comprehensive battery of survey instruments. This is a self-selected sample, generated through the Duke Family Support Program, a statewide technical assistance program for families of memory-impaired older adults. Although not random, the sample is large, heterogeneous, and from a broad geographic area. Most of the sample consisted of elderly females providing in-home care. The results of the analyses may not be generalizable to minority caregivers because there are few black caregivers in the study. The results should, however, suggest whether or not to test similar hypotheses in minority groups.

Initial analyses examined the impact of caregiving on four measures of caregiver well-being or conversely, caregiver burden: physical health, mental health, social participation, and financial resources (Duke Center for Aging, 1979; George & Bearon, 1980). Levels of caregiver well-being were compared to available population norms to determine the degree to which caregiving carried a burden relative to random community samples of elderly. Characteristics of the caregiver, patient, and caregiving context also were examined as predictors or correlates of caregiver well-being. Findings from this program of research with implications for nursing practice will be summarized in the following paragraphs. More detailed accounts of these analyses appear in Clipp and George (1990a, 1990b), Colerick [Clipp] and George (1986), George (1987), George and Gwyther (1986).

In terms of physical health and financial resources, caregivers in the Duke study appeared similar to random samples of community elderly. Caregivers were, however, carrying heavy burdens in the areas of mental health and participation in social and recreational activities. Specifically, caregivers averaged three times as many stress symptoms as the comparison samples and were less able to pursue social activities at preferred levels. As situational demands increased, caregivers relinquished much that interested them in terms of activities and hobbies. Caregivers who received adequate help from their support networks, however, were able to participate in social activities on a more frequent basis (George, 1984). Finally, we learned that caregiver burden is greatest for spouses and in-home providers and for caregivers with perceptions of inadequate support from friends and family (George & Gwyther, 1986).

Subsequent analyses focused on caregivers who institutionalized their patients between Time One and Time Two. We believed it important, from both clinical and practical perspectives, to understand the psychosocial influences on caregivers' placement decisions. Characteristics of the patient and the caregiver were identified as potential predictors of institutionalization. Surprisingly, we found that the decision to institutionalize is more strongly influenced by factors in the social environment (e.g., patient-caregiver relationship, caregiver's need for social support, caregiving context) than by the physical condition of the patient (Colerick [Clipp] & George, 1986).

In terms of social support, caregivers in the Duke sample reported receiving very little help from either formal or informal service providers. Although more caregivers reported receiving help from family and friends than from formal sources, levels of objective social support were low in absolute terms. Moreover, caregivers with full-time, in-home responsibilities were least likely to use formal service programs and reported the lowest levels of objective social support. More than half of the caregivers reported needing additional help with their role (George, 1987). Although certain caregivers (elderly, in-home providers) are needier than others in terms of support, we learned that caregiver need does not necessarily elicit support (Clipp & George, 1990b). Specifically, caregivers with the greatest burden in terms of stress symptoms, poor health, and severe caregiving demands were more likely than other providers to perceive their levels of support as inadequate and to receive the least amount of tangible assistance.

All of this leads to the question of stress management among caregivers. A review of the literature reveals that the majority of research on caregiver "burden" focuses on mental health consequences (see Brown, Birdy, & Wing, 1972; Thompson & Doll, 1982 for extensive reviews). For example, one of the earliest studies of caregiver stress (Sainsbury & Grad de Alarcon, 1970), on 119 caregivers, found more than half of the sample to have neurotic symptoms including insomnia, headache, irritability, and depression due to concern about the care recipient's behavior. More recently, George and Gwyther (1986) found caregivers to report three times the psychiatric symptoms, more negative moods, and lower life satisfaction than reported by random community samples. Caregivers have been noted to have lower morale (Fengler & Goodrich, 1979), and to describe themselves as angry, sad, depressed, and tired most of the time (Rabins, Mace, & Lucas, 1982). Other studies have shown that characteristics of the caregiving experience such as life-style alterations, competing demands, isolation, and restricted time and freedom are associated with mental health symptoms such as anxiety, depression, sleeplessness, and emotional exhaustion (Archbold, 1978; Cantor, 1983; Davis, 1978; Horowitz, 1982). Institutionalization of the demented patient usually occurs after a prolonged period of the patient's deterioration that causes psychic distress for the caregiver and undermines his or her ability to cope with the situation (Robinson & Thurnher, 1979).

The presence and severity of psychiatric symptoms in the caregiver affect the degree to which the dependency needs of others can be met. Caregivers who are highly anxious, depressed, or sleep deprived are less resourceful in coping with certain demands of in-home care such as, in the case of dementia, hostile outbursts or night wandering. As tolerance varies among providers, so do ways of problem solving and coping with stress. Given the prevalence of anxiety, depression, and sleeplessness among this group of "hidden patients" (Fengler & Goodrich, 1979) we thought it reasonable to assume that one potential method of coping would involve the use of psychotropic drugs, namely antianxiety agents, antidepressants, and sedatives.

PSYCHOTROPIC DRUG USE

Analyses on the Duke caregivers (Clipp & George, 1990a) reveal that 30% of the 510 caregivers use psychotropic drugs on at least an occasional basis. How does this compare with the general population of elderly persons? Guttman (1978) found daily use of psychotropic agents to be 13.6% for sedatives-tranquilizers and 1.1% for antidepressants. Warheit and associates (Warheit, Arey, & Swanson, 1976) estimate that 17.5% of elderly in Alachua County, Florida are currently taking sedatives, stimulants, and tranquilizers. Percentages are higher for hospitalized elderly (32%) (Salzman & Van der Kolk, 1980) and highest for institutionalized elderly, for whom it is estimated that 40% of all drugs prescribed are psychotropic agents (Zawadski, Glazer, & Lurie, 1978). Although these studies have different methodologies and report findings based on different classes of psychotropics, the overall picture is one of high use among the institutionalized elderly but less than 20% use for the general elderly population. The substantially higher prevalence (30%) found in the caregiver sample suggests that many more elderly caregivers use psychotropic drugs than is true of the older population and that caregivers may bear closer resemblance to hospitalized elderly than to community-dwelling elderly in the use of these drugs.

What factors predict drug abuse among caregivers? Evidence from the Duke sample suggests that older female providers who perceive themselves to be in poor health and, consequently or otherwise, visit their physicians frequently are more likely than others to use psychotropic medications. Perceived social support also emerged as a strong predictor of drug use, especially antidepressant use. Many of the caregivers in this sample had given up friends, hobbies, or careers and felt that they needed more help in caring for the patient than they were currently receiving from friends and family. This group, who felt that support was lacking, were nearly four times more likely to take antidepressants. We were surprised, however, to note a lack of relationship between patient illness characteristics and drug use among caregivers. Clinical literature as well as everyday experience suggest that as the patient's condition deteriorates the care burden increases (Mace & Rabins, 1981; Poulshock & Deimling, 1984). The Duke studies refute this argument by showing that the severity of the patient's condition is not associated with caregivers' use of psychotropics. Rather, it is the broader caregiving context and the psychosocial aspects of providing care to a demented patient that seem to undermine the caregiver's ability to cope.

IMPLICATIONS FOR NURSE SPECIALISTS

As the population ages, the need for increased elder care options will only grow more urgent. Some of the same problems associated with child care, such as quality and expense, are magnified with regard to elder care. Because of the health and disability issues involved, elder care can impoverish families. It has been anticipated, in fact, that caregiver survival will be the major workplace issue of the 1990s (Older Women's League, 1989).

In assessing the degree of burden in caregiving relationships, nurse specialists should be particularly sensitive to several issues. First, women are, overwhelmingly, the primary caregivers of dependent older family members despite the increase in work force participation by women in the past 20 years. Therefore, women are particularly vulnerable to caregiver burden because of the multiple roles they assume. Furthermore, women tend to respond to role overload by decreasing time spent in social and recreational activities, rather than time spent with the care recipient. Nurse specialists should think of caregivers as "hidden patients" (Fengler & Goodrich, 1979), especially in-home providers whose patients are cognitively or behaviorally impaired. Particular attention should be given to symptoms of depression and anxiety such as feeling overwhelmed, isolated, exhausted.

Second, patient needs that a family caregiver cannot meet should be identified in the nursing assessment so that appropriate links to community agencies such as respite care or home health nursing can be made. It has been demonstrated that support group participation is significantly related to (a) increased knowledge about disease processes, (b) increased knowledge about relevant community services, and (c) decreased feelings that no one under-stands what one is experiencing (George & Gwyther, 1988). These findings demonstrate the effectiveness of community-based support groups, and their participation should be urged especially for caregivers with perceived social support inadequacy. Nurses need to expand their focus beyond the family to include neighbors and friends as other potentially important parts of their clients' support networks. Programs have been developed to integrate formal and informal services (Hooyman, 1983).

Third, caregiver strain is more highly correlated with cognitive impairment and behavioral disturbance in the patient than with limitations in physical function alone (Zarit et al., 1980). Knowledge of the patient's functioning, cognitive, behavioral and physical, will shed light on the probable stress level experienced by the caregiver. In addition, spouses and adult-child caregivers are more vulnerable to stress than other caregivers because of the long hours of in-home care and the emotionally intense relationships they share with the patient.

A final and important implication of caregiving research concerns the caregiver's social support. Nurse specialists cannot make the assumption that caregivers in need of support in their caregiving role receive it. Or that support to the caregiver remains constant over time. Unlike many difficult life events in which individuals benefit from supportive others, the stress associated with caregiving is often long-term and unrelenting. Responsibilities may begin before a diagnosis is made where, in the case of dementia, the caregiver must adjust to subtle signs of forgetfulness or behavioral instability. During subse-quent phases of the illness, which may range from months to years, increasing demands are placed on the caregiver as the patient's condition worsens. Family members and friends may offer concern and assistance early in the illness when functional status has not significantly deteriorated. Over time, as the dementia progresses and caregiver burden increases, support may diminish or seem nonexistent to the caregiver.

Clinical specialists should also be aware that changes in the care context may also influence patterns of support. Some patients die in the early phases of illness. A good number remain at home for years, living with their caregivers. Others make the institutional transition when the burden of care exceeds the provider's ability to cope. Only recently has evidence been offered that levels of support are sensitive to such transitions (Clipp & George, 1990b). For example, caregivers whose social support is constantly low or decreasing over time tend to be in-home, elderly providers with high reported stress, from large households supported by the lowest incomes. They need the most help yet receive the least assistance.

ELDER ABUSE

Virtually no literature on elder abuse existed prior to 1978, except a few studies concerned with maltreatment of patients in nursing homes (see Pillemer, 1988; Pillemer & Moore, 1989 for reviews). The phenomenon of child abuse was acknowledged in the 1960s, wife abuse in the 1970s and Steinmetz (1978) suggested that the 1980s would usher in public awareness of the battered aged—elderly parents who live with, are dependent on, and battered by their adult, caretaking children. A number of studies have been published since that prediction yet there remains a lack of consensus on the definition of elder abuse as a social problem. As Johnson (1986) states:

> Differences in terminology and meaning make it impossible to compare research findings, to collaborate on detection instruments, or, in the broader context, to establish a national forum for preparing a standard definition in order to develop public policy on the subject of elder abuse. In addition, until we can adopt a standard definition of elder abuse, causal theory cannot be explored. Theory building relies on a clearly defined, measurable proposition with consistent definition. (p. 168)

Investigators in this area usually draw from T. A. O'Malley, Everitt, O'Malley, and Campion (1983) who describe abuse as the willful infliction of physical pain, injury, or debilitating mental anguish, unreasonable confinement, or the willful deprivation by a caretaker of services that are necessary to maintain physical and mental health. Anetzberger's (1987) description includes hitting, shoving, and slapping, all of which cause pain, injury, and in some instances even death to the victim. Most researchers distinguish between abuse and neglect on the grounds of "willfulness" regarding the caregiver's actions (Matteson & McConnell, 1988). Other terms used in definitions of abuse include abandonment, making threats, verbal assaults, sexual abuse, exploitation, denial of opportunity to exercise adult rights, and unrealistic confinement. As in the case of caregiver burden, the impact of elder abuse as a social problem is proportional to the rapidly increasing elderly population, particularly the oldest-old segment. In the next 50 years, or by 2040, the number of individuals age 85 and older will increase from 2.2 to 13 million. These more vulnerable, often frail elderly are at the greatest risk of becoming dependent and at risk of being abused (Steinmetz, 1988).

THEORIES OF ELDER ABUSE

Between 1978 and 1982, most research on elder abuse in the community was designed to document it as a social problem and to describe its scope.

Theoretical approaches to the causes of abuse included environmental stresses such as low income and unemployment, learned violence patterns within the family, agism, psychopathology and behavioral disorders in the abuser such as mental illness or alcoholism, dependency in the older person, and caregiving stress (Matteson & McConnell, 1988; Villmoare & Bergman, 1981). The early research is characterized by small, nonrandom samples, vague definitions of abuse, and lack of control groups. In addition, estimates of abuse prevalence in these studies are probably underestimated because most investigators surveyed professionals in the community rather than victims to determine frequency of contact with abusing families. This is a problem because only a small percentage of community elderly are connected to formal care systems.

Research after 1982 made significant strides by moving beyond descriptions of elder abuse as a problem to correlational and causal analyses. We now know that elders living with others are at higher risk of being abused than elders living alone (Wolf, Godkin, & Pillemer, 1984, 1986) because the opportunities for maltreatment are increased. Steinmetz's book (1988) is based on a 1980 descriptive study of a nonrandom sample of 104 caregivers in Delaware. She describes the stress and conflict that arises in families as caregivers attempt to meet the needs of their dependent elders. Interpretations are made within a symbolic interaction perspective and are based on perceptions of the caregiver. Nearly a fourth of the caregivers admitted to using physically abusive methods to control the elder; nearly half of the variance in the reported abuse was explained by factors such as caregiver stress, total mobility dependency, and various actions on the part of the elder such as refusal to eat or take medicine, calling the police, or invading the caregiver's privacy. Steinmetz' long program of work on family violence supports the notion that the stress of caring for a dependent elder can place the caregiver at risk for using abusive means of control (i.e., victim dependent on abuser).

Pillemer and Finkelhor (1988) challenge this notion that elder abuse is attributable to the "crises" created by the needs of an elderly parent for care, or that stressed caregivers may become abusive. They completed the first large scale random sample survey of elder abuse, on 2,000 elderly persons in Boston. They report the prevalence rate of overall maltreatment to be 32 elderly persons per 1,000. Rather than lending support to prevailing assumptions that perpetrators are young caregivers and victims are older women, their findings suggest that spouses are the most likely abusers and that men and women were equally likely to be abused although women suffered more serious forms of maltreatment. In addition, physical violence emerged as the most widespread form of maltreatment, in comparison to previous reports suggesting more common forms of psychological abuse and neglect. Specifically, 45% of the sample reported having something thrown at them; 63% reported being pushed, grabbed, or shoved; 42% admitted to being slapped; and 10% stated that they had been hit with a fist, bitten, or kicked (Pillemer & Finkelhor, 1988).

More recent work by Pillemer and Finkelhor (1989) compared elderly abused victims with a nonabused control group to specifically test the hypothesis that elder abuse results from the burden of caring for infirmed and dependent elders. Their findings present a new portrait of the perpetrator-victim dyad, that of relatively well-functioning elderly who have responsibility for (e.g., provide financial resources, housing) or must interact with deviant, ill, and socio-emotionally unstable relatives. In other words, the maltreatment reflects the abuser's personal problems and dependency on the older person rather than the victim's disability or dependency on the abuser. This study makes an important shift in focus from the victim to the abuser. "Instead of well-meaning caregivers who are driven to abuse by the demands of an old person, abusers appear to be severely troubled individuals with histories of antisocial behavior or instability" (Pillemer & Finkelhor, 1989, p. 186). Other studies also suggest substantial psychological impairment on the part of the abuser including higher rates of alcoholism and criminal arrests that are believed to lead to dependency on the elderly relative (Anetzberger, 1987; Pillemer, 1985; Wolf et al., 1986).

It is important to note, however, that Pillemer and Finkelhor measure caregiver burden in terms of the severity of the patient's condition (i.e., number of sick days in previous year; performance of nine ADLs; extent of dependence of patient on caregiver for various forms of tangible assistance such as cooking, household repairs, and personal care). An assumption is made that the burden of care increases as the patient's illness worsens. In the Duke caregiving research described earlier in this chapter, we find a consistent *lack* of relationship between caregiver burden and severity of the patient's condition (Colerick & George, 1986; Clipp & George, 1990a, 1990b), suggesting that the physical demands of patient care are not what undermines the caregiver's ability to cope. Rather, it is the perceived lack of social support and the inability to participate in social and recreational activities that compromises the caregiver's management skills. The Duke data suggests that a broader definition of caregiver burden, one that includes psychosocial aspects of the care context, may be useful in studies attempting to examine the relationship between caregiver stress and elderly abuse.

IMPLICATIONS FOR NURSE SPECIALISTS

Elder abuse has received little attention among health care providers despite surveys that document physicians' exposure to the problem (Hickey & Douglas, 1981; H. C. O'Malley, Segel, & Perez, 1979). Holtzman, Bromberg and Heiden (1989) surveyed 1,321 dentists and found that over 10% treated a victim of abuse or held suspicions about certain patients being abused, in their practice. Responsibility for elderly abused clients should be taken by an interdisciplinary team composed of professionals from nursing, social work, medicine, dentistry, and law. Any one of a number of services may be needed for targeted families including medical and mental health assessment, home health care, visiting nurse service, transportation, meals-on-wheels, caregiving respite, legal aid, and emergency shelter.

The nurse specialist's role in the multidisciplinary management of elderly mistreatment cases is complex. Nurses are often, by the intimate nature of their work, in unique positions to identify abused elders firsthand. They must avoid, however, forming negative bias against any suspected perpetrator that could injure the bonds of trust in the nurse-patient relationship. T. A. O'Malley and associates (1983) outline several steps in the process of treatment for elder abuse: identification, access, assessment, intervention, follow-up, and prevention.

Identification requires awareness that the abused older person will probably not report the abuse. Nurses must be sensitive, therefore, to what are often subtle signs of maltreatment such as neglected medical problems, malnutrition, and failure to thrive. More overt manifestations include unexplained trauma, recurring injuries, frequent falls, and severe cognitive impairment. Dehydration, depression, oversedation, or an isolated caregiver should also trigger suspicion. Upon encountering one or more of these presentations, the nurse should review the care needs of the client and exactly how and by whom these needs are being met. Research to date suggests that nurses should look for abused elders in families with considerable dependency, families in which substantial burden is expressed by the caregiver, families with a history of violence patterns, and in families in which a deviant member is dependent on an elderly relative for financial resources or housing. Patients with conditions that have multiple, interacting disabilities such as Alzheimer's disease or CVA may be at risk for abuse as well (Matteson & McConnell, 1988).

Access to an abused person in the home may be difficult due to the rights of competent adults. H. C. O'Malley et al. (1979) found that in 40% of abuse cases, professionals were not able to gain access to the individual in order to assess the situation and intervene appropriately. In subsequent work T. A. O'Malley et al. (1983) argue that nurses, because of their reputation as helping professionals, nonthreatening manner, and ability to emphasize the relationship between illness and function are key individuals for gaining access to abused patients in the home.

Assessment should be carried out by a multidisciplinary team to determine the degree of immediate danger for the elderly person. Several questions should be probed (T. A. O'Malley, 1983). Is he or she competent to make decisions? Is separation between patient and family necessary? What services are needed to help the patient, caretaker, or other family members? Will the patient or family accept intervention?

Intervention is designed to protect the patient from immediate harm and prevent future episodes of abuse. T. A. O'Malley's model suggests that health care professionals determine, as a starting point, if the patient is impaired and dependent on family for basic needs or if care needs are minimal and the abused elder is involved with a "non-normal caregiver." Based on this determination, the professional asks a series of questions such as "can the victim's needs be met by other sources?", "does the elder want separation?", "can the abuser's behavior be modified?". These questions lead to various solutions such as "obtain a court order to vacate," "provide support services to family," "explore alternate living arrangements," "provide intervention for abuser" (T. A. O'Malley et al., 1983, p. 1002). Matteson and McConnell (1988) augment T. A. O'Malley's model with guidelines for ethical decision making when decisions involve value judgments such as whether or not the elder should remain at home.

Follow-up care for the older person is based on the premise that, in most cases of chronic disability, care needs will increase. The course of dementia, for example, is always downward. Nurses should be alert to the fact that, despite acceptance of intervention by patient and family, the risk for further abuse remains high due to long-term patterns of family interaction. If the abused elder remains in the home, support for the caregiver may decrease tension in the relationship. The work of Pillemer (1985, 1988) and Pillemer and Finkelhor (1989) suggest that services should be directed to the abuser who is often dependent on the victim. These may include psychological or employment counseling as well as financial guidance to assist the abuser in establishing residential independence from the older person. Most questions, however, regarding the long-term effects of intervention in cases of abuse remain unanswered.

Prevention of elder abuse is best achieved by intervening before it occurs (T. A. O'Malley et al., 1983). Nurses should regard any elderly person in frequent interaction with a relative or caretaker as a potential target for abuse, regardless of the degree of disability involved. More precise identification of risk factors for abuse are emerging from current research as well as empirically driven theories of causation. Nationally based prevalence rates, however, are still unknown (Wilson, 1989). Nurses occupy key positions in all stages of the treatment process because of their unique relationship with the patient and their focus on disease prevention and health promotion.

CONCLUSION

Caregiver burden and elder abuse constitute stresses that place the older individual at risk for a decline in health status. Although most geriatric assessment protocols examine functional abilities, there is wide variation in the attention such assessments pay to social problems in aging (Kane, Kane, & Rubenstein, 1989). The purpose of including a social component in geriatric evaluation is to characterize an older person's functioning in a particular social context.

In the assessment of caregiver burden or elder abuse it is important to screen both the caregiver and the patient in terms of their relationship. It may be difficult to identify social problems in current cohorts of older persons because they lived in an era when interpersonal problems were not openly acknowledged. In many cases the nurse must rely on information gained through social conversation in the interview setting.

According to McConnell and Matteson (1988), an informal format is usually preferable to a structured interview, especially with older persons who may be uncomfortable discussing social or psychological issues. Certain screening questions are particularly helpful in targeting problems in social relationships. To reiterate, if the older person has obvious disabilities, it is important to ask who in the family or social network is available to provide assistance. Is there a primary caregiver? Is the caregiver also a confidante? By asking the older individual and the caregiver, if possible, to describe a typical day the nurse gains a unique perspective on patterns of role relationship and the stresses of day-to-day life. For excellent reviews of instruments designed to measure social functioning see Lekan-Rutledge (1988, chapter 2) and Lindsey (1988, chapter 6).

In some cases, nurses must be prepared to obtain conflicting information on patient functioning depending on whether the patient or caregiver is queried. Evidence suggests that, under certain conditions, health declines in older persons tends to be discounted by self and recognized by caregivers in assessments of health (Colerick [Clipp] & Elder, 1987). This means that the older patient and the caregiver provide unique data in geriatric assessment; both should be considered "the client," especially when potential outcomes for either include stress symptoms or physical harm. Nurse specialists are in a position to identify problematic caregiver-patient relationships and intervene so that providers receive the support they need to continue caring for their dependents in the community. The well-being of the older person depends on the well-being of the provider, and on appropriate nursing assessment and intervention.

REFERENCES

Allan, C., & Brotman, H. (compilers). (1981). *Chartbook on aging in America. Prepared for the 1981 White House Conference on Aging. Washington, DC: Government Printing Office.*

Anetzberger, G. J. (1987). *The etiology of elder abuse by adult offspring.* Springfield, IL: Charles C Thomas.

Archbold, P. (1978). *Impact of caring for an ill elderly parent of the middle-aged or elderly offspring caregiver.* Paper presented at the 31st Annual Meeting of the Gerontological Society, Dallas, TX.

Brown, G., Birdy, L., & Wing, L. (1972). Influence of family life on the course of schizophrenia disorders: A replicator. *British Journal of Psychiatry, 121,* 241-258.

Cantor, M. H. (1983). Strain among caregivers: A study of experience in the United States. *The Gerontologist, 23,* 597-604.

Carnevali, D. L., & Patrick, M. (Eds.). (1986). *Nursing management for the elderly* (2nd ed.). Philadelphia: J. B. Lippincott.

Clipp, E., & Elder, G. H. (1987). Elderly confidents in geriatric assessment. *Comprehensive Gerontology, 1,* 35-40.

Clipp, E., & George, L. K. (1990a). Psychotropic drug use among caregivers of patients with dementia. *Journal of the American Geriatrics Society, 38,* 227-235.

Clipp, E., & George, L. K. (1990b). Caregiver needs and patterns of social support. *Journal of Gerontology, 45S,* 102-111.

Colerick, E. J. [Clipp], & George, L. K. (1986). Predictors of institutionalization among caregivers of Alzheimer's patients. *Journal of the American Geriatrics Society, 34,* 493-498.

Davis, B. (1978). *Stress in individuals caring for ill elderly relations.* Paper presented at the 31st Annual Meeting of the Gerontological Society, Dallas, TX.

Dean, A., & Lin, N. (1977). The stress-buffering role of social support. *Journal of Nervous and Mental Disease, 6,* 403-417.

Delafuente, J. C., & Stewart, R. B. (Eds.). (1988). *Therapeutics in the elderly.* Baltimore, MD: Williams & Wilkins.

Duke Center for the Study of Aging and Human Development. (1979). *Multidimensional functional assessment: The OARS methodology.* Durham, NC: Duke University, Center for the Study of Aging and Human Development.

Fatheringham, J., Shelton, M., & Haddinott, B. (1972). The effects on the families of the presence of a mentally retarded child. *Canadian Psychiatric Association Journal, 17,* 283-289.

Fengler, A., & Goodrich, N. (1979). Wives of elderly disabled men: The hidden patients. *The Gerontologist, 19,* 175-183.

George, L. K. (1984). The dynamics of caregiver burden (final report submitted to AARP Foundation). Durham, NC: Duke University, Center for the Study of Aging and Human Development.

George, L. K. (1987). Easing caregiver burden: The role of informal and formal supports. In R. A. Ward & S. S. Tobin (Eds.), *Health in Aging: Sociological issues and policy directions* (pp. 133-158). New York: Springer.

George, L. K., & Bearon, L. B. (1980). *Quality of life in older persons: Meaning and measurement.* New York: Human Sciences Press.

George, L. K., & Gwyther, L. P. (1986). Caregiver well-being: A multidimensional examination of family caregivers of demented adults. *The Gerontologist, 34,* 253-259.

George, L. K., & Gwyther, L. P. (1988). Support groups for caregivers of memory-impaired elderly: Easing caregiver burden. In L. A. Bond & B. M. Wagner (Eds.), *Families in transition: Primary prevention programs that work* (pp. 309-331). Newbury Park, CA: Sage.

Gioiella, E. C., & Bevil, C. W. (1985). *Nursing care of the aging client: Promoting healthy adaptation.* East Norwalk, CT: Appleton & Lange. @RT = Guttman, D. (1978). A study of drug-taking behavior of older Americans. In C. Beber & P. Lamy (Eds.), *Medication management and education of the elderly* (pp. 18). Washington, DC: Excerpta Medica.

Hanson, S. L., Sauer, W. J., & Seelbach, W. C. (1983). Racial and cohort variations in filial responsibility norms. *The Gerontologist, 23,* 626-631.

Hickey, T., & Douglas, R. L. (1981). Neglect and abuse of older family members: Professionals' perspectives and case experiences. *The Gerontologist, 21,* 171-176.

Holtzman, J. M., Bromberg, T. J., & Heiden, K. (1989). *Incidents of elder abuse identified by dentists.* Paper presented at 42nd Annual Meetings of the Gerontological Society, Minneapolis, MN.

Hooyman, N. (1983). Social support networks in services to the elderly. In J. Whittaker & J. Garbarino (Eds.), *Social support networks: Informal helping in the human services* (pp. 134-164). New York: Aldine.

Horowitz, A. (1982). *The role of families in providing long-term care to the frail and chronically ill elderly living in the community.* Final report submitted to the Health Care Financing Administration, Department of Health and Human Services.

Johnson, T. F. (1986). Critical issues in the definition of elder mistreatment. In K. Pillemer & R. Wolf (Eds.), *Elder abuse: Conflict in the family* (pp. 167-196). Dover, MA: Auburn House.

Kane, R. A., Kane, R. L., & Rubenstein, L. Z. (1989). Comprehensive assessment of the elderly patient. In M. D. Peterson & D. L. White (Eds.), *Health Care of the Elderly* (pp. 475-519). Newbury Park, CA: Sage.

Lekan-Rutledge, D. (1988). Functional assessment. In M. A. Matteson & E. S. McConnell (Eds.), *Gerontological Nursing: Concepts and practice* (pp. 57-91). Philadelphia: W. B. Saunders.

Lindsey, A. M. (1988). Social support: Conceptualizations and measurement instruments. In M. Frank-Stromborg (Ed.), Instruments for clinical nursing research (pp. 107-119). East Norwalk, CT: Appleton & Lange.

Litman, T. (1971). Health care and the family: A three generation analysis. *Medical Care, 9,* 67.

Lowenthal, M., & Haven, C. (1968). Interaction and adaptation: Intimacy as a critical variable. *American Sociological Review, 33,* 20-30.

Mace, N., & Rabins, P. (1981). *The 36-hour day.* Baltimore, MD: Johns Hopkins University Press.

Matteson, M. A., & McConnell, E. S. (1988). *Gerontological nursing: Concepts and practice.* Philadelphia: W. B. Saunders.

Morycz, R. (1980). An exploration of senile dementia and family burden. *Clinical Social Work Journal, 8,* 16.

Older Women's League. (1989). *Failing America's caregivers: A status report on women who care.* (Mother's Day Report). Washington, DC:

O'Malley, H. C., Segel, H. D., & Perez, R. (1979). *Elder abuse in Massachusetts: A survey of professionals and paraprofessionals.* Boston: Legal Research and Services for the Elderly.

O'Malley, T. A., Everitt, D. E., O'Malley, H. C., & Campion, E. W. (1983). Identifying and preventing family-medicated abuse and neglect of elderly persons. *Annals of Internal Medicine, 98,* 998-1005.

Pillemer, K. (1985). The dangers of dependency: New findings on domestic violence against the elderly. *Social Problems, 33,* 146-158.

Pillemer, K. (1988). Maltreatment of patients in nursing homes: Overview and research agenda. *Journal of Health and Social Behavior, 28,* 227-238.

Pillemer, K., & Finkelhor, D. (1989). Causes of elder abuse: Caregiver stress versus problem relatives. *American Journal of Orthopsychiatry, 59,* 179-187.

Pillemer, K., & Finkelhor, D. (1988). The prevalence of elder abuse: A random sample survey. *The Gerontologist, 28,* 51-57.

Pillemer, K., & Moore, D. W. (1989). Abuse of patients in nursing homes: Findings from a survey of staff. *The Gerontologist, 29,* 314-320.

Poulshock, S., & Deimling, G. (1984). Families caring for elders in residence: Issues in the measurement of burden. *Journal of Gerontology, 39,* 230.

Rabins, P., Mace, N., & Lucas, M. (1982). The impact of dementia on the family. *Journal of the American Medical Association, 248,* 333-335.

Robinson, B. (1983). Validation of a caregiver strain index. *Journal of Gerontology, 38,* 344.

Robinson, B., & Thurnher, M. (1979). Taking care of aged parents: A family cycle transition. *The Gerontologist, 19,* 586-593.

Sainsbury, P., & Grad de Alarcon, J. (1970). The psychiatrist and the geriatric patient: The effects of community care on the family of the geriatric patient. *Journal of Geriatric Psychiatry, 1,* 23-41.

Salzman, C., & Van der Kolk, B. (1980). Psychotropic drug prescriptions for elderly patients in a general hospital. *Journal of the American Geriatrics Society, 28,* 18-22.

Select Committee on Aging House of Representatives. (1987). *Exploding the myths: Caregiving in America* (Committee Publication No. 99-611). Washington, DC: Government Printing Office.

Steinmetz, S. K. (1978). Battered parents. *Society* (July/August): 54-55.

Steinmetz, S. K. (1988). *Duty bound: Elder abuse and family care.* Newbury Park, CA: Sage.

Thompson, E., & Doll, W. (1982). The burden of families coping with the mentally ill: An invisible crisis. *Family Relations, 31,* 379.

Villmoare, E., & Bergman, J. (Eds.). (1981). *Elder abuse and neglect: A guide for practitioners and policy makers.* San Francisco: National Paralegal Institute.

Ward, R. A. (1985). Informal networks and well-being in later life: A research agenda. *The Gerontologist, 25,* 55-61.

Warheit, G., Arey, S., & Swanson, E. (1976). Patterns of drug use: An epidemiologic review. *Journal of Drug Issues, 6,* 223-237.

Wilson, N. L. (1989). Elder abuse: Who, what, and how to help [Reviews of *Duty bound: Elder abuse and family care* and *Elder abuse: Conflict in the family*]. *The Gerontologist, 29,* 711-713.

Wolf, R., Godkin, M., & Pillemer, K. (1984). *Elder abuse and neglect: Findings from three model projects.* Worcester: University of Massachusetts Medical Center, University Center on Aging.

Wolf, R., Godkin, M., & Pillemer, K. (1986). Maltreatment of the elderly: A comparative analysis. *Pride Institute Journal of Long Term Health Care, 5,* 10-17.

Zarit, S., Reever, K., & Bach-Peterson, J.J. (1980). Relatives of the impaired elderly: Correlates of feelings of burden. *The Gerontologist, 20,* 649.

Zawadski, R., Glazer, G., & Lurie, E. (1978). Psychotropic drug use among institutionalized and noninstitutionalized medicaid aged in California. *Journal of Gerontology, 33,* 825-834.

13

Cultural Diversity Among Older Americans

LAURIE M. GUNTER

Objectives: At the completion of this chapter the reader will be able to:

(1) Analyze the need for and the development of transcultural nursing.
(2) Critique selected issues that may confound the concept of culture.
(3) Implement a cultural assessment plan that recognizes the needs of persons with diverse cultural backgrounds in a variety of organizational settings.
(4) Synthesize approaches that facilitate an appreciation of diverse cultural experiences among nursing personnel, older adults, and families.

INTRODUCTION

This nation faces dramatic changes and challenges in the near future, according to a report prepared by the U.S. Senate Special Committee on Aging (1987-88) in conjunction with the American Association of Retired Persons, the Federal Council on Aging, and the U.S. Administration in Aging. It was noted in these trends and projections that in 1986, 13% of whites were 65 years of age and older compared to 8% of nonwhites and 5% of Hispanics (U.S. Senate Special Committee on Aging, 1987-1988). No statistics were given for Asian or Native American persons as separate population groups in this report.

Differences in the percentage of aged persons among the three ethnic groups identified was explained as resulting from higher fertility for the nonwhite and Hispanic populations in comparison to the white population (U.S. Senate,

1987-1988). It is probable that some of this difference can be attributed to life-style, access to health care and other resources of the nation, as well as to socioeconomic factors involving differential occupational and educational opportunities.

In addition to differences in proportion of population for minority groups, they have less money than the white group. For example, the poverty rate among black elderly was 31.0%—which was nearly triple that among whites— and for Hispanic elderly, it was 22.5%, more than double the rate among white elderly at 10.7% (U.S. Senate, 1987-1988).

According to the U.S. Senate Special Committee on Aging report, differences can also be discerned between whites and nonwhites in terms of life expectancy. Other differences noted were for labor force participation, cognitive impairment in nursing homes, death rates, residence in nursing home and community, living arrangements, educational attainment, and voting in elections. According to Pettigrew (1964), differences among cultural groups should not be attributed to the inherent superiority of one race nor to the inherent inferiority of another race but to nongenetic threats to human dignity, higher standards of living, and access to equal opportunity for the goods and services available in U.S. society. Similar differences will be found among other groups, thus requiring attention to the special needs of the culturally diverse groups of older Americans.

Purpose

The purpose of this chapter is to make suggestions for providing relevant nursing services to a diverse group of older adults. In many instances these services will be provided by a nursing staff that is stratified by socioeconomic class and consist of personnel with various cultural experiences and ethnic backgrounds (Spector, 1985). The milieu in which this service is provided will affect all persons involved, clients/patients, families, friends, as well as all types and levels of personnel. The goal is to encourage the design of a nursing milieu that will contribute to the satisfaction of all involved and provide appropriate modifications in nursing care for those whose beliefs, practices, and resources may differ from those of the persons providing the care.

This chapter will provide definitions of terms used in the discussion of cultural diversity; a brief examination of the development of transcultural nursing, the need for this area of specialization, and the identification of theoretical approaches; an analysis of confounding issues that contribute to a lessened respect for some groups and to discrimination in the American culture; and evaluation of assessment plans and suggestions for managing cultural diversity in the implementation of nursing care. Although an understanding of cultural diversity is important in the provision of relevant health services to all people in society, the nonwhite and Hispanic populations have significantly smaller proportions of elderly persons than the white population. Consequently, it is likely that little if any cultural diversity will be seen in many health care settings.

Definitions

The following definitions are for use in the transcultural nursing subfield:

"*Culture* is the learned and transmitted knowledge about a particular group with its values, beliefs, rules of behavior and life-style practices that guide persons in their thinking and actions in patterned ways" (Leininger, 1978, p. 491). Culture can also be defined as an integrated pattern of human behavior including thought, speech, and action. It is learned, changed, and taught to succeeding generations.

Ethnicity is the social differentiation of people based on such cultural criteria as a sense of peoplehood, shared history, a common place of origin, language, dress, food preferences, and participation in distinct group practices (Matteson & McConnell, 1988). *Ethnic group* is a collection of individuals who share a unique cultural and social heritage passed on from one generation to another. *Race* can be defined as a family, tribe, people, or nation belonging to the same ancestors. Races are relatively isolated mating groups with distinctive gene frequencies (Pettigrew, 1964). Some races show different incidences of certain conditions, such as cognitive impairment and suicidal tendencies (U.S. Senate, 1987-1988).

"*Ethnocentrism* is the tendency of an individual (or group) to hold feelings and beliefs that one's own lifeways are the most desirable, acceptable or best and to act in a superior manner to another culture's lifeways" (Leininger, 1978, p. 492). Ethnocentrism implies the lack of *cultural relativism,* which is the belief that cultures are neither inferior nor superior and that there is no single scale for measuring the value of a culture (Friedman, 1981). From this belief springs the importance of studying families from other cultures to counter the tendency to believe that the way "our families operate is the way in which all (normal) families and groups should and do function (Friedman, 1981). The use of *stereotypes* is an expression of ethnocentrism and is defined as preconceived beliefs about classes of individuals, groups, or objects, that have not been subjected to objective examination.

Acculturation implies not only a degree of assimilation or internalization of the dominant culture by different ethnic groups, but also the exposure to and influence of subcultures on the majority groups. America as a pluralistic society has members of diverse ethnic, racial, religious, and social groups that maintain their traditional cultures within the confines of a common culture. Over time and as a result of interaction and exchange more similarities are discernable than differences, as people strive to promote and work for the common good of all cultural groups.

> Transcultural or Cross-Cultural nursing is the learned subfield of nursing which focuses on the comparative study and analysis of different cultures and subcultures with respect to nursing and health-illness caring practices, beliefs and values, with the goal of generating scientific and humanistic knowledge and of using this knowledge to provide culture-specific and cultural-universal nursing care. (Leininger, 1978, p. 493)

Another definition of transcultural nursing is the acceptance of health care beliefs, values, and practices of persons with different cultural experiences and to practice nursing without ethnocentrism or feelings of superiority because of these differences.

DEVELOPMENT OF AND NEED FOR TRANSCULTURAL NURSING

Leininger (1970, 1978) a nurse and an anthropologist, established the subfield of transcultural nursing as a legitimate field of study. She emphasized the need to conduct comparative studies of health care practices of various cultural groups and the application of these findings in the practice of nursing. Nurses have always been involved in the care of people from diverse cultures but were apparently more intent on having patients accept their ideas and methods rather than considering the values of some folkways and medical practices. Ethnocentrism was pervasive in nursing practice and was unlikely to be questioned. Around the mid-century, social changes as a result of wars that included travel to all or most of the world; more open educational opportunities for men and women, including nurses; as well as racial and minority groups' dissatisfaction with discriminatory practices, made evident the need for knowledge and understanding that could be obtained from the study of anthropology.

Morse (1988) provides a brief history of cross-cultural nursing and a rationale for the various concepts used in this area. She also discusses various organizations that have been formed to promote cross-cultural nursing practices. She listed several reasons for cross-cultural nursing including the following needs: (1) to elicit cultural values and beliefs so that honest and flexible approaches to care based on mutual respect can be provided, (2) to understand normal behaviors in different cultural groups and to recognize behavioral responses to illness, and (3) for additional information on biological (or racial) variation and on normal growth patterns, so that the abnormal can be identified and appropriate interventions designed.

Another need in the provision of nursing care and services is for an ethic that includes respect, justice, and equality for all of the various groups giving and receiving nursing services. Gunter (1981) attempted to outline some aspects of this ethic that would respect the culture, values, and beliefs of individuals and groups. Included in this guide are the following suggestions: (1) protect choices, values, beliefs, and rights of clients to enter the decision-making process, (2) promote self-actualization and the potential for further development, (3) express respect in the nurse-patient relationship, and (4) avoid "agism" and allowing negative attitudes toward aging to affect practice.

Closely related to the preceding guidelines are the following ethical principles that can guide behavior in clinical practice: (1) safeguard patients' rights, (2) develop sound intra- and interprofessional relationships, (3) establish positive relationships with the families of patients and between patients/clients and families, and (4) determine the safety of client participation in research.

Burnside (1988) describes a theoretical approach to the study of transcultural nursing. The theoretical components include cultural, status, and support subsystems, in addition to self-concept and present life situation that all influence present behavior. In 1979, Gunter and Estes published an interactive model in which culture is included in all domains of nursing and aging (Figure 13.1). According to this model, gerontic nursing is a health service that integrates nursing and scientific knowledge about the aging process. From this knowledge basis, nursing care is provided to increase health behaviors; minimize the impact of losses and impairments due to age; provide comfort and support during distressing conditions, including dying and death; and facilitate the treatment of diseases in the aged.

It can be seen from the above statements that ethics and philosophy as well as scientific investigation provide the basis for an understanding of culture. Discussions of culture are open to disagreement and modification, but the important point is the need for examination of one's own attitudes, beliefs, and behavior in regard to interpersonal and professional relationships. Introspection and knowledge of oneself are required to cope effectively in situations where differences are expressed. There are several issues that may confound the analyses of transcultural nursing. These include the following and will be examined in the next sections: socioeconomic status, racism, stereotyping, sexism, agism, generational differences, and social change.

CONFOUNDING ISSUES

Socioeconomic status is the most problematic of the confounding issues. The poor of whatever subcultural background are more similar to other poor, than

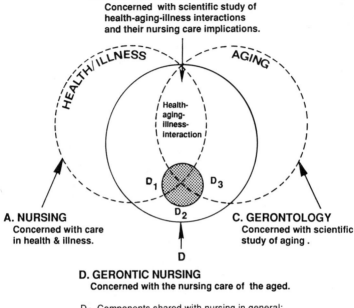

B. NURSING GERONTOLOGY
Concerned with scientific study of
health-aging-illness interactions
and their nursing care implications.

A. NURSING
Concerned with care
in health & illness.

C. GERONTOLOGY
Concerned with scientific
study of aging .

D. GERONTIC NURSING
Concerned with the nursing care of the aged.

D_1 Components shared with nursing in general:
generic nursing knowledge & methods.

D_2 Components unique to gerontic nursing:
application of knowledge and modified
nursing methods.

D_3 Components shared in common with other
practitioners in area of aging:
gerontological knowledge.

 Culture is included in all domains

Figure 13.1. Domains of Concern in the Areas of Nursing and Aging: Unique and
Overlapping Components

Source: Gunter & Estes (1979).

they are to the wealthy. In this society, individuals and families are arranged in
graded strata with varying degrees of prestige, and/or property, and/or power.
Within these strata people have common life-styles and life-changes, attitudes,
and ideologies of self and society. A disproportionate number of certain minority or ethnic groups fall in the lower socioeconomic classes. As a result, they
suffer more severe deprivation and receive less personal respect in the health

care system. They are more likely to have experienced unemployment, more preventable diseases, malnutrition, homelessness, and more social problems.

Racism embraces the doctrine that there is a connection between racial and cultural traits, and that some races are inherently superior to others (Atchley, 1985; Gould & Kolb, 1964). According to Rose (1951), a group is a minority if it is the object of prejudice and discrimination from the dominant groups and if the members think of themselves as a minority. It is not a minority because its members have a distinctive racial or national background or because its members adopt a religion or language, although minority status is sometimes attached to at least one of these characteristics.

Racism fuses national, ethnic, linguistic, religious, and racial groups into an amalgam, the alleged inferiorities of which are spuriously attributed to race alone (Gould & Kolb, 1964). Racism involves the assertion that inequality is an absolute and unconditional, that one race is inherently and by its very nature superior or inferior to others quite independently of all other factors (Gould & Kolb, 1964).

Types of racism and manifested behavior related to racism have been outlined by Weil (1983). The types of racism are institutionalized, institutional, and individual racism. The manifestations of related behavior range from overt-conscious, overt-unconscious, subtle-conscious, subtle-unconscious, lack of interest or dissociation, ignorance, and "cultural blindness" or ethnocentricity. From this perspective, it should be emphasized that ethnocentricity is a form of racism and therefore should be given more attention in transcultural nursing texts, curricula design, and research activities.

Stereotyping denotes beliefs about classes of individuals, groups, or objects that are preconceived and is an expression of ethnocentrism. These beliefs do not result from fresh appraisals of each phenomenon but from habits of judgment and expectation (Gould & Kolb, 1964). One of the problems of examining how cultural differences affect an older adult's perception of illness, hospitalization or stay in a nursing home, nursing care, or the positive and negative influences of different cultures on coping strategies, pain, and loneliness, is that of perpetuating stereotypes that are not applicable to any individual and therefore harmful to the personhood of the client/patient. A major issue revolves around how to avoid teaching stereotypes that are harmful to the person, but to provide the nurse with the needed information to facilitate therapeutic care to individuals with diverse cultural backgrounds (Gunter, 1988).

Sexism is another confounding issue in transcultural nursing. An example of this is the sentence given in a court of law to a new immigrant to this country who killed his wife for infidelity. The judge gave him a very light sentence because in his country of origin it was expected and acceptable to kill one's wife for infidelity. This is an injustice based on sex, similar to the inequities that older women receive not only in the health care system but also in other aspects of American society, as compared to the treatment of older men. Systematic observation and comparison of older men and older women may lead to surprising insights.

Agism is also a confounding variable in the consideration of culture. Leininger (1978, p. 352) states "that aging in any society is largely culturally learned, culturally expressed, and this knowledge and behavior are culturally transmitted from one generation to the next." Attitudes toward aging differ from culture to culture. In American culture, these attitudes have been negative with the dominant tendency to view aging as diminishing capability and productivity in all activities of life. The term "agism" has been applied to these negative attitudes and stereotypes. Although these attitudes appear to be changing toward more positive views, some punitive actions toward the aged can be seen, such as the proposal to implement a rather high surtax on only the aged to pay for a catastrophic health insurance that would benefit about 10% of older adults. Fortunately, this tax was repealed due to the protest of the elderly and their organizations (see Chapter 9, "Public Policy Impacting on Nursing Care of Older Adults," concerning this surtax). Little consideration was given to the fact that older adults are major taxpayers who support all levels of education and use very few of these resources.

Generational differences may influence cultural assessment. It is important to emphasize that all older persons are not the same. In fact, throughout the aging process people become more different than younger persons due to life experiences. Young people with more similar experiences are more alike than older people who become more heterogenous as they age. Consequently, the young-old have a different history and life experience than the old-old. They may have, as a group, more education, more economic resources and benefits, better nutrition and health care than the older age groups. These differences need to be taken into account in the nursing situation.

Social and historical changes impact on people of every culture. The only constant in life is change. Much of what has been learned about aging in the past will be changed in the future. Everything changes; even culture and the aging process change. Instead of learning facts about the impact of culture, the need is to learn how to gather information that may be applicable to the problems encountered in a changing world. Some of the information needed will be about the cultural practices of specific clients. But more important is the necessity to use this knowledge to provide services that will be respectful and relevant to meet the clients/patient's needs. Include in this examination one's own attitudes toward groups who differ from one's own culture, sensitivity to bigotry and discrimination, interest in the provision of care in relation to equality and justice. Professional responsibilities include the need to review Professional Codes of Ethics and to consider the implications for the care of minorities. Also, it is necessary to review legal responsibilities in response to care for minorities.

The following sections evaluate the status of nursing planning and caring for older persons with diverse cultural backgrounds but with common needs and aspirations. In addition, methods to improve health care for minority populations are provided.

ASSESSMENT OF CULTURAL DATA

The Editors of *Geriatric Nursing* (1987) suggested 10 ways to make nursing care of older adults more enjoyable. One way is to stop, look and listen, hear, think, and respond. This advice could not only assist the nurse to obtain accurate assessments and provide individualized treatment, but also to do so with little additional time or resources.

It should be noted that curriculum development and practice in transcultural nursing are hindered by the fact that there are many ethnic groups and that each of the four major minority groups in America is composed of multiple populations with distinct histories and cultures. For example, the Asian group consists of Chinese, Filipinos, Japanese, Asians, Indians, Koreans, Vietnamese, Hawaiians, Samoans, and Guamaians. Native Americans are grouped with the Eskimo and Aleut populations. The Hispanic or Spanish population is also diverse and includes people from islands and countries from the South Pacific to the Atlantic Ocean. The black population is also, in many instances, biracial and multicultural and includes people from Africa, Jamaica, and Haiti as well as some Hispanics and other nonwhites.

Nor is it feasible to provide specific knowledge about each group in view of the constant interaction between groups, common experiences, and life circumstances in which cultural practices tend to become diffused and blended to make for more similarities than differences within socioeconomic groups. These ideas are not intended to deny the existence of isolated groups, some of which seek to preserve their cultural isolation and others of which have less choice in the matter of their relationship to the major groups in society. In addition, there are increasing numbers of immigrants who have not yet been exposed to the American culture. These new groups may need special consideration in view of possible language barriers. In any of these circumstances health providers have a responsibility to assure equity and justice in access to health care that is financially supported by the nation, and to provide care that is respectful and sensitive to cultural differences and variations (American Nurses' Association, 1980; Seabrooks, Kahn, & Gero, 1987). It is for this reason that educational programs and health service organizations should include content and arrangements that encourage the participants to respect and accept human differences encountered in their practice.

There are at least three areas to examine in a cultural assessment, including the client/patient, staff, and organizational milieus. Each area will be investigated in the following sections.

The first step in the assessment process is to gather information about the extent of cultural diversity in clients/patients to be served. This data may be obtained from existing records and by simple observation. Not many service organizations will serve a greatly diverse population because of socioeconomic and geographic factors. The fact that a limited number of different minorities are involved in one setting at any one time makes it easier to obtain the cultural data needed. Talk with patients/clients and all persons concerned, and compile additional data as needed to understand their problems and concerns. Collect data to show the composition of the case load, the nursing needs, family and support systems, attitudes, health beliefs, and health practices.

Once the parameters of population diversity are defined, a long-term plan for developing a data bank may be designed. This can be done by collecting information on a form, such as the one shown in Table 13.1. Only those descriptions of practices that appear to be unique should be included and it should be clearly explained that these descriptions are not to be used for purposes of stereotyping. These should be used as references and as hypotheses to be explored when behavior and practices are not clearly understood. This form was designed to collect information on personal care activities. Unfortunately there is less information in the literature on personal care rituals than on other areas.

There is more information on types of health practitioners, rituals, medications, and child-rearing practices than on the activities of daily living that are so important in the care of older adults. Thus there is a need to obtain information or assessment data on personal care practices from minority elders. This can be accomplished over a period of time with staff making additions and deletions based on their direct contact with the elders involved and through research in this area.

In 1981, Kayser-Jones investigated personal hygiene practices in a nursing home in the United States and one in Scotland. The majority of articles, however, on cross-cultural issues among older adults focus on demographics, family, economic and social problems, as well as medical illnesses and treatment, and not on personal care activities (Asano, Maeda, & Shimizu, 1984; Brower, 1984; Cruz-Lopez & Pearson, 1985; Kiefer et al., 1985; Lopez-Aqueres, Kemp, Plopper, Staples, & Brummel-Smith, 1984; Martin, 1984; Older Asians, 1987; Saunders, 1984; Shoemaker, 1981; Waring & Kosberg, 1984; Yu & Wu, 1985). Spector's (1985) book provides, in addition to a description of the cultural background of most health care practitioners, some helpful health care information for specific ethnic groups. The reader is also referred to the *Journal of Transcultural Nursing* for additional information on cross-cultural issues in nursing. In 1984, Leininger published a reference book

Table 13.1
Areas for Assessment of Personal Care Practices of Minority Elders

ADLs[a]	Coping Strategies	Environment	Family or Other Significant Support	Community Support	Attitudes Toward Caretakers/Professionals
Eating, Feeding, Nutrition	Problem Solving	Home Housekeeping	Caretaking Role	Availability	Preferences
Bathing	Stress	Safety & Supporting Factors	Social Support/ Reassurance	Acceptance	Rejections
Dressing	Pain/ Discomfort	Institution Arrangements			
Toilet	Loneliness	Artifacts			
Continence	Religion, Prayer, Meditation				
Mobility/ Disability					

Note: This form may also be used as a comparative assessment of minority elders.

a. Indicates *Activities of Daily Living.*

225

to assist nurses to locate transcultural resources in several areas including teaching, clinical practice, curriculum, and research. Leininger (1988) also describes nutritional practices of diverse ethnic groups.

The next step in the assessment process should focus on the staff. By far the most salient force in determining the extent to which respectful and appropriate nursing care is provided to culturally diverse groups is the nursing staff as a whole. Not just professional or licensed nurses, but all personnel. The most urgent and challenging problem in considering the impact of culture on the care of older persons is the cultural differences between nurses' aides, professional staff, and the clients/patients they serve. If this problem can be confronted and resolved, the milieu of the entire organization can be changed. Assessment of the staff's attitudes, experiences, and knowledge can be obtained during small group discussions and from agency records.

The need to improve the working conditions and relationships of the nurse aides and professional staff in long-term care settings has been documented in the literature (Pillemer & Moore, 1989; Tellis-Nayak & Tellis-Nayak, 1989). Tellis-Nayak and Tellis-Nayak (1989) describe the caregivers in nursing homes as people who are poor but striving and others who are demoralized. Research by Pillemer and Moore (1989) indicated that abuse is extensive enough in nursing homes to merit public concern. Little is known about abuse in the home of frail elderly. The solutions that are usually suggested are better education and pay. These are needed without question, but much more is needed in terms of providing an understanding and respectful environment in which to work. Too little attention is given to the attitudes expressed toward minorities and poor people. Minorities and the poor are ignored as people and treated as unworthy in many small ways, whether they are patients or staff. It may be safe to suggest that the way aides are treated in an institutional setting will determine the way patients are treated.

The organizational milieu should be examined in all areas, by the clinical nurse specialist (CNS) and the nursing administrator. Review the organization's purpose, philosophy, structure, resources, use of volunteers, community relationships, and personnel policy manual. Become attuned to informal staff discussions, changes of shift reports, complaints, incident reports, and problems that need attention and solution. Touring the facility as an objective observer can help one understand the impact that the institution may have on a person with a diverse background. This allows the observer to make valuable suggestions for improving the quality of care.

MANAGING CULTURAL DIVERSITY

A major concern in the health care industry is cost containment. To provide relevant and humane health care to a culturally diverse population need not require more financial output. Indeed, such care may not only be offered without increasing costs, it may actually be more cost-effective than traditional care. Care offered in the context of group's beliefs and values will result in adherence to prescribed regimens, acceptance of health teaching, and preventive methods, thereby decreasing disease and disability. More satisfying work and interpersonal relationships will contribute to the welfare of clients/patients and their families as well as staff.

The following sections offer suggestions to assist nurses in managing cultural diversity in health care settings in three areas; nursing staff development, organizational/institutional activities, and community functions. The following suggestions should not increase health care costs but may reduce costs, by encouraging compliance and facilitating healthy life-styles.

Nursing staff development in the area of transcultural nursing should include an employment interview to determine the applicant's previous experiences in living and working in multicultural situations, and languages spoken and read. Some staff may be used to interpret clients/patients language and behavior and to assist other staff to meet special needs. Avoid systematically assigning minority staff to similar minority clients/patients, however.

Orientation programs for staff should include knowledge of community resources and a description of the mix of cultures. Also include an orientation to the philosophy of the institution toward cultural diversity, and approaches that have been useful in problem solving.

Staff development programs need to include discussions of cultural problems and suggested approaches. Long-range plans should be made for regular inclusion of cultural diversity topics and for repetition of these programs on at least a yearly basis. Time may be limited for specific programs on the impact of culture, therefore it should be emphasized that actions speak louder than words.

Arrangements can be made for some staff to attend special events related to the cultural composition of the patients/clients. For example, obtain theater tickets or other special event tickets. Free tickets might be obtained from sponsors on receiving an explanation of the purpose and need.

Organizational and institutional health care managers can encourage the use of arts and artifacts that may be appreciated by those clients/patients with diverse cultural backgrounds. Family support groups can be organized to promote an understanding of what is happening in the organization and to learn how they may be of assistance to each other, the staff, and the institution. The institution can plan variation in meal patterns, and menus can be planned to reflect the cultural make-up of the staff and clientele. "Open house" at regular intervals can orient a culturally diverse community to the organization and promote mutual understanding. Institutional managers can promote cultural well-being by celebrating various traditions as a means of respecting the cultural backgrounds of the consumers of health care.

Community activities that can promote healthy choices in a culturally diverse population include the encouragement and use of volunteers from the represented minority groups to assist with communications, relationships, emotional support, support groups, and staff development. Encourage community involvement in the organization's activities. Invite club members and teachers to bring students in for field trips in which the aging processes and problems are discussed. Explain the agency's purpose, philosophy, and community goals. Enlist community assistance in solving problems. Let the people know what help is needed to provide high quality care. Request assistance from college and university departments of anthropology and of nursing to provide specific information about the clientele and their cultural backgrounds. Encourage departments in colleges and universities to obtain clinical experience in the agency and to conduct research related to knowledge needed to provide better care. Use public, college, and university libraries to obtain needed information about specific cultural groups. Facilitate communications among the staff, patients/clients, and the community to solve the cultural problems encountered.

CONCLUSIONS

The purpose of this chapter was to assist health care personnel to provide more sensitive and relevant services to a wider spectrum of older patients or clients. It is not expected that every professional provider will be expert in providing care to each minority or subcultural group in the United States. This would be impossible because of the large variety of persons who identify with various groups. It is expected, however, that all persons providing health care services to minorities and subcultural groups should be able to express an appreciation of and an acceptance for human and cultural differences; recognize the impact that negative attitudes, agism, and stereotyping have on the delivery of health care to minority persons, as well as on all patients; internalize a code of ethics that demonstrates concern for the welfare and health of people without prejudices toward differences, such as personal attributes; appreciate that no one subset of human cultures is superior in all ways to another set; and recognize that values can be obtained through cultural interchanges.

Summary

This chapter has included definitions of several terms that are encountered in discussions about cultural diversity, and a brief overview of the need for transcultural nursing. Suggestions are provided for the assessment and collection of cultural data and for the management of cultural diversity. These suggestions are practical and realistic. They can be implemented with little if any additional cost. It is hoped that persons who find themselves working among "different" cultural groups will take the time to learn about their cultural values and practices so that they will be sensitive to the health care needs and preferences of diverse groups and can modify the care provided in an appropriate manner.

REFERENCES

American Nurses' Association. (1980). *Nursing, social policy statement.* Kansas City, MO: American Nurses' Association.

Asano, H., Maeda, D., & Shimizu, Y. (1984). Social isolation of the impaired elderly in Japan. *Journal of Gerontological Social Work, 6*(4), 65-79.

Atchley, R. C. (1985). *The social forces in later life.* Belmont, CA: Wadsworth.

Brower, T. (1984, July/August). A look at China's eldercare. *Geriatric Nursing,* 251-253.

Burnside, I. (1988). *Nursing and the aged: A self-care approach.* New York: McGraw-Hill.

Cruz-Lopez, M., & Pearson, R. (1985). The support needs and resources of Puerto Rican elders. *The Gerontologist, 25,* 483-487.

Friedman, M. (1981). *Family nursing: Theory and assessment.* New York: Appleton-Century-Crofts.

Geriatric Nursing. (1987). A guide to caring for the elderly. A handout prepared by the editors.

Gould, J., & Kolb, W. (1964). *A dictionary of the social sciences.* New York: Free Press.

Gunter, L. (1981, August). Notes on a guide to gerontic practice (Editorial). *Journal of Gerontological Nursing, 7,* 457-458. @RT = Gunter, L. (1988) Notes on a method for teaching transcultural nursing. *Recent Advances in Nursing, 20* (000), 122-135.

Gunter, L. & Estes, C. (1979). *Education for Gerontic Nursing.* New York: Springer.

Kayser-Jones, J. (1981, January/February). Comparison of care in a Scottish and a United States facility. *Geriatric Nursing,* 45-50.

Keifer, C., Kim, S., Choi, K., Kim, L., Kim, B., Shon, S., & Kim, T. (1985). Adjustment problems of Korean-American elderly. *The Gerontologist, 25,* 477-482.

Leininger, M. (1970). *Nursing and anthropology: Two worlds to blend.* New York: John Wiley.

Leininger, M. (Ed.). (1978). *Transcultural nursing concepts, theories and practices.* New York: John Wiley.

Leininger, M. (1984). *Reference sources for transcultural health and nursing.* Thorofare, NJ: Slack, Inc.

Leininger, M. (1988). Transcultural eating patterns and nutrition: Transcultural nursing and anthropological perspective. *Holistic Nursing Practice, 3,* 16-25.

Lopez-Aqueres, W., Kemp, B., Plopper, M., Staples, F., & Brummel-Smith, K. (1984). Health needs of the Hispanic elderly. *Journal of the American Geriatric Society, 32,* 191-197.

Martin, C. (1984). Aging in developing countries. *Journal of Gerontological Nursing, 10,* 8-11.

Matteson, M., & McConnell, E. (1988). *Gerontological nursing: Concepts and practice.* Philadelphia: W.B. Saunders.

Morse, J. (Ed.). (1988). *Recent advances in nursing.* London: Churchill Livingstone.

Older Asians (Chae, M.) CEU exam questions (1987). *Journal of Gerontological Nursing, 13,* 46-48.

Pettigrew, T. (1964). *A profile of the Negro American.* Princeton, NJ: D. Van Nostrand, Co.

Pillemer, K., & Moore, D. (1989) Abuse of patients in nursing homes: Findings from a survey of staff. *The Gerontologist, 29,*(3), 314-20.

Rose, A. (1951). *Race, Prejudice and Discrimination.* New York: Knopf.

Saunders, V. (1984). Profiles of elderly Armenians. *Journal of Gerontological Nursing, 10,* 26-29.

Seabrooks, P., Kahn, R., & Gero, G. (1987). Cross-cultural observations. *Journal of Gerontological Nursing, 13,* 18-22.

Shoemaker, S. (1981). Navaho nursing homes: A fusion of philosophies. *Journal of Gerontological Nursing, 7,* 531-536.

Spector, R. (1985). *Cultural diversity in health and illness.* East Norwalk, CT: Appleton & Lange.

Tellis-Nayak, V., & Tellis-Nayak, M. (1989). Quality of care and the burden of two cultures: When the world of the nurses aide enters the world of the nursing home. *The Gerontologist, 29,* (3) 307-13.

U.S. Senate Special Committee on Aging. (1987-1988). *Aging in America; Trends and Projections* (DHHS Publication No. LR 3377 [188] D 12198). Washington, DC: Government Printing Office.

Waring, M., & Kosberg, J. (1984). Morale and the differential use among the black elderly of social welfare services delivered by volunteers. *Journal of Gerontological Social Work, 6,*(4), 81-93.

Weil, M. (1983). Southeast Asians and service delivery: Issues in service provision and institutional racism. In *Bridging cultures: Southeast Asian refugees in America* (pp. 136-161). Los Angeles: Special Service for Groups, Asian American Community Mental Health Training Center.

Yu, L., & Wu, S. (1985). Unemployment and family dynamics in meeting the needs of Chinese elderly in the United States. *The Gerontologist, 25,* 472-476.

14

Cross-National Trends in the Health-Care of the Aged

JEAN SWAFFIELD

Objectives: At the completion of this chapter, the reader will:

(1) Analyze demographic trends in selected countries and examine their relevance to gerontological nursing;
(2) Analyze approaches to formulating gerontological policies in selected countries;
(3) Evaluate methods of financing health care and make comparisons in health spending cross-nationally;
(4) Critique patterns of health care delivery internationally;
(5) Evaluate current international approaches to gerontological nursing education.

INTRODUCTION

Other chapters in this book have viewed gerontological nursing from different perspectives within society in the United States. A purpose of this chapter is to analyze the nursing care of elders from a cross-national view. An international perspective can widen the horizons of gerontological nursing issues (Henderson & Nite, 1978).

This chapter will explore cross-national trends with an emphasis on demography, health financing, responses to dependency, and the progress of gerontological nursing education in terms of worldwide issues, including responses to the Alma Ata declaration, Health for all by the year 2,000 (World Health Organization, 1985).

SELECTED INTERNATIONAL
DEMOGRAPHIC TRENDS

Social, political, economic, and demographic considerations can all influence patterns of change, as can wars and diseases. Early census were used for tax collecting and military conscription. In modern times Quebec had a census in 1665, Iceland in 1703, America in 1790, and Britain and France in 1801. Whereas in 1860, 24 countries enumerated populations, one fifth of the world total, today two thirds of the world counts its people (Cox, 1976). A 10-yearly census was included in the United States 1776 Constitution.

Census data can highlight balances between age groups, particularly applicable in gerontology to establish the numbers of elderly people, allowing predictions and projections of future trends to be made. European demographic trends are comparatively similar; Table 14.1 illustrates the number of elderly 60 and older, as a percentage of the total population and the increase in these percentages over the 6-year period. Figures 14.1 & 14.2 illustrate age group data for both individual European countries and major world blocks.

Statistics for Europeans more than 60 years of age average 18.7%, comparative United States and USSR 1987 figures were 16.1% and 13.2% respectively. By the year 2,000 nearly 20% of Europe's population will be 60 or older (World Health Statistics Quarterly, 1982). The increase in the elderly population can be seen in both absolute and proportionate terms as resulting from a sustained downward trend in the birth rate occurring at a time of decreased mortality rates of all ages. The twenty-first century faces a new phenomenon of a proportionally aging population, referred to by Fogarty as the graying of Europe (World Health Organization, 1984).

Statistics, however, cannot stand alone without careful analysis and interpretation as each country has a characteristic demographic history. An insight into some of these differences is important in formulating an understanding of demographic statistics and trends and the consequent social policy implications. Some countries have made projections about the potential increase in the aging population over the next few years. Pollard and Pollard (1981) predict that from 1976 to 2001, the number of Australians aged 65 plus will more than double, the aged population increasing from 8.6% to 12% of total population.

Greece, due to previous internal upheavals, World War II, and immigration, is one of the least industrialized countries but has the fastest aging population in the world (Dontas, 1987). In 1986, 13% of the population was 65 or older, but it is the unequal distribution within the country that is problematic; 16% live in the rural areas, compared with 10.5% in the urban centers, contrasting with the opposite trends for the young men who flock to the big cities.

Demographically, Poland's elderly, as a percentage of total population, is the lowest among Western European countries and is average among socialist

Table 14.1
Percentage of Elderly Over 60 in European Countries and 6-Year Increases

	1981	1987
Belgium	14.5	19.7
Denmark	14.4	20.3
France	13.9	18.2
Germany	15.3	20.4
Greece	13.1	18.0
Ireland	10.8	14.6
Italy	13.6	18.6
Luxembourg	13.5	18.2
Netherlands	11.6	16.7
Portugal	10.4	17.0
Spain	10.8	16.9
United Kingdom	14.9	20.6

Source: Adapted from Eurostate Demographic Statistics (1981, 1987).

countries; a lower percentage only being found in the Soviet Union, Romania, and Yugoslavia. Polish society is predicted to reach the present age structure of Western countries by the middle of the next century (Synak, 1987). The aged in Poland fluctuated between 1953-1985; however, the proportion of old people in the total population has decreased recently. Although life expectancy in most industrialized countries has risen, with women living 3-5 years longer than men, Polish women live 8 years longer (Statystyczny & Statystyczny, 1987). Recently the life expectancy for both sexes has decreased, leading to speculation that this is due to increasing environmental pollution and deteriorating hygiene and medical care (Synak, 1987). In 1980, 4.7% of Turks were at or more than 65 years of age (State Statistical Institute, 1987) in contrast to other countries, and this is considered low.

The demographic shifts within the United States are detailed in Chapter 1 of this book. U.S. figures indicate differing demographic shifts (U.S. Bureau of the Census, 1983). The low birth rate between 1920 and 1940 means fewer 1990 retirements. When the "baby boom" cohort of the 1950s begins to retire, however, a drastic change will be observed. Interestingly, an amendment to the Social Security Act in 1983 raised the retirement age to 67 years in the United States, from the year 2000 (Hendricks & Calasanti, 1986). The death rates of both males and females at age 85 and older in the United States were lower in 1975 than in other developed countries (Myers, 1978). Rice (1979) projected that there would be 38 million elderly by the year 2000 compared to the official projection of 32 million, from census analysis.

In Britain the 1981 census showed that women aged 60 and older, with men aged 65 and older, represented 14.9% of the total population, was predicted to

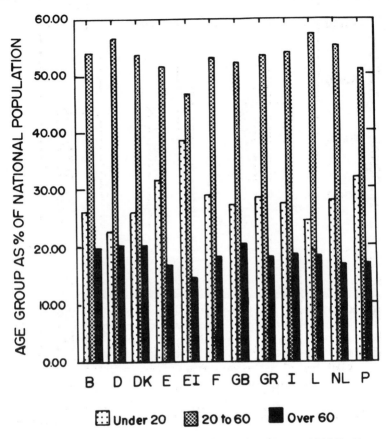

Figure 14.1. European Community Population by Age Group (1985 Data)

Source: Adapted by author from Eurostat Demographic Statistics (1987).
Note: B: Belgium; D: West Germany; DK: Denmark; E: Spain; EI: Eire; F: France; GB: Great Britain;
GR: Greece; I: Italy; L: Luxembourg; NL: Holland; P: Portugal.

rise to 20.6% by 1987, with the very elderly citizens increasing within the
elderly population itself. Between 1981 and 2001 the total number of elderly
persons is projected to rise by just over 7%, while the numbers aged 75 are
expected to increase by 31%. Increases among the very elderly are even more
dramatic: between 1981 and 2001 when the over 85s are expected to increase
by nearly 90%, almost half a million (Office of Population Censuses and
Surveys [OPCS], 1983a, 1983b, 1987).

Until recently the number of elderly in underdeveloped countries tended to
be small and unrecorded. This is expected to change dramatically, with growth
particularly marked in Asia, China and India. China and India can expect 270

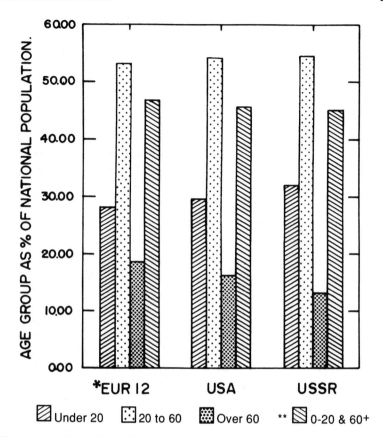

Figure 14.2. Major World Block Population

Source: Adapted by author from Eurostat Demographic Statistics (1987).
Note: *EUR 12: European community, defined in Figure 14.1.
**Major world block population comparisons, including summation of nonproductive sector (i.e., those less than 20 and more than 60).

million elderly by the turn of the century; the total population of the developing world is expected to increase by 95%; whereas the elderly population will rise by 240% (World Health Organization [WHO], 1987).

Summary

This section has highlighted demographic trends in selected countries, indicating the need to interpret data against each country's demographic history. It has also compared trends in aging between countries. The proportion of elderly in the first two decades of the next century will rise sharply in most regions of the world, especially in Asia, North America, and Europe. Having established these demographic trends within particular countries, the significance of these figures in terms of policy implications for the elderly must be assessed. Cost of care is a primary consideration in policy formulation in all countries and will be examined in the following section.

TRENDS IN HEALTH-CARE FINANCE

Completely socialized health-care systems occur in Eastern Europe, the USSR, Cuba, and China, whereas Scandinavia and the United Kingdom have incompletely socialized systems. Combined insurance, private fees, and socialized systems occur in France, the United States and the Netherlands (Fry & Hasler, 1986).

The National Health Service (NHS) in Britain was established in 1948, funded centrally except for certain patient charges, providing a full range of health services to everyone in Britain. In 1986-1987, 86% of NHS finances were raised by general taxation, 11% from NHS contributions, and 3% from prescription and other charges (National Association of Health Authorities, 1987).

Most industrialized countries have created broad, formalized social security systems for the elderly together with almost free health services. Other countries have only government funded care for the elderly, with some further categories. For instance, the United States has both private insurance and government funding, Medicare, and for the poor and disabled, Medicaid. Although some American health care is private insurance financed, most policies exclude coverage for catastrophic and long-term chronic illness. Elderly and low-income households could rarely afford adequate cover from their own resources, leading in 1968 to federal government schemes, contributing 40% by 1987 (Office for Economic Cooperation and Development, 1987). In addition, many people in the United States are left without access to health care or are unable to pay for needed services.

Third world health systems are organizationally undeveloped; local approaches to medicine exist, blending influences of former colonial countries or major aid organizations (Elling, 1981). Rapid changes in political ideology can produce corresponding changes in health provision, for example systems based on socialist models in Cuba and Nicaragua (McLachlan & Maynard, 1982; Stephen, 1979). Third world health care is frequently compounded through inherited problems from the Western World, including the diseases of industrialization, unsuitable technology, partially assimilated western culture, and the unsupervised activities of multinational corporations (T. Townsend & Davidson, 1982).

THE PROBLEM OF CROSS-NATIONAL COMPARISONS

Theoretically it should be possible to compare national health care expenditures in relationship to Gross National Product (GNP). This, however, is complicated as services differ between countries; while some countries have developed only hospital care others have highly developed community care as well.

Other differences involve government structures, policies, culture, values, philosophy, and sources of health care revenue. Comparisons are difficult when public and private insurance, and government and private pensions schemes exist. Health services even vary considerably within individual countries. Despite these difficulties, Maxwell (1981) attempted a comparison through a specially formulated analysis. From 1977 figures, he estimated health expenditures against GNP for 10 industrialized countries. Sweden, West Germany, and the United States spend 9% to 10%; 6 others between 6.4% and 8.2%. Only Britain was substantially lower, 5.2%. No evidence exists, however, that the United Kingdom's relatively low level of health care expenditure has resulted in lower levels of health (Patrick & Scambler, 1986).

PRESENT DAY SPENDING AND APPROACHES TO LIMITS ON EXPENDITURE

While national economies experienced growth, corresponding increases in health expenditure were not a concern. When, as at present, there is an economic downturn, such expenditure is questioned. It is considered no longer feasible to continue pumping a greater proportion of resources in health care without increased accountability.

Americans spent $27 billion on medical care in 1960, $387 billion in 1984, with serious consequences for the national economy; for example, automakers estimated that work force health insurance comprised nearly 10% of the cost of building a car. When Medicare was introduced in July, 1966, it spent $4.7 billion; in 1984 it spent $64 billion, including add-ons from Medicaid (Healthcare, 1987; University of Michigan, 1986). Whether measured absolutely, as a percentage of national budgets, or as GNP, the resources committed to support and care for the elderly and the general social policies increased rapidly from 1950 to 1970, being checked or reversed by the end of the 1970s.

In the United Kingdom, NHS funding appears to have increased between 1980-1981 and 1985-1986 by 46%; however, increases in staffing and equipment costs largely negate this improvement in terms of increased services (Health Service Trends, 1987). Countries are now refusing to allow health-care costs to increase at rates established in the past; efficiency and effectiveness are expected. Britain's Audit Commission's new managerial approach concentrates on economy, efficiency, and effectiveness. Resource Allocation Working Party formulas and "cash limits" were the first changes to be applied (Department of Health & Social Security, 1987). Recently, the British government has made General Practitioners more accountable for their practice, and elderly funding is soon to be the responsibility of the Local Authority. New approaches to NHS funding include income generation, while discussions are taking place to change private and social insurance (Robinson, 1988). Health care professionals are involved in pilot schemes for Resource Management Initiatives (Kings Fund Institute, 1988). Efficiency savings, through rationalization of patient services, competitive tendering for ancillary services, and reduction in labor costs were approximately 5% of total revenue expenditure in 1987 (House of Commons, 1987).

Canada has introduced "controlling" methods to prevent unlimited spending on health care. This system is seen as the most effective in the world (Hennen, 1986).

The United States has also sought greater efficiency. It introduced Diagnostic Related Groups (DRGs), a change from customary retrospective fees to a fixed price for a given service (see Chapter 9). Payment for treating 470 DRG disease categories was agreed. Although resulting in savings, total costs are still rising. Besides DRGs, Health Maintenance Organizations (HMOs) and Preferred Provider Organizations (PPOs) have been introduced to give treatment at a fixed price, usually to those in employment; the 5% membership in 1980 was expected to rise dramatically by 1990 (Health-care, 1987). As a result more patients were treated in doctor's surgeries than in expensive hospitals. The HMO trade association showed that HMO members spend less time each year in the hospital than the national average; 320 and 1,500 fewer patients days in hospital for every 1,000 members under 65 and over 65 respectively (Health-care, 1987). International comparisons demonstrate that administration costs rise with dependence on insurance funding and as a percentage of total expenditure vary considerably: United Kingdom, 5%; France and West Germany, 10%; and 21% in the United States (Maxwell, 1981).

IS SPENDING ON HEALTH CARE FOR THE ELDERLY THE WAY TO CURE ILL HEALTH?

Another problem in comparing national funding, demonstrated by regional expenditures in one country, is the distinction between illness and health promotion. In Scotland, per capita health spending is higher than in Britain as a whole, yet Scotland has the poorest health in the United Kingdom, especially for heart diseases (Brown & Cook, 1983; Health Education Council, 1987; T. Townsend & Davidson, 1982). Arguably, money for preventative care is much more relevant within health provision than money spent on hospital care, which does not necessarily produce lowered mortality and morbidity rates. A comparison of British, Swedish, and American health services found that although Sweden put emphasis on child care and the United States on elderly care, the dominant reason why Swedish mortality rates are lower than any U.S. state is a high minimum standard of living for everyone and cultural homogeneity (Anderson, 1972).

Various studies show that the health needs, met and unmet, of older people are greater than those of other population groups, as is their greater use of services. In the United States, the elderly account for 38% of inpatient hospital days, 33% of visits to the offices of medical specialists, and 90% of nursing home care. Yet the increasing proportion of elderly has only added 1% per annum of real cost of health care over the past 30 years, implying an overall health improvement for the group (Selby & Schechter, 1982). It would be wrong, however, to assume that all elderly people are ill and need monies for dealing with ill health. Promoting health remains a viable approach for the elderly as well as recognized by the World Health Organization [WHO] through the European Foundation for the Improvement of Living and Working Conditions (Fogarty, 1986).

WHO is promoting primary health care as a means of providing more appropriate and cheaper health care in both developed and developing countries. Future health policies must be directed to disease prevention and health promotion by introducing changes in life-styles and improvements in the economic and social environment.

FURTHER HEALTH CARE FUNDING FOR THE ELDERLY

Although most health policies are supported by increased taxes and benefit contributions, some authors propose that the employment of the elderly is one way to a better financed economic support ratio (P. Townsend, 1981; Walker, 1982). The actual retirement age has been falling everywhere, especially for men, with a lag among farmers and self-employed. The percentage of male workers still economically active at age 65-70 is relatively high in Ireland and Greece, but low in France and Germany (WHO, 1987).

Halting the trend to earlier retirement reduces the number of young-old needing economic support and would maintain or enlarge the tax and contribution base. Forced changes in retirement dates may reduce volunteer aid to health care organizations. Although the acceptance of such voluntary aid is culturally bound—in Britain and America it is viewed positively, whereas in Denmark and Germany there is a reluctance to utilize volunteers—the effect of these changes cannot be predicted (Fogarty, 1986). One final consideration needs addressing, however: Even though there is a preference among many old people and their families for "intimacy at a distance" for as long as they can remain independent, the cost of health care is inevitably underestimated as most care is not given by hospitals and professionals but by informal carers (Office of Population Censuses and Surveys [OPCS], 1986). Pike (1989) argues that the system of elderly care would collapse if all care had to be provided by statutory bodies or private companies.

In Britain the Carers National Association was set up to campaign for better support for carers through a Bill of Rights and the relief of isolation. Most care is given by relatives and friends of elderly and other dependent people. It is estimated that 6 million Britons are regularly involved in giving care, with 1.4 million devoting more than 20 hours a week to the task, saving the state 15 billion pounds a year (OPCS, 1986; Pike, 1989). Myles (1984) suggests that it is political as well as demographic considerations that determine who is old, who gets what, and how it is distributed.

PATTERNS OF INSTITUTIONALIZATION AND HEALTH-CARE DELIVERY SYSTEMS INTERNATIONALLY: POLICY MAKING FOR THE ELDERLY

Phillipson and Walker (1986) suggest that the description of aging by means of demographic statistics has largely substituted for social analysis of the changing meaning and experience of old age. Whereas the planning of elderly care needs to refer to demographic trends, changes, and projections, social policy decisions must be based on political considerations reflecting values and cultures together with historical experiences of previous problems. This method is not frequently used. Questions to be asked concerning policy decisions include: Having established the numbers of elderly, is this a homogenous grouping? Are universal responses required to the situation in terms of institutionalization or community care? Are the aged to be dependent on a fitter generation for further health care finance? and, Are there lessons to be learned from international patterns of health care delivery for the elderly? The following section is an attempt to address these questions.

Although scientific advances have increased longevity, the industrial world places greater emphasis on productivity and therefore fitness and mental ability to work. Two major trends appear to dominate the politics of elderly care (MacIntyre, 1977). The "humanitarian" view emphasizes the need for public policy to create conditions to minimize the personal pain of growing old. The "organizational" approach emphasizes the need to minimize the cost to the productive sector of society of the aged as a social group. Age is also synonymous with disposal, and the aged are often viewed as a problem. Fixed and compulsory retirement entail an artificial split from the productive sector of the population.

Categorization of the elderly as a group overstates the view that old people are a homogeneous group. This approach considers biological aging as more important than the determinants of the quality of life, such as social, economic, or environmental circumstances. Major differences exist between people's social and economic status in old age (Gallup Poll, 1988; Guillemard, 1987; Walker, 1981). Guillemard, in "Retraite—une mort sociale," cited in Synak (1987), examined the living patterns of retired members of a French pension fund to determine the quality of their lives and differences in approaches to being elderly. She found that 37% were lively and actively engaged or challengers, and that 36% were family centered and leisured with strong, satisfying methods of contacts; 13% were spectators, not especially happy or unhappy, drifting on the margin of life, interested in TV, housekeeping, shopping, and food; 14% were withdrawn with little purpose in life, spending much time sleeping or doing nothing, rarely going out and essentially waiting for death with a low level of satisfaction meanwhile. These classifications showed that it was not only resources, such as health, money, or housing (possessions), but potential and experiences in earlier life that determined groupings.

The majority of British elderly live at home quite happily in retirement either with relatives or alone (Gallup Poll, 1988). All elderly people do not require the same social policies just because they are old. Social and economic factors, life experiences, and physical abilities all impact on policy, implying that the elderly do not necessarily become dependent and should not be considered as a homogenous group.

ARE UNIVERSAL RESPONSES REQUIRED?

Historical responses to aging differ in each country with a realization that some planning is required for the future. Comparisons between countries have only been made slowly, each country's position depending on its internal development and industrialization. Gerontologists from 16 countries preparing a report, "Aging 2000" (World Assembly on Aging, 1982) stated

> most countries have not found adequate solutions to the problems caused by the aging of their populations; many do not have the beginnings of adequate social policy for preventing or coping with such problems. There is an urgent need for more information on elderly and aging societies as a basis for sound policies and programmes. (p. 13)

IS DEPENDENCY INEVITABLE?

Evers (1981) suggests that an open-ended commitment to providing institutional care for a rising number of dependent elderly sick people also implies an open-ended drain on economic resources. One in 20 elderly Britons require institutional care; the other 19 may need community support. When polled, 81% of senior citizens said they wanted to be cared for at home (Gallup Poll, 1988). Other countries are experiencing changes in the need for long-term care facilities for the aged. In 1981, the Federal Council on Aging projected that 2 million Americans would be in long-term care institutions by the year 2000 as against 1.3 million in 1978. In Japan, institutional care for the elderly is extremely rare; however, the problem of the frail elderly has become very acute. Culturally, the closed Japanese society has always relied on the extended family to provide the required care for the elderly. Western influences following the end of the Second World War have led to more women working, resulting in a collapse of the traditional roles within the family. Household sizes are decreasing as families are becoming more mobile. All of these factors combine to accentuate the need for government planning (Ogawa, 1989).

The health of the elderly, expressed by their disability and limited activity, could determine their ability to function independently. In 1978, 38% of the U.S. elderly population had a chronic condition resulting in loss of major activity compared to 11% of the total population (Givins, 1979). An Office of Population Censuses and Surveys (1988) survey of 55 million Britons found 6 million disabled, 4 million in old age;, however only 6% of old age pensioners live in an institution (Scottish Home & Health Department (SHHD) 1984). It appears that admission to a hospital for long-term care arises from a lack of social networks, rather than a necessity for continuous nursing care. Many hospitalized patients soon become dependent, however, through the care given within institutions (Goffman, 1961; Munnichs & Van Den Heuvan, 1976; & P. Townsend, 1981). The ethos of formal services is still predominately provision for old people rather than by them ignoring the need to take into account their capacity to cope and contribute. Recognition of self-rated health status is important instead of promoting dependency for the elderly (Heikkinen, 1983). Four approaches are required for the elderly to maintain a healthy life: services preserving the continuity of life-style, compensating services, life enhancing services, and care services (Heikkinen, 1984).

CROSS-NATIONAL TRENDS IN GERONTOLOGICAL NURSING

Traditionally custodial care for the elderly has been paramount; it has been task orientated, lacking direction or philosophy, and resulting in increased dependency within institutions, encouraging learned helplessness (Seligman, 1975) and loss of self-esteem (Robb, 1967; P. Townsend, 1964). Nurses have emphasized physical care, carried out with few staff without goal directions, leading some researchers to comment that geriatric nursing shares the central problem of all nursing; nurses do not know why they do what they do (Wells, 1980). Some reports in England still reflect this state of affairs (Health Advisory Service, 1986). In the last decade, some changes have occurred in gerontological nursing, especially in North America, followed slowly in Britain. The major change is from geriatric to gerontological nursing, a move from responding to disease processes to helping those with diseases experienced during old age to maximize their capacity throughout the aging process. A strong nursing division of the American Nurses' Association (1987) developed the Council on Gerontological Nursing, publishing its own standards of gerontological nursing practice. Clinical nurse specialists in gerontological nursing train at the graduate level, obtaining master's degrees. An attempt is being made to see each elderly person as a unique historical evolution of beliefs, life experiences, health practices, and habits, presenting a challenge to the nurse (Hogstel, 1981). In most industrial countries, however, nurses' negative attitudes still reflect society's perception. In the United States this is evident in the research by Hatton (1977), in Britain by Fielding (1986), in Australia by Curtis (1987), and by Kappeli (1986) in Switzerland. It is recognized that exposing students to the well and normal aged before caring for chronically ill patients may improve nurses' attitudes toward the elderly.

Curtis (1987), in reviewing the literature relating to aged care in Australia, indicates that the current trend in nursing homes and hostels is towards an increasingly dependent population of elderly and that there is a link between the qualifications and competence of nursing staff and the quality of care and life of the residents. In arguing for an increase in staffing levels to meet the need, she also draws attention to the need for the accompanying provision of orientation courses for staff and for ongoing education. Abbey (1987) suggests distance education as an option for geriatric nurses.

Efforts are being made to replace custodial with individualized care for elderly persons in the community, with greater emphasis on interdisciplinary team approaches. The role of the gerontological nurse has become educator, innovator, and advocate. The use of the systematic nursing process would be more successful if the elderly's strengths were identified and used to maximize independence (Baltes, Honn, Barton, Orzech, & Largo, 1983). Geriatric nursing was finally introduced in the syllabus of British student nurse training in 1973, when the Joint Board of Clinical Nursing Studies produced a 6-month course for state registered nurses and enrolled nurses (Pinel, 1976). The British Geriatrics Society (BSG) has defined geriatric medicine as concerned with the clinical, rehabilitative, social, and preventative aspects of illness and health in the elderly.

America is attempting to prove that the most innovative means of achieving a systematic change in health care delivery systems for the elderly is through the impact of educational and research efforts of professionals, targeted on promoting their wellness. Heikkinen (1984) argues that in Europe current research and training in gerontology and geriatrics is insufficient to provide medical and social workers with adequate knowledge, positive attitudes, and proper skills to serve old people who, in contrast, are the main consumers of medical services.

The need to teach gerontologic content has been recognized in Israel and has been integrated in basic nursing education (Golander & Hirschfeld, 1981). The gap between a lack of preparation and knowledge is being bridged by continuing education courses in gerontologic nursing. Nurses are involved in research of the older adult (Golander, 1987) and nurses are included in legislative policy formation. In contrast, in some countries nursing education and practice is reminiscent of nursing in America in years gone by; Liu (1983), however, suggests that the goal of nursing in China is to be located in the university system. In the USSR, nurses make no judgments and are subordinate to the physician (Duncan, 1982). In Japan, nursing care of the aged is taught as a part of the basic three-year nursing course and there are few teachers who specialize in nursing care of the aged, where curriculum content is regulated by the government (Endo, 1981). Nursing research for the aged in Japan has not progressed significantly; however, the number of publications has increased since 1970 (Endo, 1981).

Nurses who provide care for older adults in both Norway and Denmark have increased responsibility and many benefits (Jordheim, 1980; Meador, 1980). Nurses in these countries are able to make many independent judgments concerning health care needs of the older adult, including ordering some medications and treatments. Employees of some health care facilities stay free in cottages in the mountains or near the seashore. Nurses in Norway serve as inspectors for nursing homes and can climb the career ladder.

The nursing shortage is acute in many countries around the world, including Australia, Canada, Japan, the United Kingdom and the United States. Some European countries have a low turnover of nurses due to excellent personnel polices for registered nurses, however in Britain there is a high turnover rate among home health nurses (Sobel, 1981).

SUMMARY

Cross-nationally people are living longer and there is an increased need for a continuum of health care services for this age group. The cost of health care has become an international concern and most governments are seeking to regulate payment by improving effectiveness and efficiency of service. Most developed nations provide a system of national health care insurance for all citizens. Health care policy should be based not only on demographics but also on the cultural history of a country. The older adult population in the United States is extremely diverse and heterogenous, whereas in Sweden the life-style of the citizens is more alike, suggesting that in the United States a variety of services will be needed by some but not by others. Health promotion and home health care services have been recognized internationally as the most beneficial approach to cutting health care cost and improving the satisfaction of the older age group who prefer to remain independent at home as long as possible. Cross-nationally, nursing education is moving to institutions of higher education; and practice is more focused on prevention and providing a continuum of services rather than on institutionalization and dependency. In conclusion, it would seem that internationally more networking, comparison of approaches, and knowledge of other countries' achievements can only be of benefit in making policy involving the elderly.

REFERENCES

Abbey, J. (1987). Distance education: An option for geriatric nurses. *The Australian Journal of Advanced Nursing, 4,* 4-11.

American Nurses' Association. (1987). Standards and scope of gerontological nursing practice. Division of Gerontological Nursing. Kansas City, MO: American Nurses' Association.

Anderson, O. W. (1972). *Health-care: Can there be equity?* New York: John Wiley.

Baltes, M., Honn, S., Barton, E., Orzech, M., & Largo, D. (1983). On the social ecology of dependence and independence in elderly nursing home residents: A replication and extension. *Journal of Gerontology, 38,* 556-564.

Brown, G., & Cook, R. (1983). *Scotland: The real divide.* Edinburgh: Mainstream Publishing.

Cox, P. (1976). *Demography* (5th Ed.). Cambridge, UK: Cambridge University Press.

Curtis, C. (1987). Aged care in Australia: A review of the literature. *The Australian Journal of Advanced Nursing, 4,* 5-15.

Department of Health and Social Security. (1987). Sharing resources for health in England: Report of the Resource Allocation Working Party. London: HMSO.

Dontas, A. S. (1987). Primary social and health services for the aged in Greece. In S. Gregorio (Ed.), *Social gerontology: New directions.* London: Croom Helm.

Duncan, L. (1982, July/August). Observations of elder care in the U.S.S.R. *Geriatric Nursing,* 257-259.

Elling R. (1981). Political economy, cultural hegenomy and mix of traditional and modern medicine. *Social Science and Medicine,* 15A, 89-99.

Endo, C. (1981). Nursing care of the aged in Japan. *Journal of Gerontological Nursing, 7,* 681-688.

Evers, H. K. (1981). Tender loving care: Patients and nurses in geriatric wards. In L. Copp (Ed.), *Care of the aging.* Edinburgh: Churchill Livingstone.

Eurostat Demographic Statistics. (1981). Office of Official Publications of the European Community. Luxembourg: Author.

Eurostat Demographic Statistics. (1987). Office of Official Publications of the European Community. Luxembourg. Author.

Fielding, P. (1986). *Attitudes revisited: An examination of student nurses' attitude towards old people in hospital.* London: Royal College of Nursing.

Fogarty, M. (1986). *Meeting the needs of the elderly. The European Foundation for the improvement of living and working conditions.* Shanklin, Ireland: Loughlins House.

Fry, J., & Hasler, J. (1986). *Primary health-care 2,000.* Edinburgh: Churchill Livingstone.

Gallup Poll. (1988). Conference report. Cited in *Journal of Advanced Nursing* (1989), *14,* 346-348.

Givins, J. D. (1979, November). *Current estimates from the health interview survey: United States 1978.* National Center for Health Statistics. *Vital and health statistics,* Series 10, No. 130.

Goffman, E. (1961). *Asylums.* Harmondsworth, UK: Pelican.

Golander, H. (1987). Under the guize of passivity. *Journal of Gerontological Nursing, 13,* 26-31.

Golander, H., & Hirschfeld, M. (1981). Nursing care of the aged in Israel. *Journal of Gerontological Nursing, 7,* 677-680.

Guillemard, A. (1987). Retraite—une mort sociale. Cited by Synak in S. Gregorio (Ed.), *Social gerontology: New directions,* London: Croom Helm.

Hatten, J. (1977). Nurses attitude toward the aged: Relationship to nursing care. *Journal of Gerontological Nursing, 3,* 21-26.

Health Education Council. (1987). The health divide: Inequalities in health in the 1980's. *Health Education Authorities Association.* London: HMSO.

Health Advisory Service. (1986). *Annual report 1985/1986.* Sutton Surrey.

Health-care—The battle to contain cost. (1987, October, 3). *The Economist, 305,* 44-46.

Health Service Trends. (1987). The Chartered Institute of Public Finance and Accountancy Health Service Financial Management Association. London: Author.

Heikkinen, E. (1983). The elderly in eleven countries: A sociomedical survey. *Public Health in Europe (WHO Publication No. 21). Copenhagen: World Health Organization.*

Heikkinen, E. (1984). Implications of demographic change for the elderly population. In *Demographic trends in the European region.* (WHO Publications, European Series 17, 161-175). Copenhagen: World Health Organization.

Henderson, V. & Nite, G. (1978). *Principles and practice of nursing.* New York: Macmillan.

Hendricks, J., & Calasanti, T. (1986). Social policy and ageing in the United States. In C. Phillipson & A. Walker (Eds.), *Aging and social policy.* Aldershot, UK: Gower.

Hennen, B. (1986). Canada. In J. Fry & J. Hasler (Eds.), *Primary health-care 2,000.* Edinburgh: Churchill Livingstone.

Hogstel, M. D. (1981). *Nursing care of the older adult.* New York: John Wiley.

House of Commons. (1987). *Public expenditure on the social services. Social Services Committee, session 1986-1987.* London: HMSO.

Jordheim, A. (1980). Old age in Norway—A time to look forward to. *Geriatric Nursing.*

Kappeli, S. (1988). Nurses' management of patients' self-care. *Nursing Times, 82,* 40-43.

King's Fund Institute. (1988). *Health finance: Assessing the options, King's Fund Institute.* London: Author.

Liu, Y. (1983). China: Health care in transition. *Nursing Outlook, 31,* 94-99.

MacIntyre, S. (1977). Old age as a social problem. In R. Dingwall, C. Heath, M. Reid, & M. Stacey (Eds.), *Health care and health knowledge.* London: Croom Helm.

McLachlan, G., & Maynard, A. (Eds.). (1982). *The public/private mix for health: The relevance and effect of change.* London: Nuffield Provincial Hospitals Trust.

Maxwell, R. J. (1981). *Health and wealth.* Lexington, MA: Lexington.

Meador, R. (1980). Old age in Denmark—a time to enjoy. *Geriatric Nursing,* 48-49.

Munnichs, J. M. A., & Van Den Heuvan, W. J. A. (Eds.). (1976). *Dependency or interdependency in old age.* The Hague: Martinus Nijhoff.

Myers, C. (1978). Cross national trends in mortality rates among the elderly. *The Gerontologist, 18,* 441-448.

Myles, J. (1984, November). *Does class matter? Explaining America's modern welfare state.* Chicago: University of Chicago Press.

National Association of Health Authorities. (1987). *N.H.S. Handbook NAHA* London: Macmillan.

Office for Economic Cooperation and Development. (1987). *Financing and delivering health-care.* Paris: Author.

Office of Population Censuses and Surveys. (1983a). *Census data 1901-1981 and government actuary projections* (OPCS, PP2, No. 13). London. HMSO.

Office of Population Censuses and Surveys. (1983b, March). *Population projections, mid 1981* (PP2/83/18). London: HMSO.

Office of Population Censuses and Surveys. (1986). Informal carers. London: HMSO.

Office of Population Censuses and Surveys. (1987). *Great Britain: Demographic review 1984* (Series Dr No. 2). London: HMSO.

Office of Population Censuses and Surveys. (1988). *The prevalence of disability among adults* (Report 1). London: HMSO.

Ogawa, N. (1989). Population ageing audits impact upon health resources requirements at government and familial level in Japan. *Ageing and Society, 9,* 383-405.

Patrick, D. L., & Scambler, G. (1986). *Sociology as applied to medicine* (2nd ed.). London: Bailliere Tindall.

Phillipson, C., & Walker, A. (1986). *Aging and social policy.* Aldershot, UK: Gower.

Pike, A. (1989, December, 18). *Financial Times,* 30.

Pinel, C. (1976). Geriatrics as a speciality. *Nursing Times, 72,* 1601-1603.

Pollard, A. H., & Pollard, G. N. (1981). The demography of aging in Australia. In A. Howe (Ed.), *Towards an older Australia.* Brisbane: University of Queensland Press.

Rice, D. P. (1979, October). Long life to you. *American Demographics,* 9-15.

Robb, B. (1967). *Sans everything—A case to answer.* London: Nelson.

Robinson, R. (1988, ᵘpring/Summer). New approaches to the finance and delivery of health-care. *Public Money and Management,* 51-56.

Scottish Home and Health Department (1984). *Scottish health service costs for the year ended 31st March.* Edinburgh: HMSO.

Selby, P., & Schechter, M. (1982). Aging 2,000—A challenge for society. (Published for the Sandoz Institute for Health and Socio-Economic Studies) London: M.T.P. Press.

Seligman, M. E. (1975). *Helplessness.* San Francisco: Freeman.

Sobel, M. (1989, September). Growing old in Britain. *Aging,* 8-16.

Statystyczny, R., & Statystyczny, M. R. (1987). In S. Gregorio (Ed.), *Social gerontology: New directions.* London: Croom Helm.

State Statistical Institute. (1987). 1980 census of population: Social and economic characteristics of population (provincial data). Ankara. In S. Gregorio (Ed.), *Social gerontology: New directions.* London: Croom Helm.

Stephen, W. J. (1979). *An analysis of primary medical care: An international study.* Cambridge, UK: Cambridge University Press.

Synak, B. (1987). The elderly in Poland: An overview of selected problems and changes. In S. Gregorio (Ed.), *Social gerontology: New directions.* London: Croom Helm.

Townsend, P. (1964). *The last refuge: A survey of residential institutions and homes for the aged in England and Wales.* London: Routledge & Kegan Paul.

Townsend, P. (1981). The structured dependency of the elderly: A creation of social policy in the twentieth century. *Aging and Society, 1,* 5-28.

Townsend, T., & Davidson, N. (1982). *Inequalities in health.* Harmondsworth, UK: Penguin.

U.S. Bureau of the Census. (1983). *Statistical abstract of the United States* (104th Ed.). Washington, DC: Government Printing Office.

University of Michigan. (1986, July/August). *Research News,* 1-13.

Walker, A. (1981). Towards a political economy of old age. *Aging and Society, 1,* 73-94.

Walker, A. (1982, Summer). Dependency and old age. *Social Policy and Administration, 16*(2), 115-135.

Wells, T. J. (1980). *Problems in geriatric nursing care.* Edinburgh: Churchill Livingstone.

World Assembly on Aging (1982, August). Plan of action from the meeting of the United Nations Assembly on Aging in Vienna.

World Health Organization. (1984). *Demographic trends in the European region.* Copenhagen: Author.

World Health Organization. (1985). *Targets for health for all. Targets in support of the European regional strategy for health for all.* WHO Regional Office for Europe. Copenhagen: Author.

World Health Organization. (1987). *World health statistics annual.* Geneva: Author.

World Health Statistics Quarterly. (1982). *35,* 135, Geneva: World Health Organization.

P A R T   I I

The Maintenance, Treatment, and
Restorative Nursing Care of
Older Adults Who Have Actual or
Potential Health Care Problems

ILLNESS IN AGING AND THE ROLE OF
THE GERONTOLOGICAL NURSE

15

Conceptualization of Chronicity in Aging

ELIZABETH MURROW BAINES
F. MADELYNN OGLESBY

Objectives: At the completion of this chapter, the reader will be able to:

(1) Analyze the prevalence and effect of chronic illness in the elderly.
(2) Critique selected theoretical approaches to nursing care of older adults who experience chronic illness.
(3) Evaluate assessment tools utilized to assess the elderly.
(4) Analyze the impact of family caregiving on older adults. Apply nursing care strategies that assist in chronic illness care for the elderly.

INTRODUCTION

Older adults experience more chronic conditions than acute episodes. In the United States, however, the focus of health care service is on medical treatment and acute care facilities. The majority of expenditures for older adults are for episodic treatment and institutionalization. In 1987, government programs spent approximately $102 billion for health care for older adults and of this amount, hospital expenses accounted for the largest share (42%), followed by physicians (21%), and nursing homes at 20% (Fowles, 1989). In contrast, total expenses for home based care for disabilities associated with chronic conditions in the elderly in 1982, have been estimated to be $4.2 billion (Liu, Manton,

& Liu, 1985). Fowles (1989) indicated that it costs older adults an average of $5,360 per year for health care, more than three times the $1,290 spent by younger persons in this country. Approximately one fourth of the $5,360 spent for health care is personal expense for older persons (Fowles, 1989).

Not only is more money spent for medical treatment and institutionalization for the elderly than for chronic illness care, there are also misconceptions about who provides the care. Although health care services are usually conceptualized as being performed by professionals in institutions, the majority of caring is done by family members and friends in the home. According to Chappel, Strain, and Blandford (1986) at least 80% of all health care is provided by family members, even when some formal care is being administered by health care professionals. In addition, the middle-aged daughter has been identified in research as the primary provider of care to parents; however, older adults provide at least half of the care given to other older adults in the home, despite their vulnerability to chronic conditions and decreased resources (Bennett, 1983).

Chronic illness has been described as the major health care problem in this country and attempts have been made to define chronicity (Atchley, 1988; Craig & Edwards, 1983; Fowles, 1989; Lawrence & Lawrence, 1979). The literature indicates that chronic illness is a disease or disability, frequently requiring life-style changes for both the person afflicted and those people involved, and it has the potential for requiring resources and services. The term "chronic illness" refers to a long-term condition characterized by the progressive decline in function and is caused by nonreversible pathology or injury (Craig & Edwards, 1983). Chronic illness affects all ages, although a higher proportion of elderly people suffer chronic conditions. The growing prevalence of chronic illness is due both to control of infectious disease and to technology. Some of the most frequently occurring chronic conditions among the elderly include the following: arthritis (48%), hypertension (37%), heart disease and hearing impairments (30%) each, orthopedic impairments (17%), cataracts (16%), sinusitis (15%), diabetes (10%), and tinnitus (9%) (Fowles, 1989). According to Craig and Edwards, the trajectory of chronic illness is generally in a downward direction. The trajectory varies, however, as plateau and remissions occur. The goal for the person afflicted with a chronic illness, and his or her significant others, is adaptation and normalization of selected life-style.

This chapter evaluates the incidence and outcome of chronic conditions among the elderly, analyzes selected theoretical approaches to chronic illness care, critiques instruments to assess chronicity, analyzes the impact of family caregiving on older adults, and suggests approaches to nursing care for older persons afflicted with chronic conditions.

CHRONIC ILLNESS IN OLDER ADULTS

The number and percentage of older adults in the population is rapidly increasing. In 1988, approximately 12.4% of the population of the United States was 65 years of age and older (U.S. Bureau of the Census, 1990). This means that about one person in every eight (30.4 million) is 65 years of age or older (Fowles, 1989). Projections of the number and percentage of older persons in the population indicate that in the year 2030, there will be 66 million older adults representing 22% of the total population in the United States (Atchley, 1988; Fowles, 1989). Similar projections were made by Perlman (1982), who suggested that the elderly are the largest group at risk for home care and that this age group is expected to double in number in the next 50 years. Persons more than 75 years of age will increase at a more rapid rate and persons in this age group require more health care services than younger age groups. It has been suggested that these population projections may be conservative and that the elderly population may grow at an even faster rate (Personnel for Health Needs of the Elderly, 1987).

Projections have been made about the extent of chronic illness in older adults (Atchley, 1988; Frankfather, Smith, & Caro, 1981; Personnel for Health Needs of the Elderly, 1987). According to Frankfather, Smith, and Caro approximately 80%-85% of those who are 65 years of age and older have one or more chronic illnesses or debilitating diseases. Fowles suggested that most older persons have at least one chronic condition. The illness itself is not always the prevailing issue, however (Lefton & Lefton, 1979). The effect of the chronic illness on the life-style of the individual and family may become the central concern.

Not only are there a variety of projections about the incidence of chronic illness in the older population, but there are also conflicting reports about the type and amount of assistance required by older persons who have long-term conditions (Beland, 1987; Feller, 1983; Fowles, 1989; Horowitz, 1985; Macken, 1986; Shanas, 1974, 1979; Stone, Cafferata, & Sangl, 1987). Estimates range from 2.8 million older adults living in the community who need the assistance of another person in managing self-care activities (Feller, 1983) to approximately 6 million (Fowles, 1989). Self care or activities of daily living (ADLs) include bathing, dressing, eating, transferring from bed or chair, walking, getting outside, and using the toilet. Home management or instrumental activities (IDLs) include preparing meals, shopping, managing money, using the telephone, and doing housework and are needed by 7.1 million elderly (Fowles, 1989). Most elderly who require aid in home management reported receiving assistance; in contrast, less than half who had difficulty with personal care had help (Fowles, 1989; Personnel for Health Needs of the Elderly, 1987). The majority of private and public funding is based on the elders' abilities to preform ADLs (Stone & Murtaugh, 1990). Only 411,000 elders meet the restrictive criteria, but over 4 million would be eligible under more expansive criteria (Stone & Murtaugh, 1990).

Folden (1990) indicated that approximately 8% of older adults are homebound due to chronic conditions and Liang, Gall, Partridge, and Eaton (1983) suggested that 5% of the population more than 65 years of age must stay at home due to disabilities. Horowitz (1985) and Shanas (1979) reported that older persons living in the community, who have chronic disabilities and stay in bed all or most of the day, may exceed the number who are bedfast in institutions. In 1974, Shanas studied old people in six countries to examine their health status. The results indicated that in each country from 2% to 4% were bedfast at home. In 1979, Shanas reported about 3% of a national noninstitutionalized population of older persons were bedfast and 7% were housebound. Using statistics from the National Health survey, Feller (1983) reported an estimated 848,000 adults living outside of institutions usually stay in bed all or most of the time due to a chronic health problem. Feller reports a sharp increase in the percentage of persons remaining all or most of the day in bed: between 65 and 75 years of age (11.3 per 1,000); 75 years of age and older (30.4); and 51.2 for persons 85 year of age and older. No significant differences were found between females and males in the rates of adults who stay in bed all or most of the time.

The increasing incidence of Acquired Immunodeficiency Syndrome (AIDS) in the older adult could require more formal and informal health care services for those afflicted. There are 1,718 reported cases of AIDS in the 65 years of age and over population in the United States (Center for Disease Control, HIV/AIDS Surveillance Report, 1990). The majority of older adult AIDS victims are male (1,326) and the primary route of transmission of the human immunodeficiency virus (HIV) is transfusion, in contrast to the primary route of transmission for other age groups. However, the potential for needing health care assistance over an extended period of time is high for all age groups with AIDS.

Not only do older persons experience more chronic illnesses and receive more treatments in the home than younger persons, but they are also hospitalized more frequently and for longer periods of time for acute conditions (Atchley, 1988; Fowles, 1989). Using the federal government's prospective payment plan, the hospitalized older adult is being discharged much more severely ill and in need of complex nursing care. Many are ineligible for paid home health care (Gamroth, 1988; McGovern & Newbern, 1988; Meiners & Coffey, 1985; E. Phillips, Fisher, MacMillan-Scattergood, & Baglioni, 1989; Public Policy and Aging Report, 1987). The average length of stay in an acute care hospital has decreased 5.6 days since 1968 and an additional 2.1 days since 1980 (Fowles, 1989). The prospective payment system encourages skimping on diagnostic tests and results in hospital readmission instead of facilitating a continuum of needed care and services (Public Policy and Aging Report, 1987).

In a newsletter from South Carolina Women (1990), a sorrowful example of early discharge without adequate follow-up care was given. A women 71 years of age who had cared for her husband with terminal cancer for 11 years stated, "The last thing I remember of the hospital was being told they needed his bed and I was to take him out of there. No advice as to what I was to do with him, just take him away" (p. 1).

In a study to determine potential predictors of institutionalization of chronically ill older persons, Worchester and Quayhagen (1983) found that recent hospitalization for physical illness and subsequent recommendation by the physician were the highest predictor variables for placement in nursing homes. Community based services provided in the home and designed to increase the functional status of disabled elderly could delay or prevent institutionalization and increase the number of persons maintained at home (Personnel for Health Needs of the Elderly, 1987). In an analyses of data from the 1982 National Long-Term Care Survey with supplemental data from the American Housing Survey, however, Newman, Struyk, Wright, and Rice (1990) found that formal, paid home care did not reduce the risk of institutionalization; instead, it was associated with greater risk of institutionalization. Leibson, Naessens, Krishan, Campion, and Ballard (1990) found increased mortality and nursing home transfers following the introduction of DRGs but indicate the increases are explained by risk factors other than early discharge from hospitals (see Chapter 1 for additional health statistics for older adults).

In summary, there are increasing numbers of older persons in the population and many will experience one or more chronic illness requiring another person's assistance with the activities of daily living and home management. Older adults who live in the community utilize more nursing services and assistive devices than other age groups. Early discharge from hospitals increases the need for skilled nursing service among older adults, and the lack of needed care places the older adult at risk for readmittance to an institution and additional cost in both human and economic terms.

MODELS OF CHRONIC ILLNESS CARE

There are numerous models that have been developed by nurses and other health care professionals to examine chronic illness and its effect on the family and society (Bass & Noelker, 1987; Craig & Edwards, 1983; Gallagher, 1985; Hymovich, 1987; Kahana & Young, 1990; Lawrence & Lawrence, 1979; Lefton & Lefton, 1979; MacVicar & Archbold, 1976; J. Miller, 1983; Nerenz & Leventhal, 1983; Pallett, 1990; Strauss et al., 1984). Few if any of the conceptual frameworks proposed have created an acceptable paradigm for the caregiver-care recipient process.

The framework proposed by Strauss et al. (1984) suggested that one must think of any disease or chronic illness as causing problems of daily living for the person so unfortunate as to be afflicted and that the family must confront presenting problems. Archbold (1980) utilized an earlier version of Strauss et al.'s (1984) framework to view data on six families who were caring for an elderly parent who had suffered a stroke. The results indicated that strain, ambivalence, life-style changes, decision making and support systems are key issues to understanding the caregiver experience. In 1984, Baines utilized some concepts of the Strauss's model to investigate the problems and coping of older family caregivers of care recipients who were also elderly. The findings suggested that Strauss' model is useful when considering medical problems and life-style adjustments; however, it does not include nursing approaches.

In the model developed by Lefton and Lefton (1979), the importance of a team approach to chronic illness in an institution was emphasized. The model suggested that there is a need for more than medical care in the treatment of chronically ill persons and their families. The framework focuses on an institutional arrangement for the delivery of services by a team of health care professionals. Despite the attempt by Lefton and Lefton to place the patient in a central position, the limitations of this approach include the fact that most older adults are not in institutional settings. According to the authors, this approach remains to be empirically tested. Lefton and Lefton's model, however, does assign nursing a priority role on the hospital team.

Craig and Edwards (1983), in their eclectic model of chronic illness care, suggested that the primary role of the nurse is to assist the individual and family to adapt to the illness and its ramifications. Some concepts in this model include caring, reappraisal, and adjustment.

In 1987, Littlefield utilized Roy's model of adaptation for nursing in an investigation of the functional status of older adults who were chronically mentally ill. Another approach that has been applied in chronicity care is Orem's Self Care model.

Orem's self-care model has been suggested as a framework for nursing care of the aged (Burnside, 1988). This framework enables the nurse to view the competing demands of caregivers of the elderly (Bunting, 1989), to examine the ability of caregivers to assess the functional status of care recipients (Biggs, 1990), to assess elders (Bower & Patterson, 1986), and to investigate older family caregiver stress and the functional status of elder care recipients (Schindler, 1989). Burnside, however, suggested that because patients are being discharged home from hospitals with complex nursing care needs, self-care may be impossible for many of them.

A theory similar to Orem's was developed by Nerenz and Leventhal (1983), entitled the "self-regulation theory of chronic illness." This model includes concepts of information processing and adapting to the disease.

In 1981, Goldstein, Regnery, and Wellin attempted to construct a framework involving role theory as an approach to investigating family caregivers of the chronically ill. Their study investigated caregivers experiencing role conflict, fatigue, and constriction. Stoller and Pugliesi (1989) investigated roles of competing responsibilities of caregivers and found that some outside roles were associated with improved well-being.

Stress theory has also been utilized as a framework for describing chronic illness care. According to Lawrence and Lawrence (1979), chronic illness is usually either a primary or secondary stressor to the individual. Those suffering from chronic illness go through a process of adaptation to stress in distinct stages (Lawrence & Lawrence, 1979). This model is limited to the description of the adaptation to stress in the chronically ill person, it does not consider the potential for stress in family caregivers. In 1990, Jenkins utilized Neuman's Systems Model to investigate the stress of the caregiver-care recipient dyad. The study of stress has been recommended as a fertile field of investigation among nurses (Fagin, 1987) and as an arena that has considerable room for continued improvement (Lowery, 1987).

In 1976, MacVicar and Archbold proposed a framework for family assessment in chronic illness. This approach utilized Hill's crisis model to examine the characteristics of the illness, the family's perception of the condition and the family's potential resources.

Hymovich (1987) suggested that the clinical usefulness of some of the proposed models for assessment and adaptation to chronic illness has rarely been documented. In 1979, Hymovich proposed a model in which the developmental tasks of the individual experiencing the chronic illness and the involved family were assessed and the perceptions, resources, and coping abilities were identified. The model proposed that nursing interventions be based on these assessments. In a subsequent revision, Hymovich's (1987) model includes seven major components for viewing chronic illness care: the precipitating event, system, mediating variables, capabilities, needs, time, and intervention. Hymovich's model is comprehensive because it includes the majority of concepts related to chronic illness care and adds the dimension of time not usually included in models of chronic illness.

In 1983, Loomis and Wood proposed a multivariate model for nurses based on the American Nurses' Association (ANA) definition of nursing (American Nurses' Association, 1980) in which all human response systems interact with all actual or potential health problems as well as with the clinical decision-making process. The utility of Loomis and Wood's model is the multivariate approach, use of the nursing process, and ANA definitions of nursing, as well as the provision of a mechanism for evaluation.

Another model that lends itself to adaptation to chronicity care is the framework proposed by Carnevelli, Mitchell, Woods, and Tanner (1984). According to Carnevelli et al. (1984), nursing's domain for diagnosis and treatment focuses on the client's activities of daily living, the environment within which the daily living takes place, and functional health status. Carnevelli et al.'s (1984) framework contains many concepts related to chronic illness care and indicates the interaction of nursing intervention.

In summary, many models have been proposed to view chronic illness care and its effect on families, but few have been tested. There is little agreement among health care professionals about which framework is the most effective; however, there is a general consensus that a comprehensive, multidimensional model is urgently needed to serve as a guide for both research and service programs for persons with chronic conditions and for those people who assist them.

INSTRUMENTS TO ASSESS CHRONICITY IMPACT

Some theoretical models of chronic illness care include guidelines for assessment (Carnevelli et al. 1984; Craig & Edwards, 1983; Hymovich, 1979, 1987; Loomis & Wood, 1983; MacVicar & Archbold, 1976). Other conceptual approaches, however, report few assessment measures (Goldstein et al., 1981; Lawrence & Lawrence, 1979; Lefton & Lefton, 1979). The majority of instruments that have been developed to assess chronicity in older adults examine the functional status in the person being treated in a variety of settings (Ballard & McNamara, 1983; Becker & Cohen, 1984; Beland, 1987; Burton, Cairl, Keller, & Pfeiffer, 1983; Fortinsky, Granger, & Seltzer, 1981; Gurland et al., 1977-1978; Lawton, 1983; Liang et al., 1983; Panicucci, 1983; Pfeiffer, 1981; Quinn & Ryan, 1979; Talbot, 1985). *Functional status* can be viewed as the person's ability to perform the activities of daily living (Becker & Cohen, 1984). The following section is a critique of selected assessment instruments for use with older adult care recipients and caregivers.

The Older American Resources and Services (OARS) instrument assesses functioning in the aged person in five areas: social, economic, mental health, physical health, and activities of daily living (Multidimensional Functional Assessment, 1978). Specific disadvantages of this tool are its length, time required for administration, and omission of spiritual and environmental variables, as well as the influence of the functional disability on involved persons. In 1981, Pfeiffer developed an abbreviated version of the OARS questionnaire, the Functional Assessment Inventory (FAI). Both the OARS and the FAI include a component to determine the level of cognitive functioning of the person being assessed, the Short Portable Mental Status Questionnaire (SPMSQ). Gatz, Pedersen, and Harris (1987) examined psychometric properties of the mental health scale from the OARS and reported that global test scores can be misleading, especially when applied to different age groups.

Several other questionnaires examine the mental and cognitive functions of older adults (Lawton & Storandt, 1984; Matteson & McConnell, 1988).

In 1987, Helmes, Csapo, and Short reported the development of a Multi-dimensional Observational Scale for Elderly Subjects (MOSES). This scale assesses functioning, self-care, behavior, and mood. A similar instrument is the Physical and Mental Impairment of Function Evaluation (PAMIE) by Gurel, Linn, and Linn (1972). Another approach to measuring functional status is the Geriatric Evaluation by Relatives Rating Instrument (GERRI) that is designed to ask relatives of elderly outpatients with symptoms of mental decline, functional assessment questions (Schwartz, 1983).

Some researchers utilize ADL scales to measure functional status (Rubenstein, Schairer, Wieland, & Kane, 1984; Silliman, Fletcher, Earp, & Wagner, 1986; Wolinsky, Coe, Miller, & Prendergast, 1984). The Katz ADL scale is a measure of basic functioning requiring a skilled observer to rate the presence of six specific ADLs including bathing, dressing, going to the toilet, transferring, continence, and feeding (Rubenstein et al., 1984). According to Rubenstein et al. these six basic functions are usually lost in specific sequence when persons become disabled and they are generally restored in reverse sequence with recovery or successful rehabilitation.

The Physical Self Maintenance Scale (PSMS), developed by the Philadelphia Geriatric Center, is similar to the ADL assessment and includes measurement of six functional areas (Rubenstein et al., 1984). According to Rubenstein et al., the PSMS differs from the Katz ADL scale in that any health care personnel can administer the tool.

In 1977-1978, Gurland et al. conducted a cross-national study to detect potential health problems in the elderly and to make referrals when needed. They utilized the Comprehensive Assessment and Referral Evaluation (CARE) instrument.

In 1983, Ballard and McNamara (1983) designed a health status scale that included problems with ADLs as well as nursing care needs. According to the authors, the health status score proved to be the best indicator of need for nursing service in the home for cancer patients.

In 1987, Beland reported the development of an instrument to classify long-term patients by type of service (CTMSP). Beland indicates that service requirements, rather than illnesses or disabilities, permits the translation of a need into a plan of action.

According to Matteson and McConnell (1988) the Barthel Index, which measures ADLs in older people, is a useful complement to clinical judgment when predicting rehabilitation potential and outcomes of services. Similar findings were reported by Ahroni (1989) who investigated 28 persons in the community with chronic conditions, utilizing the Barthel Index. The results indicated that functional status was a good indicator of the perceived need for home health services. Fortinsky et al. (1981) utilized a demographic profile to measure social and economic support and the modified Barthel Index to examine the degree to which a person can function independently in performing the activities of daily living. Fortinsky et al. (1981) suggested that the modified Barthel Index obtained detailed information about ADLs of older adults living in the community. Gulick (1986) describes the usefulness of self-assessment of health among chronically ill older adults.

Despite the variety and type of assessment instruments developed, their effectiveness has been questioned. Cohen and Feussner (1989) suggested that the mission of developing a comprehensive geriatric assessment tool has not been achieved despite the attention it has received. The Medicaid guidelines to implement assessment and care planning for nursing home residents has provided incentives to develop assessment tools (Kane, 1990; Long-Term Care Letter, 1990). Rubenstein et al. (1984) cautioned against using functional assessment instruments validated for a specific sample with a different population. Plutchik (1979) indicated that some practical and conceptual issues of tools for the elderly include the questions of goals, or what the assessment is for and how valid the scale is. Comprehensive geriatric assessment of hospitalized elders was found to assist family caregivers (Silliman, McGarvey, Raymond, & Fretwell, 1990). Lawton and Storandt (1984) have also described factors influencing assessment, methodological issues, purposes, and types of instruments available.

When assessing chronicity the functional abilities of the person involved should be examined as well as the status of the caregiver (Brown, Potter, & Foster, 1990). Some researchers have attempted to devise instruments to measure caregiver stress and strain (Baines, 1984; Bass & Noelker, 1987; Hymovich, 1984; Kosberg & Cairl, 1986; B. Robinson, 1983; Worcester & Quayhagen, 1983; Zarit, Todd, & Zarit, 1986). The Chronicity Impact and Coping Instrument: Parent Questionnaire, was developed to measure stress and coping methods of parents of children who were chronically ill (Hymovich, 1984). Baines modified the Hymovich instrument to make it suitable for the measurement of stress and coping in the older adult. Items specific to a child's developmental level were deleted and items related to the developmental needs of an older adult were added, but the majority of the original items and categories were retained in the modified version entitled Caregiver Stress and Coping Instrument (CSCI).

Worchester and Quayhagen (1983) developed the Caregiver Stress Scale (CARES) composed of three situational stress subscales: medical-physical, psychological-behavioral, and environmental-personal. Worcester and Quayhagen also developed a Caregiver Satisfaction instrument.

In 1983, B. Robinson reported the validation of a Caregiver Strain Index (CSI). This 13-item questionnaire examines a list of things people have found difficult when caring for a person discharged from the hospital. In a similar study, Zarit et al. (1986) investigated changes over time for caregivers of dementia patients with a focus on potential for institutionalization. Zarit et al. (1986) utilized a Burden Interview to investigate perceived burdens of family caregivers on their emotional and physical health, social life, and financial status as a result of caring for a relative. The researchers also utilized a Mental Status Questionnaire and the Face Hand Test developed by Kahn in 1960. Zarit et al. (1986) described the development and testing of the Burden instrument.

Another instrument, the Cost of Care Index (CCI), was developed as a case management tool to assist professionals in family assessments and to identify actual or perceived problem areas of families in the care of elderly relatives (Kosberg & Cairl, 1986). The 20 items in this questionnaire are similar to those in Zarit et al. (1986).

In summary, there are instruments that assess the functional status of older adults and measure stress in family caregivers. Some have been tested for validity and reliability and are based on conceptual models, but few if any examine all issues involved in chronicity care or the outcome or quality of care provided. Therefore, a need exists for a comprehensive assessment tool, based on a holistic theoretical framework that examines the person with a chronic illness and the effect on the persons involved, and that evaluates the outcome of services provided.

CHRONICITY IMPACT ON FAMILY CAREGIVERS/CARE RECEIVERS

Research on caregiving indicates that providing care in the home has the potential to create serious concerns for the family and society (Archbold, 1980; Baines, 1984; Biegel & Blum, 1988-1989; E. Brody, Johnsen, Fulcomer, & Lang, 1983; S. J. Brody, Poulshock, & Masciocchi, 1978; Cantor, 1983; Caserta, Lund, Wright, & Redburn, 1987; Dwyer & Miller, 1990; Fengler & Goodrich, 1979; Gaynor, 1989; Lawton, Kleban, Moss, Rovine, & Glicksman, 1989; B. Miller & Montgomery, 1990; Sanford, 1975; Silliman & Sternberg, 1988; Stoller, 1982). The literature on caregiving also suggested that rewards are possible in family caregiving, but have received less attention (Rabins, Fitting, Eastham, & Zabora, 1990; Stone, 1987).

Not only has family caregiving been a subject of considerable attention in professional journals, it has also been a topic in several newspapers and magazines (Coleman, 1988; Dychtwald & Flower, 1989; M. George, 1989; McKenzie, 1990; Simon, 1988; Wood, 1987, 1988). The media attention given to caregiving suggests a public interest and concern about family caregiving. Gerontologists recognize most families do not abandon or willfully neglect older members; however, some social trends have left the care of dependent elders to those least able to assume this responsibility, other older adults. These societal trends include more women in the work force, increased mobility of families, escalating costs of medical and institutional care, dwindling resources, and changing population patterns. These and other societal trends come at a time when there is increased governmental pressure on families to provide more care in the home. It has been suggested that as long as family members continue to provide care for other members little will be done by the government or other agencies that have no incentive to relieve the burden (Wood, 1987).

Caregiving research has focused on adult children (Archbold, 1983; Bowers, 1987; E. Brody, 1981; B. Miller, 1989; Townsend & Poulshoch, 1986; Troll, 1988) and on spouses and older adults as caregivers (Baines, 1984, 1990; Barusch, 1988; Crossman, London, & Barry, 1981; Dura, Haywood-Niler, & Kiecolt-Glaser, 1990; Given, Stommel, Collins, King, & Given, 1990; Gregory, Peters, & Cameron, 1990; Moritz, Kasl, & Berkman, 1989; Parmelee, 1983; Pruchno, 1990; K. Robinson, 1989; Stetz, 1989). The majority of caregivers are women (South Carolina Women, 1990) and employment may be negatively affected in caregivers who work (E. Brody, Kleban, Johnsen, Hoffman, & Schoonover, 1987; Dellasega, 1990; Scharlach & Boyd, 1989).

There is some disagreement in the literature concerning the degree of disruption caused by caring for a person who needs assistance and the relationship to that person. Research has indicated that the closer the bond between caregiver-care receiver the more stressful the caregiving role, with spouses in the highest risk group for isolation and changes in health status (Cantor, 1983; Parmelee, 1983; Young & Kahana, 1989). In contrast, B. Robinson (1983) found no difference in caregiver strain between men or women or the relationship of the family member to the expatient. The potential for abuse in the caregiving situation has been investigated (Stein, 1989).

Whereas the majority of caregiver research has utilized caregivers of older adults who were cognitively impaired (Alzheimer's disease) or had mental disorders (Gwyther & George, 1986; Haley, Brown, & Levine, 1987a, 1987b; Harvis & Rabins, 1989; Hirschfeld, 1983; Morgan, 1989; Pearson, Verma, & Nellett, 1988; Wilson, 1989), some caregiver studies have examined persons with cancer (Edstrom & Miller, 1981; Stetz, 1987) or stroke (Silliman et al., 1986). In caregiving research of the older adult it is difficult to separate the interaction of physical and mental conditions of caregivers and care recipients and in some persons physical and mental disabilities may exist simultaneously (Schulz, Visintainer, & Williamson, 1990). Schulz et al. conducted a review of the literature on caregiving to examine the consequences of this experience.

Family caregiving is an international problem (Graycar & Kinnear, 1983; Nakatani, Sakata, & Maeda, 1989; Wilder, Teresi, & Bennett, 1983) as well as an urban and rural concern (Hayslip, Ritter, Oltman, & McDonnell, 1980; Reichel, 1980; Talbot, 1985) (see chapter 14, Cross-National Trends in Health Care of the Aged).

Most of the literature on family caregiving is in agreement, that despite the burden, home care is preferred at any cost to institutionalization of the impaired aged (S. J. Brody et al., 1978; Caldwell, 1982; Eggert, Granger, Morris, & Pendleton, 1977; Frankfather, et al., 1981; Johnson & Catalano, 1983; Oktay & Sheppard, 1978; Pegels, 1980; Perlman, 1982; Plass, 1978; Sanford, 1975). Home health care is less expensive and most older persons prefer home care (Oktay & Sheppard, 1978; Skellie, Mobley, & Coan, 1982).

In summary, family caregiving is an international, national, and local concern of major importance, affecting the health care and well-being of many older adults, families, and societies. The majority of caregivers for older adults are women whose employment may be affected by the demands of caregiving. Despite the high level of stress of caregiving for most families, the advantages of home care outweigh the disadvantages of institutionalization.

APPROACHES TO CHRONIC ILLNESS CARE

The literature indicates that a variety of programs and services are being tested to assist family caregivers and care recipients, including hospice, respite, and day care (Etten & Kosberg, 1989; L. George, 1986; Lawton, Brody, & Saperstein, 1989; Lawton, Brody, Saperstein, & Grimes, 1989; Sklar, 1981), and educational training programs and workshops (Biegel, Shore, & Gordon, 1984; E. Johnson & Spence, 1982; Quayhagen & Quayhagen, 1989; Rodway, Elliott, & Sawa, 1987; Selan & Schuenke, 1982). Support groups (Baines, 1989; Barnes, Raskind, Scott, & Murphy, 1981; Toseland & Rossiter, 1989), counseling sessions (Toseland, 1989) and volunteer/religious resources (Haber, 1984; Halpert & Sharp, 1989; Heller, Walsh, & Wilson, 1981; Sheehan, 1989) have been utilized to help stressed caregivers and support care recipients. Some programs have been successful and others have reported limited benefit for caregivers and care recipients. Failure to identify specific components of burden may explain the inability to verify the effectiveness of different forms of interventions in relieving caregiving stress (Kosberg, Cairl, & Keller, 1990).

According to E. Brody (1981), whatever the nature of the caregiver's strain, it is clear that the lag between needs and available family-oriented programs for the care of the chronically ill is great. E. Brody recommends expanding home care and homemaker services, providing quality institutions, giving financial support to families to defray care costs, providing reimbursement for day care and respite care, and other options to meet diverse family situations. Caregivers in Archbold's (1980) research identified adequate transportation as being necessary to relieve the stress of parent-caring.

Heller et al.'s (1981) program trained older adults to help other older adults. There are conflicting views, however, concerning the dependability and effectiveness of this approach. Sager (1983) and Perlman (1982) indicated that there is no evidence that other relatives, friends, and neighbors make the significant contributions of time and energy to caregiving in the home.

Paid caregiving in the home has been proposed (Arling & McAuley, 1983; Kane, 1989; Linsk, Keigher, & Osterbusch, 1988). In 50 United States jurisdictions, 35% or 70% permitted some form of family caregiver payment (Linsk et al., 1988). Most jurisdictions imposed limitations and regulations to prevent abuse. In 1987, only 4 states had passed bills granting family leave and only 1 included elder care in its provisions (Wisensale & Allison, 1988).

Horejsi (1982) pointed out the irrationality of policies that almost require families to destroy themselves before communities offer services that might have forestalled such outcomes. Social policy changes and rationing of health care has been suggested as methods of containing costs and providing services to people with health care needs (Dychtwald & Zitter, 1988; Hogan, 1990; Holzman, 1989). According to a panelist McConnell (National Forum on Caring, 1988), politicians receive relatively little mail about the problems and needs of caregivers. Nurses as advocates of the elderly can assist in changing this situation. Arling and McAuley (1983) indicated that for nonfinancial factors such as restriction on time and emotional strain, financial payment alone may not be effective in relieving the social and psychological pressures of caregiving.

Hirschfeld (1983) recommended home health visiting services by professional nurses to offer practice suggestions to caregivers and to provide a nonjudgmental listener to help the caregiver work through emotional problems. Other recommendations by Hirschfeld included preventive maintenance and curative home care for both caregiver and dependent person. Thornbury and Martin (1983) suggested that home care by nurses for older adults does make a difference in the health status of their clients and interventions to relieve caregiver stress were given by Baldwin (1990) and L. Phillips (1989). Shared care by formal and informal caregivers has been investigated (Hasselkus, 1988; Noelker & Bass, 1989; Schirm, 1989) and games between caregivers and care recipients were examined by Rempusheski and Phillips (1988).

In 1990, Baines investigated the effect of formal nursing care provided in the home, for older family caregivers of posthospitalized elder care recipients. The results indicated that caregiver stress and functional status of the elder care recipient was significantly improved in the treatment group receiving formal nursing service and in the paid home health care subjects. The sample included 90 caregiver-care recipient dyads, all subjects were 65 years of age and older. Stress was measured in the caregiver with the CSCI, and functional status was assessed in the care recipient with the FAI within one month posthospitalization, in six weeks, and in six months. Nursing interventions were provided by nurse researchers once a week for four weeks for subjects in the treatment group.

Family caregiving situations are characterized by heterogeneity (Gwyther & George, 1986; Stone, 1987; Zarit et al., 1986). The fact that each family caregiving situation is different and diverse needs exist in families may complicate research efforts and service delivery; however, the magnitude of family caregivers' problems warrant further exploration and program implementation. Additional studies are needed to evaluate the outcomes of all types of service programs and to plan new programs.

Another area that has received little examination is the effect of family caregiving on the quality of care received by the dependent person. These and other areas of family caregiving should be investigated over a long period of time, with standardized instruments, appropriate control, and with a large sample (Barer & Johnson, 1990; Dura & Kiecolt-Glaser, 1990; Gallagher, 1985; Horowitz, 1985; Watson & Kendell, 1983; Zarit, 1989).

In conclusion, as an increasing number of families are expected to provide care for disabled members, there is a need for health care personnel and service providers to be aware of the risks and benefits of family caregiving. A multidimensional functional assessment instrument is needed that is based on a holistic conceptual framework. Educational and training programs for family caregivers are needed. There is a need for research that examines the outcomes of service programs to assist the chronically ill aged and the family caregivers. In the past, the majority of health care has focused on medical car and acute care services; however, the elderly who have more chronic illness than acute care needs may be better served by a community based health care system that provides respite and day care, and social and home nursing services from a perspective that promotes wellness and rehabilitation. Because older family caregivers continue to provide the largest amount of caregiving for older persons with functional impairment, and the elderly are at greater risk for their own health problems, additional support for elderly caregivers must be made available in the near future.

REFERENCES

Ahroni, J. (1989). A description of the health needs of elderly home care patients with chronic illness. *Home Health Care Services Quarterly, 10,* 77-92.

American Nurses' Association. (1980). *Nursing, social policy statement.* Kansas City, MO: American Nurses' Association.

Archbold, P. (1980). Impact of parent caring on middle-aged offspring. *Journal of Gerontological Nursing, 6,* 79-85.

Archbold, P. (1983). Impact of parent-caring on women. *Family Relations, 32,* 39-45.

Arling, G., & McAuley, W. (1983). The feasibility of public payments for family caregiving. *The Gerontologist, 23,* 300-306.

Atchley, R. (1988). *Social forces in later life.* Belmont, CA: Wadsworth.

Baines, E. (1984). Caregiver stress in older adults. *Journal of Community Health Nursing*, *1*, 257-263.

Baines, E. (1989). Groups for all. *Geriatric Nursing, 10*, 296-297.

Baines, E. (1990, April). *An investigation of older family caregiver stress*. Paper presented at the meeting of the American Society on Aging Conference, San Francisco, CA.

Baldwin, B. (1990). Family caregiving: Trends and forecasts. *Geriatric Nursing, 11*, 172-174.

Ballard, S., & McNamara, R. (1983). Quantifying nursing needs in home health care. *Nursing Research, 32*, 236-241.

Barer, B., & Johnson, C. (1990). A critique of the caregiving literature. *The Gerontologist, 30*, 26-29.

Barnes, R., Raskind, M., Scott, M., & Murphy, C. (1981). Problems of families caring for Alzheimer patients: Use of a support group. *Journal of the American Geriatrics Society, 29*, 80-85.

Barusch, A. (1988). Problems and coping strategies of elderly spouse caregivers. *The Gerontologist, 28*, 677-685.

Bass, D., & Noelker, L. (1987). The influence of family caregivers on elders' use of in-home services: An expanded conceptual framework. *Journal of Health and Social Behavior, 28*, 184-196.

Becker, P., & Cohen, H. (1984). The functional approach to the care of the elderly: A conceptual framework. *Journal of the American Geriatric Society, 32*, 923-929

Beland, F. (1987). Identifying profiles of service requirements in a non-institutionalized elderly population. *Journal of Chronic Disease, 40*, 51-64.

Bennett, R. G. (1983). Care of the demented: long-term care institutions, home and family care, and hospice. In R. Mayeux & W. G. Rosen, (Eds.), *Advances in neurology*. New York: Raven Press.

Biegel, D., & Blum, A (Eds.). (1988-1989). Special Issue: Aging and family caregivers. *Journal of Applied Social Sciences, 13*, 1-8.

Biegel, D., Shore, B., & Gordon, E. (1984). *Building support networks for the elderly: Theory and applications*. Beverly Hills, CA: Sage.

Biggs, A. (1990). Family caregiver versus nursing assessments of elderly self-care abilities. *Journal of Gerontological Nursing, 16*, 11-16.

Bowers, B. (1987). Intergenerational caregiving: Adult caregivers and their aging parents. *Advances in Nursing Science, 9*, 20-31.

Bower, F., & Patterson, J. (1986). A theory-based nursing assessment of the aged. *Topics in Clinical Nursing, 8*, 22-32.

Brody, E. (1981). "Women in the middle" and family help to older people. *The Gerontologist, 21*, 471-480.

Brody, E., Johnsen, P. T., Fulcomer, M. C., & Lang, A .M. (1983). Women's changing roles and help to elderly parents: Attitudes of three generations of women. *Journal of Gerontology, 38*, 597-607.

Brody, E., Kleban, M., Johnsen, P., Hoffman, C., & Schoonover, C. (1987). Work status and parent care: A comparison of four groups of women. *The Gerontologist, 27*, 201-208.

Brody, S. J., Poulshock, W., & Masciocchi, C. (1978). The family caring unit: A major consideration in the long-term support system. *The Gerontologist, 18*, 556-561.

Brown, L., Potter, J., & Foster, B. (1990). Caregiver burden should be evaluated during geriatric assessment. *Journal of the American Geriatrics Society, 38*, 455-460.

Bunting, S. (1989). Stress on caregivers of the elderly. *Advances in Nursing Science, 11*, 63-73.

Burnside, I. (1988). *Nursing and the aged*. New York: McGraw-Hill.

Burton, B., Cairl, R., Keller, D., & Pfeiffer, E. (1983). *Functional assessment inventory: Training manual.* Tampa: University of South Florida, Suncoast Gerontology Center.

Caldwell, J. (1982). Home care. *Hospitals, 56,* 68-72, 82-83.

Cantor, M. (1983) Strain among caregivers: A study of experience in the United States. *The Gerontologist, 23,* 597-604.

Carnevelli, D., Mitchell, P., Woods, N., & Tanner, C. (1984). *Diagnostic reasoning in nursing.* Philadelphia: J. B. Lippincott.

Caserta, M., Lund, D., Wright, S., & Redburn, D. (1987). Caregivers to dementia patients: The utilization of community services. *The Gerontologist, 27,* 209-214.

Center for Disease Control. (1990, January). *HIV/AIDS surveillance report* (pp. 1-22). Atlanta, GA.

Chappell, N., Strain, L., & Blandford, A. (1986). *Aging and health care: A sociological perspective.* Canada: Holt, Rinehart & Winston.

Cohen, H., & Feussner, J. (1989). Comprehensive geriatric assessment: Mission not yet accomplished. [Editorial comment]. *Journal of Gerontology, 44,* M175-177.

Coleman, B. (1988). Family pressures drive search for home care. *AARP News Bulletin, 29,* 1 & 13.

Craig, H., & Edwards, J. (1983). Adaptation in chronic illness: An eclectic model for nurses. *Journal of Advanced Nursing, 8,* 397-404.

Crossman, L., London, C., & Barry, C. (1981). Older women caring for disabled spouses: A model for supportive services. *The Gerontologist, 21,* 464-470.

Dellasega, C. (1990). The relationship between caregiving and employment. *American Association of Occupational Health Nurses Journal, 38,* 154-159.

Dura, J., Haywood-Niler, E., & Kiecolt-Glaser, J. (1990). Spousal caregivers of persons with Alzheimer's and Parkinson's disease dementia: A preliminary comparison. *The Gerontologist, 30,* 332-336.

Dura, J., & Kiecolt-Glaser, J. (1990). Sample bias in caregiving research. *Journal of Gerontology, 45,* P200-204.

Dwyer, J., & Miller, M. (1990). Determinants of primary caregiver stress and burden: Area of residence and the caregiving networks of frail elders. *Journal of Rural Health, 6,* 161-184.

Dychtwald, K., & Flower, J. (1989). Living longer, living better? *Family Circle, 102,* 41-48.

Dychtwald, K., & Zitter, M. (1988). Changes during the next decade will alter the way eldercare is provided, financed. *Modern Healthcare, 18,* 38.

Edstrom, S., & Miller, M. (1981). Preparing the family to care for the cancer patient at home: A home care course. *Cancer Nursing, 4,* 49-52.

Eggert, G., Granger, C., Morris, R., & Pendleton, S. (1977) Caring for the patient with long-term disability. *Geriatrics, 32,* 102-114.

Etten, M., & Kosberg, J. (1989). The hospice caregiver assessment: A study of a case management tool for professional assistance. *The Gerontologist, 29,* 128-131.

Fagin, C. (1987). Stress: Implications for nursing research. *Image: Journal of Nursing Scholarship, 19,* 38-41.

Feller, B. (1983) Americans needing help to function at home. *Advance Data, 92,* 1-11.

Fengler, A., & Goodrich, N. (1979). Wives of elderly disabled men: The hidden patients. *The Gerontologist, 19,* 175-183.

Folden, S. (1990). On the inside looking out: Perceptions of the homebound. *Journal of Gerontological Nursing, 16,* 9-15.

Fortinsky, R., Granger, C., & Seltzer, G. (1981). The use of functional assessment in understanding home care needs. *Medical Care, 19,* 489-497.

Fowles, D. (Ed.). (1989). *A profile of older Americans.* Washington, DC: American Association of Retired Persons.

Frankfather, D., Smith, M., & Caro, F. (1981). *Family care of the elderly.* Lexington, MA: Lexington.

Gallagher, D. (1985). Intervention strategies to assist caregivers of frail elders: Current research status and future research directions. In C. Eisdorfer (Ed.), *Annual review of gerontology and geriatrics* (pp. 249-282). New York: Springer.

Gamroth, L. (1988). Long-term care resource requirements before and after the prospective payment system. *Image: Journal of Nursing Scholarship, 20,* 7-11.

Gatz, M., Pedersen, N., & Harris, J. (1987). Measurement characteristics of the mental health scale from the OARS. *Journal of Gerontology, 42,* 332-335.

Gaynor, S. (1989). When the caregiver becomes the patient. *Geriatric Nursing, 10,* 120-123.

George, L. (1986). Respite care: Evaluating a strategy for easing caregiver burden. *Duke University Center for the Study of Aging and Human Development: Advances in Research, 10,* 1-7.

George, M. (1989). Who will help you when you help your parents? *Aide, 20,* 14-19.

Given, B., Stommel, M., Collins, C., King, S., & Given, C. (1990). Responses of elderly spouse caregivers. *Research in Nursing & Health, 13,* 77-85.

Goldstein, V., Regnery, G., & Wellin, E. (1981). Caretaker role fatigue. Nursing Outlook, 29, 24-30.

Graycar, A., & Kinnear, D. (1983). Caring for elderly relatives. *Australian Family Physician, 12,* 267-269.

Gregory, D., Peters, N., & Cameron, C. (1990). Elderly male spouses as caregivers. *Journal of Gerontological Nursing, 16,* 20-24.

Gulick, E. (1986). The self-assessment of health among the chronically ill. *Topics in Clinical Nursing, 8,* 74-82.

Gurel, L., Linn, M., & Linn, B. (1972). Physical and mental impairment of function evaluation in the aged: The PAMIE scale. *Journal of Gerontology, 27,* 83-90.

Gurland, B., Copeland, J., Sharpe, L., Kelleher, M., Kuriansky, J., & Simon, R. (1977-1978). Assessment of the older person in the community. *International Journal of Aging & Human Development, 8,* 1-8.

Gwyther, L., & George, L. (1986). Symposium: Caregivers for dementia patients: Complex determinants of well-being and burden. *The Gerontologist, 26,* 245-247.

Haber, D. (1984). Church-based programs for black care-givers of non-institutionalized elders. *Gerontological Social Work in Home Health Care,* 43-55.

Haley, W., Brown, S., & Levine, E. (1987a). Experimental evaluation of the effectiveness of group intervention for dementia caregivers. *The Gerontologist, 27,* 376-382.

Haley, W., Brown, S., & Levine, E. (1987b). Family caregiver appraisals of patient behavioral disturbance in senile dementia. *Clinical Gerontologist, 6,* 25-34.

Halpert, B., & Sharp, T. (1989). A model to nationally replicate a locally successful rural family caregiver program: The volunteer information provider program. *The Gerontologist, 29,* 561-563.

Harvis, K., & Rabins, P. (1989). Dementia: Helping family caregivers cope. *Journal of Psychosocial Nursing, 27,* 7-12.

Hasselkus, B. (1988). Meaning in family caregiving: Perspectives on caregiver/professional relationships. *The Gerontologist, 28,* 686-691.

Hayslip, B., Ritter, M., Oltman, R., & McDonnell, C. (1980). Home care services and the rural elderly. *The Gerontologist, 20,* 192-199.

Heller, B., Walsh, F., & Wilson, K. (1981). Seniors helping seniors: Training older adults as new personnel resources in home health care. *Journal of Gerontological Nursing, 7,* 552-555.

Helmes, E., Csapo, K., & Short, J. (1987). Standardization and validation of the mutlidimensional observation scale for elderly subjects (MOSES). *Journal of Gerontology, 42,* 395-405.

Hirschfeld, M. (1983). Homecare versus institutionalization: Family caregiving and senile brain disease. *International Journal of Nursing Studies, 20,* 23-32.

Hogan, S. (1990). Care for the caregiver: Social policies to ease their burden. *Journal of Gerontological Nursing, 16,* 12-17.

Holzman, D. (1989). Medicaid dispensed on ration plan. *Insight, 5,* 54-56.

Horejsi, C. (1982). Social and psychological factors of family care. *Home Health Care Services Quarterly, 3,* 56-71.

Horowitz, A. (1985). Family caregiving to the frail elderly. In C. Eisdorfer (Ed.), *Annual review of gerontology and geriatrics* (pp. 194-244). New York: Springer.

Hymovich, D. (1979). Assessment of the chronically ill child and family. In D. Hymovich & M. Barnard (Eds.), *Family and health care.* New York: McGraw-Hill.

Hymovich, D. (1984). The chronicity impact and coping instrument: Parent questionnaire. *Nursing Research, 32,* 275-281.

Hymovich, D. (1987). Assessing families of children with cystic fibrosis. In L. Wright & M. Leahey (Eds.), *Families and chronic illness* (pp. 131-146). Springhouse, PA: Springhouse Publishing.

Jenkins, A. (1990). An investigation of the relation between caregiver stress levels and care-recipient functional status. Unpublished master's thesis, Clemson University, Clemson, SC.

Johnson, C., & Catalano, D. (1983). A longitudinal study of family supports to impaired elderly. *The Gerontologist, 23,* 612-618.

Johnson, E., & Spence, D. (1982). Adult children and their aging parents: An intervention program. *Family Relations, 31,* 115-121.

Kahana, E., & Young, R. (1990). Clarifying the caregiving paradigm. In D. Biegel & A. Blum (Eds.), *Aging and caregiving: Theory, research and policy* (pp. 76-97). Newbury Park, CA: Sage.

Kane, R. (1989). Toward competent, caring paid caregivers [Editorial]. *The Gerontologist, 29,* 291-292.

Kane, R. (1990). Standardized assessment as a means rather than an end [Editorial]. *The Gerontologist, 30,* 291-292.

Kosberg, J., & Cairl, R. (1986). The cost of care index: A case management tool for screening informal care providers. *The Gerontologist, 26,* 273-278.

Kosberg, J., Cairl, R., & Keller, D. (1990). Components of burden: Interventive implications. *The Gerontologist, 30,* 236-242.

Lawrence, S., & Lawrence, R. (1979). A model of adaptation to the stress of chronic illness. *Nursing Forum, 18,* 33-42.

Lawton, M. (1983). Environment and other determinants of well-being in older people. *The Gerontologist, 23,* 349-357.

Lawton, M., Brody, E., & Saperstein, A. (1989). A controlled study of respite service for caregivers of Alzheimer's patients. *The Gerontologist, 29,* 8-16.

Lawton, M., Brody, E., Saperstein, A., & Grimes, M. (1989). Respite services for caregivers: Research findings for service planning. *Home Health Care Services Quarterly, 10,* 5-32.

Lawton, M., Kleban, M., Moss, M., Rovine, M., & Glicksman, A. (1989). Measuring caregiving appraisal. *Journal of Gerontology, 44,* 61-71.

Lawton, M., & Storandt, M. (1984). Clinical and functional approaches to the assessment of older people. In P. McReynolds & G. Chelune (Eds.), *Advances in psychological assessment.* San Francisco: Jossey-Bass.

Lefton, E., & Lefton, M. (1979). Health care and treatment of the chronically ill: Toward a conceptual framework. *Journal of Chronic Diseases, 32,* 339-344.

Leibson, C., Naessens, J., Krishan, I., Campion, M., & Ballard, D. (1990). Disposition at discharge and 60-day mortality among elderly people following shorter hospital stays: A population-based comparison. *The Gerontologist, 30,* 316-322.

Liang, M., Gall, V., Partridge, A., & Eaton, H. (1983). Management of functional disability in homebound patients. *Journal of Family Practice, 17,* 429-435.

Linsk, N., Keigher, S., & Osterbusch, S. (1988). States' policies regarding paid family caregiving. *The Gerontologist, 28,* 204-212.

Littlefield, J. (1987). An investigation of the functional status of older adults who are mentally ill and the utilization of group therapy. Unpublished master's thesis, Clemson University, Clemson, SC.

Liu, K, Manton, K., & Liu, B. (1985). Home care expenses for the disabled elderly. *Health Care Financing Review, 7,* 51-58.

Long-Term Care Letter. (1990, August). *States hustle to implement minimum data set before the year's end* (vol. 2, p. 1). Providence, RI: Brown University.

Lowery, B. (1987). Stress research: Some theoretical and methodological issues. *Image: Journal of Nursing Scholarship, 19,* 42-46.

Loomis, M., & Wood, R. (1983). Cure: The potential outcome of nursing care. *Image: Journal of Nursing Scholarship, 15,* 4-7.

Macken, C. (1986). A profile of functionally impaired elderly persons living in the community. *Health Care Financing Review, 7,* 33-49.

MacVicar, M., & Archbold, P. (1976). A framework for family assessment in chronic illness. *Nursing Forum, 15,* 180-194.

Matteson, M., & McConnell, E. (1988). *Gerontological Nursing.* Philadelphia: W. B. Saunders.

McGovern, K., & Newbern, V. (1988). DRG impact. *Journal of Gerontological Nursing, 14,* 17-20.

McKenzie, H. (1990). *Caregiving.* Washington, DC: National Council on Aging.

Meiners, M., & Coffey, R. (1985). Hospital DRG's and the need for long-term care services: An empirical analysis. *Health Services Research, 20,* 359-384.

Miller, B. (1989). Adult children's perceptions of caregiver stress and satisfaction. *Journal of Applied Gerontology. 8,* 275-293.

Miller, B., & Montgomery, A. (1990). Family caregivers and limitations in social activities. *Research on Aging, 12,* 72-93.

Miller, J. (1983). *Coping with chronic illness: Overcoming powerlessness.* Philadelphia: F. A. Davis.

Morgan, D. (1989). *Caregivers for elderly Alzheimer's victims: A comparison of caregiving in the home and institutions* (Report to the Andrus Foundation), Washington, DC: American Association of Retired Persons.

Moritz, D., Kasl, S., & Berkman, L. (1989). The health impact of living with a cognitively impaired elderly spouse: Depressive symptoms and social functioning. *Journal of Gerontology, 44,* S17-27.

Multidimensional Functional Assessment: The OARS Methodology. (1978). Durham, NC: Duke University, Center for the Study of Aging and Human Development Press.

Nakatani, Y., Sakata, S., & Maeda, D. (1989, June). *Burden of Japanese caregivers of the demented elderly and variables affecting their burden.* Paper presented at the 14th International Congress of Gerontology, Acapulco, Mexico.

National Forum on Caregiving (1988). *Parent care* (vol.3, p. 1). Lawrence: University of Kansas, Gerontology Center.

Nerenz, D., & Leventhal, H. (1983). Self-regulation theory in chronic illness. In T. Burish & L. Bradley (Eds.), *Coping with chronic disease* (pp. 13-37). New York: Academic Press.

Newman, S., Struyk, R., Wright, P., & Rice, M. (1990). Overwhelming odds: Caregiving and the risk of institutionalization. *Journal of Gerontology, 45,* S173-183.

Noelker, L., & Bass, D. (1989). Home care for elderly persons: Linkages between formal and informal caregivers. *Journal of Gerontology, 44,* S63-70.

Oktay, J., & Sheppard, F. (1978). Home health care for the elderly. *Mental Health and Social Work, 3,* 35-47.

Pallett, P. (1990). A conceptual framework for studying family caregiver burden in Alzheimer's-type dementia. *Image: Journal of Nursing Scholarship, 22,* 52-58.

Panicucci, C. (1983). Functional assessment of the older adult in the acute care setting. *Nursing Clinics of North America, 18,* 355-363.

Parmelee, P. (1983). Spouse versus other family caregivers: Psychological impact on impaired aged. *American Journal of Community Psychology, 11,* 337-349.

Pearson, J., Verma, S., & Nellett, C. (1988). Elderly psychiatric patient status and caregiver perceptions as predictors of caregiver burden. *The Gerontologist, 28,* 79-83.

Pegels, C. (1980). Institutional vs. noninstitutional care for the elderly. *Journal of Health Politics, Policy, and Law, 5,* 205-212.

Perlman, R. (1982). Family home care. *Home Health Care Services Quarterly, 3,* 1-11 & 45-55.

Personnel for Health Needs of the Elderly through the Year 2020. (1987). Report # 205-735-736-32533. Washington, DC: Government Printing Office.

Pfeiffer, E. (1981). Functional assessment of elderly subjects in four service setting. *American Geriatrics Society, 29,* 433-437.

Phillips, L. (1989). Elder-family caregiver relationships. *Nursing Clinics of North America, 24,* 795-807.

Phillips, E., Fisher, M., MacMillan-Scattergood, D., & Baglioni, A. (1989). DRG ripple and the shifting burden of care to home health. *Nursing and Health Care, 10,* 325-327.

Plass, P. (1978). Home care services: How many can they help? *Health and Social Work, 3,* 182-189.

Plutchik, R. (1979). Conceptual and practical issues in the assessment of the elderly. In A. Raskin & L. Javik (Eds.), *Psychiatric symptoms and cognitive loss in the elderly: Evaluation and assessment techniques* (pp. 19-38). Washington, DC: Hemisphere Publishing.

Pruchno, R. (1990). The effects of help patterns on the mental health of spouse caregivers. *Research on Aging, 12,* 57-71.

Public Policy and Aging Report. (1987). *Medicare reform: Where are we headed? 1,* 1-3, & 8-11. Chicago: Policy Research Association.

Quayhagen M., & Quayhagen, M. (1989). Differential effects of family-based strategies on Alzheimer's disease. *The Gerontologist, 29,* 150-155.

Quinn, J., & Ryan, N. (1979). Assessment of the older adult: A "Holistic" approach. *Journal of Gerontological Nursing, 5,* 13-18.

Rabins, P., Fitting, M., Eastham, J., & Zabora, J. (1990). Emotional adaptation over time in care-givers for chronically ill elderly people. *Age and Ageing, 19,* 185-190.

Reichel, W. (1980). Care of the elderly in rural America. *Maryland State Medical Journal, 29,* 76-79.

Rempusheski, V., & Phillips, L. (1988). Elders versus caregivers: Games they play. *Geriatric Nursing, 9,* 30-34.

Robinson, B. (1983). Validation of a caregiver strain index. *Journal of Gerontology, 38,* 344-348.

Robinson, K. (1989). Predictors of depression among wife caregivers. *Nursing Research, 38,* 359-363.

Rodway, M., Elliott, J., & Sawa, R. (1987). Intervention with families of the elderly chronically ill: An alternate approach. *Gerontological Social Work with Families,* 51-59.

Rubenstein, L., Schairer, C., Weiland, G., & Kane, R. (1984). Systematic biases in functional status assessment of elderly adults: Effects of different data sources. *Journal of Gerontology, 39,* 686-691.

Sager, A. (1983). A proposal for promoting more adequate long-term care for the elderly. *The Gerontologist, 23,* 13-17.

Sanford, R. (1975). Tolerance of debility in elderly dependents by supporters at home: Its significance for hospital practice. *British Medical Journal, 3,* 471-473.

Scharlach, A., & Boyd, S. (1989). Caregiving and employment: Results of an employee survey. *The Gerontologist, 29,* 382-387.

Schindler, K. (1989). An investigation of the relationship between the functional status of the older adult and the level of stress in the older adult caregiver. Unpublished master's thesis, Clemson University, Clemson, SC.

Schirm, V. (1989). Shared care by formal and informal caregivers for community residing elderly. *Journal of the New York State Nurses Association, 20,* 8-14.

Schulz, R., Visintainer, P., & Williamson, G. (1990). Psychiatric and physical morbidity effects of caregiving. *Journal of Gerontology, 45,* P181-191.

Schwartz, G. (1983). Development and validation of the geriatric evaluation by relatives rating instrument (GERRI). *Psychological Reports, 53,* 479-488.

Selan, B., & Schuenke, S. (1982). The late life care program: Helping families cope. *Health and Social Work, 7,* 192-197.

Shanas, E. (1974). Health status of older people: Cross-national implications. *American Journal of Public Health, 64,* 261-268.

Shanas, E. (1979). The family as a social support system in old age. *The Gerontologist, 19,* 169-174.

Sheehan, N. (1989). The caregiver information project: A mechanism to assist religious leaders to help family caregivers. *The Gerontologist, 29,* 703-706.

Silliman, R., Fletcher, R., Earp, J., & Wagner, E. (1986). Families of elderly stroke patients. *Journal of the American Geriatrics Society, 34,* 643-648.

Silliman, R., McGarvey, S., Raymond, P., & Fretwell, M. (1990). The senior care study: Does inpatient interdisciplinary geriatric assessment help the family caregivers of acutely ill older patients? *Journal of the American Geriatrics Society, 38,* 461-466.

Silliman, R., & Sternberg, J. (1988). Family caregiving: Impact of patient functioning and underlying causes of dependency. *The Gerontologist, 28,* 377-382.

Simon, C. (1988). A care package. *Psychology Today, 22,* 40-49.

Skellie, F., Mobley, G., & Coan, R. (1982). Cost-effectiveness of community-based long-term care: Current findings of Georgia's alternative health service project. *American Journal of Public Health, 72,* 353-358.

Sklar, B. (1981). Consortium keeps frail elderly at home. *Hospitals, 55,* 62 & 66.

South Carolina Women. (1990). *Caring for the elderly* (vol. 11, p. 1). Columbia: South Carolina Commission on Women.

Stein, K. (1989, June). *Dependency stress and elders' abusive behavior toward family caregivers.* Paper presented at the 14th International Congress on Gerontology, Acapulco, Mexico.

Stetz, K. (1989). The relationship among background characteristics, purpose in life, and caregiving demands on perceived health of spouse caregivers. *Scholarly Inquiry for Nursing Practice, 3,* 133-153.

Stetz, K. (1987). Caregiving demands during advanced cancer. *Cancer Nursing, 10,* 260-268.

Stoller, E. (1982). Sources of support for the elderly during illness. *Health and Social Work, 7,* 111-122.

Stoller, E., & Pugliesi, K. (1989). Other roles of caregivers: Competing responsibilities or supportive resources. *Journal of Gerontology, 44,* S231-238.

Stone, R. (Ed.). (1987). *Exploding the myths: Caregiving in America.* A study by the subcommittee on Human Services of the Select Committee on Aging, U.S. House of Representatives (No's. 99-611). Washington, DC: Government Printing Office.

Stone, R., Cafferata, G., & Sangl, J. (1987). Caregivers of frail elderly: A national profile. *The Gerontologist, 27,* 616-626.

Stone, R., & Murtaugh, C. (1990). The elderly population with chronic functional disability: Implications for home care eligibility. *The Gerontologist, 30,* 491-492.

Strauss, A., Corbin, J., Fagerhaugh, S., Glasser, B., Maines, D., Suczek, G., & Wiener, C. (1984). *Chronic illness and the quality of life.* St. Louis: C. V. Mosby.

Talbot, D. (1985). Assessing needs of the rural elderly. *Journal of Gerontological Nursing, 11,* 39-43.

Thornbury, J., & Martin, A. (1983). Do nurses make a difference? *Journal of Gerontological Nursing, 9,* 440-445.

Toseland, R. (1989). *Effective interventions for caregivers and care receivers: A comparison of five approaches.* Paper submitted to the AARP Andrus Foundation, Washington, DC.

Toseland, R., & Rossiter, C. (1989). Group interventions to support family caregivers: A review and analysis. *The Gerontologist, 29,* 438-448.

Townsend, A., & Poulshoch, S. (1986). Intergenerational perspectives on impaired elders' support networks. *Journal of Gerontology, 41,* 101-109.

Troll, L. (1988). New thoughts on old families. *The Gerontologist, 28,* 586-591.

U.S. Bureau of the Census. (1990). *Statistical abstract of the United States.* Washington, DC: Government Printing Office.

Watson, D., & Kendell, P. (1983). Methodical issues in research on coping with chronic disease. In T. Burish & L. Bradley (Eds.), *Coping with chronic disease* (pp. 39-81). New York: Academic Press.

Wilder, D., Teresi, J., & Bennett, R. (1983). Family burden and dementia. In R. Mayeux & W. Rosen (Eds.), *Advances in neurology.* New York: Raven Press.

Wilson, H. (1989). Family caregiving for a relative with Alzheimer's dementia: Coping with negative choices. *Nursing Research, 38,* 94-98.

Wisensale, S., & Allison, M. (1988). An analysis of 1987 state family leave legislation: Implications for caregivers of the elderly. *The Gerontologist, 28,* 779-785.

Wolinsky, F., Coe, R., Miller, D., & Prendergast, J. (1984). Measurements of global and functional dimensions of health status in the elderly. *Journal of Gerontology, 39*, 88-92.

Wood, J. (1987). Labors of love. *Modern Maturity, 30,* 28-34 & 90, 92-94.

Wood, J. (1988). More caring, more giving. *Modern Maturity, 31*, 84-85.

Worcester, M., & Quayhagen, M. (1983). Correlates of caregiving satisfaction: Prerequisites to elder home care. *Research in Nursing and Health, 6,* 61-67.

Young, R., & Kahana, E. (1989). Specifying caregiver outcomes: Gender and relationship aspects of caregiving strain. *The Gerontologist, 29,* 660-666.

Zarit, S. (1989). Do we need another "Stress and caregiving" study? *The Gerontologist, 29,* 147-148.

Zarit, S., Todd, P., & Zarit, J. (1986). Subjective burden of husbands and wives as caregivers: A longitudinal study. *The Gerontologist, 26,* 260-266.

16

Physiological Illness in Aging

JUNE C. ABBEY

Objectives: At the completion of this chapter the reader will be able to:

(1) Critique the interaction of eugeric changes, sociological expectations, and disease processes that require adaptation in the older adult.
(2) Analyze physiological changes that affect the health status of the elderly.
(3) Evaluate the role of gerontological nursing in caring for the older adult experiencing physiological change and illness.
(4) Analyze the heterogeneity of physiological changes in the older person and the potential for prevention of disease.

INTRODUCTION

Built upon a variety of genetic schemata, aging is a continuous process of change that occurs throughout life. The change, in the main, is decremental, yet often reflects environmental and experiential impact and exchange in rate. In other words, research of today reports population trends rather than information upon which to develop individual care. Frequently four different kinds of aging times are used interchangeably to support findings, interpretations, and opinions. The times are: (1) chronological time or numbers of years of life; (2) psychological lifetime, or what is in fact, the space of intellectual capability; (3) the biological lifetime or physiological ability to compensate; and (4)

AUTHOR'S NOTE: The word *eugeric* means normal aging.

functional time, defined as the ability to do or continue to do work. Other problems of research reporting of time are the lack of consequence in the intervals selected for study, or even a standard definition for old.

The World Health Organization definitions of elderly, 60-75 years; old aged, 76-90 years; and the very old as more than 90 years is hardly helpful when one considers the work activities involved in the 60-75 year old group and the physical changes that occur between 76 and 90 years. The latter classification does not allow for the increasing numbers of individual differences among the survivors nor the effects of planned interventions to modulate the aging process, such as diet and exercise. The modulation is perhaps best demonstrated by the life expectancy change between 47.3 years for a person born in 1900, with that of 73 years for a person born in 1978. Part of this 26-year increase was due to a drop in infectious disease and better sanitation. Since 1970, however, the extended life span was related to a decline in mortality of the older aged group due to cardiovascular diseases (Robb, 1984). This decrease resulted from intensive and longitudinal studies, scientific and technological medical advances, and widely disseminated education to consumers and health professionals. Of equal import to health care was the inherent promise that the progression of aging contained factors or points of modulation. The process thereupon became plastic or changeable. The illnesses of aging, seen from such a perspective, became treatable, perhaps more serious because of reduction in the ability to compensate, but not simply an expectation of aging. Health care focus for the aged began shifting from treatment to prevention and from hospital to outpatient and home care. Development of the necessary nursing care requires that the approach include (1) understanding of the eugeric changes, both fixed and mutable, that occur; (2) an appreciation of the role society's expectations play in physiological compensation; and (3) comprehension of the demands disease states make on the elderly person's nerves.

The human body is replete with reserve or back-up homeostatic mechanisms that gradually diminish in capacity to compensate for physical change. An oversimplified explanation is that "they just wear out." An equally strongly held opinion is that "lack of use is abuse." Probably, elements of each are true. Aging does occur. There are many ways to classify the known decrements. For example, losses occur in patterns: (1) total loss of function such as reproduction; (2) decrease of cellular or anatomical units as occurs with nephrons, taste buds, or muscle fibers, but function remains in the retained cells; (3) numbers of units remain with decreased function illustrated by reduced sensory nerve fiber conduction rates; and, (4) changes secondary to other functional feedback loss. The level of the approach is determined by the field of interest of the proposer. The purpose of this paper is to relate overall formats that will best aid the clinician or clinical researcher. One of the first principles to consider is: What are the common signs and symptoms of the eugeric elderly person. Which are evidence of decreased function? Which respond to intervention? **Which require intervention?**

FUNCTIONAL CHANGE AND
NURSING APPROACHES

One of the most common signs of aging is a change in body size and shape. Until about 40 years of age people grow in height, due to becoming more erect and vertebral body growth. Stature then begins a gradual decline with leg length first. The loss occurs by joint changes and foot arch flattening. Later compaction of intervertebral disks occurs and spinal curvature flexion increases. When deltoid muscle mass lessens the shoulder width decreases, although the chest circumference increases when the lungs begin to lose their elasticity. This lessens the inward pull on the rib cage. The thorax that looks pinched generally occurs in the very old and indicates that ribs can no longer support the intercostal muscles. All of the foregoing depict a decrease in function.

The major area of intervention indicated is assessment of activity limiting change, and preventive exercise as early as the changes are noted. Special walking shoes can contribute to more comfortable walking. The deltoid size can be increased by weight lifting, and aerobics can strengthen and enlarge the thorax. Loss of elastic recoil of the lungs lessens expiratory flow velocities. Therefore any rapid exchange requires respiratory muscle input. These skeletal muscles have lengthened relaxation and contraction times and require considerable subject effort, so fatigue sets in. Elderly people cannot sustain panting long. These changes can be postponed by physical activity and exercise.

The body composition ratio of lean body mass to fat mass decreases. Fat and the body weight increase is thought to be due to an inactive life-style. The change in intracellular-extracellular body water fluid ratio to less than 2:1 suggests that either a loss in cell mass or cellular dehydration has occurred. Noninsulin dependent diabetes (NIDD) has been suggested as a cause, but additional study is necessary. NIDD is common in the aging population. Rowe, Minaker, Pallotta, and Flier (1983) found there is an age-associated decline in sensitivity of peripheral tissues to insulin. The bulk of reported data indicate that normal aging is not associated with change in number or affinity of insulin receptors (Minaker, Meneilly, & Rowe, 1985). A reduction in cell mass to body weight is shown by a drop in the total body potassium from 54mEg/Kg to 50mEg/Kg in men and from 46mEg/Kg to 38mEg/Kg in women of 70 years of age. All organs participate in the loss of lean body mass that is age related. This finding is reinforced by the accompanying extracellular increase in sodium to potassium concentration from 1.0:1 to 1.2:1 (Kenney, 1989). The loss of lean body mass indicates a tissue loss in active tissue such as organs and muscles. Dehydration of the elderly is often a concurrent problem with diabetes, and whereas fluids may not be imperative, the aging person is often dehydrated.

Blood volume is stable until approximately age 80 years. As expected, the ratio of blood volume to lean body mass increases. The red blood count, hemoglobin concentration, and hematocrit also continue to be within normal limits and only subtle differences are found between the cells of aging persons and the young. There are few significant changes in white blood cells except in the granulocyte. These show lobulation, decreased granulation, and increased osmotic resistance. Despite a reduction in the amount of red bone marrow with age, the remaining characteristics of the marrow continue to be the same as in the young. The ability to increase red blood cell production and cause yellow bone marrow to convert to red to produce cells remains adequate, but slow, during injury or time of crisis. These are minor changes in the plasma chemical composition and no apparent differences in plasma osmotic pressure occurs with age. Not unexpectedly, protein end products, such as urea, creatine, uric acid, and nitrogenous end products in plasma increase as nephron units decrease in number. Plasma bicarbonate concentration shows a steady decline of 1% per decade after age 50. Plasma pH stabilizes at about 7.38 or the corrective level of PCO_2. All in all, the blood and plasma remains well controlled in constituents and volume. The changes should not present symptoms or findings in and of themselves, and in mild stress should be adequate. The aged are at risk for potential acidosis if they incur a respiratory infection or stress. Blood volume regeneration is slower. The older patient with NIDD does not develop metabolic acidosis as quickly as do patients with insulin dependent diabetes. There continue to be sufficient normal red cells, with an adequate life span and hemoglobin concentration to maintain oxygenation.

By contrast, connective tissues change markedly throughout life from a highly aqueous jelly-like substances in infancy to the increasingly solidified matrices of the aged. Connective tissue contains two major types: (1) ground substance, which consists of mucopolysaccharide as hydrated gels; and (2) the fibrous proteins of collagen, elastin, and reticular fibers. A barrier, or basement membrane, exists to define the boundaries between connective tissue and endothelial or epithelial layers. As such, all exchange substances between blood and the cell must go through the basement membrane twice. With aging, the gels increase in density as water is lost and fiber density thickens. Cellular mobility lessens, and diffusion is reduced, as both cellular nutrition and the repair for healing process become slowed.

Collagen fibers increase in size and number with aging. As across linkage bandings occur, solubility reduces with density and stability increase, and turnover lessens. The matrix gradually changes to have the mechanical characteristics of a fabric of increasing rigidity. Cartilage is another tissue that transforms radically with aging. This elastic, slippery tissue in young people is found in joints, particularly at weight bearing sites such as the knees, fingers, elbows. As it ages, the increasing fiber density limits motions and provides nidi for bony deposits. Cartilage can be converted to true bone.

Connective tissue is widely distributed throughout the anatomy, and the effects of aging on this tissue are awesome and widespread. A brief list of these areas include stiffening joints from encircling fibrous tissue; rigidity of costal cartilages with limitation of movement of the thorax; compaction of intervertebral disks when the nucleus pulposus loses hydration and its flexibility; loss of elastic recoil by the lungs; and impaired cardiac function. When distensibility and elasticity is lost to reduced matrix flexibility and results in contractility reduction, cardiac valves stiffen and the aorta becomes rigid.

Bone loses minerals in aging, in direct contrast to the tendency of calcium to deposit in fibrous tissue. The osteoporosis of aging can result in as much as a 10% loss of bone salts. This results in a remodeling of long bones due to bone absorption, and the minerals released deposit and form bone on the external periosteal surface. The bone appears to be thicker because the diameter increases, but the wall or cortex itself becomes thinner. As the bones weaken, the risk for fracture, from even minor injury, grows. The incidence of osteoporosis is greater in women than men. The development is a function of four factors: (1) the skeletal status at maturity; (2) hormonal factors; (3) nutritional factors during bone loss; and (4) the effect of immobilization. For bones, maturity is defined to occur shortly after 30 years of age. Recent research has determined the amount of bone is greater in males than females throughout life and that this difference is the principal factor contributing to the prevalence of osteoporoses of women in old age. Girls have 20% less bone mass in relation to body weight. The index of bone mass is a factor of height and appears to be directly related to calcium intake (Exton-Smith, 1985). Although ingestion of fluoride has been reported to decrease rarefaction in bones, evidence is inconclusive.

Hormones related to postmenopausal osteoporosis are parathyroid hormone; estrogen; 1,25-dehydroxy-vitamin D; calcitonin; and possibly progesterone and corticosteroid. Short-term estrogen therapy leads to a decrease in bone resorption without affecting bone formation. Researchers conclude, however, that the lack of estrogen is not the sole cause or cure of osteoporosis. Exton-Smith (1985), in summarizing hormonal factors influencing osteoporosis, notes that recent work by Gallagher et al. demonstrates that estrogen treatment of postmenopausal women significantly increases both serum 1,25-dehydroxy vitamin D and calcium absorption.

Nutritional factors also affect bone loss, particularly after menopause. The most prominent is that increased dietary protein causes an elevated renal excretion of calcium. Dietrick, Whedon and Shorr (1948), did the initial work that confirmed that immobilization caused marked negative calcium balance in normal young men. Rapid demineralization is also elicited in men who are weightless during space travel (Tilton, Degioanni, & Schneider, 1980). The loss is also stimulated by the immobilization of movement due to splints or casts used in treating leg fractures. Some investigators believe that a sedentary life, with minimal activity and weight bearing, predisposes elderly persons to bone resorption and osteoporosis onset. The signs and symptoms include fragile long bones and multiple fractures. There are kyphotic posture changes that contribute to limited chest excursion because the acute anterior spinal flexion prohibits deep breathing. The acute spinal curvature can also augment kinking of the vertebral arteries, which is a contributing factor to transient ischemic attacks reported by the elderly. The ensuing curtailment of activity is readily apparent.

Calcium absorption from the small intestine depends on the availability of vitamin D. Of the major forms in which it occurs, 1,25-dehydroxy cholecalciferol (1,25-(OH_2) D) probably is the definitive to the intermediary hormonal form of vitamin D (DeLuca, 1976). Extracellular calcium ion concentration changes when the acid-base balance shifts, and therefore increases with acidosis and decreases in alkalosis. If pulmonary exchange is adequate, concentration balance is well maintained. Ionized calcium is involved in a number of important physiological functions. These are: clotting of blood, regulation of nervous system transmissions, enzymatic activation and inhibition, muscle contractibility, hormonal activity, through cyclic adenosine monophosphate, for example releasing factors, growth hormone, parathyroid hormone, bone formation and calcium dependent antigen-antibody reactions (Liberti, Callahan, & Maurer, 1973). New, more accurate, methods for diagnosing and monitoring blood chemistry hormonal levels, and bone density scans, permit quicker diagnosis and appropriate treatment. However, osteoporosis and osteomalacia are disabling conditions. These require not only patient therapy, but also support for, and teaching of, family members to cope with the patient and to promote physical and mental activity.

The signs and symptoms of bony changes associated with aging are readily apparent, as height and posture changes occur that reflect vertebral and extremity changes. The concomitant symptoms are fragile bones, particularly the lower arm and the proximal femur. Osteoarthritis or joint disease is common. These patients frequently are unstable and lose their balance easily. All of which leads to decreased mobility, modified chest expansion and pulmonary exchange, limited energy expenditure, and hence the risk of inadequate protein intake. Intervention is best begun as prevention with weight bearing activity and exercises; a combination estrogen, vitamin D, and its metabolites at menopause; and adequate nutrition which includes protein and the B vitamins. Even better prevention occurs early in life with proper and adequate nutrition, regular and intensive outdoor exercise to promote vitamin D formation, calcium absorption and deposition in weight bearing bones, and the build up of dense bones.

Recent research by Hickson at the University of Illinois, strongly suggests that muscle mass will increase in the aged with isometric and isotonic exercise, despite evidence of lipofuscin accumulation and fatty infiltration. Without exercise, loss occurs in red muscle to a greater extent than in white. The loss is inversely related to the amount of the muscle that continues to be used, and is therefore not uniform. The number and size of the muscle fibers grow smaller.

The effective length lessens because fibers lose sarcomeres. Connective fibrosis tissues replaces the lost fibers. The net result is a reduction of active fiber length, limitation by fibrous tissue of "stretchability," elasticity of compliance, a lessening of effective range of motion, and decreasing ability of muscle to exert tension or to contract maximally. No change occurs in the resting muscle potential of aging muscle. The end plate potential suffers from slowing of frequency, possibly due to synthesis slowing or reduction, and hence lessened axonal transport in motor nerves. The refractory period is increased, and there is prolongation of each individual action potential. The outcome of these changes are slowed action and reaction and decreased strength of contraction.

SOCIOLOGICAL IMPACT, PHYSIOLOGICAL PROCESS AND PREVENTION POTENTIAL

The foregoing changes result in some of the most discernable signs and symptoms of aging. The person actually slows down and loses strength. The signs are gradual at first as muscles not used as much as others decline first. Societal expectations contribute as family members initially assume the considerate and well-meaning roles of "runners," "gofers," "fetchers," and "I'll get it for you's." The interaction starts insidiously as children learn to do tasks responsibly, and gradually increases throughout the teens and early adulthood. The problem has been augmented by the development of laborsaving devices both at home and in industry and will grow with the shift from agriculture to industry and mass spectator sports. Current research shows that exercised muscle grows in mass and numbers of fibers. The intervention that promises most success in retaining skeletal and cardiac muscle function, is use. In fact, one could say that nonuse is abuse. These coupled with the need of bones for weight bearing to retain and maintain their integrity suggests that both isometric and isotonic exercise are the best interventions for care. It is well to note that the loss of motor neurons has not, as yet, been shown to decrease with muscular activity. The aged person, therefore, must recruit motor neurons from a wider area to move muscle groups. The activity is thus perceived as expenditure of greater effort and energy.

The skin manifests many function alterations due to aging processes. What results from eugeric processes and those due to radiation from harmful light waves such as ultraviolet light from the sun is oftentimes difficult to determine. An overview of the skin is that it consists of three layers, epidermis, dermis, and cutis. These are perforated by sebaceous glands and hair follicles. The epidermis, a mixture of five cell types, contains three of major significance: (1) the keratinocyte, which forms the keratinized protective horny layer; (2)

the melanocyte, which makes melanin; and (3) Langerhans' Cell, which acts as part of the macrophage system in peripheral immunity response. Chronic exposure to sunlight depresses Langerhans' Cells and increases melanocyte activity. All of these tissues undergo regression with normal aging. With the exception of melanoma, the most common skin cancers, basal and squamous cell carcinomas, are rather benign with low rates and metastases. Skin diseases rarely cause disabilities. Nevertheless, the often underestimated prevalence of "a skin problem of sufficient intensity to consult a physician" is 66% of the 70 years and older population (Johnson & Roberts, 1977).

Skin changes often have psychological impact on the aged person as disfigurements, discolorations, and deteriorations are readily apparent and progressive. Graham (1983) found that aged who are physically more attractive are also more social, more optimistic, and feel that they are in better health. The epidermal area decreases in the aged and contact adhesion with the dermis lessens; thus a shearing force will more easily damage the skin. Langerhans' Cells diminish and this causes a lessened cell-initiated immunity in aged skin. Silver, Montagna, and Karacan (1965) found a decreased number of active glands and less sweat secretion per gland in response to temperature elevation. The elderly thus become vulnerable to heat stroke because of (1) decreased heat loss to evaporation of sweat, and (2) compromised vasculature bed response for corrective heat loss through radiation.

Giacometti (1965) presents an informative review of hair changes in the aging. Scalp hair growth diminishes markedly after the age of 65. Color changes are found in most people at 45 years of age. Color changes and baldness patterns are inherited. There seems to be no greater risk for any internal disease associated with early graying of the hair.

Free nerve endings are affected little by aging; however, it cannot be assumed that there is no change in pain threshold. On the contrary both pain threshold and reaction to pain time increase (Procacci, Bozza, Buzzelli, & Cortz, (1970). That is to say, between 50 and 90 years, there is a loss of sensitivity to pain. Reactions to acute inflammatory conditions are also muted. This coupled with the impaired cell-immunity puts the aged person at risk for herpes zoster. A curious association between the titer of antenuclear antibodies and the aged has been noted by Hallgren, Kersey, Peczalska, Greenberg, and Yunis (1973). Autoimmune antibodies also increase reactions to various tissues, thus explaining the prevalence of autoimmune demotologic disorders of pemphigus and bullous pemphigoid in the elderly. Cellular immunity deficiency of the aged is currently an active area of research in cancer and ultraviolet irradiation on T-cell suppression.

Aging skin research has not established an age-related increase in skin permeability such that an elderly person is at risk for dehydration. The stratum conium does not thin and its barrier function remains intact. By contrast, the microvasculature does decrease, therefore topical absorption of medication or other substance is slowed and may be erratic. Goodson and Hunt (1979) report that extensive surgeries can be successfully performed on the old-old (older than 85 years). Substantial differences do, however, occur in wound repair (Claes, Pattersson, & Göthman, 1966) and most abdominal surgical wound dehiscence occur in the elderly. More recently, in a most rigorous study on superficial lesions, Grove (1982) compared two different age groups. The 65-75 year old group lagged behind the 18-25 year old group at every stage of repair and the older group's time intervals for restoration were significantly more variable. Perhaps the most useful comment on wound healing is to note that "after surgery medical complications are more serious and numerous in the elderly" (Kligman, Grove & Balin, 1985, p. 838).

To summarize the skin (1) is the major collector interface of information from the environment to the body; (2) provides a water-loss barrier for the body; (3) regulates thermal heat-loss and -gain through high vascularity convection, dispersion, and shunting; (4) protects against invasion by macrophage and immune response; and (5) affords a psychological presence, for the entity of being. The signs and symptoms are evident. Thinning and graying of the hair are not modifiable. Probably of more import is that the elasticity of skin also cannot be changed. Skin will sag and wrinkles will occur. Wound healing does take longer. Still, research on prevention of aging of the skin, its structures, and functions is a fledgling science. Only recently have sun screens been available, and, even more recently, has any action been taken to educate the young to protect their skin.

One would be remiss not to talk about teeth and the mouth in the physiology of aging because of their effect on nutrition. Two factors have greatly influenced the overall ability of people to prevent the loss of their own teeth. These are (1) fluoridation of water supplies, which reduced cavities; and (2) improved oral hygiene, which prevents periodontal disease. Despite almost constant abrasion and exposure to microorganisms, the teeth are durable and continue to be so for a life span. Major changes do, however, occur during aging. The enamel thins and becomes pigmented. Pulp cavity size lessens, and the dentin becomes more opaque as it fills the space. Both perfusion and sensitivity diminish. The chewing surfaces become smoother. The "long-in-the-tooth" appearance of aging results from thinning of their periodontal ligament and recession of the gums away from the tooth. The junction between the enamel and the cement substance is exposed. The indentation between the two acts as a pocket that collects food debris and microorganisms. Gum epithelium thins. Teeth shift and the bite changes, which predisposes loosening and subsequent loss of teeth.

The lining of the mouth shows loss in the rate of cellular proliferation and repair of abrasions. The mouth becomes dryer because both salivary gland activity and production of mucin decreases. The older person also drinks less water. The numbers of taste buds lessen gradually throughout life to where at

70 approximately 30% remain. The loss occurs from the front of the tongue to the back. This results in loss of sensitivity to sweet and salty tastes. Thus bitter and sour tasting remains effective. Diabetic neuropathy can alter taste, and more recently reports of hypertension causing an increased threshold to salt have appeared. Some elderly retain their appreciation for taste. Whether this is an actual maintenance of taste buds or an integrated memory with a high order of facilitation needs further study. Of more importance is that the elderly person who retains an interest in the taste of food and all of its comforting connotations, is likely to eat better.

The mouth's other singular function is to talk. A sore tongue, inflamed gums and loose teeth can preclude this very necessary part of living and communicating. The sign, not talking, is easily noted; the symptom of pain, discomfort or simply apprehension, can be missed or attributed to other causes. The accompanying withdrawal and retreat can lead to depression. The interventions of intense and regular oral hygiene can and do slow down progression to tooth loss and gum disease. Checking the mouth on a schedule will preclude the gradual onset of any unexpected but threatening process.

The alimentary tract ages primarily in three ways that affect surface area for absorption. These are (1) proliferation of the numbers of epithelial cells decreases. The rate falls about 25% between 25-70 years of age; (2) neuronal loss from the enteric nervous system, namely the autonomous myenteric and submucous plexi that control and coordinate tract movement, timing of secretion and absorption, and the amount and interval of vascular perfusion; and indirectly but significantly, (3) cardiac output reduction that determines inflow and outflow of nutrients to the tract. The net effect is (1) a decrease in available surface area for exchange; (2) a loss in synchrony in movement of the contents of all levels, but most particularly in the esophagus; (3) an increase in absorption time in the large intestine accompanied by constipation; (4) small areas of intestinal weaknesses with diverticuli formation; (5) increased formation of intestinal gas; and (6) uncoordinated peristalsis that leads to high intralumen pressures. Of the special function organs of the tract, the eugeric pancreas creates few problems. The functional reserves of the pancreas according to current research remain adequate for its primary functions. According to Kenney (1989) there is "no evidence of age-dependent impairment of digestive secretions" (p. 76). The liver begins to lose tissue mass at approximately 40 years of age. Maximum secretory transport rate is maintained but the blood perfusion rate declines at about 1.5% per year from that found in young (18-25 years) adults. By 65 years of age the perfusion rate is reported to be at about 60% of young adults. Protein synthesis seems to be well preserved into the seventh decade. The reduction of regional perfusion appears to be the primary cause of the decline of hepatic capacity to metabolize and detoxify drugs. Contributing factors are reduced activity of hepatic enzymes, and maintenance of adequate levels of nutritional requisites such as vitamin C, the B vitamins, and folate required for demethylation. There is no apparent aging change of plasma concentrations of alkaline phosphatase, serum glutamic oxytloactic transaminase, or serum, glutamic pyruvic transaminase. Ethanol detoxification remains normal.

Atrophic gastritis occurs in many people more than 50 years of age. The inflammatory process affects both the mucosa and muscle. Recent studies show that secretion of the intrinsic factor, formerly purported to decrease in amount, continues to be secreted even in the presence of profoundly curtailed acid release. Age related pernicious anemia must be elicited by other contributing factors. Although the volume of gastric secretions lessens after the age of 40, if testing is standardized to lean body mass change, the secretion remains constant. Absorption rates of ethanol and water from the stomach do not appear to be age related. The small intestine surface area for absorption significantly lessens as a function of change of height and flattening by the villi. There is, however, no pervasive proof that absorption of major nutrients is limited, and tests based upon blood concentration of these substances show that absorption remains intact in the presence of advancing age. Only two essential nutrients show absorption limitation associated with aging, these are calcium and lipids. The defect appears to be in the formation of lipoprotein, such as chylomicron, and limited syntheses of apoprotein and phospholipids. Amino acid absorption is not significantly depressed. Limitation of vitamin D is thought to be the reason for curtailed calcium absorption.

The small intestine apparently has few motility problems. This is in contrast with both the esophagus and the colon. In fact the term "presbyesophagus" is used to identify esophageal disfunction. The condition generally is first reported by men and women in their early fifties, when they notice bouts of indigestion and infrequent episodes of gastroesophageal reflex. Peristaltic waves are initiated by swallowing when the upper esophageal sphincter is relaxed. The wave travels down to the lower sphincter, which relaxes to permit entrance of the swallowed substance into the stomach. Theoretically, a wave follows each swallow and precedes the food. Oftentimes in the old person the peristaltic waves do not accompany every swallow and the lower sphincter fails to relax. The food piles up and elicits ringlike painful contractions. Studies show that the amount of total motor activity remains the same but is uncoordinated and ineffectual. Esophageal reflex is particularly dangerous in old people who are lying down because the reflux occurs quickly, usually contains gastric acid and is therefore irritating, and can result in aspiration. Hiatal hernias occur frequently in the aged. The incidence is estimated to be at around 70% in the older-than-65-years population. Constipation and diverticulosis accompany delayed motility. The problem is promoted by lack of liquid intake, soft, bland foods, and a history of taking laxatives over a long period of time. Diarrhea frequently indicates a fecal impaction rather than correction of the constipation. The loose stools in these people result from irritation and inflammation of the colon. The use of bran for treatment of the constipation and to prevent diverticulitis began within the last 15 years. When oat bran appeared to also decrease cholesterol, many people of all ages changed their diets to include digestible cellulose and "roughage. The abrupt adoption of these dietary modifications resulted in the "irritable bowel " syndrome of very soft stools with incontinence and a marked increase in flatus. These corrected when the diet was returned to "normal" and then modified more gradually. Varying degrees of bowel incontinence accompanies aging, particularly following strokes, after the age of 75, and when the autonomic and central nervous systems begins to show characteristics of aging. Generally, when something begins to go awry in the alimentary tract, the aged person becomes aware of symptoms. With eugeric aging, very little is visible to the caregiver. It is essential to allow sufficient time to question the elderly, and to build rapport that will permit and even encourage exchange. Often further radiological and laboratory tests and extensive examinations are necessary to arrive at a successful yet simple intervention.

Homeostatic regulatory systems impairment often contribute to the functional limitations of aging. Sensors and effectors can be impaired. The question then becomes what part, or parts, of the regulatory system is causing the malfunction. The overly simplified schemata is: The sensor receives, recognizes, and encodes the input stimuli. Each sensor responds to its own stimuli. The coded input then is transmitted over a neurotransmitter dependent network to an effector for the response to the stimuli. The points of failure are insufficient stimuli, decreased numbers of sensors, limited neurotransmitter, slowing of transmission rate, inaccurate coding, and aberrant response due to effector failure or incapacity to elicit an adequate response because of loss of effector units. Aging changes cause receptors to lose sensitivity and require longer stimulation to elicit a response. Regulating centers of the hypothalamus show little loss in neuron numbers but develop imprecision in maintaining the target value that elicits corrective action. Knowledge about the aging process of the autonomic nervous system outflow is limited and fragmented. Animal studies of aging effects reveal the following characteristics: (1) greater stimulus intensity is necessary to elicit end organ response in both sympathetic and parasympathetic neurons; (2) loss of the autonomic ganglia sensitivity to preganglionic stimulus; and (3) lowering of the maximum frequency with which impulses can be transmitted through the ganglionic synapses. In cholinergic parts of the systems a decrease in acetylcholinesterase concentration results from a decline in syntheses. The balance between the limited syntheses and deactivation or disposal of transmitter reduction differs from organ to organ. All of which slows and limits appropriate response.

A number of cardiovascular functions become compromised during aging. A number of these changes are attributed to the alteration of baroreceptor sensitivity. Examples are: (1) The orthostatic hypotension that occurs when many older people stand up. Where the baroreceptors are compromised neither peripheral resistance nor cardiac rate can respond adequately to offset the peripheral pooling that causes a drop in blood pressure. (2) The Valsalva maneuver performed by an older person produces greater pressure decrease during straining than that that occurs in young people. When released, there is no elevated pressure rebound. Thus clinically, fainting can accompany coughing, or straining to evacuate bowel or bladder by elderly persons. The overall picture is one of extended response time for adjustment and equilibration in the homeostatic regulatory system. This precludes rapid and prompt correction and promotes overshoot and prolonged lability of response.

Body temperature regulation is an important consideration that involves the thermal regulatory system and its ability to balance heat made with heat loss such that comfort and a protective range is maintained within the body. Heat is made through metabolic processes and muscular and glandular activities. The heat produced must be lost to the environs if the ideal internal or core temperature is to be relatively stable. Heat is lost through conduction of heat to the body surface by vasodilation and increasing circulation to the skin and periphery. At the surface, heat is lost through radiation, evaporation of sweat, and convection. Two centers in the hypothalamus control the body responses necessary for losing or retaining heat within the body. The preoptic area center activates heat dissipation mechanisms, and the posterior hypothalamus area controls the target sensing area and heat generation and conservation of heat responses of the body.

These compensatory mechanisms can be shivering, exercising of vasoconstriction, or behavioral acts such as putting on a sweater or seeking shelter. The older person is at a disadvantage because of: (1) reduced muscle mass to generate heat; (2) decreased subcutaneous insulating fat and (3) thinning of the skin; and (4) reduction of cutaneous vasculature. The decrease in cardiac output also lessens blood flow to the skin. The hands and feet frequently reflect this phenomenon and feel cold to the touch and cold to the elderly person. Older persons, however, frequently do not feel the cold as quickly as do young people. The elderly respond with similar sluggishness to increased heat and can be overcome by heat before they are aware of the danger. The lower, and oftentimes inaccurate, sensitivity puts the elderly at thermal risk. Contributing factors are diminished ability to sweat, decreased cardiac output and capacity to dissipate heat, and often inadequate fluid and salt intake or conservation. The inability to lose heat equal to that made, becomes a self generating spiral that can lead to morbid hyperthermia. Central control mechanisms are overcome at 41°C and death ensues due to respiratory failure at 44°C.

The signs and symptoms of homeostatic regulatory system impairment are often missed by both the elderly person and the caretaker. Research is now defining patterns that can be expected and thus be available for intervention. Thermoregulation is well delineated but must be taught to the elderly person and the caretakers in order that rational intervention plans can be carried out.

The other well-defined regulatory system is the maintenance of pH of body fluids. The three mechanisms for control of acid-base balance include buffering, respiratory correction, and renal elimination. Instantaneous buffering occurs when noncarbonic acid combines with the bicarbonate of extracellular fluids. If the imbalance persists, intracellular protein combines with the excess protons. Bone can also be used to buffer a protracted acidotic condition. Respiratory correction eliminates the carbonic acid formed as carbon dioxide and water when a strong acid is buffered. The kidneys account for the fixed acids and protect the buffer base by selective reabsorption or excretion. The ability of the old person to make the momentary corrections is limited by the pervasive factors of loss of lean tissue mass and bone mineral for buffering reserves, and by the decrease in body fluid volume and the lowering of bicarbonate concentration. Although considerable reserve capacity exists due to the high rates of carbon dioxide diffusability and solubility, the older a person gets the less respiratory correction is possible. This is a function of the cumulative changes of decreased pulmonary surface area, limited thoracic excursion, kyphosis, and oftentimes a history of smoking or respiratory disease that leads to lessened diffusing capacity. With increasing age, respiratory reserves become compromised and capacity for all-out effort is curtailed. This is why any respiratory difficulty is serious in the aged person.

Unlike the lungs, which cannot selectively conserve buffers, the kidneys can regulate the amount of bicarbonate reabsorbed. The kidneys also eliminate hydrogen ions in the distal tubule and finally, kidneys use ammonium ions to replace urinary cations thus actively conserve and add to the available buffers. Kidney correction of acid-base imbalance is slow and takes from hours to 5-7 days. It is also vulnerable to aging changes, particularly decreased or impaired circulation.

The aging kidney shows functional changes largely reflecting progressive immutable loss of nephrons, and a significant decrease in the corrective powers of the kidney. Vascular changes consist primarily of fewer glomerular capillary loops resulting in diminished perfusion of the kidney, decreased filtration, reabsorption, and selective adaptive compensatory elimination of end products. A case in point is that there is a steady decline in glucose reabsorption with consequent spilling into the urine. Specific renal capacities that change with aging are: (1) inability for compensatory hypertrophy; (2) progressive loss of the ability to concentrate urine and protect against water loss and dehydration; (3) lessened secretory and reabsorptive transport of threshold factors; and (4) diminished formation and excretion of ammonium. Studies show additional regulatory changes in the renin-angiotensin-aldosterone system wherein high circulating vasopressin levels occur with increased osmotic load but with a limited response to a fall in circulatory volume. This can result in dilutional hyponatremia. Although the serum pH gradually changes from 7.4 to 7.38, pH control remains adequate if the elderly person remains eugeric. If, however, a serious challenge, such as pneumonia or an infection occurs that compromises either the extracellular fluid buffers or the capacity of pulmonary compensatory "blow-off" of carbon dioxide and water, the old kidney will not be able to provide even moderately quick correction. Neither will it be able to conserve volume. By 80 years of age, approximately 50% of renal function is lost.

The respiratory and circulatory systems' primary purpose is to deliver oxygen to metabolically active cells. Oxygen is used by the cella in the formation of energy necessary for tissue repair; synthesis of humoral and tissue substance such as hormones, enzymes, and neurotransmitters; muscular activity and neuronal transmissions; and detoxification. In other words, all living cellular activity. The alveolar surfaces of the lungs are necessary for the aforementioned gaseous exchange of oxygen and carbon dioxide. This makes the ability to take air (oxygen) in and deliver it to the cells one of, if not the most important contributors to maintenance of bodily function. The system contains inherent failure points in that the lungs connect directly to the outside and are, therefore, subject to inspired contaminants and pollutants. These cause damage and changes that compound the effects of aging. Although in normal aging alveolae become smaller and shallower, inflammation causes increased secretions, blockage, and ultimately coalescence of many of these exchange units. This results in a marked decrease in surface area for exchange. The normal loss is from a total surface area of $80m^2$ at 40 years of age to $65\text{-}70m^2$ at 70 years. Spring-like coils of collagen stiffen and form cross linkages and surfactant-producing cells decreases in number, thus lung elasticity and recoil is limited. Without this counterforce, compliance increases and gaseous flow rate exchange is compromised.

Bony structure changes of the rib cage and spine also lead to diminished excursion and gaseous exchange. Although thoracic musculature and the diaphragm show little mass lost, the work load associated with chest movement increases, and the elderly person becomes aware of the amount of effort various activities require. Characteristic of muscles in general, these muscles also have lengthened contraction and relaxation intervals. Alveolar ventilation shows little diminution; however, the overall surface area for exchange declines. Evidence of blunting of the chemoreceptor sensitivity to hypercapnia and hypoxemia is reported in the clinical literature, however, during exercise the elderly have an increased ventilatory response in either condition.

Again, the naturally occurring primary changes are in connective tissue, neurological sensitivity blunting and transmission interval lengthening, and loss of muscle mass. Perhaps the single most important contributing factor is inhaled pollutants and irritants. To a large extent these insults can be prevented by elimination of smoking and use of preventive measures such as masks in high exposure sites.

After the oxygen diffuses across the alveolar membrane it either dissolves into the plasma or is picked up by eosinophils for transport in the cardiovascular system. The heart and vasculature consist of a blood conveyance system built upon volume and pressure pumps. The arterial walls are elastic with pulsatile rebound. The venous tree maintains the return hydrostatic pressure through unidirectional valves. The ideal system would have the following characteristics: (1) flexibility, (2) elasticity and compliance, (3) receptors for pressure and pulsatile rate changes, (4) ability to change rate, rhythm, volume, and pressure, and (5) muscular pumping action. All of which would seemingly suggest that the components would contain neurological receptors and effectors, muscles, and connective tissue. Logically all of the vessels connected to the pressure pump (left heart) would be subject to repeated wear from the pulse pressure, and collagen infiltration and stiffening. This would occur in the chambers and arterial walls. Changes would be loss in number and sensitivity of baroreceptor and regulatory nodes of rhythm and rate of beat. There would be a decrease in elasticity and compliance of the heart. Increased systolic pressure would be expected. Vascular capillary beds would decrease in numbers of cells and there would be increasing density of ground substance.

Research studies document the occurrence of the foregoing in persons more than 80 years of age. Cardiac output lessens at about 1% per year from age 20-80 years. The two cardiac reserve functions of increasing stroke volume or heart rate to respond to increased demand are limited by (1) stiffening of chamber walls through loss of elasticity or compliance; (2) reduced baroreceptor sensitivity of cholinergic and sympathetic blockade; (3) reduced arterial compliance; and (4) changes in neurotransmitter release. The linear decrease in heart rate is predictable. Cerebral blood flow lessens about 20% by the age of 70 years.

Longitudinal studies show a gradual increase in systolic pressure, the rate of which reflects the degree of hypertension in early adulthood. This change is not found in all cultures and is probably the result of interactions between internal and external factors. Certainly heredity and environment contribute but probably physical and emotional conditioning and diet are equally important. A widening pulse pressure is frequently found in aging and reflects the impaired distensibility of large arteries (Bierman, 1985). Whereas increased resistance in precapillary arterioles is believed to be fundamental to essential hypertension, the effects of aging on the capacitance function of veins are unknown. If diastolic and systolic hypertension occur concomitantly after the age of 55 years, it is probably not essential hypertension but rather of some other etiology. Associated factors are diabetes, renovascular disease, obesity, high salt intake, and familial history.

"Coronary heart disease is the most common sequela of hypertension in the elderly and the absolute risks in women for strokes is no lower than in men" (Bierman, 1985, p. 857). Lability of blood pressure increases with age. The proportion of brain infarction grows with severity of blood pressure elevation.

Recent studies show a number of results that strongly suggest that (1) essential hypertension results from an insulin-resistant state and limited nonoxidative pathways of insulin disposal (Ferrannini et al., 1990), (2) insulin resistance is characteristic of hypertension associated with noninsulin dependent diabetes mellitus (Christlieb, 1990), 3) decreasing insulin resistance with exercise is associated with decreased blood pressure in rats (Hwang, Ho, Hoffman, & Reaven, 1988), (4) weight reduction lessens hyperinsulinemia in humans (Krotkiewski et al., (1979), and (5) insulin accelerates the development of atherosclerosis both in vivo and invitro (Stout, 1985). The associations were significant and reinforce the emphasis on weight reduction, attention to limiting dietary fat intake, and regular exercise to maintain health and slow down the changes that accompany chronological aging.

ALZHEIMER'S DISEASE
AND RELATED DISORDERS

Aging of the nervous system is perhaps the most feared of aging processes. The signs and symptoms can be readily brought to mind: the losses of memory, the visible slowing of reflexes and instability of movement, vision changes, and loss of hearing. Reports of an increasing incidence of Alzheimer's disease compound the concern. The following section describes some neurological changes in Alzheimer's disease and related disorders, but no attempt is made to detail nursing approaches. The reader is referred to Chapters 12, 14, 15, and 17 for information on formal and informal caregiving.

Changes occur in all of the various areas of the brain at varying rates and at different intervals. Overall the brain tissue mass reaches a loss of about 7% by the age of 80 years. The early loss, between 20 and 50 years, occurs primarily in cells. This is followed by an increase in neural fiber. Brain stem nuclei loss begins late in life at about the 65th year. Onset of decreased cells in the cerebellum follows that of the cerebrum. Peripheral nerve degeneration results in loss of different fibers that yields a small decrease in conduction velocity and prolonged muscle action potential. Myelin is lost from the axons slowly. As one might expect, irregular membrane-bound protein fibrils appear within brain nuclei. Neuronal microtubules disappear to be filled in by the plaques and neurofibrillary tangles that are found in Alzheimer's disease. Neuron death eliminates synaptic contact target cells. The circuit can be reactivated by axonal sprouting from nearby neurons. The effectiveness of this process in the aged person has not been established. Many obstructions in cerebral blood flow occur as the arteries become kinked and tortuous. The rate of flow falls by 20% between 30-70 years. Both oxygen and glucose utilization continue to be well maintained. This facilitates protection of neurotransmissions, and the unique quality of the nervous system that determines all movement, thought, sensation, regulations, and response.

Nerve cells perform a number of tasks relative to transmission such as active transport, making neurotransmitters which then move along the axons to synapse, as axonal transport. This can travel in either direction away from the cell body or back to the cell itself, as the synapse influences both pre- and post synaptic target nerves. Neurotransmitters, as chemical substances, profoundly affect both behavioral and regulatory systems. These then are vulnerable to the retained cellular synthesis capability, and disposal or inactivation systems that modulate the effect. The two major types of substances are acetylcholine and catecholamine. Each of these is subject to pharmacological intervention, but extensive research on the amount of decrement or alteration due exclusively to aging is limited. Animal experimentation supports studies in humans that show norepinephrine concentration in the hind brain falls by 40%-50% between 20 and 70 years of age.

Parkinson's disease is related to aging. The cause is a decrease in available monoamine dopamine for transmission between the substantia nigra and corpus striatum nuclei. The picture is complicated by a fall in the number of dopamine binding sites. The shuffling gait and tremors of parkinsonism can be helped by administration of levodopa. Currently untreatable are the slowed monosynaptic reflexes of the Achilles tendon and plantar flexion so necessary for walking or going up and down steps. Conduction velocity is lengthened in the aged, which compromises the reaction time and synergy between muscle groups necessary for movement. Whereas free nerve endings remain, pressure touch and tactile discrimination and vibratory sensing become slow and inaccurate. The sensations of pain and thermal awareness lessen and levels of threshold stimulation change. This puts the elderly at risk as these two sensors for noxious stimuli become altered.

Changes in perception result from sensory attrition caused by alteration in sensory input or not being able to process environmental factors. The pathway consists of reception of stimuli, conversion or transduction into transmission of the sensation electrical signal to the thalamus and then to the interpretive center of the brain for processing and memory entry. Loss due to aging is linear and can be due to changes in neuronal, chemical, physical, or inaccurate processing. Major impairment can accompany either diminution of receptor elements, garbling of input, interpretive problems, decreased sensitivity, or imperfect comparative recall.

In the aged the most common correctable hearing loss is due to wax accumulation that occurs with increasingly dry cerumen secretion and external auditory canal narrowing. The ossicle and the tympanic membrane become more rigid and middle ear pressure equalization becomes limited. Actual loss of hair cells occurs and the production of endolymph lessens. Audio fibers and neurons are lost throughout the structure. High frequency sensitivity diminishes and there is acuity loss. Understanding of spoken words becomes less accurate. Part of this imprecision is probably due to a decrease in auditory reaction time and central processing "pile-up" of input. Noise or tinnitus occurs when pure-tone perception is lost.

The eye is subject to many connective tissue changes, such as retrorbital fat loss, which permits the eye to sink deeply into the bony orbit. Elastic tissue loss allows ptosis of the eyelids and can interfere with lacrimal duct drainage of tears and permit drying of the eyes. The cornea thins and is subject to edema, hazing, and ulceration. As the anterior chamber flattens when the lens thickens and stiffens, acute closed angle glaucoma can occur with a pupil dilation. The pupil diameter fixes at minimal size in response to fibrous changes of the iris. Limitation of entry of light to the retina requires increased levels of illumination for sight for persons more than 60 years of age. The lens and the aqueous humor become thicker and yellower due to decline of lens metabolism and poor circulation. With thickening and loss of flexibility the lens loses its range of accommodation for near vision. Glare is caused by micro-opacities that occur with lens thickening and that break up the light rays. The receptor loss is chiefly in the rods of the peripheral retina. Minor decrement in central vision accompanies the loss of rods. The aged person experiences difficulty in moving into a dark room because the chemical process of dark adaptation becomes slower and less effective. The number of active neurons for vision also lessens.

SUMMARY

Research on the processes entailed in physiological aging clearly demonstrates the disparate course among aged individuals. No one person fits all the findings in all instances. What is apparent is that (1) there are some patterns that can benefit from preventive measures; (2) expectations of society, friends, family members, and the aged person do have an impact on the course and intensity of aging; (3) heredity contributes the basic potential but it can be modified by care, nutrition experience, and prevention; and (4) continued activity and participation offset the "abuse of nonuse."

REFERENCES

Bierman, E. L. (1985). Arteriosclerosis and aging. In C. E. Finch & E. L. Schneider (Eds.), *Handbook of the biology of aging* (pp. 842-856). New York: Van Nostrand Reinhold.
Christlieb, A. R. (1990). Commentary on insulin resistance in essential hypertension. *Diabetes Spectrum, 3,* 308-309.

Claes, G., Pettersson, S. & Göthman, B. (1966). Results of geriatric surgery. *Acta Chirurgica Scandanavia, 357,* 85-90.

DeLuca, H. F. (1976). Recent advances in our understanding of the vitamin D endocrine system. *Journal of Laboratory Clinical Medicine, 87,* 7-26.

Dietrick, J. E., Whedon, G. D., & Shorr, E. (1948). Effect of immobilization upon various metabolic and physiologic functions of normal men. *American Journal of Medicine, 4,* 3-36.

Exton-Smith, A. M. (1985). Mineral Metabolism. In C. E. Finch & E. L. Schneider (Eds.), *Handbook of the biology of aging,* (pp. 526-527). New York: Van Nostrand Reinhold.

Ferrannini, E. Buzzigol, G. Bonadonna, R. Giocico, M. A., Gleginni, M., Graziadei, L., Pedrinelli, R., Brandi, L., & Bevilacoua, S. (1990). Insulin resistance in essential hypertension. *Diabetes Spectrum, 3,* 300-306.

Giacometti, L. (1965). Hair growth and aging. In W. Montagna (Ed.), *Advances in biology of skin.* Oxford, UK: Pergamon.

Goodson, W., & Hunt, T. (1979). Wound healing and aging. *Journal of Investigate Dermatology, 73,* 88-91.

Graham, J. A. (1983). The psychotherapeutic value of cosmetics. *Cosmetic Technology, 5,* 25-26.

Grove, G. L. (1982). Age-related differences in healing of superficial skin wounds in humans. *Archives of Dermatologic Research, 272,* 381-385.

Hallgren, H. M., Kersey, J. H., Peczalska, K. J., Greenberg, B. J., & Yunis, E. J. (1973). T and B cells in aging humans. *Federated Proceedings, 33,* 646-647.

Hwang, I. S., Ho, H., Hoffman, B. B., & Reaven, G. M. (1987). Fructose-induced insulin resistance and hypertension in rats. *Hypertension, 10,* 512-516.

Johnson, M. L., & Roberts, J. (1977). Prevalence of dermatologic disease among persons 1-74 years of age. *Advance Data.* Washington, DC: Department of Health, Education and Welfare.

Kenney, R. A., (1989). *Physiology of aging: A synopsis* (2nd ed., pp. 28-91). Chicago: Year Book Medical Publishers.

Kligman, A. M., Grove, G. L., & Balin, A. K. (1985). Aging of human skin. In C. E. Finch & E. L. Schneider (Eds.), *Handbook of the biology of aging* (p. 838). New York: Van Nostrand Reinhold.

Krotkiewski, M. Mandrous, K., Sjostrom, L., Sullivan, L., Vetterqvist, H., & Bjorntorp, P. (1979). Effects of long term physical training on bloodfat, metabolism, and blood pressure in obesity. *Metabolism, 28,* 650-658.

Liberti, P. A., Callahan, H. J., & Maurer, P. H. (1973). Physiocochemical studies of CA++ controlled antigen antibody systems. In M. Friedman (Ed.), *Protein-Metal Interaction.* New York: Plenum.

Minaker, K. L., Meneilly, G. S., & Rowe, R. W. (1985). Endocrine systems. In C. E. Finch & E. L. Schneider (Eds.), *Handbook of the biology of aging.* New York: Van Nostrand Reinhold.

Procacci, P., Bozza, G., Buzzelli, G., & Cortz, M. D. (1970). The cutaneous pricking pain threshold in old age. *Gerontology Clinics, 12,* 213-218.

Robb, S. S. (1984). The elderly in the United States: Number, proportions, health status and use of health services. In A. G. Yurick, S. S. Robb, B. E. Spier, & N. J. Ebert (Eds.), *The aged person and the nursing process* (p. 49). East Norwalk, CT: Appleton & Lange.

Rowe, J. W., Minaker, K. L., Pallotta, J., & Flier, J. S. (1983). Characterization of insulin resistance in aging. *Journal of Clinical Investigation, 71,* 1581-1587.

Silver, A., Montagna, W., & Karacan, J. (1965). The effect of age on human eccrine sweating. In W. Montagna (Ed.), *Advances in biology of skin* (pp. 129-149). Oxford, UK: Pergamon.

Stout, R. W. (1985). Arteriosclerosis and aging. In C. E. Finch & E. L. Schneider (Eds.), *Handbook of the biology of aging* (p. 24). New York: Van Nostrand Reinhold.

Tilton, F. E., Degioanni, T. T., & Schneider, V. S. (1980). Long term followup of Skylab bone demineralization. *Aviation-Space Environmental Medicine, 51,* 1209-1212.

17

Psychological Illness in Aging

BARBARA KAVANAGH HAIGHT

Objectives: Upon completion of this chapter, the reader should be able to:

(1) Assess psychological illness in aging people.
(2) Manage nursing care of aging people with chronic mental illness.
(3) Diagnose specific psychological conditions in aging people.
(4) Evaluate selected psychological interventions for aging people.
(5) Synthesize a practice approach for the psychological care of aging people.

INTRODUCTION

Much of the psychological illness in aging is reactive to losses endured through the developmental process of growing older. As people grow older they experience both social and physical change. Social change occurs through losses of significant others, isolation, and diminished support systems. Losses such as reduced sensory abilities resulting in a decreased ability to hear and see characterize physical change. Inability to cope with these social and physical changes may result in psychological stress and eventual illness. For example, as the hearing abilities of older people diminish, they may exhibit paranoid reactions. These paranoid reactions are an abnormal response to an inability to understand conversation, but after a period of time the reactions become a normal response pattern.

This chapter will examine potential psychological health concerns in well elderly people and in chronically mentally ill elderly people. Assessment tools and selected therapeutic interventions will be presented as methods for nurses to use when working with older people experiencing these stressors.

COGNITIVE AGING CHANGES

Normal cognitive changes are multiple and stressful. For example, as some people grow older their coping abilities diminish. Problem solving does not proceed in an orderly manner because of a less pointed search for information. Recent memory undergoes change and decision making becomes more cautious (Botwinick, 1987). Change also occurs in intelligence. Fluid intelligence (the ability to problem solve and think abstractly), decreases while crystallized intelligence (the result of learning and experience) increases. This change in intelligence may affect the individual's ability to problem solve and perform math functions (Baltes & Schaie, 1976). Learning also becomes more difficult because of slower processing, and if faced with stressful, demanding situations, older people are less successful in managing the situation.

PERSONALITY

Personality changes also may affect an older individual's response to life. As people age they turn more inward and become less impulsive. Men and women exchange traits resulting in men becoming more nurturing and women becoming more authoritarian (Ebersole, 1988). Besides these changes over the years, gerontologists have suggested many theories to explain the aging personality. One that remains is the continuity theory developed by Neugarten (1955). The continuity theory states that people will become more of themselves. Within this theory, Neugarten categorized people in different personality types and from this categorization was able to speculate how the types would respond to aging. Table 17.1 identifies these types and the anticipated response to aging.

Other theorists have espoused developmental changes. A popular theory that is most helpful in understanding the needs of older people is Erikson's "Eight Ages of Man." Erikson was one of the first developmentalists to believe change continued after childhood (Erikson, 1950). Others—Havighurst, Peck, and Buehler—have added tasks to these stages in an attempt to develop other theories. Erikson's stages, however, are the most discussed in the literature and are helpful to the practicing clinical nurse specialist (Ebersole, 1988). With a background knowledge of personality and normal aging changes, the nurse should then examine each individual's current environment for stressors that might result in negative psychological states, such as loneliness, apathy, anxiety, and depression.

Table 17.1
Personality Types According to Neugarten

	Type	Response to Aging
I.	Integrated—well functioning with a complex inner life and a competent ego.	Successful
	A. Reorganizer—competent with a wide variety of activities.	A. Needs to refocus energy.
	B. Focused—competent but more selective in activities.	B. Needs to have a major interest.
	C. Disengaged—competent and choosing a low activity level (rocking chair).	C. Needs to relax.
II.	Armored-Defended—striving, ambitious with high defense against anxiety.	Less Successful
	A. Holding on—aging constitutes a threat. "I'll work till I drop."	A. Good as long as pretence of youth is maintained.
	B. Constricted—defends self against aging and preoccupied with losses.	B. Views aging negatively.
III.	Passive-Dependent—demonstrates recurrent needs.	Even Less Successful
	A. Succorance-seeking—strong dependency needs and seeks support from others.	A. Problems when support systems are removed.
	B. Apathetic passivity is a striking feature of personality (man allows wife to talk for him).	B. Becomes more passive and does not fend for self.
IV.	Disorganized—gross defects in psychological functioning.	Failure Continues pattern of life.

Source: Adapted from: Neugarten, B. L. (1955) *Middle age and aging: A reader in social psychology.* Chicago: University of Chicago Press.

PSYCHOLOGICAL STATES

Loneliness

Loneliness is a phenomenon experienced by many older people. It is a condition resulting from many losses. The experienced losses often result in isolation and then in loneliness. For some, loneliness is an inner experience that is individual to the particular person. Two people may experience similar situations but only one will feel loneliness. The other will not.

Nurses in their practice have only described the condition of social isolation through nursing diagnosis. Although loneliness can grow out of social isolation, it is a totally different experience. Power's research (1988) noted that the presence of others did not always make a difference in the life of the older individual. She said the nurse needed to examine the meaning of a relationship to an older person to determine its impact on the older person's life. Therefore, loneliness is an inner, individual experience dependent on the aging individual's perceptions of a situation. Loneliness may be the result of the loss of a spouse, of a neighborhood, or of a friend and confidante. If loneliness itself is not present, the fear of it often is. Fry (1986) suggests many older people believe loneliness is inevitable. Fear of the inevitable may be a contributor to depression.

Apathy

Apathy is another state often noted in elderly people, particularly in long-term care settings (Haight & Warren, 1987). Apathy is a condition of "just existing." Carnevali and Patrick (1986) said apathy was a problem for aging people because the presence of apathy kept the people from seeking out health care and following good health care practices. Apathy also causes people to withdraw from life. It is a complete lack of caring about one's self and others. Frankl (1968) described apathy as a defense mechanism. He said it was the only way individuals could cope with the atrocities that occurred in Nazi concentration camps. Perhaps apathy is also a coping mechanism for older people, but it is one that may be detrimental. Reker's research (1987) built on Frankl's work and described apathy as meaninglessness and the result of a lack of purpose in life. Reker (1989) was consistent with Frankl's view of meaning as something that had to be personally discovered for each individual. Meaning is the force that makes life worth living. It is a significant and universal human motive that consists of making sense out of one's existence. Having a sense of personal meaning is having a purpose in life.

Anxiety

Anxiety is still another source of discontent for older people. Anxiety is a feeling of anxiousness precipitated by an unknown cause. Anxiety is often the result of common fears held by other people. For example, most older people fear disability and the loss of their mental capabilities. They also fear that their money will not last, and they will be segregated in a nursing home, and that they will no longer be in control of their own lives. One might call this fear "Borrowing Trouble." Hyer, Gouveia, Harrison, Warsaw, and Coutsouridis (1987) found that anxiety directly interfered with older people's life satisfaction. Help with problem solving and a clear assessment of the particular situation can help to relieve anxieties. Research by Whitley (1989) on defining the nursing diagnosis of anxiety, led to a statement of need for an operative measure of anxiety. Fox, O'Boyle, Lennon, and Keeling (1989), studying a group of 54 patients precolonoscopy, suggest the Endler model as an excellent predictor of anxiety. The Endler model uses a specific threat in a stressful situation to measure anxiety. Each of these states—loneliness, apathy, and anxiety—may be identified as a precursor to depression in the continuum of psychological well being.

Depression

Social isolation together with chronic illness and the loss of financial resources are the most common factors leading to depression in the elderly. Most of the depression encountered in older people is a reactive depression, a reaction to whatever life's circumstances have caused or taken away. Prevalence studies indicate that as many as 20% of all people older than 65 experience depression. Hyer et al. (1987) found that a person's state of health directly affected depression in the elderly, and Carpiniello, Carta, and Rudas (1989) associated depression in urban elderly people with widowhood, absence of a confidante, poor education, and financial difficulties. In institutions the prevalence of depression increases to 25% (Fry, 1986). Depression is a serious problem for nursing, with suicide one of the least desirable outcomes of its progression. The high suicide rate in white males over the age of 65 underlines the importance of interrupting depression. The clinical nurse specialist is well equipped to prevent a reactive depression from progressing.

The gerontological nurse clinical specialist needs to characterize the type of depression present. If the depression is endogenous, biological, or a personality trait, treatment is not within the realm of the nurse and referrals to psychiatrists should be made. To determine these differences, the nurse must focus on distinguishing pathological functions from normative temporary disordered functioning. Once the nurse makes the distinction, she must identify the situational aspects contributing to the depression. Finally, the third step is to choose an intervention to interrupt the course of the depression. The next section of this chapter will provide tools for assessment and the last section will discuss nurse oriented treatments for depression.

Chronic Mental Illness

Another major problem area for gerontological nurses is the rapidly growing number of aged people who are chronically mentally ill. Chronically mentally ill people are those who have been assigned diagnoses from the *Diagnostic and Statistical Manual of Mental Disorders* (DSM-III-R) for 10 or more years. The chronically mentally ill have become a major concern for communities since the mass discharges from psychiatric hospitals in the 1950s. Current research has focused on the quality of life of the chronically mentally ill. Huber, Henrich, and Herschbach (1988) compared the quality of life of the chronically physically ill with that of the chronically mentally ill and found that the chronically mentally ill were less satisfied with their quality of life, family, children, and health. Simpson, Hyde, and Faragher (1989) examined the quality of life of the chronically mentally ill in varied living sites and concluded that those in group homes were happier than those in institutions.

Living at home contributes to happiness and over 70% of the chronically mentally ill in this country live with relatives and friends (Esser & Lacy, 1989). This long-term and continued care situation creates a burden and stress for families and for the mentally ill person. Today many family care providers are aged themselves and a 60 year old may be providing care for an 85 year old mentally ill parent or a 40 year old mentally retarded child. The impact of the stressor of mental illness on families may be detrimental. The clinical nurse specialist must then consider the whole family as the client.

Still other chronically mentally ill elderly are homeless and in a position of double jeopardy. Deinstitutionalization forced many chronically mentally ill people to the streets, unable to care for themselves. Approximately 40% of the homeless suffer from a major medical disorder, and many of these are older people (Damrosch, 1988). Our current mental health system has cracks in its delivery system. Many older people fall into these cracks and never receive care (Blixen, 1988).

Nursing homes receive many chronically mentally ill people. Nursing homes are not prepared to provide psychological care and counseling to the chronically mentally ill and to other patients affected by their presence. Nurse aides, who have most of the patient contact, are not highly educated and as a result may hold negative stereotypes toward the mentally ill. Each of these settings need practical methods for handling the chronically mentally ill and they may be derived by the gerontological clinical nurse specialist with a background in psychiatry.

NURSING ASSESSMENT

The gerontological nurse is often the first person to notice change in older people living in the community, hospital, or extended care settings. To identify needs caused by the change effectively, the nurse must perform a functional assessment. The functional assessment serves as a screening device for all changes (physical, social, and environmental) that may contribute to psychological distress. A well-known tool for functional assessment is the OARS assessment tool, recently evaluated positively by Liang, Levin, and Krause (1989). Several other tools exist. A good resource for functional assessment tools is a book by Kane and Kane (1981) called *Assessing the Elderly: A Practical Guide to Measurement.*

When the functional assessment is complete, the nurse should further evaluate the older person using nursing diagnosis. Specht (1988) describes the importance of gerontological nurses using nursing diagnosis to direct their care. Many excellent nursing diagnoses exist for the physical assessment of older people. There exists a lack of nursing diagnoses specific to many of the psychological syndromes affecting the elderly, however. A few of the syndromes still needing diagnoses are: apathy, loneliness, caregiver burden, wandering, relocation syndrome, failure to thrive, and potential for suicide. Gerontological nurses will have additional tools for assessing the psychological problems of elderly people with the development of these diagnoses.

In addition to nursing diagnosis and functional assessment tools, other tools originally designed for research and screening may be clinically valuable. Though these tools are excellent on the whole, many of them have not been tested nor have they been found valid and reliable for an aging population. As the practicing gerontological nurse begins to use these tools, the nurse can make a contribution to research and add to the reliability and validity of tools with an older population. A description of selected assessment tools and their purpose follows. Some of the tools for assessing psychological well-being will appear in this chapter, but others may be located in the following: Brink, (1986); Kane and Kane (1981); Mangen and Peterson (1982).

Tools

The Mental Status Questionnaire (MSQ) is widely used and is an excellent tool for the assessment of cognitive function (Kahn, Goldfarb, Pollack, & Peck, 1960). Table 17.2 displays an example of the MSQ along with a legend for calculating the results. Note the basic level of the questions, which may be insulting to some older and brighter people. The nurse needs to incorporate these questions in normal conversation to prevent insulting older people who

Table 17.2
Mental Status Questionnaire (MSQ)

1. What is this place?
2. Where is this place located?
3. What day in the month is it today?
4. What day of the week is it?
5. What year is it?
6. How old are you?
7. When is your birthday?
8. In what year were you born?
9. What is the name of the president?
10. Who was president before this one?

Score shows severity of brain syndrome

0-2 errors = none or minimal
3-8 errors = moderate
9-10 errors = severe

Source: Adapted from: Kahn, R. L., Goldfarb, A. I., Pollack, M., & Peck, A. (1960). Brief objective measure for the determination of mental status in the aged. *American Journal of Psychiatry, 117*, 326.

are alert. Every question, however, must be asked to make a good assessment. Many people with cognitive impairment retain excellent social skills and are effective in covering up their disabilities. The nurse also must establish a rapport before beginning the testing, ask meaningful questions when examining recent memory, rule out sensory difficulties, and take into account the patient's cultural background. Many researchers have examined the use of the MSQ and compared the utility of this tool with others (Foreman, 1987), as well as offered additional suggestions and tools (Teng & Chui, 1987; Uhlmann, Larson, & Buchner, 1987). The following section is a critique of assessment methods utilized to evaluate psychological status including personality, loneliness, apathy, coping, anxiety, mood states, and depression.

Personality

Assessing personality in terms of Neugarten's (1955) descriptions may be helpful in trying to anticipate the person's response to aging. For instance, if the individual is the rocking-chair type one would not expect much activity. If the individual is a succorance seeker the nurse would know that particular individual needed support over a long period of time, particularly if there was a recent loss of support systems. Personality types to use in the assessment process were previously described in Table 17.1.

Loneliness

People who are lonely often seem hungry for interaction and an interview period will often yield clues to loneliness. Recently bereaved people are often quite lonely without their lost loved one. People who are coping with loneliness will often describe ways they keep busy when loneliness begins to threaten them. Those who are not coping well may be evaluated by the newly created nursing diagnosis (loneliness), not yet NANDA approved, displayed in Table 17.3. This nursing diagnosis presents major and minor defining characteristics and definitions of these characteristics and is research based (Warren & Haight, 1989). The advantage of using a nursing diagnosis is that the diagnosis focuses attention on the syndrome and begins to direct a plan of care.

Apathy

Apathy also may be assessed through nursing diagnosis. Table 17.4 displays another proposed research-based nursing diagnosis of apathy, only recently submitted to NANDA and not yet approved (Haight & Warren, 1989). Again, a nursing diagnosis created to direct a plan of care may be very effective in interrupting the syndrome of apathy and preventing or arresting the progress of depression.

Additionally, if the cause of apathy is meaninglessness, Reker's (1989) Life Attitude Profile (LAP) is an excellent added tool for assessment. One dimension of the tool, existential vacuum, is closest to the nursing diagnosis of apathy and is represented by five questions from the Life Attitude Profile: Revised (LAP-R) in Table 17.5. Martin (1990) has been researching the syndrome of apathy in patients with a psychiatric diagnosis and gives an interesting account of its classification in this patient population.

Coping

Coping has no available tool for assessment other than the stress index sources. Researchers have addressed coping through an educational program for caregivers (Chiverton & Caine, 1989) and a group skills training program (Long & Bluteau, 1988), but have offered no tool for assessment. One good way to assess coping is to perform a life review and note how the individual coped with stressful events throughout a lifetime. The life review can reveal a history of coping skills and one can more readily judge the older person's response to stress in the present. If the client is not participating in a full life review, it might be helpful to recall past stressful events and discuss the coping methods used to see if they were successful. This discussion will not only recall past coping strategies, but will focus the individual on past successes and

Table 17.3
Proposed Nursing Diagnosis for Loneliness

1.	Name:	Loneliness

2. Definition: Loneliness is the unnoticed inability to do anything while alone (Peplau, 1955). It is an unchosen state in which the individual is left feeling impotent and withdrawn from human interaction (de la Cruz, 1986).

3. Defining Characteristics:

MAJOR:	*DEFINITIONS:*
Has the feeling of abandonment	Deserted, left behind, forsaken
Complaints of "time is heavy on my hands"	Self-explanatory
Reports a loss, e.g., person, pet, health, role, etc.	Failure to keep, privation
Minimal to no social networks	Lack of support systems
Complaints of emptiness	Hollow, void, and vacant
States "feeling lonely"	Unfrequented by human being, sequestered
Perception of self as being isolated	Sees self as set apart, separate

MINOR:	*DEFINITIONS:*
Expression of distorted self-esteem	Misrepresented opinion of one's self
Displays "curling up" phenomena/posture	Fetal position
Demonstrates lack of interest in things	Self-explanatory
Decreased ability to concentrate	Inability to focus on idea, objects
Low social risk taking behavior	Meek, does not take chances in social situations
Withdrawn	Retire, remove, to keep from use, to take away
Expression of distorted self-esteem	Misrepresented opinion of one's self
Does not initiate contacts	Self-explanatory
Segregates self from others	Avoids social contact
Disturbed sleeping patterns	Difficulty falling asleep (frequent awakening)
Superficial social interaction	Lack of meaningful involvement with others

Source: Warren, J., & Haight, B. K. (1989). *Loneliness.* Paper presented at the Midwestern Nursing Research Conference, Kansas City, Kansas. (Permission to print obtained from authors.)

contribute to self-esteem, a very important contributor to life satisfaction (Taft, 1985; Thomas, 1988).

Table 17.4
Proposed Nursing Diagnosis for Apathy

1. Name: Apathy

2. Definition: Apathy has ben described as an existential vacuum. It is the absence of feeling and response and results in a lack of motivation and a subsequent withdrawal from life (Crumbaugh & Maholick, 1964).

3. Defining Characteristics:

MAJOR:	*DEFINITIONS:*
Emotional death	Absence of feeling, lack of passion
Unmoved by environmental stimuli	No response to surroundings
Disinterest	Unsympathetic, unconcerned
Just existing	Enduring
Flat affect	Emotionless
Don't care attitude	Self explanatory
Lack of motivation	No incentive or drive
Indifference	Having no interest
Lack of responsiveness to others	Lack of sensitivity, unsympathetic

MINOR:	*DEFINITIONS:*
Boredom	Languor of the mind, ennui, weary
Blunting of emotions	Dull feeling on a superficial level
Nonassertive	Lack of confidence in self
Absence of social risk taking behavior	Does not partake of social situations
Displays of lack of purpose	Lack of reason for being
Disconnected	Feelings of being apart
States feelings of uselessness	Nugatory, powerless, insignificant, no value
Uninvolved	Not taking a physical part in activities
Lack of energy	Feelings of "blahness", lack of vitality
Lack of eye contact	Avoids direct looks
Lack of goal directed behavior	Activities are not directed toward achieving a desired end
Listlessness of the body	Languid, sluggish
Lack of impulse	Absence of impelling force or impetus
Lack of desire	Lack of need, want, or longing
Slowness	Slackening of pace, lacking spirit
Lack of initiative	Lack of starting behavior, non-originator

Source: Haight, B. K., & Warren, J. (1987). "Loneliness and apathy in the elderly: A proposed nursing diagnosis." Paper presented at the Sixth Southern Regional Nursing Diagnoses Conference, Orlando, Florida. (Permission to print obtained from authors.)

Table 17.5
Reker's Life Attitude Profile-Revised (LAP-R)

Existential Vacuum: Refers to having a lack of meaning in life, lack of goals, lack of direction, and free-floating anxiety.

	1	2	3	4	5	6	7
1. I feel that some element which I can't quite define is missing from my life.	SD	D	MD	U	MA	A	SA
2. I feel the lack of and a need to find a real meaning and purpose in my life.	SD	D	MD	U	MA	A	SA
3. I try new activities or areas of interest and then these soon lose their attractiveness.	SD	D	MD	U	MA	A	SA
4. I have experienced the feeling that while I am destined to accomplish something important, I cannot put my finger on just what it is.	SD	D	MD	U	MA	A	SA
5. I seem to change my main objectives in life.	SD	D	MD	U	MA	A	SA
6. I daydream of finding a new place for my life and a new identity.	SD	D	MD	U	MA	A	SA

1	SD	= Strongly Disagree
2	D	= Disagree
3	MD	= Moderately Disagree
4	U	= Undecided
5	MA	= Moderately Agree
6	A	= Agree
7	SA	= Strongly Agree

Source: Adapted from: Reker, G. (1989, October). *Personal meaning in life: A two-component model and scale.* Paper presented at the 18th annual meeting of the Canadian Association on Gerontology, Ottawa, Canada. (Permission to print obtained from author.)

Anxiety

Anxiety presents in many forms. There is depletion anxiety accompanying depression and resulting in exhaustion and withdrawal. Another form is helplessness anxiety in which the older person feels no longer in control over his or her life and is somewhat apprehensive. The only test that does not examine anxiety as a neurotic disorder, but rather as a feeling sate, is the Profile of Mood State (POMS) (McNair, Lorr & Droppleman, 1971). The POMS scores six mood factors; confusion-bewilderment, tension-anxiety, and fatigue-energy. It is useful for assessing areas such as fatigue versus energy. The test has been used effectively in geriatric psychopharmacology studies (Fry, 1986) and so also might be helpful in identifying anxiety. Sample tests may be obtained from Educational and Industrial Testing Service, San Diego, CA, *Profile of mood states. Manual,* (McNair et al., 1971).

Mood States

Other assessment tools that are helpful are those that assess good moods or the opposite state of depression. Bradburn's (1969) Affect Balance Scale (ABS) is one that is slowly gaining acceptance in the gerontologic research community and may also be helpful in practice. This scale consists of only 10 questions and its brevity contributes to its value. Five questions are positive, testing positive affect, and 5 questions are negative, testing negative affect. The ABS with a sample scoring system is in Table 17.6.

Self-esteem and life satisfaction are additional determinants of well-being. The scales of choice to test these areas are Rosenberg's Self-Esteem Scale and Havighurst's Life Satisfaction Index-A (LSI-A) found in Mangen and Peterson (1982), *Research Instruments in Social Gerontology: Clinical and Social Psychology,* Volume 1.

Depression

Many people have presumed to measure depression. One difficulty that arises when measuring depression in elderly people is that the physical changes that occur with depression are similar to those that occur with aging. These similarities affect the validity of the depression scales. Dreyfus (1988), in a study of depression, used a depression scale specifically devised for the elderly by Brink (1986) and found this scale very helpful in a clinical setting. Brink's scale is in Table 17.7 with the scoring mechanism and a key for assessing the amount of depression. Researchers (Hyer & Blount, 1984; Nelson, 1989; Yesavage et al., 1983) continue to use this scale and report satisfactory results. In other nursing research, McDermott-Keane and Sells (1990) demonstrate the importance of using depression scales to screen out depression early in the elderly.

Not to be overlooked are the scales devised by Beck, Weissman, Lester, and Trexler (1975). Beck constructed a depression scale, a hopelessness scale, and a suicide ideation scale. He found that depressed people were not at risk for suicide unless they were also hopeless (Beck, Kovacs, & Weissman, 1979). The use of these tests together is helpful in assessing the patient's potential for suicide. If there is a question of suicide, the two tests can be used together and then validated with the suicide ideation scale, providing the clinician with an objective measure of the situation at hand. These two tests, along with the

Table 17.6
Bradburn's Affect-Balance Scale (ABS)

	Agree	Disagree	
During the past few weeks, did you ever feel . . .			
Positive Feelings:			
1. Pleased about having accomplished something:	[✔]	[ ]	+1
2. That things were your way:	[✔]	[ ]	+1
3. Proud because someone complimented you on something you had done?	[ ]	[✔]	−1
4. Particularly excited or interested in something?	[✔]	[ ]	+1
5. On top of the world?	[✔]	[ ]	+1
			Total (+4 − 1 = 3)
Negative Feelings:			
1. So restless that you couldn't sit long in a chair?	[ ]	[✔]	+1
2. Bored?	[ ]	[✔]	+1
3. Depressed or very unhappy?	[ ]	[✔]	+1
4. Very lonely or remote from other people?	[ ]	[✔]	+1
5. Upset because someone criticized you?	[✔]	[ ]	−1
			Total (+4 − 1 = 3)

Total Score = 6 (Highly Positive Affect)

Note to Nurse: WHEN YOU ASK THESE QUESTIONS, ROTATE BETWEEN POSITIVE AND NEGATIVE QUESTIONS.

Source: Adapted from: Bradburn, N. (1969). *Structure of psychological well-being*. Chicago: Aldine.

clinician's observations, provide a degree of clinical accuracy. They can be located in the following references: Beck, Kovacs, and Weissman, (1979); Beck, Weissman, Lester, and Trexler (1975); and Beck and Beamesderfer (1974).

The preceding battery of tests equips the gerontological nurse specialist with an array of objective measures to validate intuition and observation. As the nurse forms a diagnosis for the patient, an intervention plan must follow.

Table 17.7
Geriatric Depression Scale (GDS)

Choose the best answer for how you have felt over the past week:

1. Are you basically satisfied with your life? .... yes/no
2. Have you dropped many of your activities and interests? .... yes/no
3. Do you feel that your life is empty? .... yes/no
4. Do you often get bored? .... yes/no
5. Are you hopeful about the future? .... yes/no
6. Are you bothered by thoughts you can't get out of your head? .... yes/no
7. Are you in good spirits most of the time? .... yes/no
8. Are you afraid that something bad is going to happen to you? .... yes/no
9. Do you feel happy most of the time? .... yes/no
10. Do you often feel helpless? .... yes/no
11. Do you often get restless and fidgety? .... yes/no
12. Do you prefer to stay at home, rather than going out and doing new things? ... yes/no
13. Do you frequently worry about the future? .... yes/no
14. Do you feel you have more problems with memory than most? .... yes/no
15. Do you think it is wonderful to be alive now? .... yes/no
16. Do you often feel downhearted and blue? .... yes/no
17. Do you feel pretty worthless the way you are now? .... yes/no
18. Do you worry a lot about the past? .... yes/no
19. Do you find life very exciting? .... yes/no
20. Is it hard for you to get started on new projects? .... yes/no
21. Do you feel full of energy? .... yes/no
22. Do you feel that your situation is hopeless? .... yes/no
23. Do you think that most people are better off than you are? .... yes/no
24. Do you frequently get upset over little things? .... yes/no
25. Do you frequently feel like crying? .... yes/no
26. Do you have trouble concentrating? .... yes/no
27. Do you enjoy getting up on the morning? .... yes/no
28. Do you prefer to avoid social gatherings? .... yes/no
29. Is it easy for you to make decisions? .... yes/no
30. Is your mind as clear as it used to be? .... yes/no

Of the 30 questions selected for inclusion in the GDS, 20 indicated the presence of depression when answered positively while the others (Nos. 1, 5, 7, 9, 15, 27, 29, and 30) indicated depression when answered negatively. The questions were arranged in a 30-item, one-page format and ordered so as to maximize patient acceptance of the questionnaire.

Answer Key   0-10 = normal
                11-20 = mild depression
                21-30 = severe depression

Source: Brink, T. L. (1983). Development and validation of a geriatric screening scale. *Journal of Psychiatric Research, 17*(1), 37-49. (Printed with permission from Pergamon Press.)

Table 17.8
Suggested Treatment Approaches

Problem States	Treatment Approaches
Coping and Stress	Coping skills calendar
	Behavior modification
	Music and dance
	Exercise
	Relaxation training
	Problem solving
	Imagery
Apathy and Meaninglessness	Play and humor
	Pets and plants
	Life review
	Exercise
Loneliness	Pets
	Play and humor
	Reminiscence
	Group therapy
	Music
	Dance
Reactive Depression	Touch and massage
	Play and laughter
	Exercise
	Reminiscence or life review
Hopelessness and Suicide	Patient contracting
	Cognitive restructuring
	Problem solving
	Life review
Cognitive Impairment	Family counseling and support
	Reality orientation
	Validation therapy
	Pet therapy
	Music and dance
	Exercise
	Reminiscence
Anxiety	Play and laughter
	Exercise
	Relaxation training
Chronically Mentally Ill	Behavior modification
	Social skill training
	Family counseling and support groups

NURSING INTERVENTIONS

Nursing interventions for aging people are numerous and the gerontological nurse specialist has a battery of ideas from which to choose. One of the most difficult decisions is determining the most effective intervention for the condition presented at the time. Snyder (1985) suggests the use of a good decision-making tree. Suggested interventions may be implemented and results recorded. Some may be successful, or a combination of interventions may be successful. As the clinical nurse specialist uses an intervention, observations of failure and success should be recorded. Interventions should be evaluated as indicated by the patient's condition and individualized care plans devised. Table 17.8 presents suggested treatment approaches for the conditions presented earlier in the chapter.

Several excellent books are suggested for a reference library for gerontological clinical nurse specialists attending to psychological illnesses and may be found in the reference list (Bulecheck, McCloskey, & Aydelotte, 1985; Dossey, Keegan, Guzetta, & Kolkmeier, 1988; Esser & Lacey, 1989; Fry, 1986; Snyder, 1985). Persons using these intervention books should have a background in counseling or psychiatric nursing (Gilliland, James, & Bowman, 1989; Knight, 1986). The following sections describe specific nursing approaches for the older adult in psychological stress.

Problem Solving

Some older adults forget how to think in an orderly manner. They often do not incorporate good decision-making skills in their problem solving. During stressful situations, anxiety can rob them of their natural abilities to problem solve (Haight, 1989b). A very simple model of problem solving known to all nurses is the nursing process: assess the situation, plan an approach or intervention, implement the intervention, and evaluate the outcome. Then if necessary, start all over again. Another approach to problem solving is to help individuals with decision making. A simple method to use is a list of pros and cons or an explanation of the decision-making process. Table 17.9 presents the steps in the decision-making process. The information in Table 17.9 reinforces the fact that all people must go through steps to work things out and arrive at decisions. It is often helpful to share the steps of the decision-making process with clients to help them with logical thinking.

Cognitive Restructuring

Cognitive restructuring is a strategy used to teach people to replace negative thoughts with positive thoughts. The strategy assumes that a person's self-defeating thinking can be changed by altering that person's views about

Table 17.9
Stages of Decision Making

Stage:	*Key Questions:*
1. Appraising the Challenge	Are the risks serious if I don't change?
2. Surveying Alternatives	Is this (salient) alternative an acceptable means for dealing with the challenge?
3. Weighing Alternatives	Which alternative is best? Could the best alternative meet the essential requirements?
4. Deliberating about Commitment	Shall I implement the best alternative and allow others to know?
5. Adhering despite Negative Feedback	Are the risks serious if I *don't* change? Are the risks serious if I *do* change?

Source: Adapted from: Janis, I. K., & Mann, L. (1977). *Decision making: A psychological analysis of conflict, choice, and commitment*. New York: Free Press. (Printed with permission of publisher.)

contradictory beliefs. In other words, the individual will turn negative thinking into positive thinking.

One must presume that the older person is ready to make this change or one must wait until that moment occurs. It may take several weeks for the older person to recognize and admit negative thoughts. Once there is an appreciation for and recognition of the impact of negative thinking, progress will begin. To accomplish this goal the nurse and older person must follow six steps:

(1) Discuss the rationale for the procedure.
(2) Identify negative thoughts about problem situations.
(3) Practice positive thoughts.
(4) Shift to using positive thoughts.
(5) Practice positive statements.
(6) Do homework and have follow-up discussion sessions.

It is essential that the older person wants to make a change, understands the process, and commits to a plan of action. Many researchers have found cognitive restructuring an effective therapeutic modality (Gilliland et al., 1989).

Reminiscing

Another therapeutic nursing intervention is reminiscing. The literature is replete with reports of reminiscence and life review either lowering depression, raising self-esteem, or raising life satisfaction. Although the terms "life review" and "reminiscing" are used interchangeably, they are two separate modalities and should be discussed individually. The suggested treatment approaches in Table 17.8 recommend them as distinct modalities for different conditions.

Life review is one type of reminiscing under the umbrella of reminiscing. Certainly reminiscing is a part of the conduction of a life review, but a true life review becomes more complicated than simple reminiscing. First, a life review is hard work; reminiscing is often just a pleasurable moment. Life review is evaluative and integrative, reminiscing need not be. In a life review one recalls, assesses, evaluates, reframes, and then integrates. Participants cry over sad times, issues must be reworked. Reworked so much that repetition may be a part of life review. Repetition serves as a catharsis and may ease the reintegration of self. Life review deals with self and examines the actions of the self at the time, place, or event. Reminiscence occurs about events, times, places; and self does not require examination. Life review covers the life span, reminiscence does not need to do that. If one is with old high school friends, the reminiscence is usually about shared experiences in high school. Life review has structure, reminiscence does not. Table 17.10 summarizes the differences between life review and reminiscence and separates the two modalities.

The question often arises: Is life review psychotherapy? The answer is no. There are similarities between psychotherapy and life review, just as there are between reminiscence and life review. There is, however, one basic difference. In psychotherapy, the therapist helps the client sift through life's garbage. In life review, the therapeutic listener just helps the client to take out the garbage. A structured evaluative form of life review is the treatment of choice. Table 17.11 offers selected questions from a life review and experiencing form that assists the gerontological nurse to perform a structured evaluative life review (Haight, 1989a). The particular questions are not the key to the success of the life review, the key is to have the person examine the whole life span and then value the way the life was lived through selected questions like those in the summary.

Social Skills Training

Social skills and self-care skills are important tools for the chronically mentally ill. If the chronically mentally ill person can be taught to behave in a manner acceptable to society then life will be more manageable for the ill person, the caregivers, and family members. Jones and Knopke (1987) suggest physicians be more knowledgeable about the skills and needs of the chronically mentally ill. Much research has focused on simple grooming skills (Donahoe & Driesenga, 1988; Wong et al., 1988).

17.10
Differences Between Life Review and Reminiscence

Life Review	Reminiscence
Work	Pleasure
Self	Other
Evaluative	Nonevaluative
Integrative	Nonintegrative
Life Span	Occasional Times
Individual	Group
Prompted by Need or Crises	Any Cue
Reframing Events	Accepting Events
Repetition and Catharsis	May Repeat, but not needed
Structure	Random

Many of society's behaviors are complex for people who have not lived by the rules of society. For instance, there is a rule that we sleep at night and stay up all day. Deviance from this rule makes one abnormal and people only accept normality. The chronically mentally ill person must learn to understand the importance of being normal. One can learn normality by imitating behaviors and having good role models. The use of behavior modification that rewards good behavior can help to establish normality.

Social skills are necessary to guide behavior in public places. Practicing table manners at home before going to a restaurant is one way to achieve social skills. To make this practice session an enjoyable one, families can establish a "manners night." The dining room is the setting for the meal with the best linens and china. Participants dress up, socialize, and make small talk before dinner and then proceed to the dining room for dinner. While role modeling exquisite manners, the family members should talk about the way they do things. For example, one does not stuff a whole roll in one's mouth, one breaks off a piece, butters the piece, puts the knife on the bread and butter plate, and then eats the piece of roll. Good manners, aside from social skills, comprise a necessary process for acceptance by society.

An example of a self-care skill is brushing one's teeth. Poor hygiene and bad breath can offend others, therefore self-care hygiene skills are essential. Self-care is normal for well people, but ill people have to relearn the steps. Lists of routines and expected behaviors posted on a mirror can help retrain the chronically mentally ill. Table 17.12 shows skills needed for brushing one's teeth (Esser & Lacey, 1989). If behavior modification were a part of the retraining, a reward would be given at the end of a successful week. The reward reinforces the good behavior and the person relearning the skill is more apt to repeat the good work. These types of directions are also helpful for

Table 17.11
Haight's Life Review and Experiencing Form (LREF)

Selected questions from LREF:

Childhood:

1. What is the very first thing you can remember in your life? Go as far back as you can.

7. Did someone important to you go away?

Adolescence:

3. Who were the important people for you? Tell me about them. Parents, brothers, sisters, friends, teachers, those you were especially close to, those you admired, those you wanted to be like.

8. Do you remember feeling that there wasn't enough food or necessities of life as a child or adolescent?

Family and Home:

1. How did your parents get along?

5. When you wanted something from your parents, how did you go about getting it?

Adulthood:

2. Now I'd like to talk to you about your life as an adult, starting when you were in your twenties up to today. Tell me of the most important events that happened in your adulthood.

11. What were some of the main difficulties you encountered during your adult years?

    a. Did someone close to you die? Go away?
    b. Were you ever sick? Have an accident?
    c. Did you move often? Change jobs?
    d. Did you ever feel alone? Abandoned?
    e. Did you ever feel need?

Summary:

2. If everything were to be the same would you like to live your life over again?

4. We've been talking about your life for quite some time now. Let's discuss your over-all feelings and ideas about your life. What would you say the main satisfactions in your life have been? **Try for three. Why were they satisfying?**

Note: Derived from new questions and two unpublished dissertations:
Gorney, J. (1968). *Experiencing and age: Patterns of reminiscence among the elderly.* (Unpublished Doctoral Dissertation, University of Chicago).
Falk, J. (1969). *The organization of remembered life experience of older people: Its relation to anticipated stress, to subsequent adaption and to age.* (Unpublished Doctoral Dissertation, University of Chicago).

Table 17.12
Esser's Skills Needed for Brushing One's Teeth

Skill:	Items Needed:
Brushing teeth	Toothbrush
	Toothpaste
	Glass of water
	Mouthwash
What to do	Put toothpaste on toothbrush
	Brush teeth, using up-and-down strokes
	Rinse mouth with water
	Rinse with mouthwash
	Put items away

Esser's Chart of Accomplishments

Skill	✔ (Check when completed)						Date
a. Brush Teeth	S	M	T	W	T	F	S
b. (Items)							
c.							
d.							
e.							

Source: Adapted from: Esser, A. H., & Lacey, S. D. (1989). *Mental illness: A home care guide.* New York: John Wiley. (Printed with permission of publisher.)

people to maintain themselves during the middle stages of Alzheimer's disease. Alzheimer's victims only succeed in maintaining, however, not retraining (Edinberg, 1985).

Relaxation Training

Dellasega (1990) found that coping with caregiving is improved through selected relaxation modalities. Nurses may successfully deal with stress through progressive muscle relaxation as presented in Table 17.13. Guided imagery is another effective stress reduction exercise. Through guided imagery the older person can leave the nursing home, for example, go to the beach, or a lake, or a forest. The individual an hear the waves and the breeze, remember past visits, and escape the routine of nursing home life. Most stress reduction exercises are successful because the mind is diverted from the

Table 17.13
Progressive Muscle Relaxation

Settle back as comfortably as you can and let yourself relax to the best of your ability.

Now, as you relax, clench your right fist.
Clench it tighter and tighter, and study the tension as you do so.
Keep it clenched and feel the tension in your right fist, hand and forearm.
Now relax . . .
Let the fingers of your right hand become loose . . .
Observe the contrast in your feelings.

Now, let yourself go and try to become more relaxed all over.
Once more, clench your right fist really tight.
Hold it, and notice the tension again.
Now, let go, relax, let your fingers straighten out . . .
Notice the difference once more.

Now repeat that with your left fist.
Clench your left fist while the rest of your body relaxes.
Clench that fist tighter and feel the tension.
And now relax . . . . . . Again, enjoy the contrast.
Repeat that once more, clench the left fist, tight and tense.
Now do the opposite of tension—relax and feel the difference . . .
Continue relaxing like that for awhile.

Clench both fists tighter and tighter, both fists tense, forearms tense.
Study the sensations . . . . . . and relax . . .
Straighten out your fingers and feel that relaxation . . .
Continue relaxing your hands and forearms more and more.

Continue from head to toe, exercising all body parts, one at a time.

Source: Adapted from: Malloy, C., & Hartshorn, J. (1989). *Acute care nursing in the home: A holistic approach.* Philadelphia: Lippincott.

stressful situations. People can learn to practice stress reduction exercises on their own and successfully manage their stress by themselves (Haight, 1989b).

Play

We all forget to play. Where is the joy in old age, in the lives of most older people? Play is doing something for enjoyment. It can take the form of exercise, music, poetry, games, groups, and laughter. It must be entered into freely with an outcome of increased vitality and a sense of joy. The importance of play in children is well documented, but not so in adults. Clark, Lanphear, and Riddick (1987) found video game playing helped the response selection process of elderly people, and Rechnitzer (1989) reported positive effects of physical activity. What seem to be meaningless activities in some nursing homes may be meant to be play. Rhythm bands and Miss America contests all have the potential for play. Often the essential element of fun and joy is missing, and the gerontological nurse should look for these elements in activities offered to older people that are characterized as play.

Additional Nursing Modalities

Multiple nursing interventions exist for interacting with patients and treating them therapeutically. There are three excellent texts of nursing interventions (Bulecheck et al., 1985; Dossey et al., 1988; Snyder, 1985) to be found in the reference list. Nurses have great freedom to try out interventions and select those most helpful to the particular client condition.

Several kinds of group therapy exist. Groups are effective for the practice of exercise, which is effective both physically and mentally. In groups, members can support one another and enjoy many interventions such as music and dance in the company of others. Groups actually have curative factors (Yalom, 1975). They can provide company, impart information, help participants to learn interpersonal skills, and allow people to share themselves with others. They are also extremely cost effective. The gerontological nurse can deliver therapy to five or seven people at the same time through groups. Groups are especially effective for aging alcoholics. Through groups, alcoholics gain social interactions, share problems, and find they are not alone.

SUMMARY

This chapter presented psychological issues, research, assessments, and interventions for the gerontological nurse specialist. It identified selected conditions not identified by medical diagnoses, but needing treatment. In addition, the contents included innovative ways of assessment and use of tools to provide objective measures for assessment. Finally, selected modalities are offered with ready references to explore additional modalities. Gerontological clinical nurse specialists are well equipped to take a leadership role in treating these psychological problems that often are ignored by other caregivers.

REFERENCES

Baltes, P. B., & Schaie, K. W. (1976). On the plasticity of intelligence in adulthood and old age. *American Psychologist, 31,* 720-725.

Beck, A. T., Kovacs, M., & Weissman, A. (1979). Assessment of suicidal intention: The scale for suicide ideation. *Journal of Consulting and Clinical Psychology, 47*(2), 343-352.

Beck, A. T., Weissman, A., Lester, D., & Trexler, L. (1975). The measurement of pessimism: The hopelessness scale. *Journal of Consulting and Clinical Psychology, 42,* 861-865.

Beck, A. T., & Beamesderfer, A. (1974). Assessment of depression: The depression inventory. In P. Pichot (Ed.), *Psychological measurements in psychopharmacology: Modern problems in pharmacopsychiatry, 7.*

Blixen, C. E., (1988). Aging and mental health care. *Journal of Gerontological Nursing, 14*(11), 11-15.

Botwinick, J. (1987). *Aging and behavior: A comprehensive integration of research findings (2nd ed.). New York: Springer.*

Bradburn, N. (1969). *Structure of psychological well-being.* Chicago: Aldine.

Brink, T. L. (1983). Development and validation of a geriatric scale. *Journal of Psychiatric Research, 17*(1), 37-49.

Brink, T. L. (1986). *Clinical gerontology: A guide to assessment and intervention.* New York: Haworth.

Bulechek, G. M., McCloskey, J. C., & Aydelotte, M. K. (1985). *Nursing interventions: Treatments for nursing diagnoses.* Philadelphia: W. B. Saunders.

Burgio, K., & Burgio, L. (1986). Behavior therapies for urinary incontinence in the elderly. *Clinics in Geriatric Medicine,2*(4), 811.

Carnevali, D., & Patrick, M. (1986). *Nursing management for the elderly.* Philadelphia: J. B. Lippincott.

Carpiniello, B., Carta, M. G., & Rudas, N. (1989). Depression among elderly people. *Acta Psychiatrica Scandinavica, 80,* 445-450.

Chiverton, P., & Caine, E. D., (1989). Education to assist spouses in coping with Alzheimer's disease: A controlled trial. *Journal of the American Geriatric Society, 37*(7), 593-598.

Clark, J. E., Lanphear, A. K., & Riddick, C. D. (1987). The effects of video game playing on the response selection processing of elderly adults. *Journal of Gerontology, 42*(1), 82-85.

Crumbaugh, J., and Maholick, L. (1964). An experimental study in existentialism: The psychometric approach to Frankl's concept of neogenic neurosis. *Journal of Clinical Psychology.*

Damrosch, S. (1988). The homeless elderly in America. *Journal of Gerontological Nursing, 14*(10), 26-29.

de la Cruz, L. A. D. (1986). On loneliness and the elderly. *Journal of Gerontological Nursing, 12*(11), 22-27.

Dellasega, C. (1990). Coping with caregiving: Stress management for caregivers of the elderly. *Journal of Psychosocial Nursing, 28*(1), 15-22.

Donahoe, C. P., Jr., & Driesenga, S. A. (1988). A review of social skills training with chronic mental patients. *Progressive Behavior Modification, 23,* 131-164.

Dossey, B. M. Keegan, L., Guzzetta, C. E., & Kolkmeier, L. G. (1988). *Holistic nursing: A handbook for practice.* Rockville, MD: Aspen Publications.

Dreyfus, J. K. (1988). Depression assessment and interventions in the medically ill frail elderly. *Journal of Gerontological Nursing, 14*(9), 27-36.

Ebersole, P. (1988). *Toward healthy aging: Human needs and nursing response (2nd ed.). St. Louis: C. V. Mosby.*

Edinberg, M. A. (1985). *Mental health practice with the elderly.* Englewood Cliffs, NJ: Prentice-Hall.

Erikson, E. H. (1950). *Childhood and society.* New York: Norton.

Esser, A. H., & Lacey, S. D. (1989). *Mental illness: A home care guide.* New York: John Wiley.

Falk, J. (1969). *The organization of remembered life experience of older people: Its relation to anticipated stress, to subsequent adaptation and to age.* Unpublished doctoral dissertation, University of Chicago.

Foreman, M. D. (1987). Reliability and validity of mental status questionnaires in elderly hospitalized patients. *Nursing Research, 36*(4), 216-220.

Fox, E., O'Boyle, C., Lennon, J., & Keeling, P. W. N. (1989). Trait anxiety and coping style as predictors of pre-operative anxiety. *British Journal of Clinical Psychology, 28,* 89-90.

Frankl, V. (1968). *Man's search for meaning.* Boston: Beacon.

Fry, P. S. (1986). *Depression, stress, and adaptations in the elderly: Psychological assessment and intervention.* Rockville, MD: Aspen Publications.

Gilliland, B. E., James, R. K., & Bowman, J. T. (1989). *Theories and strategies in counseling and psychotherapy (2nd ed.). Englewood Cliffs, NJ: Prentice-Hall.*

Gorney, J. (1968). *Experiencing and age: Patterns of reminiscence among the elderly.* Unpublished doctoral dissertation, University of Chicago.

Haight, B. K. (1989a). Life review: Part I, A method for pastoral counseling. *The Journal of Religion and Aging,5*(3), 17-29.

Haight, B. K. (1989b). Psychological management in the home. In C. Malloy & J. Hartshorn (Eds.), *Acute care nursing in the home: A holistic approach.* Philadelphia: J. B. Lippincott.

Haight, B. K., & Warren, J. (1987). *Loneliness and apathy in the elderly: A proposed nursing diagnosis.* Paper presented at the Sixth Southern Regional Nursing Diagnoses Conference, Orlando FL.

Huber, D., Henrich, G., & Herschbach, P. (1988). Measuring the quality of life: A comparison between physically and mentally chronically ill patients and healthy persons. *Pharmacopsychiatry, 21,* 453-455.

Hyer, L., Gouveia, I., Harrison, W. R., Warsaw, J., & Coutsouridis, D. (1987). Depression, anxiety, paranoid reactions, hypochondriasis, and cognitive decline of later-life inpatients. *Journal of Gerontology,47*(1), 92-94.

Hyer, L., & Blount, J. (1984). Concurrent and discriminate validities of the geriatric depression scale with older psychiatric inpatients. *Psychological Reports, 54,* 611-616.

Janis, I. L., & Mann, L. (1977). *Decision making: A psychological analysis of conflict, choice, and commitment.* New York: Free Press.

Jones, L. R., & Knopke, H. J. (1987). Educating family physicians to care for the chronically mentally ill. *Journal of Family Practice,24*(2), 177-183.

Kahn, R. L., Goldfarb, A. I., Pollack, M., & Peck, A. (1960). Brief objective measure for the determination of mental status in the aged. *American Journal of Psychiatry, 117,* 326.

Kane, R. A., & Kane, R. L. (1981). *Assessing the elderly: A practical guide to measurement.* Lexington, MA: D. C. Heath.

Liang, J., Levin, J. S., & Krause, N. M. (1989). Dimensions of the OARS mental health measures. *The Journals of Gerontology: Psychological Sciences, 44*(5), 127-138.

Knight, B. (1986). *Psychotherapy with older adults.* Beverly Hills, CA: Sage.

Long, C. G., & Bluteau, P. (1988). Group coping skills training for anxiety and depression: Its application with chronic patients. *Journal of Advanced Nursing, 13*(3), 358-364.

Malloy, C., & Hartshorn, J. (1989). *Acute care nursing in the home: a holistic approach.* Philadelphia: J. B. Lippincott.

Mangen, D. J., & Peterson, W. A. (1982). *Research instruments in social gerontology: Clinical and social psychology (Vol. 1). Minneapolis: University of Minnesota Press.*

Marin, R. S. (1990). Differential diagnosis and classification of apathy. *American Journal of Psychiatry, 147*(1), 22-30.

McDermott-Keane, S., & Sells, S. (1990). Recognizing depression in the elderly. *Journal of Gerontological Nursing, 16*(1), 21-25.

McNair, D. M., Lorr, M., & Droppleman, L. F. (1971). *Profile of mood states: Manual.* San Diego, CA: Educational and Industrial Testing Service.

Nelson, P. B. (1989). Ethnic differences in intrinsic/extrinsic religious orientation and depression in the elderly. *Archives of Psychiatric Nursing, 3*(4), 199-204.

Neugarten, B. L. (1955). *Middle age and aging: A reader in social psychology.* Chicago: University of Chicago Press.

Peplau, H. E. (1955). Loneliness. *American Journal of Nursing, 55*(2), 1476-1479.

Powers, B. A., (1988). Social networks, social support, and elderly institutionalized people. *Advances in Nursing Science, 10*(2), 40-58.

Rechnitzer, P. A. (1989). Physical activity and our human potential: A contemporary perspective. *Canadian Journal of Sport Science, 14*(2), 68-73.

Reker, G. (1989, October). *Personal meaning in life: A two-component model and scale.* Paper presented at the 18th annual meeting of the Canadian Association on Gerontology, Ottawa, Canada.

Reker, G. T. (1987). Meaning and purpose in life and well-being: A life-span perspective. *Journal of Gerontology, 42*(1), 44-49.

Simpson, C. J., Hyde, C. E., & Faragher, E. B. (1989). The chronically mentally ill in community facilities: A study of quality of life. *British Journal of Psychiatry, 154*, 77-82.

Snyder, M. (1985). *Independent nursing interventions.* New York: John Wiley.

Specht, J. S. (1988). Nursing diagnosis: Key to improved care for the elderly [editorial]. *Journal of Gerontological Nursing, 14*(3), 7.

Taft, L. B. (1985). Self-esteem in later life: A nursing perspective. *Advances in Nursing Science, 8*(1), 77-84.

Teng, E. L., & Chui, H. C. (1987). The modified mini-mental state (3MS) examination. *Journal of Clinical Psychiatry, 48*(8), 314-318.

Thomas, B. L. (1988). Self-esteem and life satisfaction. *Journal of Gerontological Nursing,14*(12), 25-30.

Uhlmann, R. F., Larson, E. B., & Buchner, D. M. (1987). Correlations of mini-mental state and modified dementia rating scale to measures of transitional health status in dementia. *Journal of Gerontology, 42d(1), 33-36.*

Warren, J., & Haight, B. K. (1989). *Loneliness.* Paper presented at the Midwestern Nursing Research Conference, Kansas City, KS.

Whitley, G. G. (1989). Anxiety: Defining the diagnosis. *Journal of Psychosocial Nursing, 27*(10), 7-12.

Wong, S. E., Flanagan, S. G., Kuehnel, T. G., Liberman, R. P., Hunnicut, R., & Adams-Badgett, J. (1988). Training chronic mental patients to independently practice personal groom skills. *Hospital Community Psychiatry, 39*(8), 874-879.

Yalom, J. (1975). *The theory and practice of group psychotherapy* (2nd ed.). New York: Basic Books.

Yesavage, J. A., Brink, T. L., Rose, T. L., Lum, O., Huang, V., Adey, M., & Leirer, V. O. (1983). Development and validation of a geriatric depression screening scale: A preliminary report. *Journal of Psychiatric Research, 11*(2), 37-49.

18

Nutrition and Aging

M. ELIZABETH KUNKEL

Objectives: At the completion of this chapter, the reader will be able to:

(1) Analyze the biochemical and physiological changes that accompany the normal aging process that affect nutritional status in elderly persons;

(2) evaluate contributions of various dietary constituents to nutritional status of elderly persons;

(3) evaluate potential drug-nutrient interactions for their possible impact on the nutritional status of elderly persons; and

(4) analyze implications of these changes for clinical nurse specialists.

INTRODUCTION

This chapter is organized to analyze physiological and biochemical changes in aging that affect nutrition. The nutritional intake and status of the elderly is also evaluated as well as a comparison of factors related to nutrition in institutionalized and noninstitutionalized older adults. Selected drug-food interactions are also included as are implications for clinical nurse specialists.

AUTHOR'S NOTE: The invaluable assistance of Karin Kolb and Virginia P. Littlejohn in the completion of this chapter, and the support of the South Carolina Agricultural Experiment Station are gratefully acknowledged.

AGE-RELATED CHANGES IN BODY SYSTEMS

The aging process is accompanied by alterations in several biochemical parameters that have nutritional implications. These alterations include decreases in protein synthesis; protein turnover; T-cell function; and circulating levels of estrogens, calcitonin, and the physiologically active form of vitamin D. Age-associated increases in plasma concentrations of nitrogenous waste compounds, parathyroid hormone, globulins, and fibrinogen; biliary cholesterol secretion; collagenase activity; and resistance to insulin are also important nutritionally. These changes in biochemical function are associated with physiological alterations including decreases in height, weight, active tissue mass, muscle distensibility, total lung capacity, renal function, bone mass, and serum levels of albumin and hemoglobin. Most physiological functions decrease by about 1% per year after age 30 (Berman, Haxby, & Pomerantz, 1988). Aging, however, cannot be characterized as a generalized decrease in bodily functions. Some functions are relatively unaffected by aging, including hepatic function, platelet count and function, and plasma osmotic pressure.

The single most wide-reaching change in biochemical function with age is the decrease in net protein synthesis and turnover. This decrease is manifested physiologically as a loss of active tissue mass with protein metabolism remaining constant when expressed per unit of active tissue mass (Forbes, 1987; Prothro, 1989). Active tissue mass is lost at a rate of about 5% per decade after the third decade (Forbes, 1987), which leads to a lower requirement for nutrients, hormones, and mediators to achieve the same level of functioning. Alterations in protein metabolism affect connective tissue, resulting in increased cross-linking of collagen. Collagen that is more extensively cross-linked is less soluble and less elastic, which means that the muscular, skeletal, renal, cardiovascular, and pulmonary systems are less distensible and less able to endure stresses. A less elastic cardiovascular system has lower systemic perfusion of nutrients and oxygen and renal clearance rates (Rosenthal, 1987). Cardiac output decreases and total peripheral resistance increases approximately 1% per year between ages 30 to 80 years (Berman et al., 1988). These changes are associated with an increase in systolic and diastolic blood pressures with age, for example, approximately 67% of people aged 65-74 years have hypertension (National Center for Health Statistics, Drizid et al. [NCHS, Drizid] 1986). Whether this is truly an age-associated increase is questionable because blood pressures of individuals who live in isolated, primitive societies or in psychiatric institutions do not increase with age (Kenney, 1982). The decrease in cardiac output, coupled with a loss of glomeruli and a degeneration of the remaining glomeruli and tubules results in a 50% decrease in renal blood flow and a 30%-40% decrease in glomerular filtration rate (Lonergan, 1988). The body's ability to clear waste products (Euans, 1988; Rosenthal, 1987) and to concentrate urine (Euans, 1988) is impaired (Euans,

1988; Rosenthal, 1987; Shock et al., 1984); therefore, nitrogenous waste products, including creatinine (Euans, 1988; Shock et al., 1984), accumulate in the bloodstream (Whitbourne, 1985).

Total lung capacity decreases about 20% with age. This decrease is a result of increased collagen crosslinking, stiffening of the cartilaginous articulations in the ribs, and changes in spinal curvatures. The older person relies more on the diaphragm for breathing and, therefore, is more sensitive to changes in intra-abdominal pressure, whether caused by a large meal or by body position (Kenney, 1982).

Accompanying the lower active tissue mass in older people is an age-associated decrease in secretion and disposal rates of most hormones. Nevertheless, it appears that the regulating feedback loops for most hormones remain intact into old age (Whitbourne, 1985). Decreases in circulating levels of estrogens, calcitonin, and the active form of vitamin D and the concomitant increase in parathyroid hormone levels are associated with a rarefaction of the bones and may be associated with a decrease in calcium absorption noted after age 70 (Nordin, 1983). Insulin secretion in the elderly is delayed (Jackson et al., 1988) whereas peripheral resistance to insulin increases with age, resulting in decreases in the rate of glucose disposal (Fukagawa et al., 1988).

Age-associated changes in digestive and absorptive capacity have also been noted. By age 65 years, about half the population are edentulous, only one-third are fully dentate, and at least one-fifth have periodontal disease (Papas et al., 1989). Salivary secretion is decreased by age 70 years, which increases oral clearance times, decreases taste acuity, and may result in difficulty in swallowing (Whitbourne, 1985). A less efficient digestion of macronutrients with age may result more from hormonal/enzymatic changes than from changes in the functionality of the gastrointestinal system (Whitbourne, 1985). For example, passive carbohydrate absorption is not impaired by aging, but absorption of carbohydrates by active transport may be decreased with age (Beaumont, Cobden, Sheldon, Laker, & James, 1987). The lack of any significant changes in functional capacity of the large intestine associated with aging implies that the incidence of constipation in elderly people is related to factors other than the physiological aging process.

The elderly may also have a lowered responsiveness to internal cues of hunger and thirst. Rolls (1989) reported that elderly men were less likely to feel thirsty after 54 hours of water deprivation, in spite of greater hemoconcentration, than younger subjects. The reasons for the thirst deficit in the elderly have not been established, although cerebral cortical dysfunction, diminished responsiveness of osmoreceptors and/or baroreceptors, and oropharyngeal factors have been proposed (Rolls, 1989). The elderly have an increased risk of dehydration due to the diminished responsiveness to thirst coupled with the decreased ability to concentrate urine (Steen, 1988). The primary cause of fluid and electrolyte imbalances in the elderly is dehydration (Rolls, 1989). There appear to be significant age-associated changes in the chemical senses; their impact on nutritional status remains to be determined (Murphy, 1989).

The net result of the changes discussed above is that the body is less able to cope with external stresses, whether the stress results from diet, diseases, medications, or other environmental factors. The extent to which these changes are inevitable is unknown. For example, cardiovascular function of subjects from the Baltimore Longitudinal Study of Aging who were free of coronary heart disease were evaluated (Shock et al., 1984). In these subjects, maximum cardiac output did not decrease significantly with age, whereas it decreases about 1% per year in the average population (Shock et al., 1984). The extent to which age changes can be ameliorated is also unknown. For example, with the decline in renal function, it would be logical to assume that a decrease in protein intake would be warranted. Prothro (1989, p. 148) stated that "in the absence of a disease-related decline in renal function, protein restriction neither delays nor enhances the decline in renal function. . . . On the other hand, both young and elderly who have progressive renal disease benefit early in the disease from protein restrictions."

NUTRIENT INTAKES IN THE ELDERLY

Most of the studies on nutrition that have been done with elderly people are cross-sectional rather than longitudinal. It is, therefore, difficult to determine whether differences noted in nutrient intake and/or nutritional status are a reflection of changes accompanying the aging process or of differences in life-styles, environment, or other factors between older and younger people.

The National Health and Nutrition Examination Surveys (NHANES) have given a cross-sectional view of age differences in many of the components of nutritional status among adults in the United States (National Center for Health Statistics [NCHS], 1983; NCHS, Drizid, 1986; National Center for Health Statistics, Fulwood et al. [NCHS, Fulwood], 1986; National Center for Health Statistics [NCHS], 1987). Figures 18.1, 18.2, and 18.3 present data from the NHANES II survey. In each figure, the values for individuals aged 25-34 years were set at 100%. Therefore, values above or below 100% represent differences associated with age. Height, weight, and triceps skinfold thickness of males differed little between males aged 25-34 and those aged 55-64 or 65-74 years, whereas weight and triceps skinfold thickness were greater in older females compared to younger females (Figure 18.1) (NCHS, 1987). Blood pressure and serum cholesterol levels were higher for older males and females compared to 25-34-year-olds (NCHS, Drizid, 1986; NCHS, Fulwood, 1986).

Energy intakes of both males and females were lower for those aged 55-64 and 65-74 compared to those aged 25-34 years (Figure 18.2). Consumption of

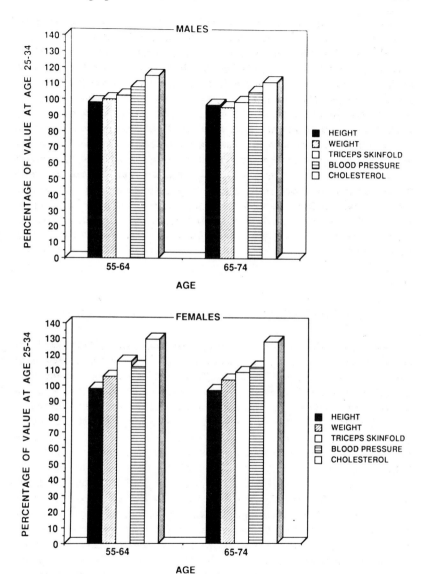

Figure 18.1. Anthropomorphic Values, Blood Pressure, and Serum Cholesterol Levels of Participants in the NHANES II Survey

Note: Values for participants aged 55-64 years or 65-74 years are expressed as a percentage of the value at age 25-34 years.

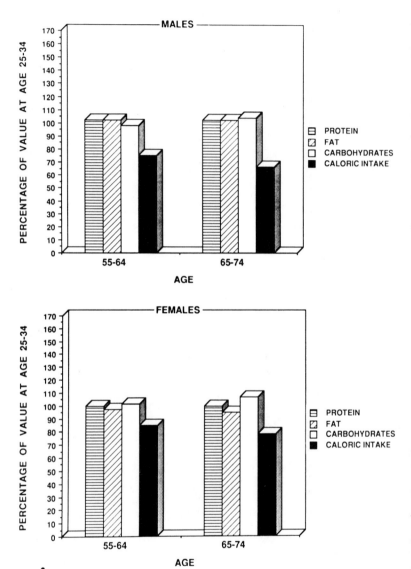

Figure 18.2. Calorie and Macronutrient Intakes of Participants in the NHANES II
Survey

Note: Values for participants aged 55-64 years or 65-74 years are expressed as a percentage of the value at
age 25-34 years. Macronutrient intakes are as grams per 1,000 kcal.

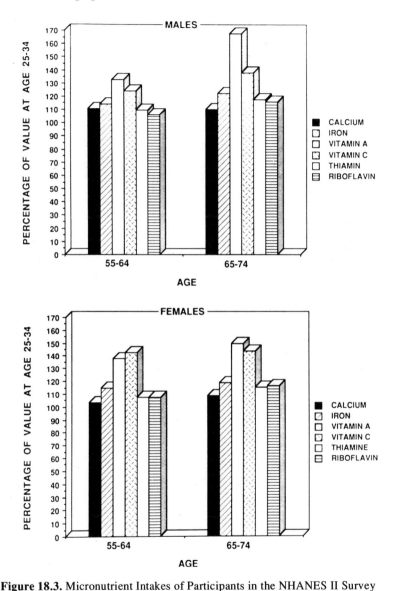

Figure 18.3. Micronutrient Intakes of Participants in the NHANES II Survey

Note: Values for participants aged 55-64 years or 65-74 years are expressed as a percentage of the value at age 25-34 years. Micronutrient intakes are as grams per 1,000 kcal.

protein, fat, and carbohydrates per 1,000 kcal was relatively constant for males, whereas proportion of carbohydrates consumed increased slightly in females (Figure 18.2) (NCHS, 1983). Other researchers have found that percentage of calories from carbohydrate, protein, and fat remained constant with age (Loewig, Westenbrink, Hulshoff, Kistemaker, & Hermus, 1989; McGandy et al., 1986), from protein increased (Wurtman, Liebermann, Tsay, Nader, & Chew, 1988), or from fat decreased (Elahi et al., 1983; Garry, Rhyne, Halioua, & Nicholson, 1989).

Based on results of longitudinal studies, Garry et al. (1989) and Elahi et al. (1983) reported that decreased intakes of fat were largely responsible for the age-associated decrease in energy intake. Elahi et al. (1983) reported decreases in intakes of saturated fatty acids, polyunsaturated fatty acids, and cholesterol, with no change in the polyunsaturated:saturated fat ratio of the diet.

Intakes of most micronutrients are adequate and are comparable between older and younger people which, coupled with the decrease in energy intake, suggests that nutrient density of the diet increases with age. Males and females aged 55-64 or 65-74 years consumed more calcium, iron, vitamin A, vitamin C, thiamin, and riboflavin per 1,000 kcal than their 25-34 year old counterparts (Figure 18.3) (NCHS, 1983). Garry et al. (1989) also found that nutrient intakes were generally adequate in their elderly subjects; the only nutrients that were consumed in potentially inadequate amounts were calcium and vitamin D by the females. McGandy et al. (1986) reported that, longitudinally, intakes of vitamin D, B vitamins, iron, and zinc decreased; of vitamin A increased; and of calcium and vitamin C did not change for males. There were no clear age-related trends in the nutrient intakes of females.

Nutrient intakes, however, are not the sole determinant of nutritional status. The impact of biochemical values, clinical variables, anthropometric values, socioeconomic factors, and past experiences on nutritional status is recognized for all age groups. The heterogeneity of life experiences in the elderly population may precipitate a wide range of values being considered "normal" and poses a particular challenge for nutritional management of people in this age group. Kergoat, Leclerc, PetitClerc, and Imbach (1987) emphasized the necessity of using several biochemical markers for detection of malnutrition in the elderly, since neither the classic serum indices nor retinol-binding protein adequately predicted patients at nutritional risk. This may be related to the changes in protein synthesis and turnover discussed earlier.

NUTRITIONAL STATUS OF THE ELDERLY

Vitamin and mineral status of the elderly is generally good. Fewer than 5% of older people have impaired iron status (Fanelli & Woteki, 1989; Manore,

Vaughan, & Carroll, 1989) or impaired zinc status (Fanelli & Woteki, 1989; Swanson, Mansourian, Dirren, & Rapin, 1988). The Low serum vitamin C was found in approximately 20% of older men and 5% of older women who had incomes below the poverty level (Fanelli & Woteki, 1989). In spite of reports of low folate intakes by more than 50% of the elderly, fewer than 10% have low serum folate levels (Suter & Russell, 1987). Similarly, the nutritional status for vitamin B_{12} (Suter & Russell, 1987) and vitamin A (Garry, Hunt, Bandrofchak, VanderJagt, & Goodwin, 1987) appears to be adequate. Inadequate vitamin D status is more prevalent in the elderly, however, and appears to be related to sunshine exposure (Lips et al., 1987). This has implications for institutionalized elderly and those who are at risk of hip fracture. Data on nutritional status for most other nutrients are inconclusive, either because of inadequate dietary intake data, inadequate excretion data, or both.

Factors Affecting Nutritional Status

Clinical measures, such as state of dentition, may also affect nutritional status. Papas et al. (1989) reported decreases of about 20% in nutrient intake for elderly subjects who had one or two full dentures. Periodontal disease and root caries were common among the participants in that study. Kunkel, Chestnut, Hoover, and Roughead (1987) found no relationship between state of dentition or gingival score and dietary adequacy in elderly subjects and suggested that the subjects had adapted to their state of compromised oral health.

Socioeconomic status is also a factor in nutritional status of the elderly. Poor people who participated in NHANES II had lower median dietary intakes of vitamin C, iron, and cholesterol; higher prevalences of obesity, low serum vitamin C, impaired iron status, and hypertension; and a lower incidence of hypercholesterolemia (Fanelli & Woteki, 1989). Food stamp use in the elderly has not been consistently associated with differences in energy status, as indicated by weight, skinfold, and energy intake (Lopez & Habicht, 1987).

Socialization associated with food also seems to impact nutrient intake. Davis, Randall, Forthofer, Lee, and Margen (1985) reported that older men who lived alone or who lived with someone other than a spouse had lower nutrient intakes than men who lived with their spouses. This does not seem to be true for older women, for whom living alone did not seem to impact eating behavior as much as it did for men. Nutrient intake of participants in congregate dining programs in the United States (Holahan & Kunkel, 1986; LeClerc & Thornbury, 1983) and in similar programs in the United Kingdom (Potts, 1987) were adequate, whereas energy and protein intakes of 35% of a group of participants in a "meals on wheels" program were inadequate (Lipschitz, Mitchell, Steele, & Milton, 1984). This difference may reflect differences in state of health, because most recipients of home-delivered meals are unable to attend a congregate meals site.

COMPARISON OF NONINSTITUTIONALIZED AND INSTITUTIONALIZED ELDERLY

There may be differences in nutritional status between noninstitutionalized elderly and institutionalized elderly. Sahyoun et al. (1988) found the two groups had comparable nutrient intakes and concluded that there was no evidence that institutionalization itself leads to impairment in nutritional status. Smith, Wickiser, Korth, Grandjean, and Schaefer (1984) reported vitamin A, vitamin C, and riboflavin status of their institutionalized population was adequate although about 5% had impaired iron status (which is comparable to data from NHANES II). About 28% of their subjects were "at risk" for a B_6 deficiency. They concluded that neither age alone nor level of nursing care required were the primary factor in producing the nutritional deficiencies that have been reported in the elderly. However, incidence of protein-energy malnutrition in institutionalized elderly has been reported to range from about 25% (Kergoat et al. 1987) to about 50% (Pinchcofsky-Devin & Kaminski, 1987). Pinchcofsky-Devin and Kaminski reported that 52% of their institutionalized subjects had some form of protein-energy malnutrition, with 24% having hypoalbuminemia, 19% marasmic-kwashiorkor, and 9% maramus. In addition, 28% of the patients had deficient immune responses and 76% were anemic.

Effects of Supplements/Nutritional Support in the Elderly

The elderly may also be more resistant to attempts to replete nutritional status than younger people. Among elderly participants in a "meals on wheels" program, those who were at risk of protein-energy malnutrition were provided with a polymeric dietary supplement 3 times a day for 16 weeks (Lipschitz et al., 1984). Provision of the supplements significantly increased energy and protein intakes and resulted in significant elevations in serum albumin, total iron binding capacity, folate, and vitamin B_{12} levels and in leukocyte ascorbate levels. However, there were no improvements in hemoglobin levels, in immunologic function tests, or in trace mineral status, suggesting that critical deficiencies were not corrected even by this rather aggressive treatment or that the abnormalities were age-related rather than nutritionally related.

FOOD PREFERENCES IN THE ELDERLY

Food preferences and eating patterns of elderly people may also be different from those of younger people. In 1985, elderly subjects reported liking foods that were softer and lower in protein and fat than they had when surveyed 10 years earlier. The foods liked the most by older persons in 1985 included potatoes, chicken, beef, pie, green beans, fish, fruit, meat, lettuce salad, and ice cream (Holt, Nordstrom, & Kohrs, 1988). Based on an analysis of the data from the Nationwide Food Conservation Survey of 1977-78, the foods eaten most frequently by elderly people in the United States were whole milk, white bread, margarine, sugar, and coffee (Fanelli & Stevenhagen, 1985). Frequent consumption of these foods is not inherently associated with diets of low nutrient density, because other, more nutrient dense foods are rarely eaten more than once a day or even daily. Akin, Guilkey, Popkin, and Fanelli (1986) categorized the eating patterns of elderly persons as light eaters, heavy eaters, or consumers of large amounts of alcoholic beverages, salty snack foods, animal fat products, legumes, or sweets and desserts. Wurtman et al. (1988) found that older people consume significantly fewer snacks than younger people, with only 15% of the calories of older people coming from snacks, whereas younger people consumed 28% of their calories as snacks. In both age groups, snacks were usually high carbohydrate foods. Even though nutritional status and nutrient intakes of the elderly are generally adequate, use of vitamin/mineral supplements is common. Garry, Goodwin, Hunt, Hooper, and Leonard (1982) found about 60% of their subjects took at least one kind of supplement, with vitamins C and A the most popular. From a large study in Boston, potential overloads from supplements of vitamin A were noted (Hartz et al., 1988; Krasinski et al., 1989). There are no conclusive data to explain the prevalence of supplement use by the elderly, particularly in those elderly who have adequate nutrient intakes without use of the supplements.

FOOD AND DRUG INTERACTIONS IN THE ELDERLY

Elderly people are the chief users of medications in the United States. Many of the drugs used by the elderly have the potential to interact with foods and result in a secondary nutrient deficiency (Roe, 1976). When multiple medications are used and their effects superimposed on those of marginal nutritional status and/or chronic disease, the impacts are much greater than for a well-nourished person taking only one medication. In one study, 32% of the elderly people were taking five or more medications concurrently (Kurfees & Dotson, 1987). Approximately 30% of the drugs taken by this population group had the potential of interacting with food, with the most common potential interaction being decreased absorption. According to the authors, potential drug-food interactions are frequently ignored by health care professionals in favor of increasing compliance with a treatment regimen. An example of medications that may impact nutritional status are those frequently used for treatment of arthritis. Nonsteroidal anti-inflammatory drugs (salicylates and prostaglandin inhibitors) inhibit platelet aggregation, thereby prolonging bleeding times, irritate the gastrointestinal mucosa leading to secondary iron deficiency anemia, and cause fluid retention and hyperkalemia. Corticosteroids used for treatment of arthritis are catabolic, diabetogenic, ulcerogenic, and lead to negative calcium balances that may result in such complications as hypokalemia, hyperglycemia, anemia, and osteoporosis. Risks are particularly acute for the elderly who frequently have underlying medical conditions, such as congestive heart failure, diabetes, or renal disease, which accentuate the negative effects of these medications (Roe, 1987). For more information on commonly prescribed medications for the elderly and their potential interactions with foods, the reader is referred to Roe (1976) or Kurfees and Dotson (1987).

IMPLICATIONS FOR
CLINICAL NURSE SPECIALISTS

The nurse caregiver needs to be aware that the majority of elders have adequate nutritional intakes, however those in institutions and homebound are at higher risk for suffering from malnutrition and dehydration. The importance of socialization and nutrition in the elderly also needs to be included in the plan of nursing care. As a researcher, the nurse can investigate the relation between life-style and nutritional status in studies that compare elders over an extended period of time. As an advocate of the elderly, the gerontological nurse should promote legislation that provides adequate nutrition to those whose economic situation is compromised. In the educational role, the nurse needs to inform the elderly and their caregivers about the potential for drug-food interactions and the importance of a balanced diet that does not usually require additional supplements. Because constipation is a frequent concern among the elderly, the gerontological nurse needs to instruct the client concerning the need for exercise and adequate fluids, as well as the fact that most research indicates constipation is not related to changes associated with the aging process, but due in large part to life-style.

SUMMARY

The authors of many studies have concluded that age per se is not an important determinant of energy and nutrient intakes among apparently healthy elderly people, but that most of the changes in intakes noted with age are related to life-styles. Elderly people in the United States who are ambulatory are generally well-nourished; incidence of malnutrition is higher among elderly people who are nonambulatory or who are institutionalized. Thus the biochemical and physiological changes associated with aging do not seem to impact significantly on the nutritional status of the elderly. Superimposing disease states and treatments on "normal" age changes frequently results in elderly people who have compromised nutritional status.

REFERENCES

Akin, J. S., Guilkey, D. K., Popkin, B. M., & Fanelli, M. T. (1986). Cluster analysis of food consumption patterns. *Journal of the American Dietetic Association, 86,* 616-624.

Avoili, L. (Ed.). (1983). *The Osteoporotic Syndrome: Detection, Prevention, and Treatment.* New York: Grune & Stratton.

Beaumont, D. M., Cobden, I., Sheldon, W. L., Laker, M. F., & James, O. F. W. (1987). Passive and active carbohydrate absorption by the aging gut. *Age and Aging, 16,* 294-300.

Berman, R., Haxby, J. V., & Pomerantz, R. S. (1988). Physiology of aging. Part 1: Normal changes. *Patient Care, 22,* 20-36.

Davis, M. A., Randall, E., Forthofer, R. N., Lee, E. S., & Margen, S. (1985). Living arrangements and dietary patterns of older adults in the United States. *Journal of Gerontology, 40,* 434-442.

Elahi, V. K., Elahi, D., Andres, R., Tobin, J. D., Butler, M. G., & Norris, A. H. (1983). A longitudinal study of nutritional intake in men. *Journal of Gerontology, 38,* 162-180.

Euans, D. W. (1988). Renal function in the elderly. *American Family Practice, 38,* 147-150.

Fanelli, M. T. & Stevenhagen, K. J. (1985). Characterizing consumption patterns by food frequency methods: Core foods and variety of foods in diets of older Americans. *Journal of the American Dietetic Association, 85,* 1570-1576.

Fanelli, M. T. & Woteki, C. E. (1989). Nutrient intakes and health status of older Americans: Data from the NHANES II. In C. Murphy, W. S. Cain, & D. M. Hegsted (Eds.), *Nutrition and the chemical senses in aging: Recent advances and current research needs. Annals of New York Academy of Sciences,* 561, 94-103.

Forbes, G. B. (1987). *Human body composition: Growth, aging, nutrition, and composition.* New York: Springer.

Fukagawa, N. K., Minaker, K. L., Rowe, J. W., Matthews, D. E., Bier, D. M., & Young, V. R. (1988). Glucose and amino acid metabolism in aging man: Differential effects of insulin. *Metabolism, 37,* 371-377.

Garry, P. J., Goodwin, J. S., Hunt, W. C., Hooper, E. M., & Leonard, A. G. (1982). Nutritional status in a healthy elderly population: Dietary and supplemental intakes. *American Journal of Clinical Nutrition, 36,* 319-331.

Garry, P. J., Hunt, W. C., Bandrofchak, J. L., VanderJagt, D., & Goodwin, J. S. (1987). Vitamin A intake and plasma retinol levels in healthy elderly men and women. *American Journal of Clinical Nutrition, 46,* 989-994.

Garry, P. J., Rhyne, R. L., Halioua, L., & Nicholson, C. (1989). Changes in dietary patterns over a 6-year period in an elderly population. In C. Murphy, W. S. Cain, & D. M. Hegsted (Eds.), *Nutrition and the chemical senses in aging: Recent advances and current research needs. Annals of New York Academy of Sciences,* 561, 104-112.

Hartz, S. C., Otradovec, C. L., McGandy, R. B., Russell, R. M., Jacob, R. A., Sahyoun, N., Peters, H., Abrams, D., Scura, L. A., & Whinston-Perry, R. A. (1988). Nutrient supplement use by healthy elderly. *Journal of the American College of Nutrition, 7,* 119-128.

Holahan, K. B. & Kunkel, M. E. (1986). Contribution of the Title III meals program to nutrient intake of participants. *Journal of Nutrition for the Elderly, 6,* 45-54.

Holt, V., Nordstrom, J., & Kohrs, M. B. (1988). Changes in food preferences of the elderly over a ten year period. *Journal of Nutrition for the Elderly, 7,* 23-33.

Jackson, R. A., Hawa, M. I., Roshania, R. D., Sim, B. M., DiSilvio, L., & Jaspan, J. B. (1988). Influence of aging on hepatic and peripheral glucose metabolism in humans. *Diabetes, 37,* 119-129.

Kenney, R. A. (1982). *Physiology of aging: A synopsis.* Chicago: Year Book Medical Publishers.

Kergoat, M. J., Leclerc, B. S., PetitClerc, C., & Imbach, A. (1987). Discriminant biochemical markers for evaluating the nutritional status of elderly patients in long-term care. *American Journal of Clinical Nutrition, 46,* 849-861.

Krasinski, S. D., Russel, R. M., Otradovec, C. L., Sadowski, J. A., Hartz, S. C., Jacob, R. A., & McGandy, R. B. (1989). Relationship of vitamin A and vitamin E intake to fasting plasma retinol, retinol-binding protein, retinyl esters, carotene, alphatocopherol, and cholesterol among elderly people and young adults: increased plasma retinyl esters among vitamin A-supplement users. *American Journal of Clinical Nutrition, 49,* 112-120.

Kunkel, M. E., Chestnut, C. K., Hoover, J. L., & Roughead, Z. K. (1987). Nutritional and dental status of Title III meal recipients. *Journal of Nutrition for the Elderly, 6,* 17-32.

Kurfees, J. F. & Dotson, R. L. (1987). Drug interactions in the elderly. *Journal of Family Practice, 25,* 477-488.

LeClerc, H. L., & Thornbury, M. E. (1983). Dietary intakes of Title III meal program recipients and nonrecipients. *Journal of the American Dietetic Association, 83,* 573-577.

Lips, P., van Ginkel, F. C., Jongen, M. J., Rubertus, F., van der Vijgh, W. J., & Netelenbos, J. C. (1987). Determinants of vitamin D status in patients with hip fracture and in elderly control subjects. *American Journal of Clinical Nutrition, 46,* 1005-1010.

Lipschitz, D. A., Mitchell, C. O., Steele, R. W., & Milton, K. Y. (1984). Nutritional evaluation and supplementation of elderly subjects participating in a "Meals on Wheels" program. *Journal of Parenteral and Enteral Nutrition, 9,* 343-347.

Loewig, M. R., Westenbrink, S., Hulshoff, K. F., Kistemaker, C., & Hermus, R. J. (1989). Nutrition and aging: Dietary intake of "apparently healthy" elderly (Dutch Nutrition Surveillance System). *Journal of the American College of Nutrition, 8,* 347-356.

Lonergan, E. T. (1988). Aging and the kidney: Adjusting treatment to physiologic change. *Geriatrics, 43*(3), 27-33.

Lopez, L. M., & Habicht, J. P. (1987). Food stamps and the energy status of the U.S. elderly poor. *Journal of the American Dietetic Association, 87,* 1020-1024.

Manore, M. M., Vaughan, L. A., & Carroll, S. S. (1989). Iron status in free-living, low income very elderly. *Nutrition Reports International, 39,* 1-10.

McGandy, R. B., Russel, R. M., Hartz, S. C., Jacob, R. A., Tannenbaum, S., Peters, H., Sahyoun, N., & Otradovec, C. L. (1986). Nutritional status survey of healthy noninstitutionalized elderly: Energy and nutrient intakes from three-day diet records and nutrient supplements. *Nutrition Research, 6,* 785-798.

Murphy, C. (1989). Aging and chemosensory perception of and preference for nutritionally significant stimuli. In C. Murphy, W. S. Cain, and D. M. Hegsted (Eds.), *Nutrition and* the chemical senses in aging: Recent advances and current research needs. *Annals of New York Academy of Sciences, 561,* 251-266.

Murphy, C., Cain, W. S., & Hegsted, D. M. (Eds.) (1989). *Nutrition and the Chemical Senses in Aging: Recent Advances and Current Research Needs.* Annals of New York Academy of Sciences, Vol. 561.

National Center for Health Statistics, Carroll, M. D., Abraham, S., & Dresser, C. M. (1983). Dietary intake source data: United States, 1976-80. *Vital and Health Statistics,* Series 11, No. 231.

National Center for Health Statistics, Drizid, T., Dannenberg, A. L., & Engel, A. (1986). Blood pressure levels in persons 18-74 years of age in 1976-80, and trends in blood pressure from 1960-80 in the United States. *Vital and Health Statistics,* Series 11, No. 234.

National Center for Health Statistics, Fulwood, R., Kalsbeek, W., Rifkind, B., et al. (1986). Total serum cholesterol levels of adults 20-74 years of age: United States. *Vital and Health Statistics,* Series 11, No. 236.

National Center for Health Statistics, Najjar, M. F., & Rowland, M. (1987). Anthropometric reference data and prevalence of overweight, United States, 1976-80. *Vital and Health Statistics,* Series 11, No. 238.

Nordin, B. E. C. (1983). Osteoporosis with particular reference to the menopause. In L. V. Avoili (Ed.), *The osteoporotic syndrome: Detection, prevention, and treatment* (pp. 13-44). New York: Grune & Stratton.

Papas, A. S., Palmer, C. A., Rounds, M. C., Herman, J., McGandy, R. B., Hartz, S. C., Russell, R. M., & DePaola, P. (1989). Longitudinal relationships between nutrition and oral health. In C. Murphy, W. S. Cain and D. M. Hegsted (Eds.), *Nutrition and the chemical senses in aging: Recent advances and current research needs. Annals of New York Academy of Sciences, 561,* 125-142.

Pinchcofsky-Devin, G. D., & Kaminski, M. V., Jr. (1987). Incidence of protein-calorie malnutrition in the nursing home population. *Journal of the American College of Nutrition, 6,* 109-112.

Potts, M. C. (1987). An evaluation of the nutrient intake of a group of elderly people attending a luncheon club. *Human Nutrition, 41A,* 352-356.

Prothro, J. (1989). Protein and amino acid requirements of the elderly. In C. Murphy, W. S. Cain, and D. M. Hegsted (Eds.), *Nutrition and the chemical senses in aging: Recent advances and current research needs. Annals of New York Academy of Sciences, 561,* 143-156.

Roe, D. A. (1976). *Drug induced nutritional deficiencies* (2nd ed.). AVI Publishing Company, CT.

Roe, D. A. (1987). Process guides on drug and nutrient interactions in arthritics. *Drug-Nutrient Interactions, 5,* 135-142.

Rolls, B. J. (1989). Regulation of food and fluid intake in the elderly. In C. Murphy, W. S. Cain, and D. M. Hegsted (Eds.), *Nutrition and the chemical senses in aging: Recent advances and current research needs. Annals of New York Academy of Sciences, 561,* 217-225.

Rosenthal, J. (1987). Aging and the cardiovascular system. *Gerontology, 33,* suppl. 1, 3-8.

Sahyoun, N. R., Otradovec, C. L., Hartz, S. C., Jacob, R. A., Peters, H., Russell, R. M., & McGandy, R. B. (1988). Dietary intakes and biochemical indicators of nutritional status in an elderly, institutionalized population. *American Journal of Clinical Nutrition, 47,* 524-533.

Shock, N. W., Greulich, R. C., Andres, R., Arenberg, D., Costa, P. T., Jr., Lakatta, E. G., & Tobin, J. D. (1984). *Normal human aging: The Baltimore longitudinal study of aging* (NIH Publication No. 84-2450). Bethesda, MD: National Institutes of Health.

Smith, J. L., Wickiser, A. A., Korth, L. L., Grandjean, A. C., & Schaefer, A. E. (1984). Nutritional status of an institutionalized aged population. *Journal of the American College of Nutrition, 3,* 13-25.

Steen, B. (1988). Body composition and aging. *Nutrition Reviews, 46,* 45-51.

Suter, P. M., & Russell, R. M. (1987). Vitamin requirements of the elderly. *American Journal of Clinical Nutrition, 45,* 501-512.

Swanson, C. A., Mansourian, R., Dirren, H., & Rapin, C. H. (1988). Zinc status of healthy elderly adults: Response to supplementation. *American Journal of Clinical Nutrition, 48,* 343-349.

Whitbourne, S. K. (1985). *The aging body: Physiological changes and psychological consequences.* New York: Springer.

Wurtman, J. J., Liebermann, H., Tsay, R., Nader, T., & Chew, B. (1988). Calorie and nutrient intakes of elderly and young subjects measured under identical conditions. *Journal of Gerontology: Biological Sciences, 43,* B174-180.

19

Alterations in Elimination:
Urinary Incontinence

MARY H. PALMER
KATHLEEN A. McCORMICK

Objectives: At the completion of this chapter, the reader will be able to:

(1) Analyze current information about the prevalence of urinary incontinence and its impact on affected older adults and their caregivers.
(2) Understand types of urinary incontinence as defined by the International Continence Society, investigating the underlying causes of each type.
(3) Identify recent research regarding the assessment and treatment of urinary incontinence in older adults.
(4) Implement nursing strategies to care for older adults with urinary incontinence in various practice settings.

INTRODUCTION

Urinary incontinence is an important geriatric condition because it affects many adults over the age of 65 years and can have a significant impact on the quality of life. It has been estimated that 10 million adult Americans are incontinent of urine (National Institutes of Health Consensus Development

AUTHORS' NOTE: This article was written by governmental employees as part of official duties; therefore the material is in the public domain and may be reproduced or copied without permission.

Conference [NIH], 1990). Nursing home residents are reported to have a higher prevalence of urinary incontinence than community-dwelling elderly. It has been estimated that 50% of nursing home residents are incontinent of urine (Kane, Ouslander, & Abrass, 1989) as compared to 9% of the community-dwelling elderly who report difficulty controlling bladder elimination (Harris, 1986). The natural history and development of urinary incontinence in older adults is not completely understood; however, it has been reported to be curable or treatable in the majority of cases (NIH, 1990). Urinary incontinence can have important physical, psychological, and social consequences for affected older adults. Loss of urine control is often a reason for displacement from one's home (Schreter, 1979) and may precipitate placement in a nursing home (Norton, 1986). Incontinent older adults in nursing homes report feelings of shame and guilt (Yu, 1987). Incontinence may lead to social isolation; the older adults, fearful of accidents, will remain at home rather than venture out and risk exposure of this condition (Mitteness, 1987a). The costs to the health care system for incontinent older adults is staggering. Hu (1986) estimated the direct costs of care to nursing homes (labor, goods, and services) to be $1.8 billion annually. Yu and Kaltreider (1987) stated that the cost to nursing homes for the care of incontinent older adults was 2.5 times greater than the cost of care for continent older adults. The financial costs of incontinence to community-dwelling older adults have not been quantified; however, the costs for disposable bladder and hygiene products, cleaning of furniture and carpets, and for laundry may be considerable (Herzog & Fultz, 1988). As a highly prevalent, potentially curable, and financially costly condition, urinary incontinence is a major gerontological/geriatrics health care issue.

Definitions of Urinary Incontinence

Until 1979 there had been no standardized definition of urinary incontinence. Definitions prior to that time focused on the unsuitability of the timing and places of voiding. The International Continence Society provided the following definition for use by researchers and clinicians to standardize terminology; urinary incontinence is, "a condition in which involuntary loss of urine is a social or hygienic problem and is objectively demonstrable" (Bates et al., 1979, p. 551). Several types of urinary incontinence were also defined: *stress incontinence* is "involuntary loss of urine when the intravesical pressure (pressure within bladder) exceeds the maximum urethral pressure but in the absence of detrusor (smooth muscle of bladder) activity," *urge incontinence* is "involuntary loss of urine associated with a strong desire to void", *reflex incontinence* is "involuntary loss of urine caused by abnormal reflex activity in the spinal cord in the absence of sensation usually associated with the desire to micturate", *overflow incontinence* is "involuntary loss of urine when intravesical pressure exceeds the maximum urethral pressure associated with bladder distention but in the absence of detrusor activity" (Bates et al., p. 551). Another type of incontinence, functional incontinence, is often reported in the literature, especially when discussing nursing home residents. *Functional incontinence* is defined as "urinary leakage associated with inability (because of impairment of cognitive or physical functioning), psychological unwillingness, or environmental barriers to toilets" (Ouslander, 1989, p. 252). The following section will examine the prevalence of urinary incontinence in older adults in the acute care, long-term care, and community setting.

PREVALENCE OF URINARY INCONTINENCE

Acute Care Setting

There are few reports of the prevalence of urinary incontinence in the acute care setting. Lack of documentation in the medical record and incontinence that is not severe enough to come to the attention of the nursing staff for changing of linens and clothing may result in underreporting of the magnitude of problem in this setting (Palmer, 1988). Also, urinary incontinence may be transient in nature, that is, urinary incontinence appears with the acute medical condition that caused the hospitalization and resolves as the patient's medical condition improves.

Sullivan and Lindsay (1984) reported prevalence of urinary incontinence in all patients aged 65 years and older ($N = 315$) admitted during a 6-week period to be 19%. Incontinence had been defined as "any inappropriate loss of urine regardless of amount or frequency or . . . requir[ing] an indwellinq foley catheter" (p. 646). Sier, Ouslander, and Orzeck (1987) reported an overall prevalence of 35% in patients aged 65 years and older ($N = 363$) admitted to the medical-surgical units during a 14-week period. Patients who had an indwelling catheter inserted during the hospital stay were identified and those who had one or more episodes of incontinence were considered incontinent of urine. Incontinence was more common in individuals over the age of 75 years and in women.

Long-Term Care Setting

As previously described, the prevalence of urinary incontinence in the long-term care setting has been estimated to be 50% (Kane et al., 1989). Data from the National Nursing Home Survey conducted in 1985 revealed the prevalence of urinary incontinence in residents aged 55 years and older was 10.7% and the prevalence of fecal and urinary incontinence was 32.5% (Hing

& Senscenski, 1986). As in the acute care setting, lack of documentation and careful assessment of urinary incontinence can lead to an underreporting of the magnitude of the problem. The primary caregiver in the long-term care setting is the nursing assistant who has a limited educational background to assess urinary incontinence (Ouslander, 1990). Also, the lack of documentation may be related to the type of documentation forms used; forms with cue words about continence status have been shown to have higher rates of documentation than open formatted forms (Palmer, McCormick, & Langford, 1989). Little is known about the incidence (new cases) of urinary incontinence in nursing homes, due to the lack of longitudinal data available to researchers.

Community Setting

The prevalence of urinary incontinence in the general population of older adults living in the community was reported to be approximately 9% (Harris, 1986). Reports of prevalence vary, however. Mitteness (1987a) reported that 31% of the 140 elderly subjects who lived in subsidized housing were incontinent of urine at least once a week. Mitteness also noted that older adults do not use the same terminology and definitions as health care professionals to describe urinary elimination and incontinence. Therefore, unless agreed upon definitions are used and there is mutual understanding between the health care provider and older adult, the prevalence of self-reported or self-described urinary incontinence may not reflect actual loss of bladder control. Many older adults have a belief that incontinence is an inevitable part of the aging process and do not seek medical help (Mitteness, 1987b). Also, the prevalence of urinary incontinence may be higher in specific groups of community-dwelling elderly. Noelker (1987) reported that 53% of impaired older adults ($N = 299$) with a family caregiver were incontinent of urine. The National Institutes of Health Consensus Development Conference (1990) reported that 15% to 30% of community-dwelling older adults have urinary incontinence. Regardless of the practice setting, urinary incontinence is a prevalent geriatric condition that is often not reported by the affected older adults or not detected by health care providers.

Physiology of Micturition

The process of socially acceptable elimination, continence, involves a complex physiologic mechanism. The innervation of micturition is not fully understood by researchers. The reader is referred, however, to a discussion of the physiology of micturition in standard physiology textbooks and in Wein (1986) and Williams & Pannill (1982). Three intact body structures—lower urinary tract, spinal cord, and frontal lobe of the cerebral cortex—are necessary to maintain continence.

The lower urinary tract consists of the bladder, urethra, urethral sphincter, and the system of innervation. The bladder serves as a reservoir of urine until emptying occurs. As the smooth muscle of the bladder, the detrusor, passively stretches and fills with urine, impulses are sent from receptors in the bladder wall along afferent nerve pathways to the spinal cord. The reflex center for bladder function is located at sacral level 2 to 4. This reflex center also relays signals to the bladder along efferent nerve pathways of the autonomic nervous system (hypogastric plexus) to continue stretching or to begin emptying urine. There is little change in intravesical pressure in the initial stages of filling. If the tension of the wall of the bladder and the radius of the bladder increases equally, the pressure remains constant (Claridge, 1965). When approximately 250 to 350 cc of urine accumulates in the bladder, the spinal reflex center signals the cortical center of control in the frontal lobe. It is at this point that the individual becomes aware of the need to void. The cortical center function is primarily one of inhibition of urination. There is also evidence that endogenous opoid peptides have an inhibitory influence on bladder contraction (Wein, 1986).

The urethra, a narrow tube leading from the base of the bladder, the bladder neck, to the outside of the body, serves as a pathway for urine to leave the body. The periurethral striated muscle, also called the urethral sphincter, remains closed during bladder filling and prevents urine from constantly leaking into the urethra from the bladder until voiding occurs. The pressure gradients within the bladder and urethra play an important role in continence. Continence is maintained when the pressure within the bladder, intravesical pressure, remains lower than the pressure in the urethra, intraurethral pressure (Williams & Pannill, 1982). The anatomic location of the bladder neck and the proximal urethra in the abdominal cavity is crucial to the maintenance of continence. It allows equal transmission of increased intra-abdominal pressure to the bladder neck and urethra (Wein, 1986). Alterations in the location of the bladder neck and proximal urethra, so that compensation of intra-abdominal pressure increases does not occur, can result in stress incontinence. Poor anatomical support permits downward rotation of the bladder neck and urethra; childbirth, pelvic surgery, and menopause are some factors that can predispose the pelvic floor to weakness (Staskin, Ouslander, & Raz, 1985).

Emptying of the bladder is delayed until acceptable toilet facilities are located. To facilitate the flow of urine out of the body, there is a coordinated contraction of the bladder after a marked increase in intravesical pressure and adaptive changes in the bladder neck and proximal urethra occurs. It is difficult, however, to delay voiding after 500 cc of urine is stored in the bladder (Ebersole & Hess, 1985).

Continence, then, involves effective functioning of the urinary tract as well as adequate cognitive functioning to interpret somatic information and an environment that is appropriate to eliminate urine (Kane et al., 1989). Urinary incontinence occurs either from a failure in the urine retention mechanism or from a lack of conscious control in the emptying process (Claridge, 1965).

There are some changes with age that may make an older adult vulnerable to develop alterations in urinary elimination. It should be stressed, however, that age alone does not cause urinary incontinence. In females, the decrease in estrogen production changes the vascular supply to the vagina and distal urethra that can lead to complaints of vaginitis and incontinence. Males experience enlargement of the prostate gland that can adversely affect the strength of urine flow, efficient emptying of the bladder, and if severe enough, it can cause outlet obstruction resulting in overflow incontinence.

Changes to the bladder, such as deposits of connective tissue into smooth muscle, affect the ability to store urine and the ability to empty efficiently (Staskin, 1986). Pathologic changes, such as irritation of the bladder from chronic infection, presence of foreign bodies, and growths can cause urinary symptoms such as frequency, urgency, and urge incontinence. Diseases or conditions that affect the peripheral and central nervous system, especially areas responsible for the neural control of bladder function, can influence the effectiveness and efficiency of micturition. Dementia, cerebral vascular accidents, Parkinson's disease, and peripheral neuropathy from diabetes mellitus are prevalent pathological conditions in older adults. Their presence has been associated with urinary incontinence (Leach & Yip, 1986; Resnick & Yalla, 1985). Decreased mobility and impaired manual dexterity, even in the presence of a normally functioning urinary tract, have also been associated with functional incontinence (Ouslander, 1989).

ANALYSIS OF RESEARCH

The assessment and treatment of urinary incontinence depend on the individual's location within the health care setting. This is due to the differing secondary physical characteristics of recipients of health care in the hospital, in the nursing home, and in the community. For example, the incontinent adult in the hospital may have normal bladder function and transient incontinence, the residents of nursing homes often have cognitive impairment and immobility in addition to frail physical health, and most community-dwelling incontinent adults are cognitively intact and mobile. Therefore, the assessment and treatment of incontinence will be described within three framework settings: (1) ambulatory/community health nursing and Geriatric Day Care Facilities, (2) long-term care facilities, and (3) hospital based practice.

Physical Examination

A health assessment is crucial to characterize and understand the reasons for incontinence. Adults in the community need a physical examination of the perineal area, abdomen, and rectum. Examination of the urine to detect urinary tract infections is also appropriate. A urinalysis will also describe the health of the bladder and kidneys. Blood serum levels of glucose, urea nitrogen, and creatinine should also be assessed. An assessment in a clinic or in the home includes filling the bladder with sterile water, and trying to provoke leakage with a cough, a sneeze, or straining (Ouslander, 1986). The determination of post-void residual urine will detect overflow incontinence in individuals with large residual volumes (greater than 100 cc). A physical examination will reveal the presence of fecal impaction, benign prostatic hypertrophy, complications of medications, atrophic vaginitis, state of hydration, and other conditions that may improve continence when treated. A complete description of the physical examination of an adult in the outpatient setting was published by Wyman (1988).

History

A detailed description of precipitating factors that cause incontinence needs to be identified by interviewing the incontinent adult. For example, the usual antecedents of urge incontinence are the sounds of running water, cold weather, the sight of a toilet, or thought of going to the toilet. A frequent report is the occurrence of accidents as one returns home and unlocks the door to the house. This syndrome is termed "key in the door syndrome" (Burgio & Engel, 1987). It also occurs in people waiting in long lines for public toilet facilities.

Adults with stress incontinence often describe physical activities that precipitate urine accidents. Common among these activities are coughing, sneezing, lifting heavy objects, bending, or stooping. They often report small urine loss when walking, or standing from a seated position. Women who participate in aerobic exercise and must wear a protective pad during "jumping jacks" often have stress incontinence. Adults with stress incontinence often describe small volume accidents. A complete nursing history for urinary incontinence is described by Wyman (1988).

Bladder Records

Bladder records or diaries have been proposed by nurses in incontinence assessment and treatment for many years (Clay, 1980). These records serve to provide a confirmation and supplement to the history by clearly identifying circumstances that provoke incontinent episodes, describing the amount of urine loss, documenting the frequency of accidents, and serving as the baseline against which to monitor progress and testing the effectiveness of treatment. A copy of a simple bladder record is in Figure 19.1. It is evident that a bladder record or diary must be completed by a cognitively intact, literate adult in the community, or a caregiver. These records, when kept for a 1- 2-week period, often document the patterns of variability of incontinent episodes that facilitates the diagnosis of the problem. The simple bladder record includes information about the time of voiding, the time of incontinent episodes, and the amount of urine volume lost, and the precipitating event.

Urodynamic Evaluation

A referral to a urologist, gynecologist, or nurse practitioner who is associated with either clinician is sometimes indicated when a complete urodynamic examination is required. Adults who may require this specialized testing include those with complex symptomatology, associated neurologic abnormalities, incomplete bladder emptying, previous incontinence surgeries, histories of failure on behavioral or drug therapies, and surgical intervention for the presence of identified polyps or tumors. A description of the urodynamic tests are also described by Wyman (1988).

Environmental Factors and Toileting Skills

The ability of adults to follow several steps in reaching and successfully completing a toileting episode is essential. Direct observation with a watch or stopwatch of one or more toileting episodes will reveal if the person can locate the toilet, calculate the time needed to reach the toilet, to undress, and to assume the appropriate position for voiding. Normal persons can reach a toilet at a distance of 50-100 feet and toilet appropriately within 30 seconds; the average time is 24.6 seconds (Burgio, Burgio, McCormick, & Engel, 1985). The environmental factors that limit continence, as well as suggested nursing modifications are described fully by Morishita (1988). The nursing modifications can be categorized as bed, chair, bathroom, toilet substitutes, and clothing. In addition, an environmental factor often overlooked is the individual's access to adequate fluid intake. The community-dwelling adult with a mobility impairment who is left in a chair at home while family members or caregivers leave, often does not have adequate fluid access throughout the day.

Psychological Impact

Of great importance to the community dwelling adult is the impact of the incontinence on social interactions and ability to leave home to attend church,

Name _____   Date _____

Instructions: (1) In the 1st column, mark the time interval every time you void
(2) In the 2nd or 3rd column, mark every time you accidently leaked urine
(3) Write "dry" if no accident occurred in the 2-hour interval

Time Interval	Urinated in Toilet	Leaking Accident	or	Large Accident	Reason for Accident
6-8 am					
8-10 am					
10-12 am					
12-2 pm					
2-4 pm					
4-6 pm					
6-8 pm					
8-10 pm					
Overnight					

Number of pads used today: _____

Comments: _____

_____

Exercises: _____

_____

_____

                                                    Total: _____

Figure 19.1. Bladder Record

Source: Burgio, K., & Engel, B. (1987). Urinary incontinence behavioral assessment and treatment. In L. Carstensen & B. Edelstein (Eds.), *Urinary Handbook of clinical gerontology* (p. 259). Elmsford, NY: Pergamon.

social functions, work, or to travel. The beginning of social isolation because of incontinence may precede functional limitations and ultimately lead to nursing home placement.

The psychological factors requiring assessment include cognitive ability, the level of depression, the presence of psychiatric disorders, the quality of life, and the motivation to become continent or to remain incontinent. Two tools used to measure cognitive ability and level of depression are the Folstein Mini-Mental State Exam (MMSE) and the Center for Epidemiological Studies-Depression Scale (CES-D) (Folstein, Folstein, & McHugh, 1975; Radloff, 1977).

Treatments: Outpatients

Table 19.1 is a summary of the treatments that change the continence outcomes in community dwelling, outpatients, and participants in Geriatric Day-Care Facilities. They are categorized into five major interventions: (1) Habit training, (2) Bladder retraining, (3) Contingency management, (4) Self-management, and (5) Biofeedback.

Habit training (temporal voiding) schedules are the most widely used method of treating incontinence. The adult avoids urinary accidents by using a fixed schedule to urinate instead of responding to bladder fullness. Treatment consists of establishing a voiding routine, usually between 2-4 hours, whether or not a sensation to void is present. Individualized schedules can be determined after a patient diary has been obtained to determine the usual bladder pattern, the frequency of continent voidings, and the frequency of accidents. The voiding interval is shortened if incontinent accidents are frequent and lengthened when the person is consistently drier during the day. Habit training is often combined with contingency management procedures that reward appropriate toileting and discourage inappropriate voiding or incontinence.

Bladder retraining, also called bladder training or bladder drill, is a procedure used to restore a normal pattern of voiding and normal bladder function. Instead of training the patient to use a fixed schedule, the bladder retraining encourages the patient to adopt an expanded voiding interval by gradually increasing the voiding intervals. Training focuses on increasing the time interval between voidings, thereby decreasing frequency, increasing bladder capacity, and eventually diminishing urgency. Contingency management involves the systematic reinforcement of appropriate toileting through the use of verbal praise of successful toileting and reminders to use the toilet after unsuccessful toileting.

Self-management (self-care) may include components of several different treatment modalities such as: habit training, bladder retraining, contingency management, and pelvic muscle exercises. Habit training, bladder retraining,

Table 19.1
Behavioral Interventions for Urinary Incontinence: Outpatients

Intervention	*Description*	*Types of Incontinence*
Habit Training	Fixed or flexible toileting schedule; adjusted to accommodate patient's pattern of incontinence.	Urge; functional
Bladder Retraining	Toileting interval is gradually increased or decreased to normal.	Urge; neurogenic bladder
Contingency Management	Systematic reinforcement of appropriate toileting; inappropriate toileting ignored or reminder given to use toilet for voiding.	Functional
Self-Management	Habit training Bladder retraining Pelvic floor exercise	Stress; urge
Biofeedback	Feedback of physiologic responses used to teach sphincter contraction (i.e., pelvic floor exercise), bladder inhibition, or abdominal relaxation.	Stress; urge

Source: Adapted from Burgio, K., & Burgio, L. (1986) Behavior therapies for urinary incontinence in the elderly. *Clinics in Geriatric Medicine, 2*(4), 811.

and contingency management have already been briefly described. Pelvic muscle exercise (also called Kegel exercise) is a contraction and relaxation of the pelvic muscle in order to increase strength. Usually, the person is asked to contract the muscle for 10 seconds and relax for 10 seconds, three times a day, for a maximum of 50-60 contractions. Sometimes the strength of the contractions are monitored through a vaginal device called a perineometer. This device provides feedback about the correct muscle being contracted, as well as the magnitude of the force of the contraction. In addition to pelvic muscle exercise, individuals may also practice interrupting the urinary stream during voiding, which will contract pelvic muscle. Self-help tapes have been developed by Help for Incontinent Persons (HIP) to train incontinent adults with simple and advanced exercises that help to strengthen the pelvic muscle (Jeter, 1989).

Biofeedback is an intervention that provides audible and/or visual feedback about bladder, abdominal pressures, and external anal sphincter activity in order to teach voluntary sphincter contraction, bladder inhibition, and abdominal relaxation. The targets of the intervention are the pelvic striated muscles for contraction, and relaxation of the abdominal muscles. Intra-urethral resistance can be trained to increase by contracting peri-urethral muscles in adults

Table 19.2
Behavioral Interventions for Urinary Incontinence: Long-Term Care

Intervention	Description	Types of Incontinence
Habit Training	Fixed or flexible toileting schedule; adjusted to accommodate patient's pattern of incontinence.	Urge; functional
Bladder Retraining	Toileting interval is gradually increased or decreased to normal.	Urge; neurogenic bladder
Contingency Management	Systematic reinforcement of appropriate toileting; inappropriate toileting ignored or reminder given to use toilet for voiding.	Functional
Staff Management	Systematic structuring and reinforcement of appropriate implementation of treatment by staff.	Functional
Bellpad	Augmented: prompted void with an electric alarm device in severely cognitively impaired.	Stress; urge
Mechanical Lift	Augmented; prompted void with a mechanical lift in severely mobility impaired.	Stress; urge

Source: Adapted from Burgio, K., & Burgio, L. (1986) Behavior therapies for urinary incontinence in the elderly. *Clinics in Geriatric Medicine, 2*(4), 811.

with stress incontinence, and voluntary inhibition of bladder contractions can be relearned by adults with urge incontinence.

Treatments: Long-Term Care

Table 19.2 summarizes the interventions that have been described in the research literature related to long-term care and nursing homes. They are categorized into six areas of treatment: (1) Habit training, (2) Bladder retraining, (3) Contingency management, (4) Staff management, (5) Bellpad Augmented Prompted Void, and (6) Mechanical Lift Augmented Prompted Void.

The habit training schedule that residents are admitted to in the long-term care setting has frequently been one hour (Hu et al., 1989; Schnelle, Sowell, Hu, & Traughber, 1988). Another study analyzed the usefulness of different schedules of prompted voiding on the improvement of incontinence (McCormick, Scheve et al., n.d.). Residents who were wet when baseline measures were taken, were prompted hourly and there was significant improvement over baseline. The residents, however, did not maintain this improvement when they were transferred to the home units that used a two-hour schedule. Among residents who were treated with a two-hour schedule, they improved and maintained this treatment effect. One group went on to be treated every three hours and also continued to improve on the longer schedule. Residents who were relatively dry while in baseline were later prompted on a four-hour schedule and they also significantly improved.

Staff management interventions have also improved outcomes for residents in the long-term care setting. These interventions consist of assigning nursing personnel to logistically feasible patient populations, teaching nursing personnel to alter their behaviors from changing patients' wet clothing and mopping urine from floors to toileting patients, monitoring *staff* behavior, and rewarding appropriate staff performance with praise (McCormick, Scheve, & Leahy, 1988). In a study to demonstrate the effectiveness of management procedures, two phases were described (L. Burgio et al., 1990). In phase I, research assistants were taught how to administer prompted voiding treatment. The staff management system included self-monitoring and recording of prompted voiding activities and supervisory monitoring and feedback based on group performance and activities. This system was initially effective, but performance began to decline in 4-5 months after initiation of the system. In phase 2, another more personal system was implemented, to restore staff performance. During phase 2, feedback was provided to each staff member individually. Results showed that once individual feedback was provided, the staff performance exceeded the initial levels achieved in phase I. In a subsequent study, the monitoring of individual performance was augmented with contingencies. A letter was placed into the nursing staff's personnel file every three months praising positive performance and giving disapproval of low performance (Hawkins, Langford, Engel, & Burgio, n.d.). Results showed that individual feedback plus contingencies produced significant improvements in the number of assigned prompted-void checks and toileting episodes completed.

Because many residents in long-term care are also cognitively impaired (demented) and do not respond to routine prompted void treatment, a study was designed to augment prompted void treatment with a bellpad. A bellpad is an electronic alarm device that rings when wet with urine (McCormick, Burgio, Engel, Scheve, & Leahy, n.d.). Results indicated that the bellpad treatment was associated with significantly increased dryness compared to baseline. In addition, improved dryness was maintained for up to three months in residents remaining on follow-up treatment. These findings indicate that even severely cognitively impaired residents continence status can be improved with nursing techniques in long-term care.

Yet another group in long-term care are those who are severely mobility impaired. They require either two personnel to lift them or the use of a mechanical lift. In another study that monitored the results of prompted void treatment augmented by a mechanical lift, the costs of incontinence treatment were also documented (McCormick, Cella, Scheve, & Engel, 1990). This study demonstrated that a mechanical lift and a two-hour toileting schedule improved continence. Because this incontinence treatment is labor intensive, the costs of treating incontinence increased but the costs of the consequences of incontinence (decubitus ulcers and urinary tract infections) decreased by $13.38 per patient day.

Treatments: Acute Care

Table 19.3 is a summary of the treatments that have been described that change continence outcomes in hospitalized patients. They are categorized into five areas: (1) Habit training, (2) Bladder training, (3) Contingency management, (4) Staff management, and (5) Biofeedback. Unlike the other areas of intervention research, data are scantily available from the United States related to the treatment of hospitalized adults for incontinence. Biofeedback, however, has been used to treat incontinence in stroke and post-prostatectomy patients. Middaugh, Whitehead, Burgio, & Engel (1989) reported that four males who had a previous stroke successfully maintained continence after participating in biofeedback assisted bladder retraining. The training procedure did not change the physiologic functioning of the bladder but assisted the individual in better managing a low volume hyperreflexic bladder.

Biofeedback was also an effective intervention for 20 males with post-prostatectomy incontinence (K. Burgio, Stutzman, & Engel, 1989). After biofeedback training sessions, there was an average 78% decrease in stress incontinence and an average 80% decrease in urge incontinence. Males with continuous leakage had less successful results, average 17% reduction in leakage. These findings indicated that there was damage to the mechanism of passive control of continence. This study showed that candidates for biofeedback should be carefully selected based on the pattern of urine loss over several days. Candidates must actively participate in therapy and be motivated to continue the therapy on their own.

ROLE FOR THE GERONTOLOGICAL NURSE

The role of the gerontological nurse in any practice setting is to assist older adults to attain and maintain their maximum level of functioning. In the acute care setting, the gerontological nurse will provide care for older adults whose incontinence is usually associated with medical and surgical conditions such as cerebral vascular accidents and post-prostatectomy. Transient incontinence

Table 19.3
Behavioral Interventions for Urinary Incontinence: Acute Care

Intervention	Description	Types of Incontinence
Habit Training	Fixed or flexible toileting schedule; adjusted to accommodate patient's pattern of incontinence.	Urge; functional
Bladder Retraining	Toileting interval is gradually increased or decreased to normal.	Urge; neurogenic bladder
Contingency Management	Systematic reinforcement of appropriate toileting; inappropriate toileting ignored or reminder given to use toilet for voiding.	Functional
Staff Management	Systematic structuring and reinforcement of appropriate implementation of treatment by staff.	Functional
Biofeedback	Feedback of physiologic responses used to teach sphincter contraction (i.e., pelvic floor exercise), bladder inhibition, or abdominal relaxation.	Stress; urge

Source: Adapted from Burgio, K., & Burgio, L. (1986) Behavior therapies for urinary incontinence in the elderly. *Clinics in Geriatric Medicine, 2*(4), 811.

may be induced by delirium, infection, restricted mobility, or be a side effect of medication. The nurse must assess the underlying cause of incontinence and employ interventions that are directed at avoiding consequences of incontinence, such as skin breakdown and emotional distress. The nurse should participate actively in discharge planning for incontinent adults; outpatient referrals for gynecologic and urologic work-ups should be made if appropriate, patient education regarding normal micturition and effects of aging should be initiated. Information about available and affordable environmental modifications to the home should be provided for the patient who is returning home. The gerontological nurse plays an important role in staff education. The latest information about nursing interventions and programs used in the acute care setting to maximize continence status should be provided to the staff. Documentation of the problem, its assessment, and the evaluation of the intervention selected is important especially if the patient remains within the health care system, such as home care, day care, or institutional care to maximize continuity of care. The gerontological nurse in the long-term care setting is often the only professional health care provider in the long-term care facility on a daily basis. Awareness of the high prevalence of incontinence among a vulnerable population, especially functional incontinence secondary to cognitive and mobility impairments, is necessary to undertake effective nursing interventions. Appropriate nursing assessment techniques are necessary; mixed types of incontinence are often present in a nursing home setting. For example, a resident may have a combination of stress and urge incontinence. The aims of the gerontological nurse should be to use staff management techniques and appropriate specialized treatment programs described in this chapter. Documentation of interventions employed to enhance the continence status and evaluation of their effectiveness will assume increased importance for regulatory agencies of long-term care facilities and for cost containment efforts within the facilities.

In the community, gerontological nurses work in conjunction with a urologist or in an independent role to provide treatment for stress incontinence, especially among ambulatory, cognitively intact adults. For home-bound older adults with a family member as a primary caregiver, individualized continence programs can be designed to reduce incontinence (Smith, 1988).

Urinary incontinence is not an inevitable outcome to a long life. Gerontological nurses can employ sound and effective interventions in any practice setting to alleviate or reduce this distressing but common condition in the older adult.

REFERENCES

Bates, P., Bradley, W., Glen, G., Griffiths, D., Melchior, H., Rowan, D., Sterling, A., Zinner, N., & Haid, T. (1979). The standardization of terminology of lower urinary tract function. *Journal of Urology, 121*(5), 551-554.

Burgio, K., & Burgio, L. (1986). Behavioral therapies for urinary incontinence in the elderly. In J. Ouslander (Ed.), Clinics in Geriatric Medicine, (4), 811.

Burgio, K., Burgio, L., McCormick, K., & Engel, B. (1985, November). *Characteristics of continent and incontinent clients of an adult day care center.* Paper presented at the meeting of the Gerontological Society of America, New Orleans, LA.

Burgio, K., & Engel, B. (1987). Urinary incontinence behavioral assessment and treatment. In L. Carstensen & B. Edelstein (Eds.), *Handbook of Clinical Gerontology* (p. 258). New York: Pergamon.

Burgio, K., Stutzman, R., & Engel, B. (1989). Behavioral training for post-prostatectomy urinary incontinence. *Journal of Urology, 141*(2), 303-306.

Burgio, L., Engel, B., Hawkins, A., McCormick, K., Jones, K., & Scheve, A. (1990). A staff management system for maintaining improvements in continence with elderly nursing home residents. *Journal of Applied Behavioral Analysis, 23*(1), 11-118.

Claridge, M. (1965). The physiology of micturition. *British Journal of Urology, 37,* 620-623.

Clay, E. (1980). Promoting urine control in older adults: Habit retraining. *Geriatric Nursing, 1*(4), 252-254.

Ebersole, P., & Hess, P. (1985). *Toward healthy aging* (2nd ed.) (pp. 218-222). St. Louis: C. V. Mosby.

Folstein, M., Folstein, S., & McHugh, P. (1975). A practical method for grading cognitive status of patients for the clinician. *Journal of Psychiatric Research, 12,* 189-198.

Harris, T. (1986). Aging in the eighties. Prevalence and impact of urinary problems in individuals age 65 years and over. *Advance Data from Vital and Health Statistics, No. 121,* Washington, DC: National Center for Health Statistics.

Hawkins, A., Langford, A., Engel, B., & Burgio, L. (n.d.). The effects of verbal and written supervisory feedback on staff compliance to assigned prompted voiding in a nursing home.

Herzog, A., & Fultz, N. (1988). Urinary incontinence in the community: Prevalence, consequences, management, and beliefs. *Topics in Geriatric Rehabilitation, 3*(2), 1-12.

Hing, E., & Senscenski, E. (1986). Use of health care—Nursing home use. In *Health statistics on older persons Analytical and Epidemiological Studies* (DHHS Publication No. PHS 87-1409). Hyattsville, MD: Public Health Service. [United States, 1986. Series 3, No. 25].

Hu, T. (1986). The economic impact of urinary incontinence. In J. Ouslander (Ed.), *Clinics of Geriatric Medicine, 4*(2), 673-687.

Hu, T., Igou, J., Kaltreider, L., Yu, L., Rohner, T., Dennis, P., Craighead, W., Hadley, E, & Ory, M. (1989). A clinical trial of a behavioral therapy on reduced urinary incontinence in nursing homes. *Journal of the American Medical Association, 261*(18), 2656-2662.

Jeter, K. (1989). Pelvic muscle exercises (audio tape). Available through Help for Incontinent Persons (HIP), P.O. Box 544, Union, SC 29379, (803)579-7900.

Kane, R., Ouslander, J., & Abrass, I. (1989). *Essentials of clinical geriatrics* (2nd ed.) (pp. 139-189). New York: McGraw-Hill.

Leach, G., & Yip, C. (1986). Urologic and urodynamic evaluation of the elderly population. In J. Ouslander (Ed.), *Clinics of Geriatric Medicine,4*(2), 23-27.

McCormick, K., Burgio, K., Engel, B., Scheve, A., & Leahy, E. (n.d.). The treatment of urinary incontinence in nursing home residents: An augmented prompted void approach for the demented.

McCormick, K., Cella, M., Scheve, A., & Engel, B. (1990, December). Cost-effectiveness of treating of incontinence in severely mobility-impaired long term care residents. *Quarterly Review Bulletin, 16*(12), 439-443.

McCormick, K., Scheve, A., Burgio, L., Engel, B., Leahy, E., & Hawkins, A. (n.d.). The effects of changing prompted voiding schedules in the treatment of incontinence in nursing home residents.

McCormick, K., Scheve, A., & Leahy, E. (1988). Nursing management of urinary incontinence in geriatric inpatients. In K. McCormick (Ed.), *Nursing Clinics of North America, 23*(1), 231-264.

Middaugh, S., Whitehead, W., Burgio, K., & Engel, B. (1989). Biofeedback in treatment of urinary incontinence in stroke patients. *Biofeedback and Self Regulation, 14*,(1), 3-19.

Mitteness, L. (1987a). The management of urinary incontinence by community living elderly. *The Gerontologist, 27*(2), 185-193.

Mitteness, L. (1987b). So what do you expect when you're 85? Urinary incontinence in late life. In J. Roth & P. Conrad (Eds.), *Research in the sociology of health care.* Volume 6, (pp. 177-219). Greenwich CT: JAI Press, pp. 177-219.

Morishita, L. (1988). Nursing evaluation and treatment of geriatric outpatients with urinary incontinence: Geriatric day hospital model: A case study. In K. McCormick (Ed.), *Nursing Clinics of North America, 23*(1), 189-206.

National Institutes of Health Consensus Development Conference (1990). Urinary incontinence in adults. *Journal of the American Geriatrics Society, 38*(3), 265-272.

Noelker, L. (1987). Incontinence in the elderly—Care by the family. *The Gerontologist, 27*(2), 194-200.

Norton, C. (1986). *Nursing for continence* (pp. 1-26). Beaconsfield Publishers: Beaconsfield, Bucks England.

Ouslander, J. (1986). Diagnostic evaluation of geriatric urinary incontinence. In J. Ouslander (Ed.), *Clinics of Geriatric Medicine, 2*(4), 715-730.

Ouslander, J. (1989). Assessment and treatment of incontinence in the nursing home. In P. Katz & E. Calkins (Eds.), *Principles and practices of nursing home care* (pp. 247-274). New York: Springer.

Ouslander, J. (1990). Urinary incontinence in nursing homes. *Journal of the American Geriatrics Society, 38*(3), 289-291.

Palmer, M. (1988). Incontinence. The magnitude of the problem. In K. McCormick (Ed.), *Nursing Clinics of North America, 23*(1), 139-157.

Palmer, M., McCormick, K., & Langford, A. (1989). Do nurses consistently document incontinence? *Journal of Gerontological Nursing, 15*(12), 11-16.

Radloff, L. (1977). The CES-D Scale: A self-report depression scale for research in the general population. *Applied Psychological Measurements, 1*, 385-401.

Resnick, N., & Yalla, S. (1985). Management of urinary incontinence in the elderly. *New England Journal of Medicine, 313*(13), 800-805.

Schnelle, J., Sowell, V., Hu, T., & Traughber, B. (1988). Reduction of urinary incontinence in nursing homes: Does it reduce or increase costs? *Journal of the American Geriatrics Society, 36*(1), 34-39.

Schreter, C. (1979). Clinical note: Incontinence on the street. A counseling/housing dilemma. *The Gerontologist, 19*(5), 509-511.

Sier, H., Ouslander, J., & Orzeck, S. (1987). Urinary incontinence among geriatric patients in an acute-care hospital. *Journal of the American Medical Association, 257*(13), 1767-1771.

Smith, D. (1988). Continence restoration in the homebound patient. In K. McCormick (Ed.), *Nursing Clinics of North America, 23*(1), 207-218.

Staskin, D. (1986). Age-related physiologic and pathologic changes affecting lower urinary tract function. In J. Ouslander (Ed.), *Clinics in Geriatric Medicine, 2*(4), 701-710.

Staskin, D., Ouslander, J., & Raz, S. (1985). Office evaluation of female incontinence. *Primary Care, 12*(4), 675-685.

Sullivan, D., & Lindsay, R. (1984). Urinary incontinence in the geriatric population of an acute care hospital. *Journal of the American Geriatrics Society, 32*(9), 646-650.

Wein, A. (1986). Physiology of micturition. In J. Ouslander (Ed.), *Clinics in Geriatric Medicine, 2*(4), 689-699.

Williams, M., & Pannill, F. (1982). Urinary incontinence in the elderly. *Annals of Internal Medicine, 97*(6), 895-907.

Wyman, J. (1988). Nursing assessment of the incontinent geriatric outpatient population. In K. McCormick (Ed.), *Nursing Clinics of North America, 23*(1), 169-187.

Yu, L. (1987). Incontinence stress index: Measuring psychological impact. *Journal of Gerontological Nursing, 13*(7), 18-25.

Yu, L., & Kaltreider, D. (1987). Stressed nurses dealing with incontinent patients. *Journal of Gerontological Nursing, 13*(1), 27-30.

20

Rehabilitation of Older Adults

MARION A. PHIPPS
MARGARET KELLY-HAYES

Objectives: At the conclusion of this chapter the reader will:

(1) Evaluate the historical development of rehabilitation nursing care of the older adult.
(2) Critique theoretical approaches to rehabilitation nursing care of the older adult.
(3) Evaluate a multifactorial method of assessing the rehabilitation needs of older adults.
(4) Implement a rehabilitation nursing approach to care of older adults in a variety of practice settings.

INTRODUCTION

Rehabilitation of the older adult may be viewed as a philosophical theme, underlying all aspects of care regardless of the care setting. Maintenance of function and independence, rather than necessarily a cure of disease, becomes the goal of elderly health care and the focus of interventions. These interventions aim at restoration of functional independence and quality of life for the older person.

In the United States today, changes in health statistics and population demographics signal a powerful impact on health care, particularly for the elderly. People are living longer and projections forecast a continued increase in the percentage of elderly in the population over the next 50 years. This segment of the population has a wide range of health concerns and needs. Many older adults are healthy, fit, active, and need no assistance, whereas others are disabled from acute and chronic health problems and need assistance with many aspects of care. In 1984, a third of the noninstitutionalized elders more than 80 years old were defined as having no difficulty in walking 1/4 mile, lifting 10 pounds, climbing stairs, or shopping (Harris, Kovor, Suzman, Kleiman, & Feldman, 1989).

Health professionals are faced with major challenges in care of the elderly. There is a need to identify approaches to keeping the well elderly active, healthy, and functioning independently. There is also the need to find approaches to care of the elderly with acute and chronic illnesses to decrease disability and increase functional well-being.

The application of rehabilitation nursing philosophy and principles to the care of the elderly can serve as a framework for meeting these challenges. Nurses skilled in rehabilitation can assist older people to attain and maintain the highest possible level of functional independence.

In this chapter we will describe rehabilitation nursing philosophy and practices in the care of the disabled elderly. The concept of disability will be defined and principles of geriatric rehabilitation will be applied to care considerations for the elderly.

DEVELOPMENT OF REHABILITATION NURSING

The principles and philosophy of rehabilitation nursing have been incorporated in the education of professional nurses since the establishment of the first nursing schools in the 1870s. In fact, the first nursing textbook published in England contained many principles of rehabilitation nursing practice. It was not until the 1940s, however, that rehabilitation nursing made specific recommendations about care of disabled individuals.

During this time in the United States, Sister Kenney revolutionized the approach to treatment of individuals with poliomyelitis (Young, 1989). Examples of her interventions included treatment of spasm and pain with range of motion, heat modalities, and muscle re-education techniques. Following World War II, the need for rehabilitation services for veterans forced changes in attitudes and technology. Rehabilitation, from this time, became viewed as a viable treatment for individuals with once disabling conditions. In concert with this movement, the first rehabilitation nursing textbook was published in 1951.

DEFINITION OF REHABILITATION NURSING

Over the past 40 years rehabilitation nursing has become recognized as an advanced specialty area with nurses practicing in areas such as stroke, spinal cord injury, and geriatric rehabilitation. In 1984, the Association of Rehabilitation Nurses, in cooperation with the American Nurses' Association defined rehabilitation nursing as

> a specialty practice within the profession. Rehabilitation nurses diagnose and treat the human responses of individuals and groups to actual or potential disability that interrupts or alters function and life satisfaction. The goal of rehabilitation nursing is to assist the individual or group in the restoration and maintenance of maximum health. (Mumma, 1987, p. 15)

Rehabilitation nursing is based upon the belief that rehabilitation is a process of restoring and maintaining a client at optimal physiological, psychological, vocational, and social functioning. Rehabilitation nurses address two basic concerns: prevention and restoration. Prevention is maintaining function to prevent deterioration of an uninvolved organ or system or preventing further injury to an already affected part. Restoration, on the other hand, deals with those specific knowledge-based practices that are part of the process of bringing an individual to his or her highest potential.

CHANGING HEALTH NEEDS OF THE ELDERLY

There is an increase in the number of elderly in our country. Between 1930 and 1980, the population of the elderly grew four times that of the under 65 population. By the year 2030, people aged 65 and older are expected to comprise 20% of the population, and 45% of this group is expected to be 75 years or older (Rice, 1989). Women older than 85 are expected to outnumber men three to one (Smith & Lipman, 1986). At the same time, chronic disease has replaced acute illness as the major source of health problems in the United States, causing more than 80% of deaths and an even greater percentage of disability (Fries, 1980). Most chronic diseases increase with age, resulting in most individuals 70 years and older having at least one functional limitation.

As the percentage of older persons with chronic diseases increases in the population, there is concern about the concomitant increase in the amount of disability in this group. The National Health Survey indicated an increased level of disability and an increased need for assistance with self-care for the elderly with more than one chronic disease (Guralnik, LaCroix, & Everett, 1989). Williams (1980) suggested that chronic illness caused some degree of limitation in self-care in 45% of noninstitutionalized elderly 65 years and older, with an increase to 60% for those 85 and older.

Disability in the elderly may occur not only because of chronic illness but also as a result of acute illness and hospitalization. While hospitalized, the older person is more vulnerable to the development of complications and functional decline than someone younger. Acute illness and hospitalization-induced disability in the elderly are particularly insidious as these problems may be considered the baseline status of the patient rather than new onset. As a consequence, correctable disability in the elderly may become chronic in nature.

With this changing pattern of survival, there is the need to consider other dimensions of the impact of illness. Katz and colleagues (1983) have described an alternate end point; that is, the expected duration of functional well-being that Katz et al. (1983) termed "active life expectancy". Instead of death, the end of active life expectancy is that point in time when an individual loses his or her independence in performing basic activities of daily living. Because technology has postponed the age of death due to cancer, cardiovascular disease, and stroke, health care providers need to focus on maximizing their efforts to the time it will have the greatest impact on remaining life. This demands an inquiry into what constitutes an active life for elders and what contributions rehabilitation interventions can make.

DISABILITY IN THE ELDERLY

The relationship between independent living and type and severity of disabilities is apparent. Although by definition the term disability assumes interaction between the individual and the environment, the word is frequently equated with separate and specific impairments. The conceptual process from which we now define disability has evolved over the past 25 years. The two main architects of the disability models were Saad Nagi (1965, 1969, 1976) and Philip Wood (1975, 1980). These two theorists, although in many areas similar in the construct of their models, differ in identifying the locus of responsibility. Saad Nagi proposed that there were three major consequences of disease or pathology. The first was impairment that represented the anatomical or physiological abnormalities resulting from a specific pathological process; the second, functional limitation which he refers to as sensory-motor functioning such as walking, climbing, and bending. Nagi's third component, disability, he defines as "inability or limitations in performing social roles and activities such as in relation to work, family or to independent living" (1979, p. 441).

Wood (1980) developed a conceptual model in many ways similar to Nagi's model but extended his theory to include the concept of handicap in the framework of disability. His definition of handicap was, "a disadvantage for a given individual, resulting from an impairment or disability, that limits or prevents the fulfillment of a role that is normal (depending on age, sex, and social or cultural factors) for that individual" (Wood, 1980, p. 4).

In 1980, the World Health Organization (WHO) published a hierarchical set of definitions of disability. According to the WHO, impairment is described as the loss or limitation of an organ of the body or mind. When an individual, because of the impairment has a loss or limitation of ability to perform a certain function, it is classified as a disability. When the impairment or the disability create a social disadvantage for the affected individual, it then becomes a handicap.

MEASUREMENT OF DISABILITY

Applying disability theory and definition to the elderly population has proven to be a difficult task for a number of reasons, the most obvious being that the elderly are likely to have multiple health problems with concomitant functional limitations (Nagi, 1976). At present, the most commonly used measurement of disability in the elderly is the measurement of basic activities of daily living (ADLs) (Branch & Jette, 1981; Charlton, Patrick, & Peach, 1983; Colvez & Blanchet, 1981; Nagi, 1976). Beyond ADLs there is little agreement on how and what should be measured.

Surveying disability trends in the United States from 1966 to 1976, Colvez and Blanchet (1981) defined disability among the elderly in terms of physical mobility, physical independence in basic activities, and ability to carry out one's normal activity. Charlton et al. (1983) expanded the measurement to also include psychological status, ability to communicate, and ability to work. The approach devised by Kane and Kane (1981) conceptualized health as a hierarchical structure: the first level is general physical health or the absence of illness, the second level is the basic performance of self-care and mobility activities that are critical for independence, and the third, ability to perform and maintain those complex activities and roles that are associated with meaningful life. Kane and Kane's conceptualization of disability provides an appropriate framework for identifying rehabilitation interventions for elders because rehabilitation interventions for the elderly can address a wide range of needs from basic self-care activities to reintegration into the community.

Changes in assessment of disability have been guided by changes in the concept of rehabilitation and our growing knowledge of the aging process. The possibility now exists that active intervention can help promote more healthy aging and retain higher levels of functioning for longer periods of life, thereby decreasing the amount of disability incurred (Guralnik & Kaplan, 1989). In general, measurement of successful rehabilitation is usually in terms of assessment and outcome of intervention for a described skill. For the geriatric population, assessment becomes the keystone for planned interventions and should include all parameters that affect "active life" functioning. Following the WHO (1980) definition of disability, we propose that disability should be measured on four levels: physical functioning, cognition, emotional well-being, and social interaction. These four levels of functioning will be organized in the following sections.

Functional Assessment

A measurement of physical functioning can be derived from many different combinations of items. The most commonly used measures are the basic activities of daily living, mobility status, and bowel and bladder continence. Although there are well over 40 ADL tools developed to document function, the most widely utilized scales are the Barthel Index (Mahoney & Barthel, 1965) and the recently developed Functional Index Measure (FIM) (see Table 20.1) that extends the range of measurement for more inclusive rehabilitation assessment. The FIM, developed by the Uniform Data System, provides uniform language, definitions, and measurements that describe disability. The conceptual basis is that the level of disability should indicate the burden of care or the cost to the individual or society for that person not to be functionally independent. In rehabilitation this type of assessment is used to establish criteria for admission, discharge, and documentation of rehabilitation gains. At a different level, complex activities of daily living are categorized under the title of "instrumental" activities of daily living (IADLs) that include the more complex activities associated with independent life such as shopping, housekeeping, and transportation. The choice of scales for ADL and IADL depends on the assessment needs and the desired outcome from rehabilitation interventions.

Documentation of physical functioning is either by performance or capacity measurements. Performance is defined as activities the individual reports that he or she actually does on a day-to-day basis; capacity is the carrying out of specific activities to judge what the individual actually is capable of performing. Field investigators in community-based populations are increasingly employing performance questions in large scale surveys of functional disability in older populations (Fulton, Katz, Jack, & Hendershot, 1989), whereas in rehabilitation, direct observation of capacity is the most commonly utilized method of evaluation (Kane & Kane, 1981). The challenge in performance assessment is to distinguish whether or not a particular activity is not performed because of a health problem or for other reasons unrelated to health. Some ADLs may not be performed because of preference or out of habit. This is especially likely in assessing Instrumental ADLs such as housekeeping, meal preparation, and shopping. Distinguishing between capacity and performance

Table 20.1
Functional Independence Measure (FIM)

L E V E L S	7 Complete Independence (Timely, Safely) 6 Modified Independence (Device) → **NO HELPER**
	Modified Dependence 5 Supervision 4 Minimal Assist (Subject = 75%+) 3 Moderate Assist (Subject = 50%+) → **HELPER** *Complete Dependence* 2 Maximal Assist (Subject = 25%+) 1 Total Assist (Subject = 0%+)

Self Care	ADMIT	DISCHG	FOL-UP
A. Feeding	___	___	___
B. Grooming	___	___	___
C. Bathing	___	___	___
D. Dressing - Upper Body	___	___	___
E. Dressing - Lower Body	___	___	___
F. Toileting	___	___	___
Sphincter Control			
G. Bladder Management	___	___	___
H. Bowel Management	___	___	___
Mobility	___	___	___
Transfer:			
I. Bed, Chair, W/Chair	___	___	___
J. Toilet	___	___	___
K. Tub, Shower			
Locomotion			
L. Walk/Wheel Chair	w ___ c ___ ___	w ___ c ___ ___	w ___ c ___ ___
M. Stairs	___	___	___
Communication			
N. Comprehension	a ___ v ___ ___	a ___ v ___ ___	a ___ v ___ ___
O. Expression	v ___ n ___ ___	v ___ n ___ ___	v ___ n ___ ___
Social Cognition			
P. Social Interaction	___	___	___
Q. Problem Solving	___	___	___
R. Memory	___	___	___
TOTAL	[ ]	[ ]	[ ]

Source: Uniform Data System for Medical Rehabilitation (1987). State University of New York at Buffalo, NY. Printed with permission.

measurements of functional disability is particularly important for the oldest-old women, those with cognitive deficits and those with poor general health (Kelly-Hayes et al., in press). Investigations involving these subgroups of the aged need to take particular note of the type of functional disability measures employed.

Cognitive Assessment

Cognitive status evaluation should be an integral part of the rehabilitation assessment. There is extensive evidence to indicate that, as people age, there are alterations seen in performance of intellectual functioning (Cummins & Benson, 1983) with the incidence and prevalence of dementia in the elderly rising rapidly with advancing age. In recent studies of dementia in community populations (Bachman et al., 1989; Evans et al., 1989) the prevalence of dementia of all types appeared to be more common than previously believed, with an overall prevalence of 10% among those 65 years of age and older. It has been estimated that one in five will become severely demented before death. In addition, more than half the nursing home residents suffer from some degree of dementia (Cummins & Benson, 1983). Because the outcome of rehabilitation is most likely predicated on new learning, this plays an important role for the type of rehabilitation interventions recommended.

The measurement tools for cognitive function can be self-administered, observer rated, or unstructured or structured interviews. They can assess simple or multidimensional categories. In recent years, several scales have been specifically designed for elder populations (Kane & Kane, 1981). Incorporation of mental status measurement can serve as a guide for specific rehabilitation efforts.

Affective Functioning

One of the most powerful deterrents to successful rehabilitation in later years is the presence of depression. Depression is often exacerbated by loss of physical well-being and independence. In some conditions, such as stroke, depression may be an actual feature of the disease (Wolf, Bachman, & Kelly-Hayes, 1990). Berkman et al. (1986) studied the association between depressive symptoms and functional disability in a cohort of elders. She found that depression varied dramatically by health characteristics, with persons having major functional disabilities demonstrating substantially higher levels of depression. Although depression is universally acknowledged to be important, there is little consensus on how to measure it in the elderly. If not recognized and treated, its presence can have profound negative impact on all rehabilitation efforts.

Social Interaction

A social definition of health and disability recognizes that individuals carry out social roles. Social and community ties may play a major role in the etiology of many diseases. Social functioning has been correlated with physical and mental functioning and enhances the ability of a person to cope with health problems. Thus it should not be underestimated as an influence on rehabilitation outcome.

In describing the nature and magnitude of disability among a noninstitutionalized elderly population, Branch and Jette (1981) identified frequency of social interaction as a major determinant for an independent life-style. In their study, disability appeared to increase with age and women reported a higher degree of unmet needs. Assessment of social coping resources and the measurement of life stresses should be included as part of a complete health assessment.

Institutionalization as a Measure of Disability

Older people of similar ages have a faster rate of physical deterioration when institutionalized than those living in the home (Bortz, 1990). It is therefore a goal of rehabilitation to prevent institutionalization for as long as possible. The overall increase in risk for impending institutionalization revolves around several variables. Worsening health is often the precipitating factor (Doty, 1986). In a longitudinal analysis of data from 1982 to 1984, the National Long-term Health Care Survey (NLTC), Manton (1988) noted that disability was strongly predictive of institutional risk. Specifically, men and women impaired in instrumental ADLs formed "an orderly progression in mortality and institutional risks between those not impaired and those with at least one ADL impairment" (p. s155a). Also, when the number of hospitalizations was used as a proxy variable for health status, the relative risk of institutionalization for people living in retirement communities with two hospitalizations was 1.2 times that of elders with only one.

The relative contribution of a single catastrophic illness such as stroke, in combination with other factors on the need for institutionalization has only recently received attention. In a prospective study of survival and the need for institutionalization among stroke cases in the Framingham cohort, Kelly-Hayes et al. (1988) found that two different patterns existed. Multivariate logistic regression revealed that acute survival was negatively affected by stroke type, severity of neurological impairments, and age. For those who survived at least 30 days, however, independent living was determined as much by social factors as severity of disability. Older women, married or not, with moderate to severe disability and minimal education, were at highest risk for institutionalization.

APPLICATION OF REHABILITATION PRINCIPLES
TO CARE OF THE ELDERLY

Zadai (1985) described the initial role of rehabilitation in the elderly to, "assess the functional limitations of aging and separate them from the pathological changes of disease. The attempt then is to design a program that counterbalances the aging or disease process and improves the individual's ability, enhancing quality of life" (pp. 54-55).

When analyzing the rehabilitation approach to care of the older person several general principles must be considered. Recognizing those physical alterations that are preventable and reversible can give the disabled elderly an increased ability to maintain independent function. Correctable causes of functional decline must be identified and treated. During the course of therapeutic interventions, further deterioration should be prevented. Providing methods of adaptation may allow the older disabled person an increased sense of well-being and control.

Rehabilitation often involves the need to learn new ways of performing skills. Older people have difficulty learning new tasks that are timed (Katzman & Terry, 1983) and tasks taught in a stressful environment. The environment for learning new skills must be carefully planned to provide the older person decreased stress and reduction of extraneous stimuli. The older individual may have an increased level of fatigue and may need more rest periods in order to participate in therapy sessions.

There may be barriers to the full participation of the older person in a rehabilitation program. Negative attitudes on the part of health professionals regarding the older person's ability to improve with rehabilitation may prevent the initiation of any attempt toward rehabilitation. Rubinstein (1987) describes the underutilization of rehabilitation as one of the unmet needs of the elderly in our country. These attitudes, in fact, may induce further disability by imposing "learned helplessness" in the older person (Avorn & Langer, 1982). In addition, negative attitudes of care providers about older persons in general may further limit rehabilitative approaches to care.

Another barrier to rehabilitation of the older person may be the person's own attitude about their potential for recovery. Motivating the older adult to participate in rehabilitation is an important aspect of care (Hesse & Campion, 1983). Nurses and therapists may need to help the older person find meaning for participation in physically demanding and stressful therapeutic regimes. The person may ask, "Why bother, I am too old for this." When staff work with the client and family to define goals of care and rationale for treatment, the client may find the impetus to engage in the difficult work of recovery. Intradisciplinary collaboration regarding assessment and interventions for functional, cognitive, affective, and social status are the cornerstone of this process.

Rehabilitation in the Institutional Setting

Older adults utilize short-stay hospitals more frequently and for longer periods of time than any age group. The rate of hospitalization and the average length of stay increases with age and it is estimated that nearly half of the expenditures for health care of the elderly are for patient care during short-stay hospitalization (Kennie, 1983; Minaker & Rowe, 1985; Warshaw et al., 1982).

Acute illness and hospitalization may be more difficult for the older person than for someone younger. Age-related changes in organ function, particularly in the renal, pulmonary, and immune systems, may diminish the older person's physiological response to acute illness. These altered homeostatic mechanisms decrease the older person's tolerance for medication regimes, surgery, and invasive procedures.

Older persons have an increased rate of complications such as adverse drug reactions, confusion, incontinence, falls, and infection. The older adult may be more prone to the development of nosocomial infections such as pneumonia and urinary tract infections. In a study of 279 patients, aged 70 and older, assessed in an acute hospital, Warshaw and colleagues (1982) discovered a high incidence of functional disability; 65% were unable to walk independently, 50% were confused, and 50% were incontinent or using a Foley catheter. Warshaw et al. state, "Hospitalization may have a negative impact on functional recovery at the same time medical and surgical interventions are successful" (p. 849).

The cause of this functional decline is multifactorial. The acute illness itself may leave the older person weakened and debilitated. Nutritional depletion and dehydration may lead to fluid and electrolyte disturbances. Morley (1986, p. 681) describes the dehydrated state of many hospitalized elderly as a "water desert". The delicate balance the elderly person had maintained prior to admission may be upset by the aggressive treatment and medications used to treat the acute problem. Kennie (1983) described the need for cautious medical interventions or minimal interference as part of good health care for the elderly.

Nursing care of the older person that is custodial in nature rather than rehabilitative in focus, may increase dependence. Avorn and Langer (1982) demonstrated that dependent behavior in nursing home residents is frequently maintained by the nursing home staff. In the institutional setting, the acuity of the patient's illness and that of other patients on the unit and the time demands on the nurse, make the provision of rehabilitative approaches difficult.

The scheduling of nursing care and evaluative procedures may be difficult for the older person, especially if these need to be done at a time when they are exhausted by their illness and would rather rest or sleep. If the older person has hearing or language problems, understanding the rationale for painful nursing treatments and medical evaluative procedures may be impossible. Confusion, anger, and fear may be the outcome. Fear of pain, treatment protocols, perceived decline, and loss of control may result in depression and dependent behavior.

The elderly may have decreased capacity to respond to the hospital environment. This environment is often designed more for efficient delivery of acute care services, rather than for meeting the needs of particular patient populations. Hospital units are generally crowded, noisy, and lacking in privacy and may be overwhelming to the older person, particularly someone with visual or hearing problems. Hospital equipment used by the patient, such as beds, chairs, tables, and commodes, is often not designed to promote patient independence, but for safety reasons is made to immobilize the patient. The design of the environment and needed patient equipment may induce dependence in the elderly.

Initiating a rehabilitation approach to care of the elderly to prevent functional decline and resultant disability may become as important as treating the acute problem. For example, when the older person is acutely ill, nursing staff need to plan interventions that help this person recover from their illness, do not impose disability, and keep him or her as mobile and active as possible. This level of care may be difficult to determine and may need to be changed as the patient's status changes. All attempts to have the person move, participate in their own care and health care decisions, and perform as much self-care as possible, should be viewed as therapeutic.

Assessment of functional status, cognition and behavior, and social supports beginning on admission and continuing throughout the patient's hospital stay will help the nurse plan care. Discussing the patient in a regularly scheduled intradisciplinary forum, in which assessment data is presented, will allow care providers the opportunity to establish realistic goals for the patient. Patient and family input into this discussion is essential.

As an example, assessment of mobility is an important component of functional assessment. Lewis (1989) approaches improving mobility in the elderly through planning care at each stage of what she describes as the mobility spectrum, starting with bed mobility and continuing to ambulation. Nurses often incorporate many of these concepts into care of older persons without recognizing the therapeutic potential of their activity.

In addition to these approaches, group exercise programs can be planned as part of the care. Payton and Poland (1983) described two studies in which exercise programs made a significant difference in the status of the elderly. Although this type of program may be difficult to support within the hectic environment of an acute care unit, there are those who could benefit from the exercise as well as the stimulation and social interaction. Paillard and Nowak (1985) developed a group exercise program for elderly patients on a 36 bed acute medical unit within a large urban medical center. They discovered that this program increased the activity tolerance of those patients who participated.

Several studies have found geriatric assessment units and geriatric rehabilitation units to be particularly effective in providing care tailored to the needs of older people with functional loss (Liem, Chernoff, & Carter, 1986; Rubinstein et al., 1984; Schuman, Beattie, Steed, Merry, & Kraus, 1981).

Rehabilitation in the Community Setting

The comprehensive approach described in the acute hospital can be applied in a variety of settings, providing a framework for nursing interventions that have a rehabilitation focus. In the community setting, where the goal of keeping the older person in their own environment for as long as possible requires a certain level of independent function or a caregiver, rehabilitation approaches are necessary. If the older adult is in need of supportive services, an in-depth assessment of functional, affective, cognitive, and social-economic factors should be performed prior to the initiation of any program of care. Obtaining this baseline data will provide community care staff, the client, and the family the information needed to plan for interventions and specific services. Keeping older persons medically and nutritionally stable, while requiring them to maintain maximum levels of mobility and self-care activity, are important aspects of these interventions. Supportive services such as visiting nurses, physical and occupational therapy, and home health aides may provide the missing link in the elderly person's ability to remain in their own home. If the older person is frail and family supports are not available throughout the day, day-care programs provide a more structured protective environment.

CONCLUSION

In this chapter we have presented a rehabilitation approach to the nursing care of the older person. It is the authors' belief, that by utilizing a multidimensional approach to the assessment and treatment of actual or potential problems, the rate of deterioration from chronic conditions can be minimized and active life expectancy extended.

Although we have described specific areas within rehabilitation nursing practice that can enhance the quality of life for this population, we believe that there are many areas of needed nursing investigation. These include: measurement of environmentally induced disability, consensus building regarding standards of practice, identification of nursing interventions as a separate form of therapy; association of cognitive decline and physical well-being; and the burden of the accumulative effects of co-morbid diseases. With the application of rehabilitation principles to all aspects of care, we can hopefully offer the elderly a more positive approach to treatment of their illnesses.

REFERENCES

Avorn J., & Langer, E. (1982). Induced disability in nursing home patients: A controlled trial. *Journal of the American Geriatrics Society, 30,*(6), 397-400.

Bachman D., Linn R., Wolf, P. A., Knoefel, J., White, L., & D'Agostino, R. (1989). Influence on cognitive decline with advancing age: Preliminary results of the Framingham study. *Neurology,* (Supp. 1), *39,* 285.

Berkman, L., Berkman, C., Kasl, S., Freeman D. H., Leo, L., Ostfeld, A. M., Coroni-Huntley, J., & Brody, J. (1986). Depressive symptoms in relation to physical health and functioning in the elderly. *American Journal of Epidemiology, 124,* 372-388.

Bortz, W. N. (1990). The trajectory of dying: Functional status in the last year of life. *Journal of the American Geriatric Society, 38,* 146-150.

Branch, L., & Jette, A. (1981). The Framingham disability study: Social disability among the elderly. *American Journal of Public Health, 71,* 1202-1210.

Charlton, J. R. H., Patrick, D. L., & Peach, H. (1983). Use of multivariate measures of disability in health surveys. *Journal of Epidemiology and Community Health, 37,* 296-304.

Colvez, A., & Blanchet, M. (1981). Disability trends in the United States population 1966-76: Analysis of reported causes. *American Journal of Public Health, 71,* 464-470.

Cummins, J. L., & Benson, D. F. (1983). *Dementia: A clinical approach.* Boston: Buttersworth.

Doty, P. (1986). Family care of the elderly: The role of public policy. *Milbank Memorial Fund Quarterly, 64,* 34-75.

Evans, D. A., Funkenstein, H. H., Albert, M., Scherr, P. A., Cook, N., Chown, M. J., Herbert, L. E., Henneken, C., & Taylor, J. O. (1989). Prevalence of Alzheimer's disease in community population of older persons. *Journal of the American Medical Association, 262,* 2551-2556.

Fries, J. (1980). Aging, natural death and the compression of morbidity. *New England Journal of Medicine, 303*(3), 130-135.

Fulton, J., Katz, S., Jack, S., & Hendershot, G. (1989). Physical functioning of the aged: United States, 1984. National Center for Health Statistics. Vital and Health Statistics, Series 10, No. 167.

Guralnik, J., & Kaplan, G. (1989). Predictions of healthy aging: Prospective evidence from the Alameda County study. *American Journal of Public Health, 79,* 703-708.

Guralnik, J. M., LaCroix A. Z., & Everett, D. F. (1989). *Morbidity and Mortality Weekly Report, 38,*(46), 788-789.

Harris, T., Kovor, M. G., Suzman, R., Kleiman, J. C., & Feldman, J. J. (1989). Longitudinal study of physical disability in the oldest old. *American Journal of Public Health, 79*(8), 698-702.

Hesse, K., & Campion, E. (1983). Motivating the geriatric patient for rehabilitation. *Journal of the American Geriatrics Society, 31*(10), 586-589.

Jette, A., & Branch, L. (1981). The Framingham disability study: Physical disability among the aging. *American Journal of Public Health, 71,* 1211-1216.

Kane, R. A., & Kane, R. L. (1981). *Assessing the elderly.* Lexington, MA: Lexington Books.

Katz, S., Branch, L., Branson, M., Papsidero, J., Beck, J., & Greer, D. (1983). Active life expectancy. *New England Journal of Medicine, 309*(20), 1218-1224.

Katzman, R., & Terry, R. (1983). *The neurology of aging.* Philadelphia: F. A. Davis.

Kelly-Hayes, M., Wolf, P. A., Kannel, W.,B., Sytowski, W., D'Agostino, R., & Gresham, G. (1988). Factors influencing survival and the need for institutionalization following stroke: The Framingham study. *Archives of Physical Medicine and Rehabilitation, 69,* 415-418.

Kelly-Hayes, M., Jette, A. M., Wolf, P. A., D'Agostino, R. B., Odell, P. (in press). Defining the difference between physical limitations and disability among elders in the Framingham cohort. *American Journal of Public Health.*

Kennie, D. (1983). Good health care of the aged. *Journal of the American Medical Association, 249,*(6), 770-773.

Lewis, C. (1989). *Improving mobility in older persons.* Rockville, MD: Aspen Publications.

Liem P., Chernoff, R., & Carter, W. (1986). Geriatric evaluation unit: A three year outcome evaluation. *Journal of Gerontology, 41*(1), 44-50.

Mahoney, F. J., & Barthel, W. (1965). Functional evaluations: The Barthel Index. *Maryland State Medical Journal, 14,* 61-65.

Manton, K. G. (1988). A longitudinal study of functional change and mortality in the United States. *Journal of Gerontology Social Science, 43,* s153-161.

Minaker, K., & Rowe, J. (1985). Health and disease among the oldest old: A clinical perspective. *Milbank Memorial Fund Quarterly, 63*(2), 324-349.

Morley, J. (1986). Nutritional status of the elderly. *The American Journal of Medicine, 81*(11), 679-694.

Mumma, C. (Ed.). (1987). *Rehabilitation nursing: Concepts and practice* (2nd ed.). Evanston, IL: Rehabilitation Nursing Foundation.

Nagi, S. Z. (1965). Some conceptual issues in disability and rehabilitation in the elderly. In M. B. Sussman (Ed.), *Sociology and rehabilitation.* Washington, DC: American Sociological Association.

Nagi, S. Z. (1969). *Disability and rehabilitation: Legal, clinical and measurement.* Columbus: Ohio State University Press.

Nagi, S. Z. (1976). An epidemiology of disability among adults in the United States. *Milbank Memorial Fund Quarterly, 54,* 439-467.

Paillard, M., & Nowak, K. (1985). Use of exercise to help older adults. *Journal of Gerontological Nursing, 11*(7), 36-39.

Payton, O., & Poland, J. (1983). Aging process: Implications for clinical practice. *Physical Therapy, 63*(1), 41-47.

Rice, D. (1989). Demographic realities and projections of an aging society. In S. Andrepoulos & J. Hogness (Eds.), *Health care for an aging society,* pp. 15-46. New York: Churchill Livingstone.

Rubinstein, L. (1987). Geriatric assessment: An overview of its impact. *Clinics in Geriatric Medicine, 3*(1), 1-15.

Rubinstein, L., Josephson, K., Weland, G., English, P., Sayre, J., & Kane, R. (1984). Effectiveness of geriatric evaluation units. *New England Journal of Medicine, 311*(26), 1664-1670.

Schuman, J., Beattie, E., Steed, D., Merry, G., & Kraus, A. (1981). Geriatric patients with and without intellectual dysfunction: Effectiveness of standard rehabilitation program. *Archives of Physical Medicine and Rehabilitation, 62*(12), 612-618.

Smith, K., & Lipman, A. (1986). Social needs of the disabled elderly: An interdisciplinary assessment of long-term care needs. *Topics in Geriatric Rehabilitation, 1*(2), 58-69.

Uniform Data System for Medical Rehabilitation. (1987). Buffalo, NY: State University of New York Press.

Warshaw, G., Moore, J., Friedman, W., Currie, C., Kennie, D. C., Kane, W., & Mears, P. (1982). Functional disability in the hospitalized elderly. *Journal of the American Medical Association, 248*(7) 847-850.

Williams, T. F. (1980). Comprehensive functional assessment: An overview. *Journal of the American Geriatrics Society, 31*(11), 637-641.

Wolf, P. A., Bachman, D., & Kelly-Hayes, M. (1990). Stroke and depression in the community: The Framingham study. Manuscript submitted for publication.

Wood, P. H. N. (1975). *Classification of impairments and handicaps.* Geneva: World Health Organization.

Wood, P. H. N. (1980). The language of disablement: A glossary relating to disease and its consequence. *International Rehabilitation Medicine, 2,* 86-92.

World Health Organization. (1980). *International classification of impairments, disabilities, and handicaps* (A manual of classification relating to consequences of disease). Geneva: World Health Organization.

Young, M. (1989). A history of rehabilitation nursing. In *Fifteen years of making the difference.* Skokie, IL: Association of Rehabilitation Nurses.

Zadai, C. (1985). Pulmonary physiology of aging: The role of rehabilitation. *Topics in Geriatric Rehabilitation, 1*(1), 1-15.

21

Selected Ethical and Legal Issues in Aging

Sister ROSE THERESE BAHR

Objectives: At the completion of this chapter the reader will be able to:

(1) Evaluate ethical issues affecting older adults and the role of the gerontological nurse.
(2) Critique legal issues involving health care for older Americans.
(3) Analyze human subjects' concerns related to research involving older adults.
(4) Implement nursing strategies to assist older adults to obtain and retain basic human rights.

INTRODUCTION

When society is examined closely in relation to its care of the elderly population, one sees the values embraced by that society. In American society a phenomenon never experienced before in this country is occurring—the graying of its citizenry. In the United States 12%-13% of the population is more than 65 years of age with the fastest growing segment being those 85 and older, who may be experiencing frailness and chronic debilitation (National Center for Health Statistics, 1989). It is estimated that over 20 million elderly persons reside in long-term care facilities, programs, or homes such as board and care homes, nursing homes, adult day-care programs, hospices, respite care, penal or correction institutions, acute care hospitals, and single room occupancy hotels or rooms in metropolitan cities throughout the nation (Harper, 1990; Thompson, 1986). It is this large assemblage of older individuals that is drawing the attention of health policy makers, legislators, ethicists, educators, futurists, and health professionals—especially in the arena of gerontological nursing. The major focus of these groups is the sense of being overwhelmed by the sheer numbers of persons seeking assistance from the health care delivery system. Gerontological nurses are in the front lines of providing care and are caught in the middle of the major controversies regarding such care. The focus of this chapter is to examine selected ethical and legal issues facing older adults and implications for gerontological nursing.

ETHICAL ISSUES

Ethical issues abound when discussing the older adults in the United States. Issues are related to authority for decision making, autonomy, beneficence, justice, paternalism, euthanasia, reduction of programs for the elderly in the community, preadmission screening prior to being given permission to enter a long-term care facility, and inherent rights of older adults in society. There are numerous issues—more than the scope of this chapter will allow—regarding description and indepth analysis. One thing is certain, ethics involves individuals and society (Harper, 1990; Aroskar, 1987).

Rights of Older Adults

Every individual including the older person has rights that are accorded because of his or her innate humanness (Benjamin & Curtis, 1981). When the person becomes ill or debilitated, those rights remain. The right to life, liberty, and the pursuit of happiness are basic rights accorded every individual. Other rights that older people should enjoy include the right to refuse treatment or medication, to informed consent, to see family and visitors as they choose, to receive mail unopened, to privacy, to prompt medical care and treatment, to be free from procedures that are injurious to their health status, to express their religious preferences freely and without ridicule, and to freedom from restraints or any other device or mode of treatment that is only for staff convenience (Keglovits, 1983). These rights should be common knowledge for any health professional and should be incorporated into any plan of care formulated for older adults. But within each of these rights is the potential for ethical dilemmas. Gerontological nurses must be extremely alert to situations that have the capability of creating injustices for older adults, whatever the health delivery setting.

The ethical issues to be addressed in this chapter include: restraint use for the elderly, elder abuse, and suicide. Each of these issues will be discussed in light of the impact on society at large and gerontological nursing in particular.

Restraint Use for the Elderly

When one contemplates the right to liberty that each older person enjoys by virtue of being a human individual, the ethical dilemma conjured up in the mind when the inordinate use of restraints are employed becomes exceedingly overpowering. The powerlessness imposed on an older adult when in restraints is beyond description if one has not experienced such shacklement. The restraint becomes the vehicle of control rather than the older person maintaining control over his or her person and environment.

Gerontological nurses have a moral responsibility to assess each and every older adult for his or her particular circumstances prior to the automatic inclusion of restraints as an integral part of the nursing care plan. The following questions should be included as part of the assessment. Should this older person who may wander and fall be restricted in movement and mobility by being fastened to a piece of furniture, such as a bed, wheelchair, geri-chair? Should the focus be on the dignity and respect each older person is entitled to or should the nurse consider more favorably the potential litigation from an administrative/professional point of view (Calfee, 1988; Harper, 1990). Restraints, including mechanical and chemical, are becoming an embarrassment across the nation as legislators, policymakers, and nurse researchers are demonstrating major issues in the ethical realm that constitute an affront against the person of the older adult. In December, 1989, in Washington, D.C., a congressional symposium and hearing were held at the request of gerontological nursing on the many ethical issues surrounding the use of restraints in long-term care settings. The symposium was titled "Untie the Elderly." Much research was presented demonstrating that few situations called for the use of restraints if excellent assessment of the older adult/resident was performed and a care plan implemented with the focus on the rights of the older person, not the wishes of the family or the health facility policies. The restraint usage demonstrates a critical need of gerontological nurses to understand the physiological changes within the older person when becoming immobile through such a mechanism. The person's physical and psychological well-being begins to diminish immediately. Psychological depression, apathy, and low spirit-titre projects the individual into a negative orientation of "don't care anymore." This debilitating stance can move the person toward suicidal thoughts and behaviors.

In terms of the debilitating physiological changes, the restrained older person experiences cardiac and respiratory changes because of the restricted position in the bed or sitting for long hours without change of position in geri- or wheelchairs. Fluid intake is restricted because the individual cannot freely drink beverages because his or her hands are usually tied in such a manner that reaching is impossible beyond a small range of motion.

Restraint-free environments are slowly making their way into long-term care facilities where qualified gerontological nursing staff carry out the philosophy of care that older adults do not lose their rights to freedom of movement or decision making. The person who can judge what is best for their care is the older person him- or herself, in conjunction with informed family members and health professionals. The Health Care Financing Administration (HCFA) suggested a ruling that "the resident has a right to be free from unnecessary drugs and physical restraints and is provided treatment to reduce dependency on drugs and physical restraints." This proposed rule was made a condition for Medicare program participation in October, 1989 (Federal Register, 1989, p. 5322).

SUICIDE AMONG OLDER ADULTS

As noted earlier, 13% of the U.S. population is 65 years and older and 17%-25% of the annually reported suicides occur in this group. Suicide among older people is on the rise in the United States. Suicidal rate for older adults rose from 17.1 (per 100,000) in 1981, to 21.5 (per 100,000) in 1986 (Brant & Osgood, 1990).

It is estimated that 1.5 million older adults live in 24,000 long-term care facilities in the United States (National Center for Health Statistics, 1986). These institutionalized persons are sicker, older, and may not have any significant person such as family that may show care and concern for them. These are conditions that may place them "at risk" for suicide. To help prevent suicide among the group should be a concern for gerontological nurses from a professional, ethical, and humanitarian perspective.

Limited research in the area of suicide among institutionalized elderly has been conducted. In 1986, a national study of this phenomenon was conducted by Osgood, Brant, and Lipman (1987), with questionnaires mailed to 1,080 administrators and directors of nursing in long-term care settings nationally. Data were collected in years 1984 and 1985 on incidences of overt suicides—for example, hanging, shooting, and life-threatening behaviors of an intentional nature, refusal of fluid, food, medication. Responses to the questionnaires came from 463 facilities (43%); at least one instance of suicidal behavior during the data collection period was reported by 84 facilities. Others had identified 1 to 9 suicidal behaviors (Osgood et al., 1987).

Gerontological nurses are presented with ethical dilemmas when potential suicidal behaviors emerge in the course of providing care to institutionalized older adults. Of great concern is the need for nurses to perform in-depth psychosocial assessments on older adults who are lonely; suffer from losses; are socially isolated, rejected, or abandoned by family/significant other; depressed; or socially withdrawn. Of particular importance to detect are the major and multiple losses the older person is facing, for example, spouse, friends, control, money, pets, physical mobility, independence, sensory-perceptual losses, home, freedom, autonomy, privacy, and possessions (Osgood et al., 1989). An older adult who is becoming more and more dependent suffers the loss of self-esteem and self-worth as well. Nurses who practice with older adults must always be alert to comments made by the person, and any self-destructive remark is to be taken seriously. Proper referrals should be made following discussion with the person and the family. Long-term care settings should have a nurse consultant, such as a geropsychiatric nurse with proper credentialing, who can assist the staff nurses properly assess and plan interventions. These interventions should be planned in such a way that they will assist the older person to perceive his or her life as worthwhile, meaningful, and with a future. The climate in a long-term care facility must foster mental health and treat any and all conditions pointing to self-destruction as a crisis for intervention. The *Ethical Code for Nurses* suggests that no harm be done to clients receiving nursing care. More astute observation and assessment skills are needed by gerontological nurses in institutional settings (Harper, 1990; Kramer, 1986).

Another recently reported ethical phenomenon is the "assisted suicide" of older adults who freely choose to terminate their lives through drugs, for example, potassium overdose administered intravenously by a physician or health provider. Major ethical controversy has emanated from the one reported case in May, 1990 from the State of Washington where a 56 year old woman afflicted with an early stage of Alzheimer's disease had the physician insert the needle into her arm and initiate the flow of normal saline solution. When she was ready for the procedure, she herself turned the clamp that allowed the potassium to drip into her body via the IV tubing. She was dead within seconds. This case has set a precedent for the medical world and much publicity was given via newspaper, television, and radio. Even though the physician has been criticized by his medical colleagues in the American Medical Society, older adults now see this procedure as a painless approach to terminating their lives at will and when they have determined they choose not to live any longer. The ethical ramifications from this one case will have far-reaching implications in our society. Gerontological nurses need to be aware of the emergence of this type of thinking within medical circles that could impact on the role of the nurse caring for older adults within institutional settings and in community settings.

ELDER ABUSE

A growing national problem of grave ethical concern in gerontological nursing is the area of elder abuse. This phenomenon is defined as "any action on the part of an elderly person's family . . . or professional caretaker to take advantage of his person, property, or emotional well-being through threat of violence, use of disciplinary restraint or use of negligence on the part of the caretaker to provide basic needs" (Kimsey, Tarbox, & Bragg, 1981, p. 468) (see Chapter 12).

The scope of the problem of elder abuse is increasing at a phenomenal rate. Congressional hearings and a national study were undertaken by the House Selection Committee on Aging in 1978. A report entitled *Elder Abuse: An Examination of a Hidden Problem* (U.S. House of Representatives, 1981) provided the following information:

(1) Elder abuse is a full-scale national problem which exists with a frequency and rate only slightly less than that of child abuse.

(2) An estimated 4% of the nation's elderly, one million older Americans, are victims of some sort of abuse, from moderate to severe, each year.

(3) While one out of three cases of child abuse is reported, only one out of six cases of elder abuse comes to the attention of the authorities.

(4) The victims are likely to be very old—75 or older. Women are more often abused than men. The victims are usually in a position of dependency; i.e., they rely on others, often the persons who abuse them, for their care and protection.

(5) The probable abuser will undoubtedly be experiencing great stress. Alcoholism, drug addiction, marital problems, and long term financial difficulties are often factors in abuse of older persons.

(6) The most likely abuser is the son of the victim (21% of cases) followed by the daughter (17% of cases). The third most frequent abuser is the spouse who acts in a caregiver role, with the male spouse more likely to be the abuser than the female spouse.

(7) Older persons are less likely to report abuse, because they are ashamed, do not wish to bring trouble to the family, are afraid of reprisals or do not have the physical ability to register complaints. (Oaker & Miller, 1983, pp. 431-432)

Gerontological nurses once again come to the forefront of this ethical dilemma when making home visits, assessing older clients/patients/residents in hospital units or long-term care settings. Fulmer and Ashley (1986) projected the possible cumulative effects of age, disease and neglect leading to abuse as noted in Figure 21.1.

Table 21.1 by Fulmer and Ashley describes clinical examples that project indicators of neglect with possible cause. According to this model, indicators of neglect are a result of age, disease, and abuse.

Elder abuse in the physical realm includes beatings, whippings, hittings, and burns (including scalding) that may result in fractures and/or bruises, physical harm, self-neglect, and difficulty or failure in care of personal needs. Neglectful behaviors by caretakers may include food and medication deprivation, lack of proper or sufficient clothing or shelter and essential devices such as eyeglasses,

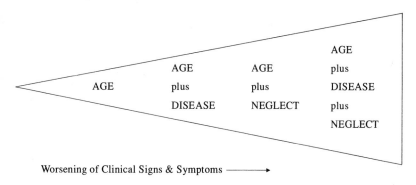

Figure 21.1. Possible Cumulative Effects of Age, Disease, and Neglect Leading to Abuse

Source: Fulmer, T., & Ashley, J. (1986). Neglect: What part of abuse? *Price Institute Journal of Long Term Home Health Care, 5*(4), 21. (Permission to reprint granted.)

dentures, walkers, canes, wheelchairs, and hearing aids. Sometimes the delay experienced by older persons in the care provided by family/neighbor/friend in such areas as manhandling of administration of medication, infections caused by incontinence, and inappropriate diet, is border-line abuse (Block, 1983).

Psychological abuse may result from such behaviors toward the elderly as placing the individual in seclusion or locked in his or her room to prevent the behavior of wandering, being humiliated and treated as a child, verbal assaults, name calling, threats against the freedom of choice, and poor environmental conditions, as well as inappropriate feeding, grooming, and personal care (Harper, 1990).

Gerontological nursing approaches to reduce the ethical dilemma and prevent elder abuse include:

(1) Closely examine older adults during home visits,
(2) Examine older individuals for signs of abuse on admission to any health care facility,
(3) Determine if older adults are reluctant to self-report abusive behaviors at home for fear of retaliation or abandonment by the caregiver,
(4) Determine if the spouse or caretaker seems fearful when the nurse is in the home,
(5) Report any suspected cases of elder abuse for further investigation to safeguard the rights of the older persons regarding preservation of life (Harper, 1990).

Table 21.1
Two Examples of Indicators of Neglect, with Possible Causes

		Possible Causes		
Indicator of Neglect	*Age*	*Age Plus Disease*	*Age Plus Neglect*	*Age Plus Disease Plus Neglect*
Fracture	Osteoporosis	Osteoporosis plus stress fracture	Osteoporosis plus inadequate assistance with ambulation	Osteoporosis plus stress fracture due to inadequate assistance with ambulation
Poor Hygiene	Decreased visual acuity	Decreased visual acuity plus rheumatoid arthritis	Decreased visual acuity plus inadequate self-washing leading to poor hygiene	Decreased visual acuity plus rheumatoid arthritis (pain) leading to inadequate self-washing & resultant poor hygiene

Source: Fulmer, T., & Ashley, J. (1986). Neglect: What part of abuse? *Pride Institute Journal of Long Term Health Care, 5*(4), 21. (Permission to reprint granted.)

In summary, the ethical issues in gerontological nursing of restraint use, suicide among older adults, and elder abuse span the home setting and hospital/long-term care settings. Gerontological nurses are morally responsible for the well-being of older adults entrusted to their care and must be observant for any ethical violations that may bring harm or injury to their personhood.

In addition to ethical issues, many legal issues are faced by older adults. The next section will discuss selected legal issues that influence gerontological nursing practice.

LEGAL ISSUES

Issues of living regarding older adults sometimes move ethical phenomena into the legal system of justice for discussion, deliberation, and decisions where fairness to all parties is present. Three legal issues of critical importance in the contemporary United States that have major ramifications for older adults and gerontological nursing include quality of life issues, especially Do Not Resuscitate (DNR) orders by family and/or physician; mental competence issues regarding guardianship and durable power of attorney; and rationing or limiting of care due to limited resources—for example, health care dollars to be spent on older adults versus younger children with provision of basic health needs.

QUALITY OF LIFE

A great difficulty exists in adequately defining "quality of life" because it is such an individual experience. Each person has his or her own perception of what quality of life means for them. What may be a pitfall for one person in terms of some circumstance/event may be seen as a positive aspect of life for another individual. So, too, with older adults. Gerontological nurses cannot assume that disabilities such as arthritis, cardiac disease, or major chronic illnesses reduce the quality of life for aging people. Older adults perceive the quality of life in terms of the influence of their culture, education, previous life-style, family strengths, health care beliefs, and community life integral to their lives.

In long-term care settings, gerontological nurses are dedicated to improving the quality of life or institutionalized elderly by health promotion, holistic nursing interventions, and maximizing functional independence and capacity. The Institute of Medicine (1986) in its report titled *Improving the Quality of Care in Nursing Homes* indicated the importance of quality of life as "intimately related to the quality of care, but encompassing a resident's sense of well-being, level of satisfaction with life and feeling of self-worth and self-esteem" (p. 371). The National Citizens Coalition for Nursing Home Reform conducted a study (Karen, 1988) and asked residents of nursing homes to indicate the quality of life issues important to them. These issues include environment, facility philosophy, interactions, security, choice and informed decision making, activities, privacy,and personal, social, and spiritual life. Factors found by Holder and Frank (1988) for additional aspects of quality of life include maintaining the most desirable physical status including exercise, activities, minimizing pain and discomfort, and maximizing functional potential; personal control, self-determinism, participation in civic functions, involvement in group activities and group decision making, cheerfulness, and kindness shown to older adults by others; excellent listening skills, attitudes of persons one lives with that are supportive, empathic, positive, and constructive as well as sympathetic; surroundings that are comfortable, attractive, and clean; positive relationships with peers, family, and staff; and, presentation of one's self in the chosen life-style from a positive perspective.

Many legal questions surround the quality of life issues but none more than DNR (do not resuscitate) orders and the accompanying issue of employing or not employing the cardiopulmonary resuscitation (CPR) procedure (Moseley, 1989; "Life-Sustaining", 1987). Many gerontological nurses may have difficulty not invoking this procedure when a medical crisis occurs and may react negatively when families and or physicians invoke the legal status of the DNR code. Because it is the nurse who attends the aging person throughout the terminal stage of illness and the dying process it becomes extremely frustrating to attempt to keep the person comfortable when a life-threatening struggle ensues and the nurse is requested to stand by and do nothing to intervene. The critical question is very present: At what point does a poor quality of life emerge in the life of an individual that warrants a "slow code" or "no code" decision? The burden is placed on gerontological nurses to carry out the legally written order. To question the order may invoke anger from both the physician and family who believe that the procedure is in the best interest of the aging, terminally ill person. If a slow-code means failure to provide physical comfort and psychological support, however, it is never justified.

Within the legal context of quality of life and basic rights of older adults regarding decision-making are the additional issues that create dilemmas for health professionals including the right to death with dignity and the implementation of the person's wishes for treatment/non-treatment described in a document identified as the "living will." As medical science discovers advanced methods for prolongation of life, more and more "right to die" cases are being presented to the legal courts for decisions to terminate life-sustaining technologies such as respirators and food/fluid continuation in comatose persons. The right of each older person to the final stages of living in a dignified, respectful manner is inherent within his/her personhood as a human being. To experience one's dying process and eventual death in a peaceful manner and environment surrounded by caring, supportive individuals (family, spouse, friends, health professionals) is to achieve the ultimate right inherent in the quality of life. Noteworthy is the increasing number of families who are requesting that their loved ones return to the home setting for such eventual demise with perhaps the utilization of hospice personnel. This trend suggests that older adults prefer the familiarity of their homes with people they love to care for them when their final moments of life arrive. Truly to be treated respectfully and with dignity during the dying process and death is the wish of each person, but especially the older adult who can review life as a worthwhile journey and who now passes on his or her life's achievements to those he or she loves (Degner & Beaton, 1987; Hastings Center, 1987; Office of Technology Assessment, 1987). As more and more legal cases are tried in the courts, however, the right to die with dignity is slipping away from the control of the older individual and the family to agencies in our society. This loss of control becomes a critical area that needs major attention from gerontological nurses. Advocacy for older adults for the maintenance of mastery over their own lives without legal intervention is a professional responsibility for nurses who are qualified in the care of older adults.

Discussions occurring in legal circles regarding the living will and its implementation has given rise to much speculation for health professionals (Harper, 1990). A living will is a document that describes in detail what treatments are preferred or not preferred by the individual in circumstances where his or her quality of life has decreased due to physical/mental conditions and where the individual no longer has the capacity or capability of decision making in keeping with his or her wishes. This document is signed in the presence of a legal representative. Health professionals, especially gerontological nurses, must be acutely aware upon assessment of older adults in institutionalized settings whether a living will has been filed with a lawyer by this person, whether family members are aware of the existence of such a document and agree with its contents, and whether the state in which care of the older person is initiated holds the document bound by legal ramifications. Not all states in the United States recognize the living will as a legal document but it does contain the older person's medical treatment preferences, which should be honored in most circumstances. This issue continues to provoke major discussions in legal and ethical circles. Gerontological nurses must keep abreast of these developments so as to be advocates for the older adults in their care.

Legal questions arise over what standard is applied when assessing another person's life and its quality (Moseley, 1989). In the final stages of life it is only the person who is able to decide if his or her continued quality of life warrants the possible burdens of the CPR procedure or a DNR order. Truly these are thought-provoking issues to be pondered by gerontological nurses in all settings of care.

MENTAL CAPACITY/COMPETENCY DETERMINATION

Legal battles are fought over issues related to the definition of mental capacity/competency of individuals. The President's Commission report (1983) referred to persons "with decision-making capacity" and those "who lack decision-making capacity." Words such as "competent" or "incompetent" were not used in the report. These words are used interchangeably in terms of legal usage, however.

The Hastings Center (1987, p. 55) defined decision-making capacity as the ability of the person to "comprehend information relevant to the decision; deliberate about the choices in accordance with personal values and goals; and communicate (verbally or nonverbally) with caregivers." Despite which definition of cognitive ability is used, nurses who care for the elderly frequently encounter problems related to this area.

Gerontological nurses become involved in legal issues when the mental capability or capacity of an older adult is assessed as less than adequate to continue responsibility for his or her own life, from a personal perspective and for the decisions to be made to maintain normalcy of living. Documentation in the nursing charts of the behaviors of older adults may be subpoenaed and brought to court for determination if another person should be designated as the legal guardian of the older adult. According to Henderson and McConnell (1988), guardianship is a legal procedure that allows another person to exercise individual rights for an aging individual who is no longer mentally competent. It is designed to protect the individual and their property when the older person is not able to manage their affairs (Harper, 1986). Sometimes the power of attorney is granted to another individual, which is seen as voluntary guardianship where a competent individual freely selects a surrogate decision maker to handle all aspects of their affairs.

Gerontological nurses should be alert to any mental changes and developments or onset of decisional incapacity in older adults under their care. When such changes are noted and verified through thorough testing, the gerontological nurses should draw attention to this condition in the older adult by making the proper referrals and informing the physician and/or family for further action.

RATIONING OF HEALTH CARE

A very controversial legal issue in contemporary America is the rationing of health care with the targeted population being older adults. This discussion has emerged from viewpoints offered on the subject by former Governor Richard Lamm of Colorado and Hastings Center Director, Daniel Callahan. Their remarks suggest that when "a moderate shortage of health care resources exist, rationing of resources is necessary" (Callahan, 1987; Lamm, 1986). They comment further that health care should be provided "to those who will benefit most and rationed from those who will benefit less, such as the elderly" (Callahan, 1987; Lamm, 1986; Perrin, 1989). It is well known that approximately 35 million Americans lack health insurance and access to health care (Perrin, 1989).

Lamm has suggested that rationing of care occurs in today's society already, but it is neither planned or justly rationed. Millions of dollars in health care are spent for individuals with highly complex conditions and utilization of highly advanced medical technology. He states that rationing is now accomplished chronologically, geographically, scientifically, economically, and by disease and employment (Perrin, 1989). Suggestions were made that rationing of health care by age would be more just and provide better use of limited resources. This appears to many gerontological nurses and other groups to be discriminatory against the elderly of our society (American Nurses' Association, 1980a).

Callahan (1987) puts forth the argument that a natural life span should conclude with a natural death. That period in the aged persons' life comes when one's work in life has been accomplished and the persons for whom the individual is responsible are now independent and no longer are in need of the guidance of the older person. Another aspect of the natural life span argument is identified in the consideration of the dying process of the aged person in that it should not be too wracked with too much pain and the death of the person is not perceived as an offense to anyone's sensibility (Perrin, 1989). Callahan suggests that when the end of the natural life span for an individual has occurred, somewhere between ages 78-82 years of age, no life-extending technologies should be employed to attempt to avoid a natural death. Further, he notes that without the use of the natural life span as a guide, it could be unclear to health professionals when to determine, as acute episodes of illness occur in the continuum of life, when the person is dying (Callahan, 1987). In contrast, in most civilized nations the elderly, though less productive in a material sense, have always been valued for their wisdom, insight, and love to guide the younger, less experienced generations. Not to value one generation based on material productivity is to devalue all stages of human life that exist in both the natural and spiritual realms.

Hearings of allocation of health care resources are taking place in the Senate and House of Representatives, as well as on the State level—Oregon, for example. These activities will be followed by legislators drafting decisions concerning health care allocations basing their guidelines on actions that demonstrate that resource scarcity does indeed exist and deciding on what principles to utilize when distributing those resources (Perrin, 1989). In addition, the prospective payment plan, diagnostic review groupings (DRGs) limits the use of acute care facilities by the elderly who need nursing and medical care in hospitals.

Gerontological nurses need to become highly knowledgeable about these arguments and the legislative proposals emanating from these discussions. Political savvy is a responsibility for each gerontological nurse to appreciate the intricacies of the philosophical arguments presented and the resulting decisions that will be legally binding on the current group of older adults and for those many generations of persons to come. To set limits merely on the factor of age is demeaning and sets limits to the potential growth and development of each and every older person. Each gerontological nurse is urged to become an advocate of the aged so that the precious talents of these individuals are not lost simply through the dynamics of politics and the projections of researchers. Surely the creativity of nurses can develop alternative modalities to allow the aged to live out their lives in the assurance that their health care needs at whatever age will be addressed and the proper treatment initiated to ensure a life relatively free from pain and discomfort.

RESEARCH AND OLDER ADULTS: ANALYSIS OF HUMAN SUBJECTS' CONCERNS

Ethical and legal issues in gerontological nursing give rise to innumerable research questions that need to be addressed by nurse researchers. Research agenda development through the Delphi survey process is integral to addressing critical questions/areas as identified by nurse experts. Examples of such research agenda development include the *Long Term Care Nursing Research Agenda for the 1990's* by Haight and Bahr (1990), and the *Mental Illness in Nursing Homes: Agenda for Research* by Harper and Lebowitz (1986). These agendas project the research needs of older adults in multiple settings and on multi-dimensional levels, for example patient care needs; physiological, psychological, and spiritual needs of older adults; safety measures; reduction of medication errors; lowering of psychotropic drug usage; depression in elderly clients; home health care needs; wellness and health maintenance among elderly persons; and a host of other researchable topics. The purpose of research is to improve the quality of life and nursing care to older adults.

Key to conducting nursing research is the selection of populations and samples from among older persons (Burns & Grove, 1987). This selection process may bring to the surface a host of concerns that must be addressed by the nurse researcher prior to the completion of the research proposal and the data collection phase. Three major concerns include appropriate research designs, human subjects protection, and informed consent. An analysis of these concerns follow.

Research designs used in gerontological nursing may be qualitative, quantitative, or a triangulation design that includes both qualitative and quantitative methodological approaches (Burns & Grove, 1987). When a researcher selects the qualitative design approach care must be given in selection of a population that has the capacity for reliable self-report. This concern gives attention to establishing precise selection criteria so that the data requested from the aging population will be adequate, valid, and reliable for analysis and the drawing of conclusions to the projected research question. When one is restricted in this manner for subject selection the question becomes one of appropriate representation of the data to truly provide adequate insight into the phenomena under study. This concern becomes a vital issue if the nurse researcher is attempting to gain insight into the experiential data inherent within older subjects. When the quantitative design is used, concerns arise in terms of appropriate tools for data collection. Many available tools in the literature have not been tested with an aging population. Consequently the results of these measures may not be representative of the population under study. Another concern is the administration of such instruments. Oftentimes, older subjects cannot easily answer the formatting of an instrument, which can give rise to errors in responses or a confusion as to the exact response requested. Validity and reliability data may not be available for many tools, particularly as it relates to norming for an aging population. Therefore, appropriate research design concerns may be problematic for conducting research in gerontological nursing.

A second concern is human subjects protection (Burns & Grove, 1987). The protection of older subjects is a major responsibility of the nurse researcher conducting research in gerontological nursing. One of the major issues inherent in this concern is the confidentiality of subjects. At no time may the researcher divulge the name, address, place of residence, or any other data abut the subject when reporting the research findings in publications and/or presentations. All results are reported as group data. Any materials about the subject (e.g., demographic data, respondent's completed questionnaire, and/or interview materials) are to be kept in a safe location, preferably in a locked file where only the researcher has access to the materials. Each institution where research is conducted has the major responsibility for human subject protection. A special body/committee of researchers called the Institutional Review Board or Human Subject Concern Committee oversees the protection of human subjects in all ethical and legal aspects of research (Burns & Grove, 1987). Each researcher must receive full approval of the research proposal from this body to assure that no physical or psychological discomfort will be experienced by the subject during the course of data collection; and that confidentiality will be maintained at all times. The subjects are also assured that they may withdraw from the research study at any time without penalty or reprisal on the part of the nurse researcher.

The last concern is that of informed consent (Burns & Grove, 1987). The nurse researcher has the obligation to fully inform the older person who is the potential subject or their designated guardian about the study, their responsibilities as a participant in the study, what areas of discomfort they may potentially experience, expectations of results, the role of the nurse researcher, and implications for improvement of care for older adults. Only when the potential subjects fully understands their role in the study, have had their questions answered to their satisfaction, and believe their participation will have positive outcomes for improving care may the researcher request their signature on the consent form. No amount of concern or any other form of pressure may be exerted on a potential subject. Permission to participate must be freely given.

Questions arise when the potential subject may be incapacitated in some manner, e.g., neurologically damaged, and yet research in this area would be extremely helpful to future populations. Informed consent, in these cases, is requested from the spouse, significant other, or family member—whomever the designated person is who has legal responsibility for protection of the person and their property.

Conducting research in gerontological nursing is exciting and challenging. Only through research can the scientific discipline of gerontological nursing develop the basis for improved care to older adults. This brief analysis of three major concerns in conducting nursing research provides insight into issues related to selection of appropriate research designs and instruments, human subjects protection, and informed consent. All gerontological nurses with appropriate training and education are to be nurse researchers. The field of gerontological nursing needs research to provide credibility to its function and application of research findings to improve care provided to older adults in all settings.

ETHICAL AND LEGAL ISSUES: IMPLICATIONS FOR GERONTOLOGICAL NURSING

The ethical issues affecting the lives of older adults in restraint use, rise in suicides, and elder abuse as well as the legal issues of quality of life, determination of mental capacity/competence, and the rationing of health care for older adults should be seen by gerontological nurses as calls for action. Action necessary is, first of all, to be highly informed and knowledgeable about the issues; to form informed opinions; and to communicate those opinions to legislators, ethicists, medical professionals, and interdisciplinary groups who provide care to older adults. The elderly of our country are under siege and need the support of advocates to fight what are their battles for life today and will become the battles for all of us in the future. One way to accomplish advocacy for older Americans, is the support of groups that lobby for elderly rights,including ANA and AARP. To keep perspective in gerontological nursing is to keep the older person in a clear focus. It is respect for life and individual choice that we in gerontological nursing are devoted to and we can tolerate no situation that diminishes that precious life and choice in any way. Gerontological nurses must be activists whose major concern is the well-being of older adults in settings where they may be found.

SUMMARY

Discussions centered on ethical and legal issues selected from numerous issues facing the older adult in society today. When the rights of older adults are under attack in various segments of contemporary society it is essential that professional gerontological nurses rise to the occasion and initiate advocacy for the elderly who so desperately need assistance. The autonomy, beneficence, and justice principles of ethical behaviors are key to the well-being of older adults and must be assured by the actions of gerontological nurses everywhere. The sanctity of life, honored by the Constitution of the United States, demands that we in gerontological nursing come to their aid at this time.

REFERENCES

American Nurses' Association. (1980a). *Ethical code for nurses and interpretative statements*. Kansas City, MO: American Nurses' Association.

American Nurses' Association. (1980b). *Nursing social policy statement*. Kansas City, MO: American Nurses' Association.

Aroskar, M. (1987). The interface of ethics and politics in nursing. *Nursing Outlook, 35*(6), 268-272.

Benjamin, M., & Curtis, J. (1981). *Ethics in nursing*. New York: Oxford University Press.

Block, M. D. (1983). Abuse of the elderly. In S. H. Kadish (Ed.), *Encyclopedia of crime and justice* (pp. 1635-1637). New York: Free press.

Brant, B. A., & Osgood, N. J. (1990). The suicidal patient and long-term care institutions. *Journal of Gerontological Nursing, 16*(2), 15-18.

Burns, N., & Grove, S. K. (1987). *The practice of nursing research: Conduct, critique and utilization*. Philadelphia: W. B. Saunders.

Calfee, B. E. (1988). Are you restraining your patient's rights? *Nursing, 88*,(5), 148-149.

Callahan, D. (1987). *Setting limits: Medical goals in an aging society*. New York: Simon & Schuster.

Degner, L. F., & Beaton, J. I. (1987). *Life-death decisions in health care*. New York: Hemisphere Publishing.

Federal Register. (1989, February 2). U.S. Department of Health and Human Services, H.C.F.A. Medicare, Medicaid Long Term Care Facilities, F. Vol. Rule, 10(2), p. 5322.

Fulmer, T., & Ashley, T. (1986). Neglect: What part of abuse? *Pride Institute Journal of Long Term Home Care, 5*(4), 21.

Haight, B., & Bahr, R. T. (1990). A report: Long term care nursing agenda for the 1990's. In *Indices of quality in long-term care: A proceedings*. New York: National League for Nursing.

Harper, M. S. (1986). Introduction. In M. S. Harper & B. D. Lebowitz (Eds.), *Mental illness in nursing homes: Agenda for research* (pp. 1-6). Washington, DC: Department of Health and Human Services.

Harper, M. S. (1990). Mental health and older adults. In M. O. Hogstel (Ed.), *Geropsychiatric nursing*. St. Louis: C. V. Mosby.

Harper, M. S., & Lebowitz, B. D. (Eds.). (1986). *Mental illness in nursing homes: Agenda for research. Washington, DC: Department of Health and Human Services*.

Hastings Center. (1987). *Guidelines on the termination of life-sustaining treatment and the care of the dying*. Bloomington: Indiana University Press.

Henderson, M. L., & McConnell, E. S. (1988). Ethical considerations. In M. A. Matteson & E. S. McConnell (Eds.), *Gerontological nursing*. Philadelphia: W. B. Saunders.

Holder, E. L., & Frank, B. (1988). Residents speak out on what makes quality. *Provider of Long-Term Care Professionals, 14*(12), 28-29.

Institute of Medicine. (1986). *Improving the quality of care in nursing homes*. Washington, DC: Government Printing Office.

Karen, M. J. (1988). Quality assurance in New York state: Resident-centered protocols, the basics. *Provider for Long-Term Care Professionals, 24*(12), 21-22.

Keglovits, J. (1983). Legal considerations in psychiatric nursing practice. In H. S. Wilson & C. R. Kneisl (Eds.), *Psychiatric nursing*. Menlo Park, CA: Addison-Wesley.

Kimsey, L. R., Tarbox, A. R., & Bragg, D. F. (1981). Abuse of the elderly—The hidden agenda, the caretakers and the categories of abuse. *Journal of the American Geriatric Society, 29*(10), 465-472.

Kramer, M. (1986). Trends of institutionalized and prevalence of mental disorders in nursing homes. In M. S. Harper & B. D. Lebowitz (Eds.), *Mental illness in nursing homes: Agenda for research*. Washington, DC: Department of Health and Human Services.

Lamm, R. D. (1986). Rationing of health care: The inevitable meets the unthinkable. *Nurse Practitioner, 11*(5), 581-583.

Life-sustaining technologies and the elderly. (1987). Washington, DC: Office of Technology Assessment.

Moseley, R. (1989). DNR: The continuing ethical problems. *Florida Nursing Review, 3*(4), 8-14.

National Center for Health Statistics. (1986). *Advance report of final mortality statistics. NCHS monthly vital statistics report 37* (6 suppl.) Washington, DC: Department of Health and Human Services.

National Center for Health Statistics. (1989). *Health of an aging America: 1989 bibliography.* Washington, DC: Department of Health and Human Services.

Oaker, A., & Miller, B. (1983). An overview of elder abuse. In J. L. Kosberg (Ed.), *Abuse and maltreatment of the elderly, causes and interventions*. New York: PSG Publication Company.

Osgood, N. J., Brant, B. A., & Lipman, A. (1987). Patterns of suicidal behaviors in long-term care facilities: A preliminary report on an on-going study. *Omega, 19*(1), 59-65.

Perrin, K. (1989). Rationing health care: Should it be done? *Journal of Gerontological Nursing, 15*(9), 10-14.

President's Commission for the Study of Ethical Problems in Medicine and Biomedical and Behavioral Research. (1983). *A report in the ethical, medical, and legal issues in treatment decisions*. Washington, DC: Government Printing Office.

Thompson, L. (1986, July 6). Why people age. *Washington Post*, pp. 11-12.

U.S. House of Representatives. (1981). *Elder abuse: An examination of a hidden problem.* Washington, DC: Government Printing Office.

Index

About the Editor

Elizabeth Murrow Baines, RN, Ph.D., is Professor of Nursing, College of Nursing, Clemson University, South Carolina. Her degrees include a master's in nursing, a post master's certificate of specialization in gerontology, and a doctoral degree from the University of Nebraska. She also served seven years in the Navy Nurse Corps, with one year of service onboard the *USS Sanctuary*. During this period of service she received the Naval Achievement Medal, National Defense Service Medal, Vietnam Service Medal with Bronze Star, and the Navy Unit Commendation Ribbon.

She has received research grants, including from the National Center for Nursing Research (NCNR), to investigate the outcomes of nursing intervention on the stress of older family caregivers and the functional status of the elder care recipient. She has presented research findings locally, nationally, and internationally, and has published in refereed journals and served as a reviewer. She initiated a support group for family caregivers in the College of Nursing, Nursing Center, and has been active on several local, state, and national organizations and boards. In 1988, she was awarded the "Excellence in Nursing Award" by Gamma Mu Chapter of Sigma Theta Tau.

About the Contributors

June C. Abbey, RN, Ph.D., FAAN, is Associate Dean, Research and Evaluation, and Director of the Center for Nursing Research, Vanderbilt University School of Nursing, Nashville, Tennessee. She is the Endowed Chair Holder of the Valere Blair Potter Distinguished Professor in Nursing; is a member of the Food and Drug Administration's General Hospital and Personal Use Devices Advisory Panel; and is co-investigator of a federally funded grant, "Nighttime Incontinence Care in Nursing Homes." Her many publications include topics on physiological aspects of aging, incontinence, and biomedical devices.

Faye G. Abdellah, RN, EdD, ScD, FAAN, was Deputy Surgeon General from 1981 to 1989, and is Sigma Theta Tau International's Distinguished Research Scholar. She was former chief advisor to the Surgeon General on long-term care policy, nursing and education, service, and research; and was actively involved in working with the Surgeon General in formation of health policies related to AIDS and in Surgeon General's workshops. While serving in this position, she developed the first comprehensive standards for skilled nursing and intermediate care facilities as well as the first patient classification system to be used in nursing homes. She is author or co-author of more than 131 publications on nursing, long-term care, and health research, including *Patient Centered Approaches to Nursing* and *Better Patient Care Through Nursing Research* (3rd. ed.). She is the recipient of 10 honorary degrees and of 63 professional and academic awards including the prestigious Allied Signal Award for contributions to health policies affecting older adults.

Sister **Rose Therese Bahr,** A.S.C., RN, Ph.D., FAAN, is Professor of Nursing and Chair, Division of Community Health Nursing at the Catholic University of America School of Nursing. She is a nurse gerontologist and has authored numerous articles and chapters in texts on gerontological nursing, elder abuse, ethical and legal issues facing older adults in contemporary society, as well as holistic nursing approaches in gerontological nursing. She is the co-author of the text, *The Aging Person: A Holistic Perspective,* which has received world-wide distribution and has been translated into Japanese. She is a consultant to programs preparing gerontological nurse clinical specialists in many national university settings. She currently is the Chair, Council of Gerontological Nursing, American Nurses' Association, and Program Chair for the Educational Conferences for the National Gerontological Nursing Association.

Jeanne Quint Benoliel, RN, DNSc, FAAN, is Professor Emeritus, Community Health Care Systems Department School of Nursing, University of Washington. A two-year study of women's adjustment postmastectomy at UCLA initiated her extensive research career. She has a wide range of publications and presentations to her credit. Her most recent research was a study of the influence of support on breast self-examination adherence by high-risk women and she has done extensive cancer research. She was the first holder of the Elizabeth Sterling Soule Nursing Professorship. She has served as director for funded training grants to prepare nurses for leadership in providing community-based services to advanced cancer patients and their families (Oncology Transition Services) and to offer research training in Psychosocial Oncology.

Rosangela Boyd, Assistant Professor of Recreation and Leisure Studies at Temple University, is completing her doctoral work at Clemson University. Her research interests are in the areas of aging, developmental disabilities, cross-cultural aspects of leisure, and humor.

Anna M. Brock, RN, Ph.D., is Dean of the School of Health Sciences and Chairperson of the Department of Nursing at Gannon University, Erie, Pennsylvania. She is an outstanding nursing leader who has held clinical, faculty, and administrative positions. She is a frequent speaker on nursing issues at local, state, and national conferences and is widely published. She has been honored for outstanding clinical performance and has received the teaching of the year award during a previous employment. She has conducted nursing research that has been funded from both public and private funds and is an active member and office holder of several professional organizations.

Frances M. Carp, Ph.D., is a Public Health Fellow and an American Board of Professional Psychology Diplomate in Clinical Psychology. She was Professor of Psychology at Michigan State University in East Lansing and at Trinity University in San Antonio, Texas. At the National Institutes of Health in Bethesda, Maryland, she served as Scientist/Administrator in the Aging Program of the National Institute for Child Health and Human Development, a program at that time preparing to emerge as the National Institute for Aging. She was Director of the Aging and Human Development Program at the American Institutes for Research, and Research Specialist at the University of California (Medical Center in San Francisco and Berkeley campus). She has published numerous articles in scientific/professional journals and chapters in edited books. She is author of *A Future for the Aged* and *Retirement*, and editor of *Patterns of Living and Housing of Middle-Aged and Older*, *The Retirement Process*, and *Lives of Career Women: Approaches to Work, Marriage, Children*.

Elizabeth Clipp, RN, Ph.D., received her doctorate in developmental psychology from Cornell University. She completed a predoctoral internship at the Gerontological Research Center in Baltimore (NIA), in the Laboratory of Coping and Stress, and a postdoctoral fellowship at the Center for the Study of Aging and Human Development at Duke University. Since 1985 she has been a Research Assistant Professor of Medicine in the Division of Geriatrics at Duke University Medical Center, and a Nurse Researcher in the Geriatric Research, Education and Clinical Center (GRECC) at the VA Medical Center in Durham, North Carolina. Her research interests include longitudinal measurements of physical and emotional health and quality of life among patients with chronic illness, specifically Alzheimer's disease and cancer, and their caregivers.

Martha J. Foxall, RN, Ph.D., is Associate Professor at the University of Nebraska Medical Center College of Nursing. She is also Chairperson of the Department of Nursing Administration, Education, and Science. She has an MA in education from Omaha University, an MSN in medical-surgical nursing from the University of Nebraska Medical Center, and a doctorate in adult education and gerontology from the University of Nebraska-Lincoln. Her research interests include family response to chronic physical illness and life satisfaction of older persons, especially ethnic older adults. She is the author of several articles related to these research areas.

Laurie M. Gunter, RN, Ph.D., is Professor Emeritus at Pennsylvania State University and has taught aging content to nursing students and nurses for 25 years. She has studied the attitudes and preferences of nurses and nursing students toward the elderly; life events and health in retired career women; the impact of technological change in older nurses; served as chairperson of the

American Nurses' Association Interim Certification Board until the first Geriatric Nurses were certified in 1976; and served as a member of the Executive Committee of the Division of Gerontological Nursing. She has written two books and a number of articles related to the care of the elderly. She is widely sought as a consultant, speaker, and for continuing education in the nursing care of older persons. She has held teaching positions at Meharry Medical College, University of California at Los Angeles, Indiana University, University of Washington, and the Pennsylvania State University. She has also held visiting professorships at the University of Delaware, University of Tulsa, and at the University of California at Los Angeles.

Barbara Kavanagh Haight, RNC, Dr. P.H., is a tenured Professor of Nursing at the Medical University of South Carolina where she directs the graduate program in gerontological nursing and researches the therapeutic role of the life review in elderly people. Other areas of research interest include the use of nursing diagnosis for elderly people, attitudes of students toward the nursing care of the elderly, research priorities in long-term care, determining the variables of successful reminiscence, and the use of life review as a preventive measure for depression and suicide. She is also the recipient of many awards and honors and was named the South Carolina Career Woman of the Year for 1989 by the Business and Professional Women's Club of South Carolina. She is active in the community, serving as Vice Chairperson for the Council of Gerontological Nursing of the American Nurses' Association, consultant to local nursing homes and the Veterans Administration as well as to the South Carolina Commission on Aging, and is Chairperson for the Committee of Nursing Home Nurses. She has presented nationally and internationally on the subject of life review. She is the author of numerous journal articles and chapters. She is also a member of the editorial review boards of the *Journal of Gerontological Nursing*, *Holistic Nursing Practice,* and the *Geriatric Patient Education Resource Manual.*

Opal S. Hipps, RN, EdD, is Professor and Dean of the College of Nursing at Clemson University, Clemson, South Carolina. She received her doctorate in health education administration from the University of South Carolina, Columbia. She is a member of the Southern Council on Collegiate Education in Nursing's Task Force on Graduate Education and is a member of the Executive Board of the Council of the Council of Baccalaureate and Higher Degree Programs of the National League for Nursing. She serves on the Advisory Committee on Nursing in the S.C. State Board of Nursing and the Policy Council for Nurse Recruitment and Retention for South Carolina. In addition to her involvement in professional activities, Dr. Hipps is involved in civic organizations, including serving on the Board of Directors for Hospice of the Foothilss, Seneca, South Carolina. She has published in refereed nursing journals and served as a reviewer. She has researched both gerontological and nursing education problems.

Carolyn C. Hoch, RN, Ph.D., CS, is Assistant Professor of Psychiatry at the University of Pittsburgh School of Medicine. She received her doctorate in psychiatric-mental health nursing from the University of Pittsburgh School of Nursing. Her areas of research interest are sleep and aging, sleep-disordered breathing, Alzheimer's disease, late life depression, and applications of the Roy Adaptation nursing model. She has been the recipient of grants from the National Institute of Mental Health, the Alzheimer's Disease and Related Disorders Association, the American Nurses Foundation, and Sigma Theta Tau. She is nationally recognized for her research with numerous presentations at international and national nursing, medical, and scientific meetings. She has more than 50 publications including such journals as *Western Journal of Nursing Research, Scholarly Inquiry of Nursing Practice: An International Journal, Geriatric Nursing, Journal of Gerontological Nursing, International Journal of Aging and Human Development, Archives of General Psychiatry, Biological Psychiatry, Journal of Clinical Psychiatry,* and *Sleep.*

Margaret Kelly-Hayes, RN, EdD, CRRN, is Project Director for Neurological Research at the Framingham Heart Study—the oldest epidemiological study of risk factors and disease in the United States. She received her doctorate in education from Boston University. She has been certified in rehabilitation nursing and currently holds the position of researcher and clinical specialist in the area of neurologic disability. She has represented rehabilitation nursing issues on several national committees and has recently been elected to the Stroke Council for her work in disability evaluation. She is an Associate Clinical Professor and has been a member of the Department of Neurology at Boston University School of Medicine since 1974 and an adjunct faculty member at the Boston University School of Nursing from 1974 to 1989. Since 1985, she has represented the Association of Rehabilitation Nurses on the Task Force to Develop a Uniform Data System for Medical Rehabilitation.

M. Elizabeth Kunkel, Ph.D., is Associate Professor in the Department of Food Science at Clemson University, South Carolina, and Adjunct Assistant Professor in the Division of Community Dentistry, Department of Stomatology, College of Dental Medicine, Medical University of South Carolina, Charleston. Her appointment at Clemson is half teaching and half research, with her major research interests including bone metabolism and factors affecting mineral bioavailability. She has been on the faculty at Clemson University since 1981 and on the faculty at the Medical University of South Carolina since 1983. She is a registered dietitian and a member of several professional societies including the American Dietetic Association, the American College of Nutrition, the

Society of Nutrition Education, the American Society of Bone and Mineral Research, the American Public Health Association, the Gerontological Society of America, and the Institute of Food Technologists. Since 1984, she has authored or co-authored more than 15 journal articles and more than 15 abstracts presented at national meetings.

Kathleen A. McCormick, RN, Ph.D., FAAN, is the principal investigator of many research projects in the pulmonary laboratory of the Laboratory of Behavioral Sciences in the National Institute on Aging. She is also the Surgeon General alternate to the National Library of Medicine Board of Regents and the Secretary's Alzheimer Task Force. She was formally Co-Director of the Inpatient Geriatric Continence Project, which was a 15-bed unit funded by the National Institute on Aging, and the Health Care Financing Administration to study the behavioral treatments of incontinence. She is co-author of the 1986 American Journal of Nursing Book of the Year Award Winner, *Essentials of Computers for Nurses*. She is the editor of the March, 1988, *Nursing Clinics of North America* on urinary incontinence in the elderly. Besides the Federal Nurse Award, she is the recipient of the U.S. Public Health Service J. D. Lane, Jr. Investigator Award, the Sustaining Membership Award from the Association of Military Surgeons, the Excellence in Writing Award from the National League for Nursing and Humana, and an Award of Special Recognition for Research from the University of Pennsylvania School of Nursing. In addition to being a Fellow of the Academy of Nursing in the United States, she is a Fellow of the Royal College of Nursing in Australia.

Francis A. McGuire, Ph.D., is Professor of Parks, Recreation and Tourism Management at Clemson University. He earned his doctorate from the University of Illinois. His current research addresses the role of humor in improving the quality of life of residents of long-term care facilities. He is also pursuing research topics related to leisure behavior across the lifespan.

F. Madelynn Oglesby, RNC, Ph.D., is Associate Professor in the College of Nursing at Clemson University. She received her diploma in nursing from St. Luke's Hospital in Jacksonville, Florida, her bachelor of science in nursing education at Florida State University, her master of science with a major in psychiatric-mental health from the University of Maryland, her Ph.D. in behavioral sciences from the University of Delaware, and a postdoctoral fellowship in research at the Nursing Research Unit of Edinburgh University (Scotland). She has taught nursing in a university setting since 1963, teaching psychiatric-mental health nursing, nursing research, and other nursing courses to undergraduate and graduate students at Emory University, the University of Delaware, and Clemson University. She conducted research in staffing patterns for nursing, family health nursing, and assessment of needs for specific nursing education programs. She has published in nursing journals and has participated in conferences in nursing.

Mary H. Palmer, RNC, Ph.D., is an Intramural Research Training Associate Fellow with the National Institute on Aging at the Gerontology Research Center in Baltimore. Formerly, she was an Instructor on the Graduate Faculty at the University of Maryland School of Nursing. She has a BSN and an MS in Gerontological Nursing from the University of Maryland School of Nursing. Her doctorate is in behavioral sciences and health education from the Johns Hopkins University School of Hygiene and Public Health. In 1982, she was selected as the Outstanding Student in Gerontological Nursing from the University of Maryland. She is certified in gerontological nursing by the American Nurses' Association. Her research interests include the natural history and development of urinary incontinence in nursing home residents, identification of incontinence by acute care nurses, the documentation of incontinence by health care providers, and the care of nursing home residents. She is the author of several articles on aging and nursing issues and *Urinary Incontinence,* a 1985 American Journal of Nursing Book of the Year.

Marion A. Phipps, RN, MS, CRRN, completed her undergraduate studies in nursing at the University of New Hampshire in 1969 and graduate studies in rehabilitation nursing at Boston University in 1974. Since 1980 she has been a Rehabilitation Nurse Specialist at Beth Israel Hospital in Boston. The focus of this position is clinical consultation and staff education. Since 1987 she has worked in consultation with the Herman Miller Co. in the development of an improved patient seating system. In 1988, she was selected to participate in a federally funded AIDS residency program. She is currently a member of a planning committee of a B.I.H. Robert Wood Johnson funded planning grant to examine retention of nurses. She is a member of the Association of Rehabilitation Nurses. She is past president of the New England Chapter and has served on local and national committees of this organization. She is also a member of Sigma Theta Tau, Alpha Chi Chapter, Boston College.

Veronica F. Rempusheski, RNC, Ph.D., is Director/Researcher for the Gerontological Nursing Program at Beth Israel Hospital in Boston—a position she has held since its inception in 1985. She holds associate and adjunct teaching appointments at several Boston area institutions, including Boston College, Harvard Geriatric Education Center, and MGH Institute of Health Professions. She is an active member of nursing research, gerontological nursing, and multidisciplinary gerontology and anthropology organizations internationally, nationally, regionally, and locally, including past president of the Eastern Nursing Research Society and a fellow in the Gerontological Society of America. She has practiced, conducted research, and lectured throughout the United States as well as in Canada, Japan, Poland, and Jamaica, West Indies. Her research interests include elder care/ caregiving and caregivers, grandparents, ethnic diversity, and ethnic identity of elders in home, acute care hospital, and community settings. Her articles have been published in research, practice, and administrative nursing journals, and social work and gerontology journals. She guest edited the 1989 gerontology symposium in *Nursing Clinics of North America* and is the 1990-1991 column writer/editor of "Ask an Expert" for *Applied Nursing Research.*

Joanne E. Ryan, RN, Ph.D., has developed and teaches the geriatric/gerontological nursing track in the master's program at the University of Delaware. She also alternately teaches courses on theories and models of nursing and nursing research. She co-authored with Laurie Gunter *Self Assessment of Current Knowledge in Geriatric Nursing,* which was chosen by *A.J.N.* as a Book of the Year. She also has co-authored *Rehabilitation Nursing Guide for Instructors.* Her research papers have been presented and published in conference proceedings at international conferences in Australia, New Zealand, Brazil, Canada, and England. Her research has involved identification of well elderly physical assessment data, color vision distortions in the elderly, testing for psychosocial factors of nursing home residents, and identification of therapeutic milieu factors in a long-term care facility.

Elaine E. Steinke, RN, Ph.D., is an Assistant Professor of Nursing at The Wichita State University, Wichita, Kansas. Formerly, she was an Associate Professor of Nursing at Kansas Newman College, Wichita. Her research interests are in the fields of gerontology and critical care. She has conducted a research study and has published articles on sexuality in aging. Recent publications include three chapters related to sexuality in *Geriatric Nursing Care Plans,* Frances Rogers, editor, and a research article in *Image: The Journal of Nursing Scholarship,* Summer 1988. She is frequently a guest speaker on the topic of sexuality in aging.

Jean Swaffield, BSc, MSc, RGN, RSCN, DN, DNT, PWT, FETC, is currently a Senior Lecturer in Nursing in the Department of Nursing Studies, University of Glasgow. Her nurse education and training has included general, pediatric, and community nursing, together with nurse tutor qualifications. Her first degree in government, politics and modern history was stimulated by her desire to more fully understand decision making in the Health Service and its impact on patient care. Her master's degree at Edinburgh University was in nursing education. She has always maintained an interest in caring for the elderly, particularly in the field of continence promotion. She is the Chairperson of the Association of Continence Advisors in Britain. Her current interests in nursing stem from consumer impact and her specialist research interests include peer counseling within self-help groups, a topic initiated while at the Urban Institute in Washington, DC, in 1980, patient motivation and patient self-esteem. Her interests in cross-national trends in gerontological nursing were heightened by both an eight-week study tour of the United States in 1986, sponsored by the Florence Nightingale Memorial Fund, visiting many centers of excellence across the states from coast to coast, and her MSc research dissertation on the topic of patient dependency and self-esteem.

Susan Noble Walker, RN, EdD, is Associate Professor and Interim Chairperson of the Department of Community Health, Psychiatric/Mental Health and Gerontology at the University of Nebraska Medical Center College of Nursing in Omaha, where she directs the research of master's and doctoral students interested in health promotion with older adults. She previously coordinated the master's program in gerontological nursing and was Co-Director of the Health Promotion Research Program at Northern Illinois University. She is Co-Convener of the Midwest Nursing Research Society's Health-Seeking Behaviors section and a past Chairperson of the American Nurses' Association Council on Gerontological Nursing, and was an invited participant in the U.S. Surgeon General's 1988 Workshop on Health Promotion and Aging. Her research, concerned with patterns and determinants of health-promoting lifestyle behaviors, has been funded by the American Nurses' Foundation and the National Center for Nursing Research, NIH, and has been reported widely at regional, national, and international conferences. Recent publications include "Health Promotion for Older Adults: Directions for Research" in the *American Journal of Health Promotion,* "A Spanish Version of the Health-Promoting Lifestyle Profile" in *Nursing Research,* and "Determinants of Health-Promoting Lifestyle in Ambulatory Cancer Patients" in *Social Science & Medicine.*

NOTES

NOTES